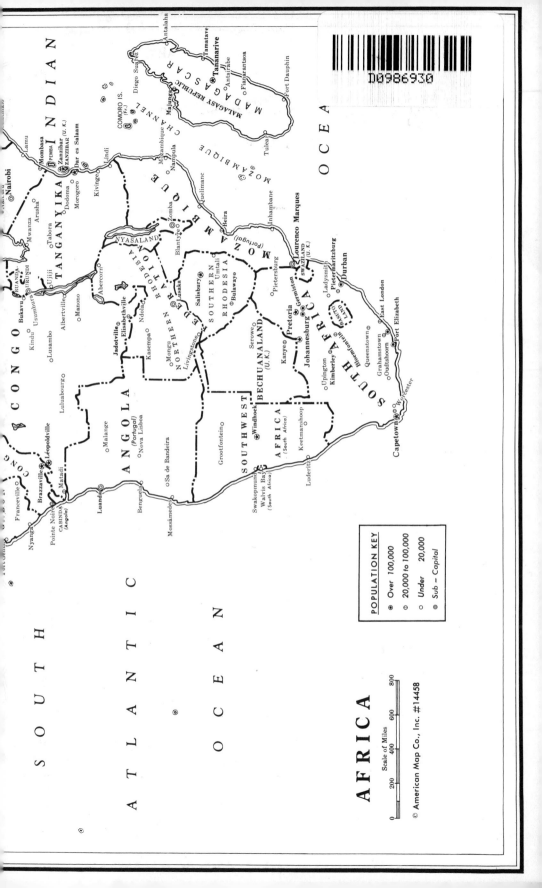

THE HANDBOOK OF Africa

THE HANDBOOK OF

Africa

EDITED BY Violaine I. Junod

ASSISTED BY Idrian N. Resnick

NEW YORK UNIVERSITY PRESS 1963

Contents

Introduction

This book was originally prepared as an African Handbook for the use of a course offered to foreign-aid technicians by the Center for Development Research and Training, African Studies Program, at Boston University. The first edition was prepared by George F. Brooks in September 1959, and revised by John Seiler in July 1960 under the supervision of V. Ferkiss and John M. Livingston. Both of these editions appeared in hectographed form.

For this publication the book has been completely revised. The format used is taken from the United Kingdom Reference Division of the Central Office of Information publications: *Fact Sheets on U.K. Dependencies.*

The purpose of the book is to provide comparable factual information on each of the fifty-odd political units of Africa, and to provide basic source material by a thorough process of footnoting. No attempt is made either to interpret or analyze the data. Facts and figures are given without qualifying comments. Thus no attempt is made to evaluate development plans or programs, to assess the efficiency of railway systems or the adequacy of health services, or to comment on the goals and aims of political parties and associations.

The value of the book lies in its bringing together for the first time a series of related facts and figures giving as complete a factual picture of the various countries' social, political, and economic life as is possible, and providing the student and interested layman bases upon which continent-wide comparisons can be made. It highlights the existing gaps in the information now available, reveals the weakness and uncertainty of much of the existing basic data, and may encourage further research and study where it is most needed. Finally, it provides many of the facts necessary to interpretation and analysis.

The editors recognize the limitations of this publication. Events in Africa move with such rapidity that what is current today is frequently a matter of history tomorrow. This is particularly true of political and social information. Furthermore the quantity and quality of the information given of necessity has depended upon the sources available so that the comparability aimed at has not always been achieved. All the material contained in this book was that most recently available as of December 31, 1961. The only post-1961 data included relates to the Government sections of Algeria and Rwanda and Burundi.

The problems of collecting statistical information on Africa are numerous. In most African countries the collection of basic data is a recent development. Methods of collecting the information vary from country to country and often within national boundaries. For certain countries, most notably Liberia and Ethiopia, scientific collection of population data of any kind has not yet been undertaken. Another major problem arises from the fact that the years during which information is collected (whether estimated or scientifically collected) are not the same. On this basis alone, total population figures do not reflect the continental situation at any one time.

In order to make the data as comparable as possible, to minimize the discrepancies between facts and figures, and accepting the practical impossibility of evaluating the reliability of the various sources of information used, the material for each country was collected in three distinct stages.

First, as much information as possible was obtained from government publications (pre- and postindependence), such as annual reports, statistical bulletins (monthly, quarterly, and annual), census data, information service publications, and trade and commercial journals.

Second, once these sources had been exhausted, documents produced by recognized international bodies such as the United Nations and its organizations, the International Labor Office, and the International Bank for Reconstruction and Development; and various Commission reports were used.

Finally, usually reliable publications of a nonofficial nature, such as *The Statesman's Yearbook* (1959 and 1961), *The Columbia Lippincott Gazetteer of the World*; journals on Africa such as *West Africa, Africa Report, Africa: trade and development, Marchés Tropicaux et Méditerranéens*; and general books on Africa by recognized scholars, such as J. D. Stamp's *Africa: Study in Tropical Development*, R. Segal's *Political Africa*, J. S. Trimingham's *Islam in West Africa*, Lord Hailey's *African Survey* (rev. ed.), and F. Lorimer's *Demographic Information on Tropical Africa*, were used to fill in the existing gaps.

For the small Spanish and Portuguese enclaves, where government and other sources were unprocurable, *The Statesman's Yearbook 1961* was the sole source used. The bulk of the data on Angola was obtained direct from the Portuguese Embassy in Washington, D.C., and most of the data on the Congo (Leopoldville) of necessity reflects the preindependence situation.

Despite this coverage of source material, many instances arose where the information was simply not available and this has been indicated in the body of the text.

PRESENTATION OF MATERIAL

In order to illustrate some of the many problems encountered in the preparation of this book, the data presented are discussed section by section.

GEOGRAPHY

Most of this information was obtained from government documents or *The Columbia Lippincott Gazetteer of the World*. Certain countries did not have the information available on a country-wide basis, e.g., Guinea. In such cases the relevant data were selected from regional studies such as those produced by the Headquarters Quartermasters' Research and Engineering Command, U.S. Army, Natick, Mass. Geographical information being by nature more or less constant, problems encountered under other sections were not relevant here.

HISTORICAL SKETCH

Historical summaries were usually provided in government publications, particularly those published by information services. No attempt is made at an interpretative presentation. The aim of this section is to provide the bare bones of a country's history to the present day.

GOVERNMENT

Information on constitutions, franchise, local government, and political parties in Africa is that most susceptible to change. During the months of preparation of this book many constitutions underwent major changes; prime ministers one day were relegated to other positions the next, and the political union between Egypt and Syria disappeared. It is recognized that many of the facts contained in this section will have been consigned to history when they finally appear in print. It can only be claimed with certainty that, except for Algeria, Rwanda, and Burundi, the information included here reflects the situation at the end of 1961. The data were obtained from government publications, journals on constitutional law, various embassies in the United States, newspaper reports, and journal reviews.

POPULATION BREAKDOWN

Information on the characteristics of populations in Africa varies widely and it is this field which suffers most from discrepancies, unreliability, questionable methods of data-collecting, and great differences in the dates when the information was obtained. It is ironical to find that, while information on human resources is so uncertain, information on livestock is usually presented with the greatest degree of certainty, at times even to the "exact" unit.

The total population figure for each country featured in this book is usually the latest official estimate, unless a census has recently been held. For the most part these figures are found in government publications.

The population-breakdown figures—main cities, age and sex distribution, and the like—do not necessarily tally with the total figures given nor with each other. The many reasons illustrate well the difficulties encountered when working with available population data in Africa: the years when the data were collected differ; some figures are estimates, others obtained from a census; the breakdown figures do not necessarily flow from the latest census held, e.g., the 1948 Kenya census is still used in government publications for tribal and other breakdowns; figures for the different "racial" communities are collected in different ways and at different times; sometimes details are available for only certain "racial" communities, a town, a district, or a region, but not for the country as a whole. Wherever possible, detailed figures flowing from one single source were used, however old the source, in order to minimize discrepancies to their utmost. In each case, of course, sources are clearly indicated.

The only figures computed by the editors are the sex distribution and, in some countries, the urban-rural distribution percentages. In the larger African countries, towns of 10,000 or more inhabitants, and in the smaller countries, towns of 5,000 or more, were used as the base for the urban percentage computation. But because town and total population figures were usually collected in different years, or some figures were estimates and others census results, the percentage given must be regarded as a very crude estimate.

The age-breakdown categories of populations can seldom be compared. The age groups listed are not necessarily the same from country to country nor from "racial" group to "racial" group within the same country. Clearcut categories are generally available for the smaller non-African communities. For the African population, the general practice is to divide the population into two broad classes—adults and children or aged and young—yielding unquestionably erroneous results.

For purposes of comparability it was necessary to standardize certain terms. Sources vary widely in their use of terms under the headings of "race," ethnic, and religious breakdowns. In this book the term "ethnic" is used to cover broad "racial" categories, recognizing that "race" in this instance does not refer to the scientifically accepted use of the word, but the sociological one. Thus the subheading "Ethnic Distribution" includes the terms European (white), Asian, Arab, colored (mixed-blood or mulatto), and African—divided, where possible, into major tribal components. If available, national groups, usually subdivisions of the European group, such as Greeks, Italians, French, and others, have been listed as well. Under the subheading "Religious Affiliation" the terms Christian, Muslim, and Animism have been used; and if further breakdowns were given, these have been listed. Animism in this book is treated as a generic term to cover all indigenous African religious and ancestral cults, "heathens" and/or "pagans."

SOCIAL DATA

Little difficulty was experienced collecting educational information. The only figure subject to caution is the percentage of the school-going-age population actually at school. For this figure three main sources were used: the Report of the UNESCO Education Conference of African States (Addis Ababa, 1961), which uses the age group 5 to 14 years of age as the base for its computation; *Outre-Mer 1958* and annual education reports which do not usually specify the age group from which the percentage is computed.

Information on vital trends in population is grossly defective and misleading. Certainty seems to exist only in regard to some non-African communities, particularly in countries where large white-settler communities are to be found. Vital statistics for the African population, where available, are usually the result of sample studies carried out over limited regions, by certain hopsitals in certain areas, or restricted to certain towns. This information was obtained primarily from annual health or medical reports and certain statistical manuals, notably *Outre-Mer 1958* for ex-French territories.

Facts and figures on diseases and health and medical institutions were generally available, but details on the number of beds and medical practitioners were not always so. Annual health and medical reports were the most often used sources.

The only two tables provided for each country appear in this section, viz: the one on Education, and the other on Health Services.

ECONOMY

As in other sections, the economic data were taken, wherever possible, from government publications. Surveys of Economic Commissions, United Nations publications, and surveys of the International Bank for Reconstruction and Development also proved useful. The information is designed to give an indication of existing facilities and the type of economic activity in the cash economy in each country. The picture presented is necessarily a rough one and is in no way intended to be a complete representation of the structure of these economies.

Measures, weights, and currency are usually given in those terms, abbreviations, signs, or symbols current in the country. Readers are referred to Appendix V for the conversion tables.

In Africa, as in other underdeveloped areas, economic statistics generally leave much to be desired. Consequently, while many of the data are presented in great detail, it would be more in keeping with reality if the reader rounded off these figures to the millionth, hundred thousandth, and so on, as the case may be.

Furthermore, there has been no attempt to evaluate the quality of the collection of data or the qualitative differences between countries. For instance, it should not be assumed that a thousand miles of primary roads in one country means the same thing as a thousand miles of primary roads in another. What one country regards as a primary road might be such that it would qualify only as secondary in another country. There are certain data that may be regarded as generally comparable in the "Transport and Communications" section: railroads and airports. But even here there may be wide differences in the quality of the facilities from country to country.

Trade statistics are generally the most reliable data in Africa. But only current account figures are available for most countries. Therefore, countries that have favorable trade balances may, in fact, have deficits in their balance of payments; it is not possible to determine whether or not this is the case from the data presented.

Careful note should be made of the fact that marketing arrangements and development assistance have entirely different meanings in the former French and the former British territories. These are described in Appendices III and IV. For this reason the section on "Marketing and Cooperative Societies" was excluded from the data on ex-French territories.

The sections on "Industry" also present problems because the information, if not read with caution, may create the wrong impression. With few exceptions, industries (manufacturing or mining) are not well developed in Africa. Consequently it might appear that a country with several industries has a relatively diversified economy. Such is rarely the case. A careful comparison of such data with export and employment figures will indicate the relative importance of such undertakings.

Finally, the "Labor" section is most useful when related to the population figures, particularly the age breakdown. It will be seen that in most cases only a small part of the working-age population (broadly defined), is engaged in wage-earning employment. This does not mean that there is unemployment in these countries. It merely means that the rest of the working labor force is not earning cash wages and is most likely engaged in agriculture.

It remains for the editors to thank all those who made this book possible: the Boston University African Studies Program staff and library services and the various embassies and information services in the United States, for making available their time, resources, and documents. We particularly wish to express our thanks to Professor Daniel McCall for his assistance on the language section; to Newell Stultz for his preparation of the material on the Republic of South Africa and South-West Africa; to Harold Marcus and James Farrell for making available to us material on Ethiopia and the Somali Republic, respectively; to the following for their reading and checking of certain sections—John M. Livingston (Geography and History), Professor William O. Brown (General sections, Population and Social Data), Jeffrey E. Butler and Professor R. Schachter (Government), and Professor Mark Karp (Economy); to Professor John D. Montgomery, Director of the Center for Development Research and

Training, for his constant encouragement and advice; to Doris Calvin and Marion Dinstel for their unfailing and willing cooperation in the use and selection of material from the African Studies Program Library; to Barbara White, Polly Seelye, and Paulina Heard for checking the manuscript, and finally to Nancy Rubin for her arduous task of typing the final manuscript.

Violaine I. Junod
Idrian N. Resnick

Boston University
April 1962

THE HANDBOOK OF Africa

Algeria

AREA: [1] *113,883 sq. m.—Northern Departments*

750,000 sq. m.—Southern Departments

POPULATION: [2] *10,300,000 (1960 est.)*

Density: [3] 30.6 per sq. km.

GEOGRAPHY [4]

The Atlas Mountains divide northern Algeria into two distinct longitudinal zones: (*a*) The Tel, a Mediterranean region, comprising most of the cultivated land, with a rainfall ranging from 16 to 40 inches annually, and (*b*) the higher plateau region, a zone of steppes where rainfall ranges from 0 to 15 inches annually. Southern Algeria consists of the Regg, a vast, stony area; the Erg, areas of dunes; the Hamada or desert highlands; and an imposing mountain range, the Ahaggar, in the southernmost area.

HISTORICAL SKETCH [5]

Algeria's early history was linked with the rise and decline of Carthage, the fortunes of Berber chieftaincies, the control of Rome into the early part of the Christian era, the Vandal invasions in the 5th century, and Arab invasions during the 6th and 7th centuries A.D. Though Christianity flourished during the later Roman period, it was replaced by Islam after the Arab invasions. The Berber tribes of Algeria resisted Romans, Arabs, and Vandals. From the 16th to the 19th centuries, Algeria was nominally part of the Ottoman Empire. The rulers of Algeria however, usually had great autonomy and thrived on privateering activities. The pretext for the French expedition in 1830 was the well-known blow with a fly whisk dealt the French Consul by the Dey of Algiers. The history of Algeria under French occupation can be divided roughly into two periods: 1832–1884, marked by an almost continuous fighting, and 1884–1954, a period of French consolidation and colonization. The area was under mili-

1

tary government for most of the first period until 1865 when it was formally annexed to France. Though juridically Algeria was considered part of France and sent representatives to the Metropolitan Parliament in Paris, the Muslim majority had no political rights and were governed by decrees and policy regulations until 1944. In the reforms of 1947, most of which were not carried out, Algeria was given an assembly with financial powers. The Assembly was composed of 120 members, half of whom were elected by the European colon and assimilated Muslim population and half by the Muslim majority. This assembly was dissolved in 1956. When Governor General Soustelle proposed gradual but final integration of Algeria with France, it was too late: the Algerian rebellion had already begun (1954). France's first reaction to the revolt was to attempt crushing the insurgents with force and to refuse to negotiate with the rebel leaders. The leaders of the rebel movement, the Front de Liberation National, formed a provisional government in 1958, with headquarters in Tunisia. Protracted negotiations to discuss terms of agreement between the French government and rebel leaders were held intermittently over the next few years. At the beginning of 1962 an agreement was finally reached and Algeria was granted its independence on July 3, 1962.

GOVERNMENT

Present Status [6]

Independent republic.

Constitution [7]

The present constitutional picture in Algeria is extremely involved and inconclusive. The following is a summary of the salient constitutional events leading to the present situation.

On April 8, 1962, a referendum was held in metropolitan France, her overseas territories, and departments, in which the electorate was asked to ratify the Evian Agreements concluded between the French Government and the F.L.N. (National Liberation Front) on March 18, 1962. Over 90 percent of the voters chose to adopt the accord, and the provisions of the Evian Agreements were implemented: a Provisional Executive under M. Abderrahamne Farés was appointed by France to rule Algeria until an elected nationalist government relieved it. The Provisional Executive was charged with the administration of the internal affairs, the maintenance of law and order, the preparations for general elections and independence, and with the task of admitting Algerians to positions in the various branches of the administration. Consequently, the 72-man National Revolutionary Council, the highest authority of the F.L.N., was allowed to form a Provisional Government under Premier Benyoussef Ben Khedda. In accordance with the Evian Agreements, this organ was to schedule general elections in order to create a Constituent Assembly of 196 members (including 16 Europeans), which in turn was to form a permanent government and draft a constitution. These elections had not yet been held when Algeria declared her independence on July 3, 1962.

On the day of independence, the Provisional Government held *de facto* control in Algeria. However, on August 7, after an intense struggle for leadership during July, the Ben Khedda regime formally divested itself of its powers in favor of the Political Bureau set up by Vice Premier Ahmed Ben Bella. Like the Provisional Government, the Political Bureau is a party institution, and its mandate is to end with the formation of a Constituent Assembly. General elections for the Constituent Assembly have already been postponed four times.

It is still unclear whether the Political Bureau is envisaged as an embryonic government or the central committee of a single party. In any event, should the Political Bureau survive, it most likely will exercise complete control over the general elections, since candidates are to be chosen on a single ballot from regional lists approved by the Bureau. In most cases nomination by the Bureau is tantamount to election, for most voting districts will put up only a single candidate for each in the Assembly.

While the Provisional Government has not actually resigned and remains the "institution of the revolution," its only remaining function is the conduct of foreign relations. The Evian Agreements state that until general elections are held ultimate authority in Algeria is to reside in the Provisional Executive. In fact this organ has no power of its own and continues to work through the Political Bureau, just as it previously worked through the Provisional Government.

A major problem now facing the Ben Bella government is the attitude of the commanders of three of Algeria's six autonomous military districts (or *willayas*). These colonels have refused to consolidate their commands with a national army until permanent political institutions are established by general elections. Contesting the Bureau's legitimacy, they demand an early meeting of the National Revolutionary Council to supplant the civilian leadership, which they contend has assumed unwarranted powers. The question remains whether the tenuous truce between the Political Bureau and the military will endure.

Local Government [8]

Municipal administration is completely lacking in some areas; the interior districts are administered entirely by the individual *willayas*.

POPULATION BREAKDOWN

Main Cities [9]

1960 estimate

Algiers (capital)	806,000
Oran	389,000
Constantine	221,000
Bône	150,000
Sidi-Bel-Abbès	105,000
Mostaganem	80,000
Sétif	74,000

Urban-rural Distribution [10]

In 1954 27% of the total population was urban. However, the Muslim population, by far representing the greater proportion of the total, was only .09% urban in Algeria (Sahara territory excluded).

Ethnic Distribution [11]

Estimated as of January 1, 1958:
Muslim: 9,240,000
Non-Muslim (European): (1,033,000 of which 140–150,000 Jews.

Religious Affiliation [12]

1954 estimate

Muslims	8,847,000
Non-Muslims	1,043,000

Languages

Arabic and French.

Sex Distribution [13]
1954 estimate

	Male	*Female*
Muslim	4,140,000 (50.7%)	4,025,000 (49.3%)
Non-Muslim	469,000 (47.9%)	511,000 (52.1%)

Age Distribution [14]
1954 estimate

	Under 20	*20–60*	*60+*
Muslim	52.5%	42%	5.5%
Non-Muslim	33%	53%	12%

SOCIAL DATA

Education [15]

TABLE I

	Enrollment 1959/60	*Teachers*
2,605 Public primary schools	724,870	19,004
105 Private primary schools	14,822	—
Primary teacher training	1,336 (trainees)	—
38 Public secondary schools	47,848	1,584
Private secondary schools	7,187	—
6 Agricultural schools	483	—
Public technical education	21,089	—
Private technical education	10,307	—
University of Algiers	6,533 (students in 1959)	
Institute of Higher Islamic Education	66	—
Institute of Political Science	n.a.	—

In 1958, 1 Muslim child out of every 4 was at school.

Expenditure on education 1957/58, 22,815 million francs. (1951/52, 10,948 million francs).

Health and Social Services

VITAL STATISTICS [16]

	1959		
	Birth rate *per 10,000*	*Death rate* *per 10,000*	*Infant mortality* *rate per 1,000*
Muslim (urban only)	+490	+199	+170
Non-Muslim	+215	+ 85	+ 39

MAIN DISEASES [17]

Eye diseases, typhoid, diphtheria, venereal disease and tuberculosis.

HEALTH SERVICES [18]

TABLE II
1959

		Beds
136	Public hospitals	34,275
15	Private institutions	2,133
5	T.B. centers	
129	Health centers	—

There were 1,870 doctors in 1959.

In 1958 there were 32 tuberculosis and 139 venereal disease dispensaries and 109 eye clinics.

SOCIAL WELFARE SERVICES [19]

Social-insurance and family-allowance schemes are controlled by the government. In addition private welfare organizations provide similar services for those not covered by government schemes.

ECONOMY

Algeria is essentially an agricultural country but has a growing industrial sector with a varied output. Its major activity is the production and export of wine.

Transport and Communications

WATERWAYS

None.

PORTS [20]

Algeria has 13 ports. The most important are Algiers, which in 1959 handled 20,646 million tons, Oran—10,077 million tons, Bône—6,090 million tons, Mostaganem—2,854 million tons, and Philippeville—3,732 million tons. She has her own merchant fleet totaling 106,099 tons.

ROADS [21]

In 1959 Algeria's total road kilometrage was 56,298, of which 8,894 km. represented national roads, 16,104 km. provincial roads, 13,610 were local roads, and 17,690 recognized rural paths. There were 182,-759 automobiles in 1959.

RAILROADS [22]

In 1959 there were 4,130 km. of railroads, 37 steam, 38 electric, and 120 Diesel engines.

AIRPORTS [23]

Algeria has some 50 airports, of which four are major airports: at Alger-Maison-Blanche, Oran-La Sepia, Bônes-Les Salèves, and Philippeville. There is an internal air-linking system and the internal landing fields are generally run and controlled by the army. Maison Blanche is a large airport, ranking third to Orly and Le Bourget, being 7,800 feet long and 200 feet wide.

POSTS, TELECOMMUNICATIONS, AND BROADCASTING [24]

Algeria has a total of some 900 post offices and agencies, a well-equipped telegraph service, and some 178,300 telephone posts of all kinds with 97,000 subscribers (1959 figures). In addition it has some 504,000 owners of radios. Radio-Algérie provides full-time service, running programs in French, Arabic, and Kabyle. It has six transmitters.

Resources and Trade

MAIN EXPORTS [25]

Foodstuffs and victuals (55% of total value of exports in 1957, of which wines were the most important), vegetable products, and minerals.

MAIN IMPORTS [26]

Transport material, textiles and textile products, machinery and electrical products, foodstuffs, metals and metal products, mineral products.

VALUE OF TRADE [27]

In millions of new francs

	1956	1957	1958	1959	1960
Exports	1,500	1,720	2,050	1,805	1,947
Imports	2,730	3,830	4,790	5,630	6,245

MARKETING AND COOPERATIVE SOCIETIES [28]

A French State monopoly of tobacco virtually controls the industry. By agreement it receives 10,000 tons of the tobacco grown each year, and the local tobacco manufacturers (C.A.F.T.A.) 6,000 tons. Its local services supervise and control the proper operation of the tobacco co-ops.

There are numerous tobacco co-ops which resell the best part of their purchases to the monopoly, the rest being sold for export. Other co-ops are found in the wine industry (e.g., there are 4 cooperative wine stores) and in agriculture.

LIVESTOCK [29]

1959 estimate

Cattle	664,000
Horses, mules and asses	882,000
Goats	1,879,000
Camels	120,000
Pigs	69,000

Industry

MANUFACTURES [30]

Many of the locally mined minerals are exported, either in semi-finished form or manufactured goods. In 1959 there were 3,220 industrial processing plants covering industries such as food processing, mechanical and industrial products, textiles and leather, construction and building material, chemicals, and petroleum.

MINING [31]

In addition to phosphates, Algeria also has iron, zinc, and some copper deposits which are being mined. Iron is its most important mineral export, coming third to her wine and vegetable exports.

POWER [32]

In 1960 local electricity production totalled 1,324.7 million kw. The year before, consumption was 1,044.5 million kw. Twelve cities have a gas service, and local coal production in 1959 netted 122,000 tons. Petroleum is found at Djebel Ouk and in the Sahara.

Finance

CURRENCY

French franc.

BANKING [33]

Bank of Algeria (bank of issue), and several cooperative agricultural banks assisted by the government are in operation. Barclays Bank (D.C.O.) has branches at Algiers and Oran.

BUDGET [34]

In million NF

1961	
Ordinary revenue	3,046
Ordinary expenditure	3,046

Taxation is the chief source of revenue.

DEVELOPMENT PLANS [35]

The Constantine Plan, covering the years 1958–1969, is divided into two 5-year periods. For the period 1959/63 estimated expenditure is $4 billion, of which 25% is to be allocated to public facilities such as education, public health, communications, and administration; 25% to housing and urban development; 25% to heavy equipment for power, soil conservation, and industry; and 25% to light equipment for agriculture, light industries, and services. The plan is financed from private and public funds and Algerian and Metropolitan France capital. The French budget is the largest contributor, with a minimum payment of $200 million per annum.

LABOR

According to the 1954 census the active population was distributed as follows: [36]

	Traditional Sector	Modern Sector
Agricultural activity	5,125,000	793,000
Nonagricultural-activity	100,000	3,437,000
	5,225,000	4,230,000

In December 1957 Algeria had some 72 trade unions, with a membership of some 320,000; 175,000 of these were affiliated to the International Confederation of T.U.; 35,000 to the International Federation of Christian T.U.; 5,000 to the Communist World Federation of T.U. and 105,000 belonged to independent trade unions.[37]

Labor legislation covers such matters as accidents, illness, family allowances, trade unions, conciliations, leave wages, etc. About 800,-000 agricultural and nonagricultural workers are covered by social security. A family-allowance scheme and social-insurance benefits (covering medical expenses, disability, maternity, old age, etc.), exist.[38]

ALGERIA NOTES

1   Ambassade de France, Service de Presse et d'Information: *Basic Data on Algeria*, New York, May 1961, p. 2.

2   *Ibid.*

3   Délégation Générale du Gouvernement en Algérie: 1960, Service de Statistique Générale, *Annuaire Statistique de l'Algérie*; Nouvelle Série, douzième volume, Alger, p. 20, Table III.

4   *Basic Data on Algeria, op. cit.*, pp. 2, 6.

5   N. Barbour (ed.), *A Survey of Northwest Africa* (The Mahgreb), O.U.P., London and New York, 1959; R. Segal, *Political Africa*; Stevens & Sons Ltd., London, 1961, p. 299; S. H. Steinberg (ed.); *The Statesman's Year-book 1961*, Macmillan & Co. Ltd., London, 1961, p. 1010.

6   "France Hands Over Power in Algeria," *The Times* (London), July 4, 1962, p. 12, col. 1; Henry Giniger, "Paris Issues Proclamation of Algerian Independence," *The New York Times*, July 4, 1962, p. 1, cols. 6–8.

7   "The Algeria Story," *Africa Report*, April 1962, p. 1; "Algeria Officers in Open Rebellion Against Premier," *The New York Times*, July 3, 1962, p. 1, cols. 4–8; "Algerian Army Commanders Denounce Govern-ment," *The Times* (London), July 3, 1962, p. 11, cols. 4–5; "Army, Policitians at Odds in Algeria," *Christian Science Monitor*, August 23, 1962, p. 4, col. 5; Thomas F. Brady, "What for Algeria?," *The New York Times*, August 1, 1962, p. 4E, cols. 1–3; Darsie Gillie, "Willaya Leaders Jeopardise Evian Agreement," *Manchester Guardian*, August 27, 1962, p. 1, col. 1; Henry Giniger, "Problems Ahead for Algeria," *The New York Times*, July 8, 1962, p. 4, cols. 1–5; Richard Scott, "New State Welcomed, but Hesitation About Cabinet," *Manchester Guardian*, July 4, 1962, p. 9, col. 8; Henry Tanner, "Algiers Officers Demand Changes in Civil Regime," *The New York Times*, August 27, 1962, p. 1, col. 1.

8   "French Share of Blame in Struggle for Power," *Manchester Guardian*, August 27, 1962, p. 7, cols. 7–8.

9   S. H. Steinberg (ed.), *op. cit.*, p. 1010.

10 *Annuaire Statistique de l'Algérie, op. cit.*, p. 19, Table II.

11 *Tableaux de l'Economie Algérienne*, Imprimerie Baconnier, Alger, 1958, p. 19.

12 Ministère des Affaires Economiques et Financières, Ministère de la France d'Outre-Mer: *Donnée Numérique sur l'Union Française*, Paris, 1956, p. 6, Table III.

13 *Tableaux de l'Economie Algérienne, op. cit.*, p. 23.

14 *Ibid.*, pp. 19–20.

15 *Annuaire Statistique de l'Algérie, op. cit.*, pp. 67–79; Information Service of the Delegation General of the French Government in Algeria, *Algeria's Development 1959*, Oct. 1959, p. 27; *Tableaux de l'Economie Algérienne, op. cit.*, p. 155.

16 *Annuaire Statistique de l'Algérie, op. cit.*, estimated from tables on p. 18.

17 *Ibid.*, p. 61, Table XIV; *Tableaux de l'Economie Algérienne, op. cit.*, p. 34.

18 *Annuaire Statistique de l'Algérie, op. cit.*, pp. 55–60; *Tableaux de l'Economie Algérienne, op. cit.*, p. 37.

19 *Tableaux de l'Economie Algérienne, op. cit.*, p. 150.

20 *Annuaire Statistique de l'Algérie, op. cit.*, p. 133, Table XVII.

21 *Ibid.*, p. 123, Table I; p. 125, Table IV.

22 *Ibid.*, p. 128, Table IX.

23   *Tableaux de l'Economie Algérienne, op. cit.*, p. 136; *Basic Data on Algeria, op. cit.*, p. 2; Notes on Africa Series, *Notes on Algeria*, No. 2, Foundation for All Africa, New York, n.d.

24   *Annuaire Statistique de l'Agérie, op. cit.*, p. 137, Table XXII, and p. 138, Table XXVII; *l'Algérie Contemporaine*, Coulouma S.A., Paris, July 1956, pp. 190–91.

25   *Tableaux de l'Economie Algérienne, op. cit.*, p. 140.

26   *Ibid.*, p. 138.

27   Délégation Générale en Algérie: Service de la Statistique Générale, *Bulletin de Statistique Générale 1961*, Numéro Supplémentaire, Alger, pp. 20–21.

28   Service de Propagande, PSEI, Information: *A Survey of Algeria*, Paris, 1956, pp. 97–101 and XI.

29   *Annuaire Statistique de l'Algérie, op. cit.*, p. 93, Table IX.

30   *Tableaux de l'Economie Algérienne, op. cit.*, pp. 115–17; *Basic Data on Algeria, op. cit.*, p. 93, Table IX.

31   *Tableaux de l'Economie Algérienne, op. cit.*, p. 113.

32   *Ibid.*, p. 108; *Annuaire Statistique de l'Algérie, op. cit.*, p. 107, Tables 1(a) and (b), and p. 109, Table VI; *Basic Data on Algeria, op. cit.*, pp. 8–9.

33   S. H. Steinberg (ed.), *op. cit.*, 1959, p. 1001.

34   *Bulletin de Statistique Générale 1961, op. cit.*, p. 31.

35   Ambassade de France, Service de Presse et d'Information: *The Constantine Plan for Algeria*, New York, n.d., pp. 10–11.

36   *Tableaux de l'Economie Algérienne, op. cit.*, p. 24.

37   United States Department of Labor, Office of International Labor Affairs: *Directory of Labor Organizations, Africa*, Feb. 1958, p. x, Table 1, and pp. 1.1–1.19.

38   *A Survey of Algeria, op. cit.*, pp. 46–47; Service d'Information et de Documentation du Gouvernement d'Algérie, *50 Main Facts About Algeria*; Fact No. 36; Ambassade de France, Service de Presse et d'Information: *Algeria at Work*, New York, p. 30.

Angola [1]

AREA: *471,351 sq. m.*

POPULATION: *4,557,979 (1951 estimate)*

Density: 9.6 per sq. m.

GEOGRAPHY [2]

Angola consists of a coastal lowland, 60 miles wide in the north and under 20 miles in the south, and a vast, dissected tableland (average altitude 6,000 feet) rising abruptly from the coastal strip, then sloping gently eastward toward the Congo and Zambezi basins. The coastal region north of Lobito has a tropical climate with an annual mean temperature between 50 and 75 degrees F. Farther south the heat is tempered by the cold Benguela current which, however, prevents the rain from reaching the coast. The upland region has a more salubrious climate with an annual mean temperature between 65 and 70 degrees F., and receives up to 60 inches of rain a year, from September to April.

HISTORICAL SKETCH

Angola was discovered in the latter part of 1483 when the Portuguese explorer and navigator Diego Cão, while searching for a sea route to India, arrived at the Congo River. In the remaining years of the 15th century, Portuguese explorers continued their voyages south along the African coast exploring the principal rivers.

Historians generally fix the founding of Luanda in the year 1575 with the arrival of Paulo Dias, the first Governor of Angola. Portugal's position in Africa was reaffirmed at the Conference of Berlin 1884–1885, when the territorial boundaries of Angola were fixed by international treaty and recognized by the world powers.

GOVERNMENT

Present Status
Province of Portugal.

Constitution
Angola falls under the Overseas Minister in Lisbon and is governed by a Governor General, assisted in the civil administration of the country by 4 Provincial Secretaries and a Legislative Council. A Government Council acts as a Provincial Cabinet and is composed of the Provincial Secretaries, the military commander, the attorney general, the director of the treasury and 2 Legislative Council members. The Legislative Council consists of 26 members, 18 elected and 8 appointed. While the Governor General has the power to override decisions of the Legislative Council, all differences of opinion must be reported fully in writing to the Overseas Minister in Lisbon for review.

Franchise
Qualified adult suffrage: qualifications—literacy in Portuguese and a tax qualification, or being the head of a family.

Local Government
Angola is divided into 13 districts headed by District Governors. These are subdivided into 62 municipalities and 21 circumscriptions administered respectively by the Municipal Councils and Administrators. The system of government of the circumscriptions is traditional.

Political Parties [3]
Movimento Popular de Libertação de Angola (MPLA), led by Ilidio Machado.
União das Populações de Angola (UPA), led by A. H. Roberto.

POPULATION BREAKDOWN

Main Cities
1950 *census*

Luanda (capital)	141,722 (now estimated at 230,000)
Nova Lisboa	28,297

Lobito	23,897
Banguela	14,690
Sá da Bandeira	11,657
Malange	9,473

Urban-rural Distribution

According to the 1950 census, some 11% of the population is urban.

Ethnic Distribution

1950 census

White	78,826	(now estimated at 200,000)
Mixed	29,648	(now estimated at 75,000)
African	4,036,687	
Other	105	
TOTAL	4,145,266	

Africans are divided into the following main tribal groups:
Kicongo
Kimbundo
Umbundo (about one-third of the entire native population)
Lunda-Kioco
Ganguela

Religious Affiliation

1950 census

Catholic	1,502,863
Other Christians	541,312
Other religions	2,097,360
No religion	3,731

Languages

Portuguese is the official language. Kicongo and Kimbundo.

Sex Distribution

1950 census

Male	*Female*
2,033,568 (49.1%)	2,111,698 (50.9%)

Age Distribution

1950 census

Under 24	*25–49*	*50+*
2,369,296	1,378,907	397,063

SOCIAL DATA

Education

TABLE I
1959

		Enrollment	Teachers
1,639	Government primary schools	85,776	2,466
81	Government secondary schools	5,361	241
23	Professional and technical schools	4,288	346
2	Normal colleges	297	—

These figures do not include elementary education provided by missions. It is estimated that if these were included the total number enrolled in 1959 would have been 681,767.

Information on the percentage of school-going age population and expenditure on education is not available.

Health and Social Services

VITAL STATISTICS

Not available.

MAIN DISEASES

Malaria, dysentery, gastritis, duodenitis and colitis, tuberculosis, and respiratory ailments.

HEALTH SERVICES

TABLE II
1959

77 Hospitals
112 Infirmaries and dispensaries
1 Mental asylum
5 Leprosaria

In addition, industrial companies and agricultural concerns maintain some 600 health stations (1960).

There were 226 medical practitioners in 1959.

SOCIAL WELFARE SERVICES

In 1959 there were 7 Offices of Retirement and Social Welfare Agencies and 3 Mutual Aid Associations in Angola. There were 13,541 beneficiaries of the Retirement and Social Welfare Plan, and 771 who were receiving pensions. There were 11,183 members of Mutual Aid Associations. Other social welfare agencies operating in Angola include the Red Cross and Caritas, a Catholic organization for charitable and social assistance.

ECONOMY

Angola has primarily an agricultural economy. However, recently large mineral deposits have been developed for export.

Transport and Communications

WATERWAYS

Angola has no navigable rivers.

PORTS

Angola has 10 ports, two of which are major: Luanda and Lobito, both of which handle over 1 million tons of freight annually.

ROADS

In 1959 Angola had 35,519 kilometers of roads.

RAILROADS

There are 3,110 kilometers of railroads consisting of 4 main lines: the Luanda Railway, the Benguela Railway, the Amboim Railway, and the Moçâmedes Railway.

AIRWAYS

There are 12 principal airports and landing fields in Angola—at Cabinda, Santo Antonio do Zaire, Ambrizete, Luanda, Port Amboim, Novo Redondo, Lobito, Chela, Nova Lisboa, Sá da Bandeira, Moçâmedes, and Toto.

POSTS, TELECOMMUNICATIONS AND BROADCASTING

Information on postal services is not available. Angola is connected by cable with East, West, and South African telegraph systems. There were 12 telephone exchanges in 1959, serving a total of 7,864 telephones. In 1959 there were 18 radio stations, offering a total of 33,690 hours' service. Seventeen of the stations were privately owned; the other is state-owned.

Resources and Trade

MAIN EXPORTS

In 1959 the principal exports were coffee, diamonds, sisal, maize, fish-meal, raw cotton, iron ore, sugar, dried fish, and lumber.

MAIN IMPORTS

In 1959 the principal imports were table wines, cotton textiles, heavy industrial machinery and apparatus, railway materials, trucks, passenger cars, petroleum, cast and wrought iron, industrial motors, parts and accessories, and light industrial machinery and apparatus.

VALUE OF TRADE

In millions of U.S. dollars

	1955	1956	1957	1958
Exports	97.5	114.4	116.9	128.3
Imports	93.5	109.9	124.0	130.0

MARKETING AND COOPERATIVE SOCIETIES

While various types of marketing, purchasing, fishing, farm-implement pooling, and credit cooperative societies exist, there are no statistics.

LIVESTOCK

	1958
Cattle	1,217,245
Sheep and goats	583,839
Pigs	292,578

Industry

MANUFACTURES

The principal industries include textiles, rubber products, cement, food processing, and chemicals. There are cigarette factories, breweries, bottling plants, and other processing plants for local consumer products, and an oil refinery that processes both local and imported crude oil.

MINING

A total of 68 mines were being worked in 1959, of which 42 were diamond mines, 8 manganese, and 18 others—notably iron, petroleum, rock salt, and asphalt mines. A $45 million program of development in the manganese and iron ore industry is being undertaken.

POWER

There are 753 power plants, with a kilowatt power of 71,518 as of 1959. In that same year, total consumption amounted to 109,396,000 kwh.

Finance

CURRENCY

Escudo. 1 escudo equals $0.025. 1,000 escudos equal 1 conto.

BANKING

The Banco de Angola is the issuing bank. Banco Commercial de Angola and the postal savings bank (Caixa Económica Postal).

BUDGET

In contos 000's

	1959
Revenue	1,837.9
Expenditure	1,705.6

DEVELOPMENT PLAN

Total estimated 1959–1964 expenditure: 4,603,000 contos.

The plan covers scientific surveys of soil and economic surveys, particularly in the fields of food production and mineral location, the development of resources—water supplies, livestock, forest conservation, mechanization of agriculture, etc.; settlement schemes; communications and transport; education and development of basic local services such as electricity installations, drainage, etc.

Labor

Not available.

In December 1957 Angola had 21,108 trade-union members.[4]

ANGOLA NOTES

1 Unless otherwise stated, all information obtained from the Portuguese Embassy, Washington, D.C., Oct. 1961.

2 *The Columbia Lippincott Gazetteer of the World*, Columbia University Press, New York, 1952, p. 72.

3 R. Segal, *Political Africa*, Stevens & Sons Ltd., London, 1961, pp. 302–303.

4 U.S.: United States Department of Labor, Office of International Labor Affairs, *Directory of Labor Organizations, Africa*, Feb. 1958, p. x; Table 1, p. 2.1.

Basutoland[1]

AREA: *11,716 sq. m.*
POPULATION: *641,674 (1956 census)*
Density:[2] *55 Africans per sq. m.*

GEOGRAPHY

Only the western quarter of Basutoland is low-lying. The rest consists of highlands, rising to 11,000 feet in the Drakensberg Range. In the center is a high plateau varying from 9,000 feet to 10,500 feet. The lowland temperature varies from 90 degrees F. in summer to 20 degrees F. in winter; in the highlands the range is much wider and temperatures below zero are not unknown. The variable rainfall averages about 28 inches a year, most of it falling between October and April.

HISTORICAL SKETCH

The Basutos came into prominence as a nation when Moshesh, a chief in the north, in 1818, gathered together remnants of clans scattered by Zulu raids. From 1856 to 1868 Moshesh (who ruled until 1874) was intermittently at war with the Boers living in the now Orange Free State province of the Republic of South Africa. In 1868 he appealed to the British for protection, through the Governor of the Cape Colony, and his tribe and territory were given recognition under the British flag. Three years later the territory was annexed to the Cape Colony by an act of the Cape legislature. Difficulties between the Basuto and the Cape Colony government followed and the issues were finally resolved when, in 1884, the country was restored to the control of the Queen through the United Kingdom High Commissioner for South Africa. In 1910 the Advisory Basutoland Council was created.

GOVERNMENT

Present Status
British colony.

Constitution
The Basutoland National Council is the legislature. It consists of 80 members: 40 elected, 22 chiefs ex-officio, 14 nominated by the Paramount Chief, and 4 officials. The Executive Council consists of the Resident Commissioner, 4 officials, and 4 unofficial members.

Franchise [3]
The elected members of the Basutoland National Council are elected by the District Councils acting as electoral colleges. Members to these are elected by taxpayers over 21 years of age.

Local Government
The nine districts of the territory are under the control of District Commissioners, and subdivided into smaller areas presided over by hereditary chiefs and headmen, who owe allegiance to the Paramount Chief. Each district has an Advisory Council whose members are popularly elected. A National Treasury was established in 1946.

Political Parties [4]
Basutoland Congress Party (BCP), led by Ntsu Mokhehle.
Basutoland Freedom Party (BFP), led by B. M. Khaketla.
Marema Tlou, Chief Seepheephe Samuel Matete.
Basutoland National Party (BNP), led by Chief Leabua Jonathan.

POPULATION BREAKDOWN

Main City
Maseru (capital), 5,000.

Urban-rural Distribution
Not available.

Ethnic Distribution [5]

European	1,926
Basuto	638,857
Asian	247
Mixed	644

Religious Affiliation [6]

Of the African population 70% are Christians and the rest animists or unspecified.

Languages

Sesotho, English (official), and Afrikaans.

Sex Distribution [7]

1956 census

	Male	*Female*
African	270,451 (42.3%)	368,406 (57.7%)
European	962 (49.9%)	964 (50.1%)
Asian	133 (53.8%)	114 (46.2%)
Mixed	305 (47.4%)	339 (52.6%)

Age Distribution [8]

1956 census

	Under 21	*21–49*	*50+*	*Unknown*
European	615	955	344	12
Asian	122	85	39	1
Mixed	336	188	98	22
African		Not available		

SOCIAL DATA

Education [9]

TABLE I
1959

African	*Gov't.*	*Cmte controlled*	*Mission*	*Total enrollment*	*Teachers*
Primary schools	4	5	1,041	128,248	2,447
Secondary schools	—	4	17	1,621	82
Technical and Vocational schools	1	—	26	688	33

TABLE I—Continued
1959

African	Gov't.	Cmte con-trolled	Mission	Total enroll-ment	Teachers
Teacher-training colleges	—	—	7	521	41
Pius XII University College (Roma)	—	—	—	139	—
European					
4 schools	—	—	—	121	—

In 1959, 14 students were studying abroad in the U.K., 9 in South Africa, 3 in the U.S.A., 3 in India, and 3 in Southern Rhodesia.

About 50% of the Africans of the 5–19 age group attend school at any one time, and 95% attend school at one time or another.

1958/59 expenditure: $579,517.

Health and Social Services

VITAL STATISTICS
Not available.

MAIN DISEASES
Poliomyelitis, diphtheria, whooping cough, typhoid fever, measles, tuberculosis, venereal disease, and deficiency diseases.

HEALTH SERVICES [10]

TABLE II
1958

	Government	Mission	Private
Hospitals	9 (485 beds)	4 (289 beds)	—
Health centers	4	—	—
Maternity and child welfare centers	15	5	8
Mountain dispensaries	3	1	—
Outpatient clinics	23	21	6
Leprosarium	1	—	—
Mental centers	1	—	—
Venereal disease clinics	16	5	—

In the same year there was one doctor per 19,356 of the African population and one bed per 835 Africans.

SOCIAL WELFARE SERVICES [11]

Boy Scout and Girl Guide movements function throughout the territory. The Homemakers Association organizes clubs for women. The Pension Board and Basuto Soldiers' Relief Fund cater to the welfare and rehabilitation of ex-soldiers.

ECONOMY

Basutoland is a pastoral country with no factories or industrial undertakings. The main effort of the U.K. Administration has been directed at soil conservation and agricultural improvements in order to increase food production and exports.

Transport and Communications

WATERWAYS

None.

PORTS

None.

ROADS

Basutoland has 970 miles of graveled or earth roads and 3 miles of tarred roads. Pack animals constitute the only means of transport in many parts. A new 50-mile mountain road is being built to link Maseru to the central mountain area at Marakabei on the Seqnyane River.

RAILROADS

One mile of the Bloemfontein-Natal main line is in Basutoland and runs along the boundary. A branch line links Maseru and Marseilles in the Orange Free State.

AIRWAYS

Airstrips are found at Maseru, Mokhotlong, Semonkong, and Qacha's Nek.

In 1958 Basutoland had 66 postal offices and postal agencies. Maseru had an exchange with 300 subscribers and there was a VHF telephone system from Buteh Buteh to Quiltang. Basutoland has no radio stations of its own.

Resources and Trade

MAIN EXPORTS
Wool, mohair, wheat and wheatmeal, cattle, beans, and peas.

MAIN IMPORTS
Merchandise, maize and maize meal, wheat and wheatmeal, sorghum.

VALUE OF TRADE [13]
In $000's

	1954	1955	1956	1957	1958
Exports	1,942	1,796	1,944	2,713	1,343
Imports	2,612	3,202	2,937	3,013	2,947

MARKETING AND COOPERATIVE SOCIETIES [14]
In November 1959 there were 17 agricultural marketing, 25 agricultural credit, 8 consumer, and 2 artisan cooperative societies with a total membership of 11,840.

LIVESTOCK
1957 estimate

Cattle	381,700
Horses	81,600
Mules	3,600
Donkeys	48,616
Sheep and goats	1,756,000

Industry

MANUFACTURING AND MINING [15]
Basutoland has no industrial undertakings.

POWER [16]
There is a power station at Maseru undergoing extension.

Finance

CURRENCY

The same as the Republic of South Africa. Rand. R2 = £1 sterling

BANKING

The Standard Bank of SA Ltd., and Barclay's Bank (D.C.O.) operate branch services at Maseru and some district headquarter stations.

BUDGET [17]

1958/59

Revenue	£1,237,792
Expenditure	£1,792,335

The main sources of revenue are import duties, excise taxes, native taxes, income taxes, wool and mohair export duties. Basutoland is treated as part of South Africa for customs purposes and receives a fixed percentage of the total customs revenue collected by the Republic.

DEVELOPMENT PLAN [18]

U.K.D. & W.F. grants for 1955/60—£1,018,264. Soil conservation has been the main item of expenditure.

LABOR [19]

The land cannot support the average family, and, apart from employment in government service or trading stores, little work is to be found in the territory. A large number of Basuto men seek work in the Republic of South Africa, mainly in the gold mines. In 1957 43,000 passes were issued for mining, 3,000 for agriculture, and nearly 8,000 for other industries.

There are 4 trade unions in Basutoland. Labor legislation provides for the registration of trade unions; the settlement of disputes; regulation of wages; condition of employment of women and children; recruitment and contracts for the employment of migrant labor; and workmen's compensation.

BASUTOLAND NOTES

1   Unless otherwise stated, all information obtained from Fact Sheets on the U.K. Dependencies, Reference Division, U.K. Central Office of Information, No. R. 4356, *Basutoland*, Oct. 1959.

2   Basutoland: Basutoland Government, *1956 Population Census*, Maseru, 1958, p. 69, Table I and p. 78, Table IX.

3   Communication received from the British Embassy, Washington, D.C., July 1961.

4   R. Segal, *Political Africa*, Stevens & Sons Ltd., London, 1961, pp. 304–306.

5   Basutoland: *1956 Population Census, op. cit.*, p. 69, Table I.

6   *Ibid.*, p. 99, Table XXIII.

7   *Ibid.*, p. 69, Table I.

8   *Ibid.*, p. 91, Table XV.

9   Basutoland: *Annual Report Summary of the Director of Education 1959*, Morija Printing Works, Morija, 1960, p. 17, Table I; p. 19, Table II; and p. 23, Tables V and VI; also Basutoland, Bechuanaland Protectorate, and Swaziland: *Report of an Economic Survey Mission*, H.M.S.O., London, 1960, p. 251.

10 Basutoland: *Annual Report of the Medical Department 1958*, Morija Printing Works, Morija, 1959, p. 21.

11 U.K.: H.M.S.O., *Basutoland 1958*, London, 1959, pp. 73–75.

12 *Ibid.*, p. 99; Basutoland, Bechuanaland Protectorate and Swaziland: *Report of an Economic Survey Mission, op. cit.*, pp. 386–87.

13 *Report of an Economic Survey Mission, op. cit.*, pp. 371–73.

14 *Ibid.*, p. 246.

15 U.K.: *Basutoland 1958, op. cit.*, p. 45.

16 *Ibid.*, p. 96.

17 Basutoland: The Treasury, Maseru, *Report on the Finances and Accounts for the Financial Year Ended 31st March 1959*, pp. 1 and 3.

18 *Report of an Economic Survey Mission, op. cit.*, p. 368.

19 U.N.: *Progress of the Non-Self-Governing Territories Under the Charter*, Territorial Surveys, Vol. 5, New York, 1960, p. 103.

Bechuanaland[1]

AREA: *275,000 sq. m.*
POPULATION: *350,000 (1960 estimate)*
Density: [2] *+1.2 per sq. m.*

GEOGRAPHY

The average altitude of Bechuanaland is 3,300 feet. The Kalahari Desert, consisting of undulating sandhills with stretches of grass and woodlands, covers much of the south and west. In the northwest the land is watered by the Olovango and Chobe rivers, the former widening into a delta, and in the season of heavy rainfall flooding Lake Ngami and the Makarikeri salt lake which, at other times, are dry. The climate is subtropical, varying to temperate in the higher altitudes. Average annual rainfall is 18 inches, but less than 9 inches in the Kalahari Desert area. In August, seasonal winds from the west carry sand and dust across the whole country.

HISTORICAL SKETCH

Britain's first contact with the area was established through Robert Moffat and David Livingstone of the London Missionary Society in the 19th century, when the territory was torn by intertribal warfare. In the last quarter of the century trouble broke out between the Bechuanas and the Boers across the border of the Transvaal, and it was the appeal of the Bechuanas to Britain for protection and the desire of Britain to confine the expansion of the Boer Republics which led to the establishment of British control over the area. In 1884 a Deputy Commissioner to the Bechuana tribes was appointed and a year later the whole of the territory was proclaimed to be under the protection of the Queen. In 1891 the High Commissioner for South Africa was given authority to exercise jurisdiction over the territory. In 1895 part of the southern region of the area, including Mafeking, was incorporated into the Cape Colony. The first joint Advisory Council of Africans and Europeans was established in 1950, and in 1960 a system of government by Legislative and Executive Councils was introduced.

GOVERNMENT

Present Status
British protectorate.

Constitution [3]
The Legislative Council consists of 31–35 members (3 ex-officio, 21 elected—10 European, 10 African, and 1 Asian members—7 nominated officials, and up to 4 unofficial members nominated by the High Commissioner). The Executive Council consists of the Resident Commissioner, 5 officials, and 4 unofficial members.

Franchise [4]
Europeans and Asians: British, 21 years and over, 12 months residence in the territory, and property or income qualification.

African: Members to the Legislative Council are elected by an African Council consisting of the Resident Commissioner and 32 members appointed or elected from the 13 divisions of the protectorate, and not more than 2 nominated unofficial members.

Local Government
In native areas administration is by "indirect rule," the tribal chief or native authority having powers and rights established by proclamation, and exercising a large measure of independence. The establishment of partly elected district or tribal advisory councils, to assist the chiefs and subordinate authorities, is being encouraged. Native Treasuries were first established in 1938.

Political Parties [5]
Bechuanaland Peoples Party (BPP), led by K. T. Motsete.
Bechuanaland Protectorate Federal Party (BPFP), led by L. D. Radittack.

POPULATION BREAKDOWN [6]

A census was taken in 1956, but details are not yet available, and the 1946 census is still officially used.

Main Cities
Kanye, Serowe, Molepolole, and Mochudi all have a population of over 10,000. Serowe is the capital.

Urban-rural Distribution [7]
About half the total population live in villages of more than 1,000 persons.

Ethnic Distribution [8]
1946 census

Bamangwato	101,000
Bakwena	40,000
Bangwaketse	39,000
Batawana	39,000
Bakgatla	20,000
Bamalete	10,000
Barolong	8,000
Batlokwa	2,000
Others	36,000

1956 census

European	3,173
Colored	676
Asian	248

Religious Affiliation
One-seventh of the African population is Christian and the rest are animists.

Languages
Tswana. English is the official language.

Sex Distribution
Not available.

Age Distribution
Not available.

SOCIAL DATA

Education [9]

TABLE I

	Enrollment 1959	Teachers 1957
179 African primary schools	32,406	662
5 African secondary schools	431	16
1 African teacher training college	86	6
9 European primary schools	451	
5 Colored primary schools	278	

About 45% of African children of school-going age attend school. In 1957 there were 8 students studying abroad: 2 in the U.K., 3 in Basutoland, and 3 in the Union of South Africa. Expenditure in 1959: £316,792 (1947—£50,030).

Health and Social Services

VITAL STATISTICS [10]

Per 1000	Birth rate	Death rate	I.M.R.
European	25	N/A	8
African		Not available	

MAIN DISEASES

Malaria, tuberculosis, diphtheria, whooping cough, pneumonia, and gastroenteritis.

HEALTH SERVICES [11]

TABLE II
1958

	Government	Mission
Hospitals	7 (456 beds)	9 (291 beds)
Dispensaries	35	26

In 1957 there were 15 government and 7 private doctors.

SOCIAL WELFARE SERVICES [12]
The government provides ±£1,000 for relief of destitution. The Boy Scout and Girl Guide movements are active in the field of youth activities. Community centers and halls are being established and various voluntary associations, such as the British Red Cross, provide services. A mobile film unit tours the countryside.

ECONOMY [13]

At present Bechuanaland's economy depends almost entirely upon its stock-raising activity; 95% of the population is engaged in stock raising and there is little paid employment in the territory. The tribes are traditionally little concerned with agriculture, being pastoralists. There is some prospect of mineral development.

Transport and Communications

WATERWAYS
None.

PORTS
None.

ROADS
Bechuanaland has 1,000 miles of graveled or earth roads.

RAILROADS
394 miles of the main Cape Town to Rhodesia line lie within the protectorate.

AIRWAYS
There are airfields at Gaberones, Mahalapye, Francistown, Maun, Serowe, Tsabong, Ghanzi, Lobatsi, Molepolole, and Palapye, and several landing grounds.

POSTS, TELECOMMUNICATIONS, AND BROADCASTING [14]
In 1958 there were 41 post offices, 383 telephone services, and 11 telegraph agencies. There were 29 private radio communication stations and 1,566 licensed radio listeners.

Resources and Trade

MAIN EXPORTS [15]

Cattle carcasses (representing 60% of total exports from 1956–58), live cattle, abbatoir by-products, hides, asbestos, beans and pulses, and sorghum.

MAIN IMPORTS

General merchandise, textiles, vehicles, wheat, maize, and other food-stuffs.

VALUE OF TRADE [16]

In £000's

	1954	1955	1956	1957	1958
Exports	2,424	2,822	2,888	2,412	2,599
Imports	2,053	2,463	3,056	2,730	3,504

The Republic of South Africa is the chief market and source of imports.

MARKETING AND COOPERATIVE SOCIETIES

There are no cooperative societies, but the Bamangwato market their milk on a cooperative basis.

LIVESTOCK

1955 estimate

Cattle	1,152,400
Horses	7,300
Mules and donkeys	27,000
Sheep and goats	457,000
Pigs	4,600
Poultry	78,800

Industry

MANUFACTURES [17]

There is a small soap factory at Lobatsi.

MINING

Asbestos, gold, manganese, and cyanite (silicate of aluminum) are produced and exported. Deposits of copper, nickel, and coal are known to exist. An agreement was signed in 1959 between the Bamangwato tribe and the Rhodesian Selection Trust Group of companies whereby the latter were granted rights to prospect in the Bamangwato Reserve.

POWER [18]

Francistown has two 90-kw. steam-driven sets and Lobatsi has two 150-kw. steam-driven units.

Finance

CURRENCY

The same as the Republic of South Africa. Rand. R2 = £1 sterling.

BANKING

The Standard Bank of South Africa, Ltd., and Barclay's Bank (D.C.O.) each have branches at Francistown and Lobatsi and operate agencies from them.

BUDGET [19]

1961/62 estimate

Revenue	£4,854,206
Expenditure	£2,970,034

The main sources of ordinary revenue are taxes and duties, posts and telegraphs, customs and excise, and a subvention from the Rhodesian Railways. Bechuanaland is treated as part of the Republic of South Africa for customs purposes and receives a fixed percentage of the total customs revenue collected by the Republic.

DEVELOPMENT PLAN [20]

U.K.D. & W. grants 1955–60: £1,765,678. Water development has been the major item of development expenditure.

LABOR [21]

Over 95% of the population is engaged in stock raising and there is little paid employment within the territory. Many of the men go to work in neighboring territories, particularly to the mines of the Republic of South Africa, for part of the year. In 1958, 19,600 went to South Africa and Southern Rhodesia, mainly on a nine months' contract.

There is one workers' organization, the Francistown African Employees' Union, with a nominal membership of 200.

Labor legislation covers conditions governing the recruitment of labor for the mines.

BECHUANALAND NOTES

1 Unless otherwise stated, all information obtained from Fact Sheets on the U.K. Dependencies, Reference Division, U.K. Central Office of Information, No. R 4355, *The Bechuanaland Protectorate*, Oct. 1959.

2 Basutoland, Bechuanaland Protectorate, and Swaziland: *Report of an Economic Survey Mission*, H.M.S.O., London, 1960, p. 169.

3 Communication received from the British Embassy, Washington, D.C., July 1961.

4 *Ibid.*

5 R. Segal, *Political Africa*, Stevens & Sons Ltd., London, 1961, pp. 307–308.

6 *Report of an Economic Survey Mission, op. cit.*, p. 169.

7 Communication received from the British Embassy, *op. cit.*

8 *Ibid.; Report of an Economic Survey Mission, op. cit.*, p. 169.

9 Bechuanaland Protectorate: *Annual Report Summary of the Education Department, 1954*, pp. 5, 8–10, Table I, and pp. 20–22, Table V; also U.N. *Progress in Non-Self-Governing Territories Under the Charter*, Territorial Surveys, Vol. 5, New York, 1960, p. 114.

10 Bechuanaland Protectorate: *Annual Medical and Sanitary Report 1958*, p. 8.

11 U.N.: *Progress of the Non-Self-Governing Territories Under the Charter*, *op. cit.*, p. 112.

12 U.K.: *Bechuanaland Protectorate 1958*, H.M.S.O., London, 1959, pp. 58–60.

13 *Ibid.*, p. 10.

14 *Ibid.*, pp. 72–75.

15 *Ibid.*, pp. 114 and 117.

16 *Report of an Economic Survey Mission, op. cit.*, pp. 101 and 117, Appendix 3.

17 U.K.: *Bechuanaland Protectorate 1958, op. cit.*, p. 49.

18 *Report of an Economic Survey Mission, op. cit.*, p. 74.

19 Bechuanaland Protectorate: *Estimates of Revenue and Expenditure 1961–1962*, p. 2.

20 *Report of an Economic Survey Mission, op. cit.*, p. 170.

21 U.K.: *Bechuanaland Protectorate 1958, op. cit.*, p. 12.

The Federation of the Cameroon

AREA:[1] *166,700 sq. m.*

POPULATION:[2] *3,187,500 (1957 estimate)*

Density:[3] 20 per sq. m.

GEOGRAPHY [4]

Cameroon is divided into four natural regions: first, the southern coastal region of plateaus and dense forests of an average altitude of 300 meters, including a narrow coastal strip, 50 km. wide in the south and 100 km. in the north. The climate is tropical all year long and rainfall averages between 1,500–2,000 mm. Second, the central region consisting of the high Adamaona plateau where the forest ends and the savanna begins. The climate is cool and there is one dry and one wet season. The average rainfall is 1,600 mm. Third, the northern region, a vast savanna plain with a hot dry tropical climate and a dry season (November to May) and a wet season for the rest of the year when rainfall never exceeds 1,600 mm. Fourth, the mountainous region in the west with an altitude of 1,500–2,000 meters. The climate is cool with rainfall ranging from 1,800 mm. to 4 m. or more.

HISTORICAL SKETCH [5]

The Portuguese are known to have established a settlement in the Douala region in 1640, but it was not until 1820 that permanent contact with Europe was established. British and then German traders established trading posts along the coastline, with little penetration into the interior. In the 1880's European powers began to vie with each other over claims to territory in these regions. The Germans signed treaties with chiefs which were recognized by France and the United Kingdom in 1885. In

37

1911 France ceded to Germany, in exchange for a free hand in Morocco, large territories in the French Congo and Gabon. These were taken back during World War I. Following World War I, the greater portion of the territory was placed under French administration as a mandate. A small section along the Nigerian frontier was mandated to Great Britain. The country continued to be administered by League of Nations mandates until the end of World War II when it was placed under the United Nations Trusteeship system. In January 1959, the French Trust Territory was granted full internal autonomy and complete independence was proclaimed on January 1, 1960. The Cameroon became a member of the United Nations on September 20, 1960. In February 1961 the southern section of the British Trust Territory of the Cameroons opted for federation with the Republic of the Cameroon.

GOVERNMENT

Present Status
Independent federal republican state.

Constitution [6]
The federal government consists of a President, who is chief of the executive and head of the state, and Vice-President elected by popular vote; a Cabinet and federal legislature of deputies (1 per every 80,000 inhabitants), at the moment selected by the two states' legislatures until the first federal elections in 1964. The President appoints and may dismiss the ministers and parliamentary secretaries; he appoints the states' parliamentary secretaries on the advice of the Prime Minister. Both he and the federal legislature may initiate laws and he can demand a second reading. In the event of continuous conflict between the federal and states' legislatures, the President may dissolve the federal legislature and call for an election within two months.

At the state level each of the two states, East Cameroon (ex-Cameroon Republic) and West Cameroon (ex-Southern Cameroon), has an elected assembly of 100 and 37 members, respectively. In West Cameroon the House of Chiefs has been maintained and will exercise powers determined by its state legislature.

Franchise
Universal adult suffrage.

Local Government [7]

Under the new constitution the country is divided into provinces and communes administered by councils of elected and nominated members. Each province falls under a minister or secretary of state representing government. Details are not available.

Political Parties [8]

Union Camerounaise, led by Ahmadou Ahidjo, President of the Republic and of East Cameroon. John Mgu Foncha is Vice-President of the Republic and Premier of West Cameroon.

Démocrates Camerounais, led by André-Marie Mbida.

Union des Populations du Cameroun, led by Theodore Mayi-Matip.

POPULATION BREAKDOWN

Main Cities [9]

Yaounde	54,347 (1957)
Douala	113,212 (1955/1956)

Urban-rural Distribution [10]

See note.

Ethnic Distribution [11]

Non-African	16,517 (*1957 census*)
African	3,171,000 (*1957 estimate*) divided into:
Pygmies	6,500
Bantu	1,055,000 (Beti, Bassa, Bakoko, Baso, Duala, Bakindu, Kaka, Djem, and Fang)
Semi-Bantu	506,000 (Bamikele, Tikar, Bamun, Kaka, Bakum)
Sudanese	84,000 (Baya, Bangantu, and Babute)
Neo-Sudanese	45,000 (Kotoko and Mandara)
Fulani	395,000
Semites	45,000
Others	725,000 (all approximate figures)

Religious Affiliation [12]

Christians	33%
Muslims	19%
Animists	48%

Languages [13]

Many local vernacular languages are spoken, of which Fang is the most important. French is the official language.

Sex Distribution [14]

1957 estimate

	Male	Female
African	1,538,700 (48.6%)	1,632,300 (51.4%)
Non-African	9,467 (57.4%)	7,050 (42.6%)

Age Distribution [15]

1957 census

	Under 16	16–50	50+
African	1,091,100	1,338,900	241,000
Non-African		Not available	

SOCIAL DATA

Education [16]

As of January 1, 1958

TABLE I

	Enrollment	Public School Teachers
649 Public primary schools 1,814 Private primary schools	293,977	1,818
18 Public secondary schools 41 Private secondary schools	6,645	51
35 Public technical schools 29 Private technical schools	3,344	81

There were 904 students studying abroad.

In 1957, 64% of the children of school-going age were at school, of which 28.6% were girls; education expenditure represented 14% of the local budget.

Health and Social Services

VITAL STATISTICS

Not available.

MAIN DISEASES [17]

Venereal disease, pian (yaws), malaria, eye and skin diseases.

HEALTH SERVICES [18]

As of January 1, 1958

TABLE II

	Beds
4 General hospitals	1,701
1 Secondary hospital	300
40 Medical centers	3,130
11 Infirmaries	247
250 Dispensaries	242
171 Private institutions	3,340
17 Maternity & specialized services	1,166 (maternity beds)

There were 191 medical practitioners: 1 per every 16,700 inhabitants. There were 28 beds per 10,000 inhabitants.

SOCIAL WELFARE SERVICES [19]

Provision is made for case work, the running of nursery schools, and women's educational groups; there is an observation center for juvenile delinquents and a medical social work service.

ECONOMY [20]

Agriculture, raising of livestock, and forestry are the basis of the economy; gold, diamond, and tin mining are carried on to a limited extent.

Transport and Communications

WATERWAYS [21]

A small section of the Benoue River, up to Garoua, is of commercial importance but only for 3 months of the year.

PORTS [22]

Douala is the only major port and handled 867,000 tons of cargo in 1958.

ROADS [23]

At the beginning of 1958 there were 600 km. of bituminized roads, 8,200 km. of nonbituminized roads, and 1,200 km. of seasonal trails.

RAILROADS [24]

In 1957 there were 517 km. of railroad.

AIRWAYS [25]

There are 4 main airports at Douala, Garoua, N'Gaoundere, and Yaounde.

POSTS, TELECOMMUNICATIONS AND BROADCASTING [26]

At the beginning of 1958 there were 95 postal agencies, 116 telegraph offices, 1,869 telephone subscribers, and 2,374 branch telephones. Cameroon runs 3 radio stations, providing a combined 152 hours' service per week.

Resources and Trade

MAIN EXPORTS [27]

Cocoa (representing about 31% of the total exports in 1957), coffee, bananas, shelled peanuts, palm kernels, tobacco, rubber, woods, and cotton.

MAIN IMPORTS [28]

Consumer goods, capital goods, foodstuffs, raw materials, and semi-finished products.

VALUE OF TRADE [29]

In millions of C.F.A. francs

	1956	1957	1958	1959	1960
Exports	13,150	15,004	22,291	26,767	23,938
Imports	16,700	18,149	21,452	20,153	20,384

LIVESTOCK [30]

1957

Cattle	1,256,000
Sheep and goats	1,600,000
Pigs	250,000
Horses and asses	67,000
Poultry	4,000,000

Industry

MANUFACTURES [31]

The bulk of the manufacturing industries are concerned with food processing such as coffee, oils, chocolate. In addition cigarettes and tobacco, soap, cement, aluminum, and household goods are produced.

MINING [32]

Tin, gold, and titanium are mined.

POWER [33]

Cameroon had an installed capacity of 101,090 kw. in 1957 with 8 stations. Consumption in that same year totaled 193,948 kwh.

Finance

CURRENCY

C.F.A. franc: 1 C.F.A. franc equals 2 old Metropolitan French francs.

BANKING [34]

La Banque d'Afrique Occidentale, the British Bank of West Africa, La Banque Commerciale Africaine, La Banque Nationale pour le Commerce et l'Industrie, Le Crédit Lyonnais and La Société Générale.

BUDGET [35]

1957 C.F.A. francs

Ordinary revenue	9,656,000
Ordinary expenditure	8,754,000

Taxation is the main source of revenue.

DEVELOPMENT PLAN [36]

A 10-year plan divided into two stages—1947/1953 and 1953/1958. Total expenditure: 56,902 million C.F.A. francs of which two-thirds was contributed by F.I.D.E.S. and the rest from the French budget, Cameroon budget, internal loans, and the semipublic sector. Expenditure for the year 1957/1958 was allocated as follows:

Rural economy	42.2%
Infrastructure	40.6%
Social services	17.2%

LABOR [37]

In 1957 the wage-earning population was estimated to be distributed as follows:

Public Sector

Civil service	8,000	
Non-Civil service	17,900	25,900

Private Sector

Agriculture, fishing, and forestry	45,150	
Mining and quarrying	2,500	
Industry	12,300	
Building and public works	12,950	
Commerce, banking, and professions	25,400	
Transport and storage	8,000	
Domestic service	7,500	113,800
TOTAL		139,700

In 1957 there were 36 employers' unions with 283 members and 424 employees' unions with a total membership of some 36,000.[38]

Labor matters were covered by the Labor Code of 1952 until independence. Postindependence information is not available.

THE FEDERATION OF THE CAMEROON NOTES

1   Kimble, George H. T. (Ed.), *Tropical Africa*, The Twentieth Century Fund, New York, 1960, Vol. II, p. 452.

2   Service des Statistiques d'Outre-Mer, *Outre-Mer 1958*, Paul Dupont, Paris, Nov. 1959, pp. 822–23, Tables 1 and 2.

3   *The Journal of Negro Education*, Vol. XXX, No. 3, Howard University Press, p. 282.

4   Gouvernement français à l'Assemblée Générale des Nations Unies sur l'Administration du Cameroun placé sous la tutelle de la France, *Rapport Annuel Année 1957*, l'Imprimerie Chaix, St. Ouen, 1959, pp. 9–10.

5   Ministère de la France d'Outre-Mer, *Le Cameroun 1946*, Agence des Colonies, Paris, N.D., pp. 1–4; also, S. H. Steinberg (Ed.), *The Statesman's Yearbook 1961*, Macmillan & Co., Ltd., London, 1961, pp. 882–83.

6   Proprietors West African Graphic Co., Ltd., *West Africa*, London, No. 2312, September 23, 1961, p. 1056.

7 *Revue Juridique et Politique d'Outre-Mer*, 15e année, No. 2, April–June 1961, Librairie Générale de Droit et de Jurisprudence, Paris, p. 235.

8 R. Segal, *Political Africa*, Stevens & Sons Ltd., London, 1961, pp. 312–15; also *Africa Report*, Vol. 6, No. 10, Nov. 1961, Washington, D.C., p. 5.

9 *Outre-Mer 1958, op. cit.*, pp. 823–24, Tables 3 and 4.

10 Since only the population figures of the cities of Yaounde and Daoula are available, it is impossible to compute an urban population estimate.

11 *Rapport Annuel Année 1957, op. cit.*, pp. 16–17; *Outre-Mer 1958, op. cit.*, pp. 822–23, Tables 1 and 2.

12 *Outre-Mer 1958, op. cit.*, p. 140, Table 1.

13 *Rapport Annuel Année 1957, op. cit.*, pp. 19–21.

14 *Outre-Mer 1958, op. cit.*, pp. 822–23, Tables 1 and 2.

15 *Ibid.*

16 *Ibid.*, pp. 825–26, Tables 8 and 9.

17 *Rapport Annuel Année 1957, op. cit.*, pp. 418–22.

18 *Outre-Mer 1958, op. cit.*, p. 825, Table 6.

19 *Rapport Annuel Année 1957, op. cit.*, pp. 231–33.

20 International Labor Office, *African Labor Survey*, Geneva, 1958, p. 21.

21 *Rapport Annuel Année 1957, op. cit.*, pp. 189–90.

22 *Outre-Mer 1958, op. cit.*, p. 827, Table 14.

23 *Ibid.*, p. 826, Table 10.

24 *Ibid.*, p. 826, Table 12.

25 *Ibid.*, p. 827, Table 15.

26 *Ibid.*, pp. 827–28, Tables 16 and 17.

27 *Ibid.*, p. 830, Table 24; also *Rapport Annuel Année 1957, op. cit.*, p. 375.

28 *Outre-Mer 1958, op. cit.*, p. 830, Table 24.

29 France: Ministère de la France d'Outre-Mer, *Bulletin de Conjecture des Territoires d'Outre-Mer*, No. 15, Paris, April 1958, p. ix; No. 21, August 1960, p. 22; France: Service des Statistiques, *Résumé des Statistiques d'Outre-Mer*, Bulletin Accéléré, Paris, Nos. 5–8 and 28, 1959 and 1961, p. 3.

30 *Rapport Annuel Année 1957, op. cit.*, p. 383.

31 *Outre-Mer 1958, op. cit.*, p. 829, Table 20.

32 *Ibid.*, p. 830, Table 23.

33 *Ibid.*, p. 829, Table 21.

34 *Rapport Annuel Année 1957, op. cit.*, p. 97.

35 *Ibid.*, pp. 350 and 352.

36 *Ibid.*, pp. 107–108 and 115.

37 *Outre-Mer 1958, op. cit.*, p. 209, Table 3.

38 *Ibid.*, p. 207, Table 1.

The Central African Republic[1]
(formerly Ubangi-Shari)

AREA: *238,000 sq. m.*

POPULATION:[2] *1,145,500 (1958 estimate)*

Density: 5 per sq. m.

GEOGRAPHY [3]

The Central African Republic lies just north of the equator. It consists of a vast rolling plateau with an average altitude around 2,000 feet; most of the land drains toward the Congo Basin. It has many rivers, including the Ubangi, tributary of the Congo River, and the Shari River, after both of which the country was originally named. Temperatures range between 70 degrees F. in the cold months to over 90 degrees F. in the hot months. Rainfall is lowest in the northern region, averaging 30 to 40 inches annually. In the south, rainfall averages between 50 and 60 inches annually.

HISTORICAL SKETCH

Relations between the French and this region began in 1887 with the extension of the French Congo northward. In 1894 it was constituted as a separate territory known as Ubangi-Shari, under the authority of a High Commander. In 1905, it was merged with Chad, and in 1910 French Equatorial Africa was formally constituted, comprising Gabon, the Middle Congo, Chad, and Ubangi-Shari.

In 1946, following the new constitution of the Fourth French Republic, Ubangi-Shari took a greater share in the management of its own affairs. It sent representatives to the French Parliament in Metropolitan France for the first time following the establishment of its own elected Representative Assembly in 1945. In October 1958 it became a self-governing republic within the newly formed French Community, and on August 13, 1960, gained its independence. It was admitted to the United Nations on September 20, 1960.

GOVERNMENT

Present Status

Independent republican state.

Constitution

The government consists of an elected Legislative Assembly of 50 members, elected for a five-year term, and a President invested by the Assembly with broad executive powers. He appoints members of the government and may terminate their functions; he is head of all administrative services and makes appointments to state posts; he promulgates laws and has power to issue regulations; he ensures the maintenance of law and order and may proclaim a state of emergency. The Legislative Assembly meets twice a year in ordinary session and may be convened in extraordinary session at the request of the President. Both the President and the members of the Assembly may initiate legislation.

Franchise

Universal adult suffrage.

Local Government

Local government is decentralized; the country is divided into 11 regions which administer their own affairs democratically. Details are not available.

Political Parties [4]

Mouvement pour l'Evolution Sociale de l'Afrique Noire (MESAN), led by David Dacko, President of the Republic. It holds 38 seats in the Assembly.

Mouvement à l'Evolution Démocratique de l'Afrique Centrale (MEDAC), led by Abel Goumba. It holds 11 seats.

POPULATION BREAKDOWN

Main Cities [5]

1958 estimate

Bangui	81,700
Bouar	16,100

Bambari	14,100
Basangoa	12,300
Berberati	11,400
Bangassou	6,700

Urban-rural Distribution [6]

About 12% of the total population lives in towns of 10,000 or more inhabitants.

Ethnic Distribution [7]
1958 estimate

Non-African	5,974
African	1,139,500

Divided into 4 major ethnic groups:

Madjia-Baya
Banda
M'baka
Azande

Religious Affiliation [8]

Christians	25%
Muslims	4%
Animists	71%

Languages

Each ethnic group listed above has a language of its own, but "Shango" is a sort of lingua franca spoken all over the country. French is the official language.

Sex Distribution [9]
1958 estimate

	Male	Female
African	562,700 (49.4%)	576,800 (50.6%)
Non-African	3,495 (58.5%)	2,479 (41.5%)

Age Distribution [10]
1958 estimate

	Under 15	15–49	50+
African	438,100	639,500	60,900
Non-African	1,745	3,421	808

SOCIAL DATA

Education [11]

As of January 1, 1958

TABLE I

	Enrollment	Public School Teachers
140 Public primary schools } 103 Private primary schools }	45,774	446
6 Public secondary schools } 9 Private secondary schools }	1,044	12
15 Public technical schools } 2 Private technical schools }	436	29

There were 35 students studying abroad in 1958.

In 1957, 28.1% of the children of school-going age were at school, of which 16.5% were girls. Education expenditure represented 19.3% of the budget in that same year.

Health and Social Services

VITAL STATISTICS

Not available.

MAIN DISEASES

Not available.

HEALTH SERVICES [12]

As of January 1, 1957

TABLE II

	Beds
2 Secondary hospitals	463
18 Medical centers	813
18 Infirmaries	239
52 Dispensaries	—
8 Private institutions	78
19 Maternity services	373

43 medical practitioners, 1 per every 27,000 inhabitants; 14 beds per 10,000 inhabitants.

SOCIAL WELFARE SERVICES [13]

Maternal and child welfare services are emphasized with an increasing development in the establishment of educational activities for women. In rural areas "paysannat" programs cover the development of agricultural communities. In 1956 some 32,000 people fell under this program.

ECONOMY

The Central African Republic is a poor country whose economy is based almost entirely on agriculture.

Transport and Communications

WATERWAYS

There are more than 370 miles of navigable waterways, but owing to the variation of water flow from season to season and the unevenness of river beds at some points, navigation is difficult.

PORTS

New installations are being constructed at Bangui, on the Congo River.

ROADS

There are 10,900 miles of roads, of which 3,600 are passable all year round by heavy vehicles.

RAILROADS

None. A railroad connecting Bangui with Berbere and Fort-Lamy in the Republic of Chad is in the planning stage.

AIRWAYS

There are airfields at Bangui, Berberati, and Bouar. Airstrips throughout the country link its various parts.

POSTS, TELECOMMUNICATIONS AND BROADCASTING

Information on postal, telegraph, and telephone services for the Central African Republic is not available. Radio Brazzaville and Radio

A.E.F., with programs in local dialects, serve all of former French Equatorial Africa.

Resources and Trade

MAIN EXPORTS [14]

Cotton, coffee, peanuts, diamonds, and sisal.

MAIN IMPORTS [15]

Food and beverages, cotton cloth, fuel, and cement.

VALUE OF TRADE [16]

In 000's of C.F.A. francs

	1956	1957	1958	1959	1960
Exports	3,250	3,100	3,400	3,798	3,427
Imports	4,050	4,100	4,640	4,287	4,956

Almost all of the country's trade is carried on within the the franc area.

LIVESTOCK [17]

	1957
Cattle	312,000
Sheep and goats	460,000
Pigs	13,000
Horses and donkeys	300

Industry

MANUFACTURES [18]

The country produces peanut oil, palm oil, beer, cotton fibers, soap, and hides and skins on a small scale.

MINING

The only mineral resources mined are diamonds and gold. A program for the prospecting of primary deposits has been initiated by the government.

POWER

Hydroelectric power is being developed in M'Bali and the Vangaria Valley to supply the Bangui generators. Transformers are being installed in Bangui.

Finance

C.F.A. francs. 1 C.F.A. franc equals 2 old Metropolitan French francs.

BANKING [19]
Banque de l'Afrique Occidentale, Banque Commerciale Africaine, Banque Nationale pour le Commerce et l'Industrie, Société Générale, Crédit, Lyonnais, and Banque Belge d'Afrique.

BUDGET [20]
In Millions of C.F.A. francs

	1958
Revenue	1,792
Expenditure	1,792

DEVELOPMENT PLAN
See Appendix III.

LABOR
The wage-earning population was estimated to be distributed as follows in 1957: [21]

Public Sector		
Civil service	2,200	
Non-Civil service	3,200	5,400
Private Sector		
Agriculture, fishing, and forestry	15,520	
Mining and quarrying	5,750	
Industry	7,220	
Building and public works	4,200	
Commerce, banking, and professions	3,800	
Transport and storage	1,700	
Domestic service	5,000	43,190
TOTAL		48,590

There were 242 trade unions in 1956 throughout ex-French Equatorial Africa. At the beginning of 1958, 2,066 employers were contributing to the Family Equalization funds and 7,746 workers were receiving allocations.[22]

The Labor Code of 1952 covered such matters as hours of work, trade unions, the setting up of Labor Tribunals and Labor Offices, health and safety, and family allowances. Postindependence information is not available.

THE CENTRAL AFRICAN REPUBLIC
NOTES

1 Unless otherwise stated, information obtained from Ambassade de France, Service de Presse et d'Information, *The Central African Republic*, New York, Dec. 1960.

2 Service des Statistiques d'Outre-Mer, *Outre-Mer 1958*, Paul Dupont, Paris, Nov. 1959, pp. 776–77, Tables 1 and 3.

3 Headquarters Quartermasters Research and Engineering Command, U.S. Army, Technical Report EP-94, Canal Zone Analogs V: *Analogs of Canal Zone Climate—South Central Africa*, Natick, Mass., July 1958, Figures 3, 5, and 8.

4 R. Segal, *Political Africa*, Stevens & Sons Ltd., London, 1961, p. 316.

5 *Outre-Mer 1958, op. cit.*, p. 777, Table 2.

6 Percentage computed from *Ibid.*, pp. 776–77, Tables 1, 2, and 3.

7 *Ibid.*, pp. 776–77, Tables 1 and 3.

8 *Ibid.*, p. 140, Table 1.

9 *Ibid.*, p. 776–77, Tables 1 and 3.

10 *Ibid.*

11 *Ibid.*, p. 778, Tables 6 and 7.

12 *Ibid.*, p. 777, Table 4.

13 U.N.: *Progress on Non-Self-Governing Territories Under the Charter*, Territorial Surveys, Vol. 5, New York, 1960, p. 29.

14 Haut Commissariat de la République en A.E.F., *L'A.E.F. Economique et Sociale 1947–1958*, Editions Alains, May 1959, Tables, p. xiv.

15 *Ibid.*

16 France: Service des Statistiques, *Résumé des Statistiques d'Outre-Mer Bulletin Accéléré*, No. 28, Paris, April 1961, p. 3.

17 *Outre-Mer 1958, op. cit.*, p. 780, Table 13.

18 *Ibid.*, Table 14.

19 S. H. Steinberg (Ed.), *The Statesman's Yearbook 1959*, Macmillan & Co., Ltd., London, 1959, pp. 1018–19.

20 *Ibid.*, 1961, p. 1026.

21 *Outre-Mer 1958, op. cit.*, p. 209, Table 3.

22 *Ibid.*, p. 217, Table 15; also U.N., *op. cit.*, pp. 27 and 29.

The Republic of Chad[1]

AREA: *495,000 sq. m.*

POPULATION:[2] *2,579,600 (1958 estimate)*

Density: 5 per sq. m.

GEOGRAPHY

Chad lies in the heart of Africa, some 2,000 to 3,000 miles from the coast. It consists of a vast peneplain deeply cut by the valleys of the Shari, Logone, and Bahr-al-Gazal rivers, with a low sedimentary basin around Lake Chad. The land slopes gradually upward from 800 to almost 5,500 feet in the Wadai Mountains in the east and to 10,000 feet in the volcanic Tibest Mountains in the north. Lake Chad is watered mainly by the Shari River and varies in surface coverage between 4,000 and 10,000 square miles. There are three distinct geographical zones: (a) wooded savanna with a semihumid tropical climate whose rainfall averages 35 to 47 inches over 6 to 7 months in the year, in summer and autumn; (b) a bush-covered steppe with a dry tropical climate with 4 to 5 months of rainfall in summer averaging 20 to 35 inches; and (c) a desert region to the north with an arid climate with less than 8 inches of rainfall per annum.

HISTORICAL SKETCH

Lake Chad region was the seat of many pre-European African empires, such as those of Bagirmi and Wadai. European exploration of the area started at the turn of the 19th century, but it was not until 1913 that the French control of all the area now known as the Republic of Chad was established.

The first Frenchman to reach Lake Chad, Emil Gentil in 1897, signed a treaty of alliance with Sultan Gaourang. In 1913 the acquisition of the Borku region completed the present boundaries of the country. It was

54

here that Felix Eboue served as Governor from 1938 to 1940, later to become Governor General of French Equatorial Africa for four years (1940–1944). Chad then acquired the status of an Overseas Territory with an elected territorial assembly and direct representation in the Metropolitan Parliament. In 1958 it became a member state of the French Community and on August 11, 1960, gained its independence. On September 20, 1960, it was admitted to the United Nations.

GOVERNMENT

Present Status
Independent republican state.

Constitution
Legislative power is vested in a National Assembly of 83 elected members who, with the Prime Minister, may initiate laws. It meets twice a year in ordinary session. Executive power is exercised by the President, who is also Prime Minister, elected by the National Assembly. He has the power to issue regulations, to make public appointments, and is responsible for all administrative services and the maintenance of law and order. The Assembly may, by an absolute majority, adopt a motion of censure of government. Within 48 hours the President may either dissolve the National Assembly or hand in his resignation. In the latter case the Assembly elects a new Chief of State.

Franchise
Universal adult suffrage.

Local Government [3]
Before independence there existed one commune mixte at Fort Lamy, governed by an administrative mayor and advisory Municipal Commission. African villages were governed by their chiefs under the control of "canton" or tribal chiefs. Postindependence information not available.

Political Parties [4]
Parti Progressiste Tchadien (PPT), led by François Tombalbaye, present Prime Minister and President—67 seats.

Parti National Africain (PNA), led by Ali Djibine Karallah—10 seats, which fused in March 1961 to form the Union Pour le Progrès du Tchad (UPT).

POPULATION BREAKDOWN

Main Cities [5]
1957 census

Fort Lamy	56,784
Fort Archambault	18,835
Moundou	25,274
Abeche	7,800

Urban-rural Distribution [6]
About 4% of the total population lives in towns of 10,000 inhabitants or more; 3% of the African population, and 64% of the non-African population.

Ethnic Distribution [7]
1958 estimate

Non-African	4,973
African	2,574,600

There are two main ethnic divisions: The Muslims in the north, divided into Arabs, Fulani, Wadain, Kanebu, and Tibu. The Africans, divided into the Sara, Hakka, Massa, and Mundang.

Religious Affiliation [8]

Christians	7%
Muslims	52%
Animists	43%

Languages
Kanem and Fulani. French is the official language.

Sex Distribution [9]
1958 estimate

	Male	Female
African	1,243,400 (48.3%)	1,331,200 (51.7%)
Non-African	3,058 (61.4%)	1,915 (38.6%)

Age Distribution [10]

1958 estimate	Under 18	18–60	60+
African	1,097,800	1,345,900	130,900

	Under 20	20+
Non-African	1,302	3,671

SOCIAL DATA

Education [11]

As of January 1, 1958

TABLE I

	Enrollment	Public School Teachers
124 Public elementary schools 30 Private elementary schools	32,610	481
3 Public secondary schools	485	16
6 Public technical schools	217	22

In 1958 there were 35 students studying abroad.

In 1957, 8.6% of the children of school-going age were at school, of which 10.5% were girls. Education expenditure represented 11.5% of the local annual budget.

Health and Social Services

VITAL STATISTICS

Not available.

MAIN DISEASES

Sleeping sickness and leprosy.

HEALTH SERVICES [12]

As of January 1, 1958

TABLE II

	Beds
3 Secondary hospitals	724
16 Medical centers	1,058
15 Infirmaries	—

TABLE II—Continued

	Beds
49 Dispensaries	—
40 Private institutions	—
14 Maternity and special services	191 (maternity beds)

There were 45 medical practitioners in 1958, 1 per every 57,000 inhabitants; 7 beds per 10,000 inhabitants.

SOCIAL WELFARE SERVICES [13]

Emphasis is placed on maternity and child welfare services, with increased attention being paid to women's education. "Paysannat" programs assist in rural community development.

ECONOMY

The economy of Chad is almost entirely agricultural. More than 2,500,000 persons derive their living from tilling the soil, stock raising, and fishing.

Transport and Communications

WATERWAYS

Most waterways are navigable for only part of the year. The Shari River connects Chad with the Congo Republic via the Central African Republic and is navigable from the beginning of July to the end of January. The Logone and Pende rivers are so winding as to limit the length of barges that can be used. The Bahr Sara River is used chiefly for floating logs.

PORTS

None.

ROADS

There are some 18,600 miles of roads and trails. Owing to the annual floods between July and January, many are impassable during a considerable period of the year.

RAILROADS

None. A line running from Banqui (C.A.R.) to Berbere, on the Shari River, is under consideration.

AIRWAYS

There are 5 large airports at Fort Lamy, Moundou, Fort Archambault, Abeche, and Pala. Smaller airfields are to be found at Bongor, Mongo, and Largeau.

POSTS, TELECOMMUNICATIONS, AND BROADCASTING [14]

Information on postal, telephone, and telegraph services is not available. Radio Chad provides 52 hours of service per week.

Resources and Trade

MAIN EXPORTS [15]

Cotton, livestock, meat and fish, leather and hides, shelled peanuts, natron, butter, elephant tusks and teeth.

MAIN IMPORTS

Lumber, soap, beer, cigarettes, textiles and clothing, and capital goods.

VALUE OF TRADE [16]

In millions of C.F.A. francs

	1956	1957	1958	1959	1960
Exports	3,900	3,500	5,172	4,103	3,271
Imports	5,300	5,800	5,982	6,147	6,237

LIVESTOCK [17]

1957 estimates

Cattle	4,000,000
Sheep and goats	4,000,000
Camels	300,000
Donkeys	300,000
Horses	150,000

Industry

MANUFACTURES [18]

Cotton and meat processing for export and local consumption; processing of hides and skins; production of peanut oil; building and public works; machine shops.

Recent prospecting has revealed deposits of rare ores such as tungsten, but the only mineral being mined is natron (native sodium carbonate).

POWER

6 million kw. is generated at Fort Lamy.

Finance

CURRENCY

One C.F.A. franc equals 2 old Metropolitan French francs.

BANKING [19]

Banque de l'Afrique Occidentale, Banque Commerciale Africaine, Banque Nationale pour le Commerce et l'Industrie, Société Générale, Crédit Lyonnais, Banque Belge d'Afrique.

BUDGET [20]

In millions of C.F.A. francs

	1958
Revenue	2,447
Expenditure	2,447

DEVELOPMENT PLAN

See Appendix III.

LABOR [21]

In 1957 the employment of wage earners was estimated to be:

Public Sector

Civil service	3,250	
Non-Civil service	8,000	11,250

Private Sector

Agriculture, fishing, and forestry	140	
Mining and quarrying	330	
Industry	4,770	
Building and public works	5,760	
Commerce, banking, and professions	5,350	
Transport and storage	1,870	
Domestic service	5,330	23,550
TOTAL		34,800

In 1956 there were 242 trade unions throughout ex-French Equatorial Africa.[22]

As of January 1, 1958, 2,227 employers were contributing to the Equalization Fund for Family Allowances, and 2,609 workers were receiving allocations and 6,512 children were benefiting.[23]

Preindependence legislation covered such matters as working hours, conditions of work, minimum wages, and accident insurance. Postindependence information is not available.

THE REPUBLIC OF CHAD NOTES

1   Unless otherwise stated, information obtained from Ambassade de France, Service de Presse et d'Information, *The Republic of Chad*, New York, Jan. 1961.

2   Service des Statistiques d'Outre-Mer, *Outer-Mer 1958*, Paul Dupont, Paris, Nov. 1959, p. 798, Tables 1 and 2.

3   L'Annuaire Vert, *Annuaire Economique 1958*, Editions C.E.P. Publicité, Casablanca (Morocco), p. 746.

4   R. Segal, *Political Africa*, Stevens and Sons Ltd., London, 1961, pp. 454–55.

5   *Outre-Mer 1958, op. cit.*, p. 799, Table 3.

6   *Ibid.*, pp. 798–99, Tables 1, 2, and 3. Since urban figures are for 1957 and population figures are for 1958, the percentages given must be taken only as a very crude estimate.

7   *Ibid.*, p. 798, Tables 1 and 2.

8   *Ibid.*, p. 140, Table 1.

9   *Ibid.*, p. 798, Tables 1 and 2.

10   *Ibid.*

11   *Ibid.*, pp. 799–800, Tables 6 and 7.

12   *Ibid.*, p. 799, Table 4.

13   U.N.: *Progress in Non-Self-Governing Territories Under the Charter*, Territorial Surveys, Vol. 5, New York, 1960, p. 29.

14   *Outre-Mer 1958, op. cit.*, p. 801.

15   Haut Commissariat de la Republique en A.E.F.: *L'A.E.F. Economique et Sociale 1947–1958*, Editions Alains, May 1959, p. xv.

16   *Ibid.*, p. ix; also France: Service des Statistiques, *Résumé des Statistiques d'Outre-Mer, Bulletin Accéléré*, Paris, March 17, 1960 and April 28, 1961, p. 3.

17   *Outre-Mer 1958, op. cit.*, p. 801, Table 13.

18   *Ibid.*, Table 14.

19 S. H. Steinberg (Ed.), *The Statesman's Yearbook 1959*, Macmillan & Co., Ltd., London, 1959, pp. 1018–19.
20 *Ibid.*, p. 1017.
21 *Outre-Mer 1958, op. cit.*, p. 209, Table 3.
22 U.N.: *Progress of Non-Self-Governing Territories Under the Charter, op. cit.*, pp. 27 and 29.
23 *Outre-Mer 1958, op. cit.*, p. 217, Table 15.

The Comoro Islands[1]

AREA: *863 sq. m.*
POPULATION: *183,000 (1960 estimate)*
Density: 212 per sq. m.

GEOGRAPHY

The territory is made up of four main islands—Mayotte, Anjouan, Mohéli, and Grand Comore—with a mountainous relief of volcanic origin. They are situated midway between the equator and the Tropic of Capricorn. The climate is tropical with a dry season from May to October and a hot, wet season from November to April. There is considerable rainfall, and temperature at sea level never falls below 68 degrees F.

HISTORICAL SKETCH

The first detailed knowledge of this area came from Arab sailors. Two Arab invasions swept over the islands, the last coming from the Persian Gulf in the 15th century. In the 16th century the islands were visited by the Portuguese, French, and Dutch navigators, and it was during this same century that the Malagasy invasions began. Quarrels over the royal succession were rife in all the islands and were only settled during the 19th century when the French took control. In 1843 the Malagasy ruler of Mayotte ceded the island to France. In 1865 the Malagasy ruler of Mohéli signed a treaty of friendship with France and in April 1886 placed it under French protection. Anjouan and the Grand Comore had placed themselves under French protection a few months earlier. In 1912 the Comoro Islands were joined administratively with Madagascar. After World War II the Comoros were separated from Madagascar and acquired the status of an overseas territory. They retained this status following the referendum of September 1958. On December 12, 1961, the French National

Assembly gave the islands internal autonomy within the framework of the Fifth French Republic.

GOVERNMENT

Present Status
French overseas territory.

Constitution
The islands are administered by a High Commissioner who promulgates laws and decrees, supervises the legality of administrative acts, and is responsible for defense and external affairs. He is assisted by a Government Council of 6 to 8 ministers responsible to the Territorial Assembly of 31 members elected for 5 years. The Council's President, elected by a two-thirds majority of the Territorial Assembly, appoints the members of the Council.

Franchise
Universal adult suffrage.

Local Government
Each of the four main islands has a District Assembly of from 6 to 22 members elected for 5 years. They are responsible for the management of local affairs.

Political Parties
Not available.

POPULATION BREAKDOWN

Island Population
1960 estimate

Grand Comore	91,000
Anjouan	62,000
Mayotte	23,000
Mohéli	7,000

Dzaoudzi, the capital, is situated on Mayotte.

Urban-rural Distribution
Not available.

Ethnic Distribution [2]
1956 census

	Non-African	1,005

1958 estimate

	African	180,660

Religious Affiliation
The indigenous population is almost entirely Muslim.

Languages
Not available.

Sex Distribution [3]
1958 estimate

	Male	Female
African	77,980 (43.1%)	102,680 (56.9%)

1956 census

	Male	Female
Non-African	554 (55.2%)	451 (44.8%)

Age Distribution [4]
1958 estimate

	Under 20	20–60	60+
African	91,920	70,440	18,300

1956 census

	Under 20	20+
Non-African	405	600

SOCIAL DATA

Education
In 1960 nearly 4,500 pupils were receiving elementary school education in 48 French schools and 200 pupils were attending 2 secondary schools. There are several apprenticeship centers, and plans are being made to expand the teachers' training school in Moroni (Grand Comore).

Health and Social Services [5]

There are two main hospitals—the Dzaoudzi and Grand Comore hospitals; 4 smaller hospitals located at other points on the islands; 5 maternity and child care centers; and about 20 health stations. In 1958 there were 10 medical practitioners, 1 per every 18,000 inhabitants, and 20 beds per 10,000 inhabitants.

ECONOMY

The economy is chiefly agricultural. Industry is limited to the processing of local products.

Transport and Communications

WATERWAYS

None.

PORTS

Dzaoudzi (main port); Mutsamudu (Anjouan); Moroni (Grand Comore), and Fomboni (Mohéli), which together handled 23,000 tons in 1960.

ROADS

In 1960 there were 435 miles of road, of which 370 were passable during all seasons of the year.

RAILROADS

None.

AIRWAYS

There are 4 airports serving the islands. There is airline service between the islands and France.

POSTS, TELECOMMUNICATIONS, AND BROADCASTING

A radio communication network, with the main station at Dzaoudzi, provides telephone and telegraph connections between the islands and Madagascar. There is a 4 kw. radio broadcasting station, Radio Comores.

Resources and Trade

MAIN EXPORTS

Vanilla (44.5% of the total value of exports in 1960), ilang-ilang essence, copra, and sisal.

MAIN IMPORTS

Vegetable products, mineral products, textiles, metals, and motor vehicles.

VALUE OF TRADE

In $ U.S. millions

	1960
Exports	3.2
Imports	3.8

The islands trade chiefly with France and Madagascar.

LIVESTOCK

1960 estimate

Cattle	18,000
Sheep and goats	95,500
Donkeys	2,500
Pigs	1,000

Industry

MANUFACTURES

The lumber industry is highly developed. Installations for processing sisal and vanilla and for drying copra are located near production centers. Anjouan has 9 perfume distilleries, Mohéli 2, Grand Comore 12, and Mayotte 15. There is a sugar refinery on Mayotte and a combined oil mill and soap factory on Grand Comore.

MINING

There are practically no mineral resources on the islands.

POWER

Electric power is provided by two thermal power plants and three hydroelectric plants.

Finance

CURRENCY
C.F.A. franc. 1 C.F.A. franc equals 2 old Metropolitan French francs.

BANKING
Not available.

BUDGET [6]

	1960
Revenue	441,267 C.F.A. francs
Expenditure	441,267 C.F.A. francs

DEVELOPMENT PLAN
A plan was drawn up in 1946 financed by FIDES. From 1946 to 1960 total expenditure had been $816 million, allocated as follows:

Production	$2 million
Infrastructure	4 million
Social equipment	2.6 million

LABOR
In 1958 employment of the wage-earning population was estimated as: [7]

Public Sector

Civil service	335	
Non-Civil service	2,562	2,897

Private Sector

Agriculture, fishing, and forestry	7,330	
Industry	80	
Building and public works	140	
Commerce, banking, and professions	440	
Transport and storage	35	
Domestic service	620	8,645
TOTAL		11,542

In 1958 there were 2 employers' unions with 190 members. There were 150 employers contributing to the Family Allowance Equalization Fund benefiting 1,314 persons.[8]

Information on labor legislation is not available.

THE COMORO ISLANDS NOTES

1 Unless otherwise stated, all information obtained from Ambassade de France, Service de Presse et d'Information, *The Comoro Islands*, New York, Feb. 1962.

2 Service des Statistiques d'Outre-Mer, *Outre-Mer 1958*, Paul Dupont, Paris, Nov. 1959, p. 694, Tables 1 and 2.

3 *Ibid.*

4 *Ibid.*

5 *Ibid.*, p. 694, Table 3.

6 S. H. Steinberg (Ed.), *The Statesman's Yearbook 1961*, Macmillan & Co., Ltd., London, 1961, pp. 1023–1024.

7 *Outre-Mer 1958, op. cit.*, p. 209, Table 3.

8 *Ibid.*, p. 207, Table 1 and p. 217, Table 15.

The Republic of the Congo
(BRAZZAVILLE)

AREA: *139,000 sq. m.*
POPULATION: [2] *764,700 (1958 estimate)*
Density: 6 per sq. m.

GEOGRAPHY

The Republic of the Congo lies on the equator. It consists of five main geographical zones: first, a low treeless coastal plain of some 40 miles width; second, a mountainous region consisting of a succession of sharp ridges with altitudes varying from 1,600 to 2,600 feet, almost entirely covered by rain forest; third, a vast depression, the Niari Valley, covered by savanna, with northern slopes rising toward the wooded central massif of Gabon, and southern slopes going toward the treeless plateau of the Cataracts; fourth, the Stanley Pool region of hills, giving way to the grassy Bateke plateaus to the north, separated from each other by deep valleys of the northern tributaries of the Congo River. The fifth largest region, and part of the Congo basin northeast of Brazzaville is covered with a dense forest. There are two distinct climatic zones: (a) the Bateke plateaus with a long dry season, an average rainfall of 60 inches per annum, and temperatures varying between 70 and 80 degrees F.; and (b) the Congo basin with rainfall throughout the year amounting to 98 inches, and temperatures varying from 75 to 78 degrees F.

HISTORICAL SKETCH

Before the arrival of the European, a number of kingdoms existed in this area which, by the end of the 17th century, had been considerably weakened. French contact originated with the exploration of Savorgnan de Brazza about 1875 to 1880. Following the Berlin Pact of 1885, when the territory's boundaries were recognized, de Brazza was put in charge of the French mission in the Congo and Gabon. In 1903 it became part of the newly formed French Equatorial Africa, whose federal headquarters were situated at Brazzaville. The Middle Congo was the first of the central African states under French control to elect a Representative Council with an African majority after World War II. Upon passage of the Loi Cadre of 1956, this became the Territorial Assembly with extended powers. In November 1958 the country became a self-governing republic within the French Community and on August 15, 1960, obtained its independence. It was admitted to United Nations membership on September 20, 1960.

GOVERNMENT

Present Status
Independent republican state.

Constitution
There is a National Assembly of 60 deputies elected for a period of 5 years. Executive power is vested in the President, elected by the National Assembly, who is also Premier. He is assisted in policy-making by the Council of Ministers, the members of which he appoints. He promulgates laws and may issue regulations. He is head of the administrative services and the armed forces. In the event of conflict between the executive and legislative over a bill, a joint committee of two deputies and two ministers meet in the presence of the highest ranking judge. If no agreement is reached, the executive may either withdraw the bill or dissolve the Assembly, in which case new elections are held within 30 days.

Franchise
Universal adult suffrage.

Local Government [3]
Local government units are being established under the new Constitution. Details are not available.

Political Parties [4]
The Union Démocratique de Défense des Intérets Africains (U.D.D.I.A.), led by Fulbert Youlou, President and Premier of the Republic, which is the local division of the R.D.A.

The Mouvement Socialiste Africain (M.S.A.), led by Jacques Apangault, which, in coalition with the U.D.D.I.A., governs the Republic. It is a local section of the French Socialist Party.

Parti Progressiste Congolais (P.P.C.), led by Felix Tchicaya.

POPULATION BREAKDOWN

Main Cities [5]

Brazzaville	99,074
Dolisie	9,390
Pointe-Noire	37,415

Urban-rural Distribution [6]

About 21.4% of the total population lives in towns of 10,000 or more inhabitants.

Ethnic Distribution [7]

1958 estimate

Non-African	10,602
African	754,100

The African population is divided as follows:

The Kongo—350,000 representing 45% of the population and including the Balali and Bakongo.

Bateke—150,000 including the Bakukuya.

M'Bochi—95,000 which consists of 10 tribes.

Sangha—which consists of 15 tribes.

Religious Affiliation [8]

Christians	49%
Muslims	0.6%
Animists	50%

Languages

Lingala and Swahili. French is the official language.

Sex Distribution [9]

1958 estimate

	Male	Female
African	360,100 (47.7%)	394,000 (52.3%)
Non-African	5,993 (56.5%)	4,609 (43.5%)

Age Distribution [10]

1958 estimate

	Under 18	18–60	61+
African	314,700	296,600	42,800
Non-African	3,723	6,861	18

SOCIAL DATA

Education [11]

As of January 1, 1958

TABLE I

	Enrollment	Public School Teachers
187 Public primary schools 295 Private primary schools	78,962	568
4 Public secondary schools 6 Private secondary schools	1,975	46
15 Public technical schools 10 Private technical schools	1,284	36

As of January 1, 1958 there were 108 students studying abroad.

In 1957, 72.2% of children of school-going age attended school, of which 22.7% were girls. Education expenditure represented 26.2% of the annual local budget.

Health and Social Services

VITAL STATISTICS

Not available.

MAIN DISEASES [12]

Sleeping sickness, leprosy, malaria, venereal disease, and tuberculosis.

HEALTH SERVICES [13]

As of January 1, 1958

TABLE II

	Beds
1 Main hospital	579
1 Secondary hospital	450
13 Medical centers	1,078
20 Infirmaries	657

TABLE II—Continued

	Beds
69 Dispensaries	229
27 Private institutions [14]	343

95 medical practitioners, 8 per 8,000 of the population; 44 beds per 10,000 of the population.

SOCIAL WELFARE SERVICES

Housing programs are being planned to cope with the increasing urban population. Family allowances and other payments are contributed by government and employers.

ECONOMY

The Congo Republic is an agricultural economy with 80% of the arable land owned and farmed by Congolese. Developments in other fields of economic activity are small.

Transport and Communications

WATERWAYS

Inland waterways are for the most part unnavigable. There is a 740-mile route between Brazzaville and Bangui which is used for both passenger and cargo services.

PORTS

Pointe-Noire has a well-equipped harbor, and plans exist to enlarge the port in order to handle manganese shipments. In 1958 it handled 860,000 tons of freight.

ROADS

There are 4,340 miles of permanent roads and 660 miles of seasonal roads which are for the most part connected with the Congo-Ocean Railroad.

RAILROADS

The 320-mile Congo-Ocean Railroad connects Pointe-Noire with Brazzaville.

AIRWAYS

There is an international airport at Brazzaville and a large airport at Pointe-Noire. In addition there are 12 airfields servicing local needs.

Telegraph, telephone, and radio communications exist, and are centered in Brazzaville, but no figures are available. Radio Brazzaville, with 3 powerful transmitters, is one of the largest broadcasting centers in Africa and can be heard in all parts of the world.

Resources and Trade

MAIN EXPORTS
Wood, vegetable products, ores, tobacco, and bananas.

MAIN IMPORTS [15]
Machinery, consumption goods, primary material, and semifinished goods.

VALUE OF TRADE [16]
In millions of C.F.A. Francs

	1956	1957	1958	1959	1960
Exports	2,150	2,500	2,950	3,530	4,429
Imports	6,750	8,450	10,730	13,869	17,316

LIVESTOCK
1957 estimate

Cattle	7,000
Sheep and goats	100,000
Pigs	15,000

Industry

MANUFACTURES
Local processing industries include some 30 oil mills, a sugar refinery, 18 saw mills, a plywood factory, several rice mills, aluminum and tin works, machine and metal workshops, and a cigarette factory. In addition there are several private construction companies and shipbuilding and repairs workshops.

MINING
Lead is mined at M'Fouati and phosphate deposits in the Holle and other regions. New gold placers and alluvial diamonds have been discovered. Prospecting is going on for zinc, copper, and radioactive ores.

POWER

The Société des Pétroles d'Afrique Equatoriale (S.A.P.F.E.), together with the Mobil Oil Co., is developing the oil fields at Pointe-Indienne. There is a hydroelectric plant at Djoue Falls, and the installation of a dam and hydroelectric plant along the Kouilou River is under consideration. At present the total electric production of the Republic is about 25 million kw. per annum.

Finance

CURRENCY

C.F.A. francs: 1 C.F.A. franc equals 2 old Metropolitan French francs.

BANKING [17]

Banque de l'Afrique Occidentale, Banque Commerciale Africaine, Banque Nationale pour le Commerce et l'Industrie, Société Générale, Crédit Lyonnais, and Banque Belge d'Afrique.

BUDGET [18]

In millions of C.F.A. francs

	1958
Revenue	2,361
Expenditure	2,361

DEVELOPMENT PLAN

See Appendix III.

LABOR

The wage-earning population in 1957 was estimated to be employed as follows: [19]

Public Sector

Civil service	3,000	
Non-Civil service	14,200	17,200

Private Sector

Agriculture, fishing, and forestry	12,030
Mining and quarrying	1,360
Industry	6,340
Building and public works	4,960
Commerce, banking, and professions	9,550

Transport and storage	6,540	
Domestic service	5,420	46,200
TOTAL		63,400

In 1956 there were 242 trade unions in the whole of ex-French Equatorial Africa.[20]

As of January 1, 1958, there were 3,403 employers contributing to the Family Allowance Equalization Fund, and 14,950 workers receiving allocations.[21]

The Labor Code of 1952 provided legislation designed to protect the workers in all French colonial areas. As a result almost all areas of employment are now covered by collective-bargaining agreements. Postindependence information is not available.

THE REPUBLIC OF THE CONGO NOTES
(Brazzaville)

1   Unless otherwise stated, information obtained from Ambassade de France, Service de Presse et d'Information, *The Republic of the Congo*, New York, January 1961.

2   Service des Statistiques d'Outre-Mer, *Outre-Mer 1958*, Paul Dupont, Paris, Nov. 1959, pp. 784–85, Tables 1 and 2.

3   Librairie Générale de Droit et de Jurisprudence: *Revue Juridique et Politique d'Outre Mer*, 15e année, No. 2, April–June 1961, Paris, p. 253.

4   R. Segal: *Political Africa*, Stevens & Sons, Ltd. London, 1961, pp. 317–18.

5   *Outre-Mer 1958, op. cit.*, p. 785, Table 3.

6   Haut Commisariat de la République en A.E.F.: *L'A.E.F. Economique et Sociale 1947–1958*, Editions Alains, May 1959, p. 8.

7   *Outre-Mer 1958, op. cit.*, pp. 784–85, Tables 1 and 2.

8   *Ibid.*, p. 140, Table 1.

9   *Ibid.*, pp. 784–85, Tables 1 and 2.

10   *Ibid.*

11   *Ibid.*, p. 786, Tables 6 and 7.

12   Documentation Office of the Presidency of the Congo Republic: S.P.C.I., *The Congo Brazzaville*, Brazzaville, May 1961, p. 28.

13   *Ibid.*, p. 785, Table 4.

14   Dr. Albert Schweitzer's famous mission hospital is situated at Lambarene.

15   France: Institut National de la Statistique et des Etudes Economiques,

Résumé des Statistiques d'Outre-Mer, Bulletin Accéléré, Paris, June 1961, p. 3.

16   L.A.E.F. *Economique et Sociale 1947–1958, op. cit.,* p. ix; France: Service des Statistiques, *Résumé des Statistiques d'Outre-Mer Bulletin Accéléré,* No. 25, Paris, April 1961, p. 3.

17   S. H. Steinberg (Ed.), *The Statesman's Yearbook 1959,* Macmillan & Co., Ltd. London, 1959, pp. 1018–1019.

18   *Ibid.,* p. 1017.

19   *Outre-Mer 1958, op. cit.,* p. 209, Table 3.

20   U.N.: *Progress in Non-Self-Governing Territories Under the Charter,* Territorial Surveys, Vol. 5, New York, 1960, p. 28.

21   *Outre-Mer 1958, op. cit.,* p. 217, Table 15.

The Republic of the Congo
(LEOPOLDVILLE)

AREA:[1] *1,810,122 sq. m.*
POPULATION:[2] *13,658,185 (1958 census)*
Density: 14 per sq. m.

GEOGRAPHY [3]

The Congo consists of a vast depression, the Congo Basin, surrounded by mountains. The Basin has an average altitude of 1,000 feet and is made up of plains and terraced plateaus extending to its edges. These plateaus rise progressively as they approach Katanga where they form several masses reaching heights from 5,500 to 6,000 feet in the Kundelungu and Kibara mountains, and 6,500 feet in the Marunga Mountains. Along the entire eastern border lies a deep, narrow valley, 875 miles long and 25–30 feet wide. The climate of the Congo is tropical with an average annual temperature of about 64 degrees F., ranging from 43 degrees F. at the highest altitude to 79 degrees F. in the central basin. Rainfall averages from 37 inches annually in Elizabethville to 67.8 inches in Stanleyville.

HISTORICAL SKETCH [4]

The exploration of the Congo Basin by Stanley in 1874 initiated Europe's contact with that region of Africa. Unable to interest Britain, particularly the powerful Manchester merchants, in the potential of this area, Stanley turned to Leopold II of Belgium. Under the King's aegis, an International African Association was formed in 1876 with the avowed purpose of bringing civilization into this area. Under the Association's flag, Leopold employed a large body of explorers and geographers to further explore and exploit the region. The subsequent rivalry between European states over access to the navigable Congo River led to the Berlin Conference of 1884–1885 when freedom of trade in the Congo Basin was guaranteed and Leopold's claim as ruler recognized. The period which followed, during which the country was subjected to a most ruthless exploitation of its human and natural resources, led to a world condemnation of the King's policy and the transfer of the country from his direct control to Belgian ministerial supervision in 1908. It was the discovery of the rich mineral deposits in the area, principally located in Katanga, which led to the development of the Belgian Congo into one of the most highly industrialized regions of the African continent. The Belgian policy, dictated by the Belgian Parliament through its territorial administrator, the Governor, placed emphasis on economic development almost to the total neglect of other factors. Large business enterprises were given concessions, both they and government acting as partners in the economic development of the country. The church had control of education. Little was done to assist the African in his political evolution, except insofar as it assisted in the general upgrading of economic efficiency. The first overt signs of discontent and restlessness amongst the Congolese came in 1959 when riots broke out in Leopoldville. The Belgian Government's response to these pressures was to promise communal, territorial elections in December of that year—indirect elections for Provincial Councils in March 1960, and indirect elections for Central Government in September 1960. Until that year no inhabitant of the country, white or African, had exercised any political right. Under very strong pressure, the Belgian Government found itself unable to keep to its time schedule and in June 1960 gave the Congo its independence. Internal tribal and regional differences of such intensity developed that the United Nations was finally called in to attempt to reintroduce law and order in a situation of complete chaos. At the time of writing, the situation is still one of precarious balance. The Katanga Province, under the leadership of Moise Tshombe, is still pressing for the recognition of its independence, while the Congolese Government, under the leadership of Cyrille Adoula, is attempting to bring about a unification of all the different elements and regions.

GOVERNMENT

Present Status
Independent republican state.

Constitution
The Constitution of 1960 is still in operation, though a new one is being prepared by the Congolese Government. It is a Republican Constitution with a Parliament consisting of two houses: the House

of Representatives composed of 137 elected deputies and the Senate, comprising 84 Senators elected by partial vote by the provincial assemblies (14 to each assembly) and eventually a maximum of 12 Senators coopted by the elected Senators, but distributed in equal numbers among the provinces. Executive power rests with the Premier and his ministers, answerable to Parliament.

Franchise [5]

Universal adult suffrage.

Local Government [6]

Each of the 6 provinces has a provincial assembly elected as a rule by universal adult suffrage, but which may also be constituted by decision of a higher authority, by the partial vote of borough and territorial councils. The government is either elected by the assembly or outside it. Local institutions comprise the native districts, cities, and boroughs under the control of the provincial government. These existed prior to 1960, but were elected by universal adult suffrage from that time.

Political Parties [7]

The number of political parties, associations, and movements in the Congo run to over a hundred. Of these the most important are:

L'Alliance de Bakongo (ABAKO), led by Joseph Kasavubu, President of the Republic.

L'Association des Baluba du Katanga (BALUBAKAT), led by Jasan Sendwe.

Confédération des Associations du Katanga (CONAKAT), led by Moise Tshombe.

Mouvement National Congolais (aile Lumumba) (M.N.C.) which was founded by the late Patrice Lumumba and is now led by Christophe Gbenye.

Mouvement National Congolais (aile Kalonji), a breakaway from the main M.N.C. under the leadership of Albert Kalonji.

Parti Solidaire Africain (P.S.A.), led by Antoine Gizenga, Vice-Premier of the Republic.

Parti de l'Unité Nationale (PUNA) led by Jean Bolikango, of which Cyrille Adoula, Premier, is a member.

POPULATION BREAKDOWN

Main Cities [8]
1958 census

Leopoldville	389,547
Elizabethville	182,638
Stanleyville	79,951
Jadotville	74,478
Luluabourg	59,535
Matadi	51,184

Urban-rural Distribution [9]
Of the total population some 9% live in towns of 10,000 or more inhabitants; some 8.7% of the African population and 61.8% of the non-African population.

Ethnic Distribution [10]
1958 census

White	112,759
Asian	1,582
Other	3,662

African   13,540,182 divided into the following major tribal groupings: the Ba-Kongo, the Ba-Lunda, the Ba-Luba, and the Ba-Mongo.

Religious Affiliation [11]

Christians	Roman Catholics	4,546,160 (1958)
	Protestants	825,625 "
Muslims		115,500 (1956)
Jews		1,520 "
Animists	There are no figures, but it can be assumed that the balance of the population is pagan.	

Languages
Lugula, Kicongo, Chiluba, and Swahili are among the principal vernacular languages spoken. Flemish and French are the official languages.

Sex Distribution [12]
1958 census

	Male	Female
African	6,681,188 (49.3%)	6,858,994 (50.7%)
Non-African	58,214 (53.2%)	51,243 (46.8%)

Age Distribution [13]
African
7,498,961 adults and 6,041,221 children.
Non-African

	Under 15	15–29	30–39	40+
Male	37,927	14,862	4,057	1,368
Female	36,396	11,090	2,621	1,136

SOCIAL DATA

Education [14]

TABLE I

Schools		1958 enrollment	teachers
647	Government & subsidized nurseries	48,433	1,147
9	Nonsubsidized nurseries	253	16
11,865	Government and subsidized primary	1,124,494	34,997
7,920	Nonsubsidized primary	296,585	10,248
339	Government and subsidized technical and agricultural	17,142	1,353
37	Nonsubsidized technical and agricultural	7,549	434
	Total number of schools	21,400	
	Belgian Congo & Ruanda-Urundi Government University	186	
	Lovanium University	264	

Of the total number of schools 410 are government institutions;
12,860 subsidized mission schools (11,806 Roman Catholic and 1,054
Protestant); 8,130 nonsubsidized (786 Roman Catholic, 6,934 Protestant, and 410 private).

1959: $38,000,000 or 15% of the ordinary budget was spent on
education.

55% to 65% of children between the ages of 5 and 14 attend school.

Health and Social Services

VITAL STATISTICS [15]

Leopoldville only.
Per 1,000

1958

57.6 Birth rate
8.7 Death rate
82.5 Infant mortality rate

MAIN DISEASES [16]

Sleeping sickness, malaria, leprosy, and tuberculosis.

HEALTH SERVICES [17]

TABLE II

	Government	Subsidized	Private	Beds
Hospitals, clinics, surgical centers, maternity hospitals	173	165	121	52,255
Rural dispensaries	1,294	471	718	20,051
Leprosarium, hospitals for trypanosomiasis, tuberculosis sanatoria, mental asylums	40	59	—	14,293

In 1957 there were 1.4 beds per 1,000 inhabitants and a total of 643 doctors, one per 20,000 inhabitants.

SOCIAL WELFARE SERVICES [18]

There were more than 70 official social centers serving some 70,000 Congolese, most of them women. In addition, missions, private companies, and European settlers organized similar centers. Some 80 companies had created special funds to assist their employees and their families. Most of these services were urban-centered. In 1947 a Native Welfare Fund was created, operating exclusively for the benefit of tribal areas, concentrating on education, equipment of communities, improvement of the rural economy, and medical activities.

ECONOMY [19]

The majority of the population of working age is engaged in subsistence activities. The economy is an export economy primarily based on mining.

Transport and Communications

WATERWAYS [20]

The Congo and its tributaries are navigable for over 9,900 miles. Two companies operate both river and lake lines: Office d'Exploitation des Transports Coloniaux (OTRACO) and Compagnie des Chemins de fer du Congo Supérieur aux Grands Lacs Africains (C.F.L.).

PORTS [21]

The Congo has two seaports: Matadi, one of Central Africa's principal ocean ports, which handled 1,322,000 tons in 1958; and Boma. Its major inland ports are Leopoldville (1,700,518 tons handled in 1958) and Coquilhatville. Matadi has harbor facilities capable of handling 10 large vessels and 2,600,000 tons at a time. Stanleyville handled 360,011 tons in 1958.

ROADS [22]

In 1958 there were some 90,235 miles of road, of which 20,995 miles were main roads, 58,291 miles local roads, and 10,949 miles private roads. In the same year it had 35,000 motor vehicles, 21,858 trucks, 677 tractors, 489 buses, and 2,546 motorcycles.

RAILROADS [23]

In 1958 the total mileage was 3,214 miles. The railways are run by four major companies.

AIRWAYS [24]

There are some 35 landing fields in the region of Leopoldville-Stanleyville-Elizabethville, in addition to numerous local airstrips. A Class I airport was built at N'djili, near Leopoldville, in 1958. Class III airports are to be found at Luluabourg, Kindu, and Coquilhatville.

POSTS, TELECOMMUNICATIONS, AND BROADCASTING [25]
The Congo has an extensive postal system. In 1958 it had 206 telegraph offices and 38 telephone networks, of which 10 were automatic, with 12,786 subscribers. It has 3 government radio stations and 6 private stations. Services were provided in French, Dutch, and regional dialects.

Resources and Trade

MAIN EXPORTS [26]
Copper (the most important export, representing some 30% of the value of total exports in 1959), gold, silver, diamonds and jewelry, coffee, and tea.

MAIN IMPORTS [27]
Fuel, iron, cast iron, and steel; machines; vehicles; cotton.

VALUE OF TRADE [28]
In $ U.S. millions

	1955	1956	1957	1958	1959
Exports	458	346	478	416	494
Imports	366	404	428	342	300

Belgium is the Congo's chief trade partner.

MARKETING AND COOPERATIVE SOCIETIES [29]
There are no marketing boards in the Congo, but systems were devised to protect the interests of the native planters, e.g., in the cotton-growing industry.

In 1958 there were 91 cooperative societies with a total membership of 205,611; 62 were producer coops, 12 consumer coops, and the rest businessmen, artists, and utilities cooperative societies.

LIVESTOCK [30]
1958 census

Cattle	1,005,761
Sheep and goats	2,645,229
Pigs	353,509
Horses, mules, and donkeys	1,740

Industry

MANUFACTURES [31]

Processing industries developed and increased considerably after World War II. Taken together, they occupy third place after agriculture and mining. The most important products are textiles, followed by chemical products, foodstuffs, building materials, footwear, cigarettes, and metal products.

MINING [32]

Mining and metallurgical industries have played a predominant role in the Congo's economic growth, representing about 60% of total exports. The most important mining products in order of importance are copper and allied metals, industrial diamonds, manganese, and coal.

POWER [33]

The Congo produces 13% of the world's hydraulic resources and 50% of the African resources. In this regard, private companies play a predominant role, in 1955 producing 9/10 of the total hydroelectric power. In 1958, 2,519,243 kw. were produced. Wood is the Congo's second most important source of energy. Coal reserves are estimated at 1,000 million tons. There are no known petroleum deposits and the Congo has to import all its petroleum products.

Finance

CURRENCY [34]

Congolese franc: 50 francs equal $1.00 U.S. currency.

BANKING [35]

Banque Nationale du Congo (issuing bank); Banque du Congo Belge, Banque Belge d'Afrique, Société Congolaise de Banque, Crédit Congolais, Kredietbank-Congo, Banque de Paris et des Pays Bas. The savings bank is the Caisse d'Epargne du Congo Belge et du Ruanda-Urundi.

BUDGET [36]

In millions of francs.
1959 estimate

Revenue	14,782,000
Expenditure	14,771,000

The main sources of revenue are taxes and customs, excise and transit duties.

DEVELOPMENT PLAN [37]

1952/61 total estimated cost: 50,982 million francs. Expenses by December 31, 1958, had been allocated to the following:

Transportation	43 %
Social works	25.8%
Improvement of public utilities	18.9%
Sources of energy	6.6%
Agricultural development	5.7%

LABOR [38]

In 1959 the Congolese labor force numbered some 1,100,000, representing nearly one-third of the adult male population. In the same year there were 5,400 female and 3,200 nonadult wage earners.

In 1956 African labor, in the money economy, was distributed as follows: [39]

Agriculture and forestry	300,791
Mining and quarrying	84,287
Manufacturing	152,758
Building and construction	124,319
Transport	91,789
Commerce	81,548
Domestic and other services	362,404 (includes 39,699 office workers)
TOTAL	1,197,896

Five trade-union federations are represented in the Congo: [40] AFAC (Syndicat Indépendent du Personnel d'Afrique); APIC (Syndicat Professionel du Personnel Auxiliaire de l'Administration du Territoire du Ruanda Urundi); C.G.S.L.B. (Central Général des Syndicats Libéraux de Belgique); C.S.C. (Confédération des Syndicats Chrétiens); F.G.T.B. (Fédération Générale du Travail de Belgique).

Legislation covers such matters as minimum wages, working hours, medical care, family allowances, accidents and disability; labor supervision and control, labor contract regulations, apprenticeship contracts; trade unions, conciliation, and labor disputes.[41]

THE REPUBLIC OF THE CONGO NOTES
(Leopoldville)

1 Belgian Congo and Ruanda-Urundi: Information and Public Relations Office, *Belgian Congo*, Vol. II, Brussels, 1960, p. 8.

2 *Ibid.*, p. 12; census information on the Congo is considered generally reliable, except for vital trends, *vide* F. Lorimer, *Demographic Information on Tropical Africa*, Boston University Press, Boston, 1961, p. 126.

3 *Belgian Congo*, Vol. I, 1959, *op. cit.*, pp. 19–21 and 25; *Belgian Congo*, Vol. II, 1960, *op. cit.*, p. 4.

4 Colin Legum, *Congo Disaster*, Penguin Books, Baltimore, 1961, pp. 16–68.

5 *Belgian Congo*, Vol. II, 1960, *op. cit.*, p. 39.

6 *Ibid.*

7 Pierre Artique, *Qui Sont Les Leaders Congolais?*, Editions Europe-Afrique, Brussels, 1960, pp. 115–31.

8 *Belgian Congo*, Vol. II, 1960, *op. cit.*, p. 15.

9 *Ibid.*, pp. 12 and 15.

10 *Ibid.*, pp. 1 and 9–11 for full listing of all tribes; Biebuyck D., & M. Douglas, *Congo: Tribes and Parties*. Royal Anthropological Institute, London, 1961, pp. 19–26.

11 *Belgian Congo*, Vol. II, 1960, *op. cit.*, pp. 164 and 171.

12 *Ibid.*, p. 12; Congo Belge: *Résultat du Recensement de la Population Non-Indigène au 3-1-58*, Série Spéciale, No. 1—Fascicule c, *Bulletin Mensuel des Statistiques Générales du Congo Belge et du Ruanda-Urundi*, April 1959, p. 262.

13 *Belgian Congo*, Vol. II, 1960, *op. cit.*, p. 12. There are no age-breakdown figures for the total African population. Demographic studies were conducted in selected areas and localities. For results, *vide* Série Spéciale, No. 3, of the *Bulletin Mensuel des Statistiques Générales du Congo Belge et du Ruanda-Urundi*, Direction de la Statistique; Congo Belge: *Résultat du Recensement de la Population Non-Indigène au 3-1-58*, *op. cit.*, p. 300.

14 *Belgian Congo*, Vol. II, 1960, *op. cit.*, pp. 146–49. Also, Communications received from Belgium Embassy, Washington, D.C., October 1961.

15 Congo Belge: *Rapport Annuel de la Direction Générale des Services Médicaux du Congo Belge*, 1958, pp. 19–20.

16   Belgian Congo: Inspectorate General of Hygiene INFR, Congo, *Health in Belgian Africa*, 1958, pp. 57–77.

17   *Health in Belgian Africa, op. cit.*, pp. 23–24 and 38; also *Belgian Congo and Ruanda-Urundi*, Office of Information and Public Relations, *op. cit.*, p. 138.

18   *Thirteen Million Congolese*, Imprimerie Héliogravure, C. van Cortenbergh, Brussels, pp. 29–32.

19   Fédération des Enterprises Congolaises: *L'Economie Congolaise a la Veille de l'Indépendance*, Brussels, 1960, pp. 45–62; International Labor Office, *African Labor Survey*, Geneva, 1958, p. 667, Table III.

20   *Belgian Congo, Vol. II*, 1960, *op. cit.*, p. 116.

21   *Ibid.; Fédération des Entreprises Congolaises, op. cit.*, pp. 66–67.

22   *Belgian Congo, Vol. II*, 1960, *op. cit.*, p. 115.

23   *Ibid.*, p. 117.

24   *Fédération des Entreprises Congolaises, op. cit.*, p. 70.

25   *Belgian Congo, Vol. II*, 1960, *op. cit.*, pp. 68–69 and 175.

26   Congo Belge: *Bulletin Mensuel des Statistiques Générales du Congo Belge et du Ruanda-Urundi*, 5e année, No. 12, Dec. 1959, pp. 113–16.

27   *Ibid.*, pp. 127–30.

28   Communication received from the Belgian Embassy, Washington, D.C., Oct. 1961.

29   *Belgian Congo, Vol. II*, 1960, *op. cit.*, pp. 130, 285.

30   *Ibid.*, p. 94.

31   *Fédération des Entreprises Congolaises, op. cit.*, pp. 58–63.

32   *Ibid.*, pp. 46–52.

33   *Ibid.*, pp. 63–66.

34   S. H. Steinberg (Ed.), *The Statesman's Yearbook 1961*, Macmillan & Co., Ltd., London, 1961, p. 919.

35   *Ibid.*

36   *Belgian Congo, Vol. II*, 1960, *op. cit.*, p. 52.

37   *Ibid.*, pp. 127–128; also *Belgian Congo, Vol. I*, 1959, *op. cit.*, p. 293.

38   *Thirteen Million Congolese, op. cit.*, p. 38.

39   International Labor Office, *op. cit.*, p. 667, Table 3.

40   *Belgian Congo, Vol. I*, 1959, *op. cit.*, pp. 169–70.

41   *Ibid.*, pp. 158–67.

The Republic of Dahomey[1]

AREA: *44,290 sq. m.*
POPULATION:[2] *1,720,000 (1957 estimate)*
Density: 38.6 per sq. m.

GEOGRAPHY

Dahomey is divided into four geographical zones running north to south: (a) a sandy, low, flat, coastal strip 1–3 miles wide; (b) a lagoon region situated in a depression north of the coastal strip, consisting of a chain of lagoons with sea outlets at Grand-Popo and Cotonou; (c) a plateau of ferruginous clay cut by a large swampy depression and several isolated mountains never reaching altitudes of more than 1,500 feet; (d) a plateau of granite and gneiss consisting of a mountain range between 1,000 and 3,000 feet high, and the fertile plains of Borgou and Kandi. There are two climatic regions: the equatorial southern part with temperatures varying from between 72 and 93 degrees F., and two rainy and two dry seasons; and the tropical northern section with a dry season (October to April) and rainy season (April to October). Rainfall ranges between 30 and 50 inches annually.

HISTORICAL SKETCH

The history of this area traces back to the 12th and 13th centuries, when the Adja tribe lived on the banks of the Mono River. As a result of internecine rivalries, three independent kingdoms came to be established: the Kingdom of Adra, centered around the town of Allada; the Kingdom of Dahomey, to the north; and the Kingdom of Java, to the south. Trading with Europeans started in the 16th century. Of the three kingdoms, Dahomey soon dominated all its neighbors. During the 17th century, under able kings, Dahomey extended its control to the sea by occupying the Kingdom of Allada. During the 18th century they were

91

subjected to the Yoruba, but retained their independence under Gezo (1818–1858), who founded the famous corps of Amazons. He signed the first trade agreement between France and Dahomey on July 1, 1851. His successors violated treaties with France and raided neighboring French protectorates with the result that the French intervened and annexed the country in 1892. Under Governor Victor Ballot (1892–1900) treaties were signed with chiefs and a system of administration introduced. In 1946 Dahomey elected deputies and senators to the Metropolitan Government, and in 1952 established its first elected Territorial Assembly. The Loi Cadre of 1956 gave the country a large measure of self-government. On August 1, 1960, it proclaimed its complete independence and was admitted to the United Nations on September 20 of that year. It is a member of the Conseil de l'Entente.

GOVERNMENT

Present Status

Independent republican state.

Constitution

Executive power is vested in a President elected directly for a period of 5 years, assisted by a Vice-President. He has power to issue regulations, control the armed forces, negotiate treaties, and ask for a reconsideration of a bill which must then be passed by a two-thirds majority of the National Assembly. He may also have a bill submitted to a referendum. He appoints and dismisses the ministers who are responsible to him. Legislative power is in the hands of the elected National Assembly, consisting of 70 members.

Franchise

Universal adult suffrage.

Local Government [3]

Before independence there were "communes mixtes" at Porto-Novo, Cotonou, Ouidah, Abomey, and Parakou. The country was divided into 10 administrative "cercles" with 20 subdivisions. Under the new constitution local government units are being set up, but no details are yet available.

Political Parties [4]

Parti Dahoméen de l'Unité (PDU), led by Hubert Maga, President of the Republic, and Sourou-Migan Apithy.

Union Démocratique Dahoméenne (UDD), led by Justin Ahoma-degbé and banned at the beginning of 1961.

POPULATION BREAKDOWN

Main Cities [5]

African population only
1957 estimate

Porto-Novo (capital)	31,000
Cotonou (1956 census)	56,000
Savalou	29,600
Abomey	18,800
Ouidah	14,300

Urban-rural Distribution [6]

About 10% of the African population lives in towns of 10,000 or more inhabitants.

Ethnic Distribution [7]

Non-African	2,998
African	1,716,500
Fon	700,000
Adja	220,000
Yoruba	160,000
Holli	15,000
Aizo	92,000
Somba	90,000
Fulani	18,000

(All approximate figures.)
Also, Peda, Pla, Mina, Pila-Pila, and Dendi.

Religious Affiliation [8]

Christians	12%
Muslims	7%
Animists	81%

Languages

French is the official language; Fon is the main African language spoken; and Yoruba.

Sex Distribution [9]

1957 estimate

	Male	Female
African	827,500 (49.9%)	832,400 (50.1%)
Non-African	925 (63.2%)	645 (36.8%)

Age Distribution [10]

	Under 14	14–59	60+
African	610,200	918,000	131,700
Non-African		Not available	

SOCIAL DATA

Education [11]

As of January 1, 1958

TABLE I

	Enrollment	Public School Teachers
230 Public primary schools 203 Private primary schools	75,406	782
4 Public secondary schools 7 Private secondary schools	2,257	34
2 Public technical schools 2 Private technical schools	561	26

There were 387 students studying abroad in 1958. In 1957, 29.1% of the school-going-age population was at school, of which 27.7% were girls. Education expenditure represented 24.6% of the annual budget that year.

Health and Social Services

VITAL STATISTICS
Not available.

MAIN DISEASES

Leprosy, sleeping sickness, cerebrospinal meningitis, yaws, malaria, and tuberculosis.

HEALTH SERVICES [12]

As of January 1, 1958

TABLE II

		Beds
2	Secondary hospitals	588
42	Medical centers	1,464
92	Dispensaries	—
9	Private institutions	—
38	Maternity and specialized services	811 (maternity)

61 medical practitioners, 1 per 28,000 of the population; 12 beds per 10,000 inhabitants.

SOCIAL WELFARE SERVICES

Not available.

ECONOMY

Dahomey's economy is primarily agricultural and dependent upon exports.

Transport and Communications

WATERWAYS

The Oueme River is navigable for 125 of its 280 miles and empties into Lake Nokoue, which is connected with the sea by the Cotonou Canal and also with the Porto-Novo Lagoon.

PORTS

Until now the ports of Cotonou, Grand-Popo, and Ouidah have been open roadsteads. A deep-water port now under construction at Cotonou will eventually berth 10 vessels and handle an annual traffic of 1 million tons.

ROADS

Dahomey has approximately 3,700 miles of roads: 779 miles of interstate roads, of which 343 miles are asphalt, 2,046 miles of all-weather roads, and 930 miles of automobile trails.

RAILROADS

There are 360 miles of track operated by the Benin-Niger Company: Cotonou to Parakou via Bohicon and Save, 272 miles; Cotonou to Pobe via Porto-Novo, 68 miles; and Cotonou to Segboroue via Ouidah, 20 miles.

AIRWAYS

There are airports at Cotonou, Kandi, Natitingou, Cana (Abomey), and Parakou.

POSTS, TELECOMMUNICATIONS, AND BROADCASTING [13]

At the beginning of 1957 there were 64 post offices, 55 telegraph offices, and 52 telephone offices. There are two radio stations providing a 48-hour service per week.

Resources and Trade

MAIN EXPORTS

Palm kernels, nuts, and oil (representing about 75% of the total value of exports in 1959), coffee, shelled peanuts, and cotton.

MAIN IMPORTS [14]

Foodstuffs, consumption goods, fuel, capital goods and semimanufactured goods, and equipment.

VALUE OF TRADE [15]

In millions of CFA francs

	1956	1957	1958	1959	1960
Exports	2,676	2,447	3,371	2,409	6,630
Imports	3,824	4,269	4,329	3,596	6,630

About two-thirds of Dahomey's trade is with Metropolitan France.

LIVESTOCK [16]

1956 estimate

Cattle	300,000
Sheep and goats	600,000
Pigs	190,000
Horses	3,000

Industry

MANUFACTURES

Manufacturing industries concentrate on the processing of agricultural products. There are 4 palm-oil mills.

MINING

All mining activities are still at the prospecting stage.

POWER [17]

In 1953 the generating capacity was 2,450 kw., and consumption was 1.205 million kwh.

Finance

CURRENCY

C.F.A. franc. One C.F.A. franc equals 2 old Metropolitan French francs.

BANKING [18]

Banque de l'Afrique Occidentale, Banque Commerciale Africaine, Banque Nationale pour le Commerce et l'Industrie, Société Générale, Crédit Lyonnais.

BUDGET [19]

In millions of C.F.A. francs

1961

Revenue	6,323
Expenditure	5,842.2

The main source of revenue comes from indirect taxation (80%).

DEVELOPMENT PLAN [20]

The development plan is being devised and has not yet been completed.

LABOR

The distribution of the wage-earning population was estimated to be as follows in 1957: [21]

Public Sector

Civil service	3,325	
Non-Civil service	4,800	8,125

Private Sector

Agriculture, fishing, forestry	1,700	
Mining and quarrying	110	
Industry	840	
Public works and building	2,320	
Commerce, banking, and professions	4,330	
Transport and storage	2,810	
Domestic service	1,800	13,910
TOTAL		22,035

The Confédération Africaine des Travailleurs Croyants (CATC) has strong affiliation in Dahomey.[22]

Preindependence labor legislation covers such matters as wages, hours of work, trade unions, contracts, accidents, family equalization funds, etc. Postindependence information is not available.[23]

THE REPUBLIC OF DAHOMEY NOTES

1   Unless otherwise stated, information obtained from Ambassade de France, Service de Presse et d'Information, Republic of Dahomey, New York, Nov. 1960.

2   Services des Statistiques d'Outre-Mer, Outre-Mer 1958, Paul Dupont, Paris, Nov. 1959, pp. 746–47.

3   L'Annuaire Vert, Annuaire Economique 1958, Editions C.E.P. Publicité, Casablanca, (Maroc) pp. 423, 425, and 526; Librairie Générale de Droit et de Jurisprudence: Revue Juridique et Politique d'Outre-Mer, 15e année No. 2, April–June 1961, Paris, p. 271.

4   R. Segal, Political Africa, Stevens & Sons Ltd., London, 1961, pp. 327–29; also Africa Report, Vol. 6, No. 10, Washington, D.C., Nov. 1961, p. 7.

5   Outre-Mer 1958, op. cit., p. 747, Table 3.

6   Ibid., percentages computed from figures on pp. 746 and 747, Tables 1 and 2.

7   Ibid., pp. 746–47, Tables 1 and 2.

8   Ibid., p. 140, Table 1.

9   Ibid., pp. 746–47, Tables 1 and 3.

10 Ibid., p. 746, Table 1.

11 *Ibid.*, p. 748, Tables 6 and 7.

12 *Ibid.*, p. 747, Table 4.

13 *Ibid.*, p. 750, Tables 14 and 15.

14 *Ibid.*, p. 751, Table 20.

15 *Ibid.*; also France: Ministère de la France d'Outre-Mer, *Bulletin des Territoires d'Outre-Mer*, Paris, No. 31, Aug. 1960, p. 22; also France: Service des Statistiques, *Résumé des Statistiques d'Outre-Mer, Bulletin Accéléré*, Paris, Nos. 8 and 28, 1959–1961, p. 3; also: S. H. Steinberg (Ed.), *The Statesman's Yearbook 1959*, Macmillan & Co., Ltd., London, 1959, p. 1008.

16 *Outre-Mer 1958, op. cit.*, p. 750, Table 18.

17 Haut Commissariat de L'A.O.F.: *Annuaire Statistique pour l'Afrique Occidentale Française*, Années 1950 à 1954, Vol. 5, Tome 1, Imprimerie Servant-Crouzet, Paris, 1956, p. 253, Table G–3–21.

18 S. H. Steinberg (Ed.), *op. cit.*, pp. 1018–1019.

19 *Ibid.*

20 *Marchés Tropicaux et Méditerranéens*, 17e année, No. 806, April 22, 1961, p. 1092.

21 *Outre-Mer 1958, op. cit.*, p. 209, Table 3.

22 George T. H. Kimble, *Tropical Africa*, The Twentieth Century Fund, New York, 1960, Vol. II, p. 216.

23 International Labor Office, *Africa Labor Survey*, Geneva, 1958, p. 654.

Egypt
(UNITED ARAB REPUBLIC)

AREA: [1] 386,198 sq. m.
POPULATION: [2] 30,641,000 (1960 census)
Density: [3] 24 per sq. m.
672 per sq. m. in cultivated areas

GEOGRAPHY [4]

Egypt is divided into three geographical regions: the Western and Eastern deserts on either side of the Nile River and the elongated, immensely fertile Nile Valley and Delta. Only some 13,000 square miles of the land are inhabited and cultivated, the rest being desert and sparsely inhabited by nomads. The Western desert forms part of the Libyan desert and has a few fertile oases. Large depressions characterize its northern sections. The Eastern desert, or Arabian desert, is dissected by many wadis leading to the Red Sea. The highest peaks border the eastern shore and attain 7,165 feet just west of the oil-producing center, Hurghada. Rainfall throughout the country is scarce, particularly in Upper Egypt. Cairo has a mean annual rainfall of 1.2 inches and Alexandria 8 inches. The annual mean temperature in each of these two cities is 69 degrees F. and 73 degrees F., respectively. Temperature in the desert regions rises to over 120 degrees F. when the khamsin (dust storm) blows.

HISTORICAL SKETCH [5]

Egypt entered recorded history at the earliest historic date known to man, 4,241 B.C., when it adopted the calendar. Its own history up to Alexander the Great (332 B.C.) is divided into 30 dynasties. Among the most notable of these were: the IVth dynasty, when the great pyramids were built (2,900 B.C.); the XIIth dynasty, when there was considerable cultural and commercial activity (2,000 B.C.); the XVIIIth dynasty (after 1,850 B.C.) when the temples of Luxor and Karnak were built. Well-known rulers were Ikhnaton, who tried to introduce a monotheistic sun cult; and his successor, Tut-Ankh-Amen, under whose rule Egypt returned to its traditional beliefs. During the XXth dynasty, the kingdom began to decline steadily (1,200 B.C.). Following the conquest of Egypt by Alexander the Great, the Ptolemies maintained a formidable empire for more than two centuries. It was only some 20 years after the rise of Islam that Egypt was conquered by the Arabs, becoming an integral part of the Muslim world. In A.D. 1,250 the Mamelukes took over control of the region and were superseded by the Ottoman Turks in 1517. But even afterward they continued to wield power as beys (princes), administering the provinces. With the ascent of Ali Bey (1768–1773) the Ottoman hold became only nominal. Napoleon occupied Egypt (1798–1801) under the pretext of reestablishing Turkish rule. The British, fearing the spread of French influence in the area, defeated Napoleon; and after the French withdrawal, Mohammed Ali founded the modern Egyptian royal line. In 1880 Egypt's finances were submitted to British and French control and the riots which subsequently broke out in Alexandria caused the British to intervene and establish their control. During World War I Egypt was declared a British protectorate. In 1922 it was given its independence, but friction between it and Britain continued, because Egypt claimed the Anglo-Egyptian Sudan. Egypt submitted an appeal to the Security Council of the United Nations in 1947 but was rejected. In 1948 she joined with other Arab states in an unsuccessful attack on the new state of Israel. In 1952 the monarchy was overthrown by a military coup led by Colonel Nasser and other officers. The Republic was proclaimed about one year later with Gamal Abdel Nasser as its first President. On February 1, 1958, President Nasser and President Kuwatly of Syria proclaimed the union of their countries and formed the United Arab Republic. The union lasted only three years, Syria revolting and once more declaring its independence in 1961.

GOVERNMENT

Present Status

Independent republican state.

Constitution [6]

Executive power is vested in the President, who appoints central as well as regional governments. Legislative power rests with the National Assembly appointed by the President.

Franchise
Universal adult suffrage.

Local Government [7]
All local councils became municipal councils in 1955. There are 216. Membership to these councils is restricted to Egyptians. The number varies from 7 to 12 elected and 7 nominated members. These local bodies have the right to impose local rates on all residents according to the law. The municipalities of Alexandria, Port Said, and Cairo are managed partly by elected and partly by nominated municipal councils.

Political Party [8]
National Union, led by Gamal Abdel Nasser.

POPULATION BREAKDOWN

Main Cities [9]
1957 census, preliminary figures to the nearest '000

Cairo	2,877,000
Alexandria	1,278,000
Canal	416,000
Suez	163,000

Urban-rural Distribution [10]
33% of the population lives in urban areas.

Ethnic Distribution [11]
1947 census

Total population 19,022,000, of which 145,912 are aliens divided as follows:

Greek	39%
Italian	19%
British	19%
French	7%
Turkish	4%
Other	12%

Religious Affiliation [12]

Muslims	92%
Christians	1%
Copts	7%

Languages

The main and official language is Arabic.

Sex Distribution [13]

1947 census

Male	Female
9,418,998 (49.6%)	9,602,842 (50.4%)

Age Distribution [14]

1947 census

Under 20	20–49	50+
49%	39%	12%

SOCIAL DATA

Education [15]

TABLE I
1958/59

	Enrollment	Teachers
6,899 State schools	2,285,872	85,180
2,854 Private schools	582,641	22,856
Universities of Cairo, Alexandria, Ein Shams, and Assiout	77,170	—

There were 95,000 students at foreign schools and institutions.

Health and Social Services

VITAL STATISTICS [16]

Per 1,000

1955

Crude Birth Rate	Crude Death Rate
40	18

MAIN DISEASES
Not available.

HEALTH SERVICES [17]

TABLE II
1957

			Beds
State:	97	General hospitals	7,039
	112	Ophthalmic clinics	2,486
	52	Fever hospitals	3,936
	44	Tuberculosis hospitals	6,566
	2	Venereal disease hospitals	125
	2	Mental hospitals	3,334
	6	Leprosaria	1,557
	90	Child welfare centers	245
	199	Collective rural centers	3,303
	2	Railway hospitals	260
Other:	11	University hospitals	5,988
	8	Health institutes	848
	5	Municipal hospitals (Alexandria)	951
	2	Child welfare clinics	
	20	Prison hospitals	676
	130	Other prison institutions	1,968

There were 8,854 medical practitioners in 1958.

SOCIAL WELFARE SERVICES [18]
The Department of Social Affairs and Labor concentrates on labor, youth, and social medical services. It controls labor bureaus; subsidizes youth leadership schemes; runs 4,000 rural youth centers; organizes cooperatives and rural social units; and supervises orphanages and homes for the blind.

ECONOMY

Egypt is an extremely poor country. Its economy is based primarily on agricultural exports. About 50% of the wage-earning population is engaged in agriculture.

Transport and Communications

WATERWAYS [19]

The Suez Canal, nationalized in 1956, handled 147,851 net tonnage of vessels in 1958. The Nile is navigable for 2,900 miles.

PORTS [20]

The chief ports are at Alexandria, Port Said, and Suez. Total tonnage handled in 1958 was 9,170,000.

ROADS [21]

Egypt had 3,313 km. of macadamized roads and 13,219 km. of non-macadamized and desert roads in 1957/58. There were 87,270 registered vehicles in 1958.

RAILROADS [22]

In 1957/58 there were 4,343 km. of railroads run by the State Railways, 917 km. by the Delta Light Railway Co. Ltd., 252 km. by the S.A. Chemins de Fer de la Basse Egypte, and 158 km. by the Fayoun Light Railway Co. Ltd.

AIRWAYS [23]

There are two major airports—at Luxor and at Cairo.

POSTS, TELECOMMUNICATIONS, AND BROADCASTING [24]

There were 6,738 post offices and stations in 1955. The Republic is connected by cable line with all parts of the world. In 1957/58 there were 868 state telegraph offices. In 1958, 196,711 telephones were installed. Radio Cairo broadcasts in 27 languages and a new transmitter of 1 million watts is being installed which will enable it to broadcast to most of Europe, Africa, and all of the Middle East.

Resources and Trade

MAIN EXPORTS [25]

Raw cotton and rice (representing 72% of agricultural exports in 1959).

MAIN IMPORTS

Machinery, iron and steel, chemicals and pharmaceutical products, motor vehicles.

VALUE OF TRADE [26]

In million £E

	1954	1955	1956	1957	1958
Exports	143.9	146.0	142.3	171.6	163.8
Imports	164.5	187.3	186.1	182.6	238.2

The Republic trades mainly with western and eastern Europe and its chief trading partner is the U.S.S.R.

MARKETING AND COOPERATIVE SOCIETIES [27]

Information on marketing not available.

In 1955 there were 2,435 cooperative societies with a total membership of some 740,000.

LIVESTOCK [28]

1958 estimate

Cattle	1,390,000
Camels	157,000
Sheep & goats	1,982,000
Pigs	17,000
Horses & mules	56,000

Industry

MANUFACTURES [29]

There were 3,482 industrial undertakings in 1957, of which 1,332 were food-processing industries; 600 textile manufacturing industries; 203 metal manufacturing industries; and 213 cement, stone, and glass works.

MINING [30]

In 1957 there were 9 metal, 54 stone-quarrying, clay and sand pits, and 12 nonmetallic mining and quarrying establishments.

POWER [31]

In 1953 the installed generating capacity was 586,000 kw. and production totaled 1,411 million kwh.

Finance

CURRENCY [32]

The Egyption pound (£E) equals U.S. $2.87156.

BANKING [33]

National Bank (issuing bank) with some 30 (1957) other banks, including among them the Bank Misr, Arab Bank, Bank Suria. In 1957 British and French banks were nationalized.

BUDGET [34]

1958/59 estimate in £E '000

Revenue	366,865
Expenditure	366,865

The chief sources of revenue are customs tariffs and receipts from the state railways.

DEVELOPMENT PLAN [35]

A 10-year plan was started in 1954 with a total estimated expenditure of £E 500 million. The major proposal was for the vast High Aswan Dam, but offers of the World Bank, the U.S., and U.K. totaling $270 million were withdrawn in 1956 and agreement with the U.S.S.R. for credit up to 400 million rubles toward the cost of the first stage of the project was reached in 1958. Work on the first stage started in 1959 and is likely to last 4 to 5 years.

LABOR [36]

According to the 1959/60 estimates, the labor force was 7,547,000, of which 5,975,000 were employed as follows:

	To nearest thousand
Agriculture	3,254
Industry	632
Construction	170
Sectors consolidating the economic structure	502
Commerce	633
Services	793

In 1958 there were 1,336 trade unions with a total membership of 319,970. Of these 94 were agricultural unions, 120 unions of government servants, 92 in the personal and recreational services, and the bulk of the balance in industry and commerce.[37]

Labor legislation covers such matters as the employment of children, working hours, accident compensation, and the employment of hired labor.[38]

EGYPT NOTES

1   S. H. Steinberg (Ed.), *The Stateman's Yearbook 1961*, Macmillan & Co., Ltd., 1961, p. 1529.

2   United Arab Republic: Information Department, *Pocket Book 1961*, Cairo, 1961, p. 5. There appears to be no available breakdown of the 1960 census.

3   *Oxford Regional Economic Atlas*, "The Middle East and North Africa," prepared by the Economist Intelligence Unit Limited and the Cartographic Department of the Clarendon Press, London, O.U.P., 1960, p. 106.

4   *The Columbia Lippincott Gazetteer of the World*, Columbia University Press, New York, 1952, p. 560.

5   *Ibid.*, pp. 561–62.

6   S. H. Steinberg (Ed.), *op. cit.*, p. 1527.

7   *Ibid.*, p. 1529.

8   R. Segal, *Political Africa*, Stevens & Sons Ltd., London, 1961, pp. 465–70.

9   U.A.R.: Government Printing Offices, *Statistical Pocket Year Book 1958*, Cairo, 1959, p. 14.

10   *Ibid.*, p. 1.

11   *Ibid.*, pp. 1 and 8.

12   *Ibid.*, p. 9.

13   S. H. Steinberg (Ed.), *op. cit.*, p. 1530.

14   U.A.R.: *Statistical Pocket Year Book 1958, op. cit.*, p. 9.

15   *Ibid.*, pp. 25–28.

16   *Ibid.*, p. 15.

17   *Ibid.*, pp. 18–24.

18   U.A.R.: *Pocket Book 1961, op. cit.*, pp. 171–82.

19   S. H. Steinberg (Ed.), *op. cit.*, p. 1537; W. S. Woytinsky, *World Commerce and Governments*, The Twentieth Century Fund, New York, 1955, p. 488.

20   U.A.R.: *Statistical Pocket Year Book 1958, op. cit.*, p. 69.

21   *Ibid.*, p. 63; S. H. Steinberg (Ed.), *op. cit.*, p. 1539.

22   U.A.R.: *Statistical Pocket Year Book 1958, op. cit.*, p. 65.

23   S. H. Steinberg (Ed.), *op. cit.*, p. 1538.

24 *Ibid.*, p. 1523; U.A.R.: *Statistical Pocket Year Book 1598, op. cit.*, pp. 67–68; *New York Times,* Jan. 17, 1962.

25 S. H. Steinberg (Ed.), *op. cit.*, p. 1536.

26 U.A.R.: *Statistical Pocket Year Book 1958, op. cit.*, pp. 79–81.

27 *Ibid.*, p. 35.

28 *Ibid.*, p. 47.

29 *Ibid.*, pp. 56–59.

30 *Ibid.*, p. 56.

31 *Oxford Regional Economic Atlas, op. cit.*, p. 96.

32 U.A.R.: *Statistical Pocket Year Book 1958, op. cit.*, p. 92.

33 S. H. Steinberg (Ed.), *op. cit.*, p. 1539.

34 U.A.R.:*Statistical Pocket Year Book 1958, op. cit.*, p. 85.

35 *Oxford Regional Economic Atlas, op. cit.*, p. 109.

36 *Egyptian Economic and Political Review,* special issue, July–August 1961, Adel Mahmoud Sabat, publ., Kasr El Dabara, pp. XIII–XIV.

37 U.A.R.: *Statistical Pocket Year Book 1958, op. cit.*, p. 47.

38 S. H. Steinberg (Ed.), *op. cit.*, pp. 1535–36.

Ethiopia

(*Including* ERITREA)

AREA:[1] *395,000 sq. m.*
POPULATION:[2] *24,600,000 (1960) estimate*
Density: 14 per km.
9 per km. (Eritrea)

GEOGRAPHY [3]

Ethiopia is situated on a high plateau with elevations from 5,000 to 9,000 feet, and mountain peaks reaching heights of 15,000 feet. The plateau is cut into a large northwestern and a small southeastern region by the Rift Valley, up to 60 miles wide and 2,000 to 3,000 feet deep. Temperatures on the plateau vary from the high 40's (degrees F.) during the nights to the high 70's (degrees F.) during the day. There are two seasons: a dry season from October to June and a rainy season from July to September. The highest rainfall is to be found in the southwestern part of the principal plateau region, where an average of 70 inches falls annually. In the Danakil desert as little as 1 inch falls per year.

HISTORICAL SKETCH [4]

Ethiopia provides some of the earliest known historical records in Africa, appearing in the writings of Homer and early Greek scholars at the time of Athens' infancy, and those of Herodotus in the 5th century B.C. It is believed that Ethiopia was settled by southern Arabian people circa 1000 B.C. There was contact with the Jews of Asia Minor until about A.D. 330, when Christianity became the religion of the empire, superseding the Jewish religion, which had been practiced by the Imperial Court. Following the spread of Christianity in the 4th century A.D., records of that time indicate that the city of Aksum had become a great center of religious study and activity. Accounts of the empire reached Europe through Marco Polo, Vasco da Gama, and other Portuguese explorers. Even the name of Prester John had been linked with Ethiopia. In the middle of the 16th century, the Portuguese helped the Empress Regent Elena repel the Muslim threat, but did not remain in the area. It was not until this century that closer relations with European countries came to be established, first under Menelik II, and then Haile Selassie, present Emperor of Ethiopia. Except for 5 years of Italian occupation (1936 to 1941) the country has never been subjected to foreign domination. In September 1952 the British administration of Eritrea handed over sovereignty of this former Italian colony to Ethiopia to which it was federated.

GOVERNMENT

Present Status

Independent imperial state.

Constitution [5]

The Ethiopian empire is ruled by an Imperial Government responsible for defense, foreign relations, and general economic policy including customs and communications. It consists of a Council of Ministers responsible to the Emperor, and a bicameral Parliament of a Senate and Chamber of Deputies of 120 members. Senate membership must not exceed half the number of Deputies. Senators are appointed by the Emperor.

Franchise

Universal adult suffrage.

Local Government [6]

Ethiopia consists of 13 General Governates, divided into 82 provinces. The Governor General of each General Governate is head of all branches of local government and exercises supervision over all officials of the General Governate. General Governate Councils, composed of senior officials, senior representatives of the various ministries, and other persons of local prominence, advise the Governor General on matters relating to welfare.

Political Parties [7]

There are no political parties in Ethiopia. Haile Selassie is the controlling factor in the political and economic life of the country.

POPULATION BREAKDOWN

Main Cities [8]
  Estimate

Addis Ababa (capital)	400,000
Dire-Dawa	40,000
Harar	40,000
Dessie	53,000
Asmara	120,000
Condar	13,000
Jimma	8,000

Urban-rural Distribution
  Not available.

Ethnic Distribution [9]
  Galla: ± half the total population.
  Amhara: ± 2 million.
  Other: Tigreans, Gogaden, Issa, Somalis, Danakil; the Sidamo, Nilotic, and Nilo-Hamitic tribes; and the Falashas.

Religious Affiliation [10]
  The Ethiopian Orthodox Church (Coptic), under its own Patriarch, is the established church of the empire, founded in the 4th century A.D. Amharas and Tigreans are Copts; the Galla are Christian, Muslim, and pagan; the Somalis are Muslim. A small group, the Falashas, are Jews.

Languages [11]
  Amharic and English are the official languages.

Sex Distribution
  Not available.

Age Distribution [12]
  In Addis Ababa only, the age composition of the population is estimated to be as follows:

Under 20	*20–49*	*50+*
35.7%	51.8%	12.4%

SOCIAL DATA

Education [13]

TABLE I
1959/60

	Enrollment	Teachers
Government		
581 Elementary schools		
28 Academic secondary schools	180,163	4,834
29 Special secondary schools		
5 Colleges		
Mission: 150 schools	20,497	804
Private: 78 schools	14,790	557
Community: 41 schools	5,095	136
Church: 60 schools	4,389	180

In 1958/59 it was estimated that 3.8% of the children between the ages of 5 and 14 were at school. For the same period, expenditure on education represented 9.8% of total expenditure, viz: Eth. $19,400,-000.

Health and Social Services

VITAL STATISTICS [14]

1957/61 estimate per 1,000

Birth rate	Death rate
42	27

Annual increase of the population, 1.5%.

MAIN DISEASES [15]

Tuberculosis, dysentery, typhus, sleeping sickness.

HEALTH SERVICES [16]

1959 (excludes Eritrea)

TABLE II

	Hospitals	Clinics	Beds	Doctors
Ministry of Health	22	133	3,106	70
Ministry of Education	7	133	40	4

TABLE II—Continued

	Hospitals	Clinics	Beds	Doctors
Missions	13	56	903	24
Government and mission	4	1	305	4
Private	5	33	106	31
H.I.M. HSI welfare trust	4	2	480	17
Others	6	19	883	22
TOTALS	61	377	5,823	172

SOCIAL WELFARE SERVICES [17]

The municipality of Addis Ababa coordinates the efforts of voluntary welfare organizations. Services run by these organizations include relief to indigents, children's homes, orphanages, remand homes, a school for the blind, rehabilitation centers, and services for women.

ECONOMY [18]

Ethiopia is an agricultural country with the majority of the population still engaged primarily in subsistence activities. Coffee is the main source of export revenue.

Transport and Communications

WATERWAYS [19]

Lake Tana is used for the transport of goods. Facilities at its port of Bahar-Dar and Zeghie are being developed. The Buro River is navigable for 30 miles during the rainy season and its port of Gambela is being improved.

PORTS [20]

Ethiopia has two ports, one at Massawa and one at Assab. In 1959 the two ports together handled 1,292 vessels and 488,740 tons of freight.

ROADS [21]

In 1952 the highway system of Ethiopia consisted of about 12,500 miles of dry-weather roads, of which over 2,812 miles were reconstructed and resurfaced by 1960, under the management of the Imperial Highway Authority.

RAILROADS [22]

There are over 490 miles of tracks from Djibouti to Addis Ababa run by the France-Ethiopian Railway Company, and 191 miles linking Massawa, Asmara, and Agordat run by H.I.M. Government.

AIRWAYS [23]

There are international airports at Addis Ababa and Asmara. Ethiopia Airlines, through a management contract with T.W.A. established in 1946 operates both internal and international airlines linking the country with Europe and other parts of Africa.

POSTS, TELECOMMUNICATIONS, AND BROADCASTING [24]

The postal system serves 54 points mainly by airmail. All the main centers are connected with Addis Ababa by telephone or radio telegraph. There were 9,770 telephones in 1959 in Ethiopia and one radio station established in 1958. In 1957 it had 50,000 receiving sets.

Resources and Trade

MAIN EXPORTS [25]

Coffee (representing some 60% of the value of total exports from 1957 to 1959), hides and skins, oilseeds, pulses, and peanuts.

MAIN IMPORTS [26]

Cotton piece goods, petroleum products, vehicles, textiles, machinery, iron and steel goods.

VALUE OF TRADE [27]

In millions of Eth$

	1955/56	1956/57	1957/58	1958/59	1959/60
Exports	162.2	183.8	177.0	170.0	204.0
Imports	165.7	163.8	192.3	207.0	211.0

The U.S. is both chief supplier of imports and chief importer of Ethiopian exports, followed by Italy, the United Kingdom, and Japan.

MARKETING AND COOPERATIVE SOCIETIES [28]

There are no special marketing services provided. There is one agricultural cooperative society at a special project at Awash.

LIVESTOCK [29]

1957 estimate

Cattle	23,070,000
Sheep and goats	37,999,000
Horses	1,170,000
Donkeys	3,444,000
Camels	862,000

Industry

MANUFACTURES [30]

Ethiopia processes textiles, fibers, food products, drink and tobacco, tanned leather and shoes, building materials, sea products, and household goods.

MINING [31]

Minerals such as marble, mica, rock salt, and gold are mined on a small scale.

POWER [32]

Local production of electricity (public utilities and industrial firms) totaled 79.1 million kw. in 1957/58.

Finance

CURRENCY [33]

Eth$ issued by the Imperial Treasury. Eth$1 equals 40 U.S. cents. Eth$ 7 = £1 sterling.

BANKING [34]

The State Bank of Ethiopia, Development Bank of Ethiopia, Banco di Napoli, Banco di Roma.

BUDGET [35]

In millions of Eth$

1960/61	
Revenue	224.5
Expenditure	224.5

The main sources of revenue are direct taxation, indirect taxes, and customs duties.

DEVELOPMENT PLAN [36]

1957/61 Total estimated expenditure: Eth$ 535 million.

Sources

Local	Eth$ 397 million
Foreign loans and aid	143 million
Direct private investments	55 million
Loan reparations	41 million

The bulk will go to social overhead capital—communications, power, and education (two-thirds).

LABOR [37]

Addis Ababa only. In 1960 it was estimated that gainfully employed Ethiopians were distributed as follows:

Manufacturing	9,320
Other industry	5,900
Transport and communications	3,650
Commerce and banking	10,500
Civil servants	13,000
Domestic service	15,000
Others	3,500
TOTAL	60,870

There is one trade union on the WONS sugar plantation and one for workers on the Djibouti-Addis Ababa railroad.[38]

A Civil Code passed in 1960 provides for sickness allowances, unemployment benefits, and the rights of workers to organize.[39]

ETHIOPIA NOTES

1 S. H. Steinberg (Ed.), *The Statesman's Yearbook, 1961*, Macmillan & Co., Ltd., London, 1961, p. 974.

2 Mesfin W. Marriam, "An Estimate of the Population of Ethiopia," in *Ethiopia Observer*, Vol. V, No. 2, 1961, p. 140. According to F. Lorimer, Ethiopia is the largest terra incognito in Africa concerning demographic information. There has never been a census other than the one taken in Addis-Ababa in 1952 and it was incomplete; *vide* F. Lorimer, *Demographic Information on Tropical Africa*, Boston University Press, 1961, pp. 79–80. Density information obtained from *Oxford Regional Eco-*

nomic Atlas, "The Middle East and North Africa," prepared by the Economist Intelligence Unit Limited and the Cartographic Department of the Clarendon Press, London, O.U.P., 1960, p. 106.

3   Imperial Ethiopian Government: Ministry of Information, *Ethiopia: Facts and Figures,* Addis-Ababa, 1960, pp. 3–4.

4   *Ibid.,* pp. 4–7.

5   *Ibid.,* pp. 9–12.

6   *Ibid.,* pp. 12–13.

7   R. Segal, *Political Africa,* Stevens & Sons Ltd., London, 1961, p. 330.

8   S. H. Steinberg (Ed.), *op. cit.,* p. 974.

9   *Ibid.,* p. 962.

10   *Columbia Lippincott Gazetteer of the World,* Columbia University Press, New York, 1952, p. 592.

11   S. H. Steinberg (Ed.), *op. cit.,* p. 974.

12   *Appraisal of Proposed Manpower Survey for Ethiopia,* addressed to the Deputy Director, USOM, Ethiopia, Mimeograph, n.d., Table 5.

13   *Ethiopia Observer,* Vol. V, No. 1, 1961, pp. 63–71; U.N. Economic Commission for Africa, UNESCO: *Final Report of the Conference of African States on the Development of Education in Africa,* Addis Ababa, May 15–25, 1961, "Outline of a Plan for African Educational Development," p. 7, Table I, UNESCO/ED/181.

14   *Ethiopia Observer,* Vol. V, No. 2, p. 146.

15   Information obtained from private source.

16   Ministry of Public Health, unclassified information sent via American Embassy, dated 1960 and sent November 1961.

17   Imperial Ethiopian Government, United Nations: *Directory of Social Welfare Organizations and Social Services in Addis Ababa,* prepared by the School of Social Work, Addis-Ababa, 1960, pp. 3–25.

18   Imperial Ethiopian Government: Ministry of Commerce, Industry, and Planning, *Ethiopian Economic Review,* No. 1, Dec. 1959, p. 5.

19   *Ibid.,* No. 2, June 1960, p. 60.

20   *Ibid.,* No. 3, November 1960, p. 131, Table 5c.

21   *Ethiopia: Facts and Figures, op. cit.,* pp. 54–55.

22   *Ibid.,* p. 55.

23   S. H. Steinberg (Ed.), *op. cit.,* p. 978.

24   George H. T. Kimble, *Tropical Africa,* The Twentieth Century Fund, New York, 1960, p. 153; S. H. Steinberg (Ed.), *op. cit.,* p. 977.

25   *Ethiopia: Facts and Figures, op. cit.,* p. 27.

26   *Ibid.*

27   Ethiopian Government: Ministry of Commerce and Industry, Bulletin No. 15, April 1959, Addis Ababa, p. 2, Table 2b; State Bank of Ethiopia: *Report on Economic Conditions and Market Trends,* No. 50, Addis Ababa, May 1961, p. 11; Ethiopia: Facts and Figures, *op. cit.,* p. 30.

28   Information obtained from private source.

29   *Ethiopia: Facts and Figures, op. cit.,* p. 19.

30   *Ethiopian Economic Review,* No. 1, December 1959, *op. cit.,* pp. 73–74.

31   S. H. Steinberg (Ed.), *op. cit.,* p. 977; *Ethiopia: Facts and Figures, op. cit.,* pp. 43–44.

32   *Ethiopian Economic Review,* No. 1, December 1959, *op. cit.,* p. 5.

33   S. H. Steinberg (Ed.), *op. cit.,* p. 978.

34   *Ethiopia: Facts and Figures, op. cit.,* pp. 35–36.

35   *Ethiopian Economic Review,* No. 3, November 1960, *op. cit.,* pp. 135–36, Tables 7a and b.

36   *Ethiopia: Facts and Figures, op. cit.,* pp. 45–47.

37   *Appraisal of Proposed Manpower Survey, op. cit.,* Table 6.

38   Information obtained from private source.

39   *Ibid.*

French Somaliland[1]

AREA: *About 8,880 sq. m.*
POPULATION: *About 81,000 (1960 estimate)*
Density: Less than 9.2 per sq. m.

GEOGRAPHY

Somaliland has three main geographical regions: a low and desolate coastal zone, about 12 miles wide in the north, lined by high cliffs between Ghubbet-el-Kharab and Djibouti; a series of closed basins in the the interior enclosed by bare plateaus in the southwest, such as the Gamarre and Yaguere, 3,280 to 4,265 feet high; and the basaltic mountain ranges north of the Gulf of Tadjoura. The climate is torrid. Djibouti has a mean annual temperature of 85 degrees F. During the hot season, May to October, when the khamsin blows from the northwest, extremes of 107 degrees F. have been recorded. A cooler season extends from October to May. There are about 26 days of rainfall in the coastal region, averaging less than 5 inches annually. In the mountain areas the annual rainfall is more than 20 inches.

HISTORICAL SKETCH

The French acquired Obock in 1862 following a treaty signed with the Danakil chiefs, but effective occupation dates from 1881. Djibouti was founded in 1888 and became the capital in 1892. In 1896 the territory became known as Côte Française des Somalis. In 1946 the territory acquired the status of an overseas territory and since 1956, under the Loi Cadre, enjoys internal autonomy. In 1958 the country chose to remain a member of the French community under the Fifth Republic.

GOVERNMENT

Present Status
Overseas territory of France.

Constitution
Somaliland is administered by a Government Council of 8 members, of which the Governor is President. The Council is elected by the Territorial Assembly of 32 elected members. The territory also elects one Deputy and one Senator who represent it in Paris.

Franchise
Universal adult suffrage.

Political Parties [2]
Parti de la Défense des Intérêts Economiques et Sociaux du Territoire (D.I.E.S.T.), led by Hassan Goulep.
Union Républicaine led by Mahmoud Harbi.

POPULATION BREAKDOWN

Main City
Djibouti	41,000

Urban-rural Distribution
Some 45,300 people live in urban centers, i.e., more than half the total estimated population.

Ethnic Distribution
1960 estimate

French	3,000
Foreigner	5,000
Danakil	30,000
Issa	24,000
Arab	6,000

Religious Affiliation [3]

Christians	6%
Muslims	94%

Languages

Arabic, Somali, and Danakil. French is the official language.

Sex Distribution

Not available.

Age Distribution

Not available.

SOCIAL DATA

Education [4]

TABLE I

		Enrollment
12	Public primary schools	1,190
3	Private primary schools	700
1	Public secondary school	77
2	Private secondary schools	76
1	Public technical school	} +300
2	Private technical schools	

There were 70 teachers in public schools in 1956, and 6 students studying outside the territory. Educational expenditure represented 4.7% of the local budget in 1956.

Health and Social Services

VITAL STATISTICS

Not available.

MAIN DISEASES [5]

Tuberculosis, leprosy, contagious diseases, and malaria.

HEALTH SERVICES [6]

TABLE II
1956

		Beds
1	Main hospital (Djibouti)	520
4	Rural dispensaries	—
1	Urban dispensary	—
1	Tuberculosis dispensary	—
7	Special services	202

There were 6 doctors in 1956 and 78 beds per 10,000 inhabitants.

SOCIAL WELFARE SERVICES [7]

These are little developed. In 1952 an approved school for juvenile delinquents was established.

ECONOMY [8]

The territory depends chiefly on its position as a transit zone. In 1949 it was constituted a "free" territory and customs duties were abolished. Agricultural production is limited because of lack of water. The country is extremely poor.

Transport and Communication

WATERWAYS

None.

PORTS [9]

The free port of Djibouti has moorings for 5 ships and in 1956 handled 731,000 tons of cargo.

ROADS [10]

There are 495 miles of all-weather roads suitable for cars and 680 miles of trails suitable for trucks or jeeps.

RAILROADS

The only railroad runs from Djibouti to Addis Ababa in Ethiopia, and is 484 miles long, of which 60 miles fall within the territory.

AIRWAYS

There is an international airport at Djibouti. In addition, there are 10 local landing strips.

POSTS, TELECOMMUNICATIONS, AND BROADCASTING

Postal service information not available. There were 851 telephones in use in 1959. Radio Djibouti provides services in French, Arabic, Afar, and Somali languages.

Resources and Trade

MAIN EXPORTS [11]

Hides and skins, sea salt, coffee, and wheat.

MAIN IMPORTS [12]

Iron and steel products and other metal ware; textiles, thread, and fabrics; food products, beverages and tobacco; mineral products.

VALUE OF TRADE [13]

In millions of Djibouti francs

	1956	1957	1958	1959
Exports	512	512	373	256
Imports	1,932	1,609	10,020	13,157

Metropolitan France is Somaliland's chief trade partner. In 1956 it took 38.9% of its exports and provided 43.6% of its imports.

LIVESTOCK

1960 estimate

Cattle	78,000
Sheep and goats	610,000
Donkeys	6,500
Camels	25,000

Industry

MANUFACTURES

Somaliland's manufacturing concerns are limited and include ship-building and repairs, building and construction work, production of compressed or liquid gas, manufacture of foodstuffs, processing of road tar, small machine shops.

MINING

Prospecting for minerals has revealed only small quantities of copper and traces of iron ore and other metals.

POWER [14]

There are three stations: one at Djibouti with a capacity of 3,600 kw., one at Arta with a capacity of 130 kw., and one at Dikhil with a capacity of 60 kw. Total output in 1956 was 5,761,550 kwh.

Finance

CURRENCY [15]

1 Djibouti franc equals 2.30 old French Metropolitan francs. The French treasury is the note-issuing authority.

BANKING

Not available.

BUDGET [16]

Millions of Djibouti francs

	1956
Ordinary revenue	914.58
Ordinary expenditure	914.58

DEVELOPMENT PLAN [17]

In the first stage of the plan 55% of the finance was received from Metropolitan France and 45% from the territory's own resources. Metropolitan France's contributions were subsequently raised to cover 75% and later 90% of the total expenditure.

Allocations

First stage		Second stage
52%	infrastructure	50%
23%	social services	27%

LABOR [18]

In 1957 employment of the wage-earning population was estimated as:
Public sector

Civil service	363	
Non-Civil service	3,046	3,409

Private sector

Agriculture, fishing, and forestry	90

Mining and quarrying	—	
Industry	350	
Building and public works	1,000	
Commerce, banking, and professions	1,690	
Transport and storage	960	
Domestic service	3,000	7,090
TOTAL		10,499

In 1956 there were 8 branches of metropolitan unions in the territory and two local unions with 2,800 members in the public sector; in the private sector there were 7 local unions associated with the Trade Union Federation with 2,000 members.[19]

All labor is controlled by the Inspectorate of Labor and Social Legislation. The Labor Code of 1952 regulates all labor matters.[20]

FRENCH SOMALILAND NOTES

1   Unless otherwise stated, information obtained from Ambassade de France, Service de Presse et d'Information, *French Somaliland*, New York, Dec. 1961.

2   R. Segal, *Political Africa*, Stevens & Sons Ltd., London, 1961, pp. 140–41.

3   Service des Statistiques d' Outre-Mer, *Outre-Mer 1958*, Paul Dupont, Paris, 1959, p. 140, Table 1.

4   *Ibid.*, p. 181, Table 2, and p. 201, Table 33; U.N.: *Progress in Non-Self-Governing Territories Under the Charter*, Territorial Surveys, Vol. 5, New York, 1960, p. 67.

5   *Outre-Mer 1958*, *op. cit.*, p. 156, Table 5, and p. 166.

6   *Ibid.*, p. 157, Table 7; U.N.: *Progress in Non-Self-Governing Territories Under the Charter*, *op. cit.*, p. 66.

7   U.N.: *Progress in Non-Self-Governing Territories Under the Charter*, *op. cit.*, p. 66.

8   *Ibid.*, p. 62.

9   *Ibid.*, p. 63.

10   S. H. Steinberg (Ed.), *The Statesman's Yearbook, 1961*, Macmillan & Co., Ltd., London, 1961, p. 1025; and U.N.: *Progress in Non-Self-Governing Territories Under the Charter*, *op. cit.*, p. 67.

11   U.N.: *Progress in Non-Self-Governing Territories Under the Charter*, *op. cit.*, p. 64.

12 *Ibid.*

13 *Ibid.*, pp. 64–65, S. H. Steinberg (Ed.), *op. cit.*, p. 1023.

14 U.N.: *Progress in Non-Self-Governing Territories Under the Charter*, *op. cit.*, p. 63.

15 S. H. Steinberg (Ed.), *op. cit.*, p. 1023.

16 U.N.: *Progress in Non-Self-Governing Territories Under the Charter*, *op. cit.*, p. 64.

17 *Ibid.*

18 *Outre-Mer 1958*, *op. cit.*, p. 209, Table 3.

19 U.N.: *Progress in Non-Self-Governing Territories Under the Charter*, *op. cit.*, p. 65.

20 *Ibid.*

The Gabon Republic[1]

AREA: *102,290 sq. m.*
POPULATION:[2] *412,700 (1958 estimate)*
Density: 4 per sq. m.

GEOGRAPHY

Gabon is divided into three geographical zones: first, the coastal
lowlands, ranging in width from 18 to 125 miles, never exceeding 1,000
feet in altitude, bordered along the south with lagoons fringed with man-
groves; second, plateaus of varying heights extending over the entire northern and eastern sections and a portion of the south; and third, mountainous regions—the Crystal Mountains in the north of 2,950 feet and over,
the Birogou Mountains in the southeast, and the Vahilu Mountains in
the center with Mount Iboundji, the highest peak, 5,165 feet. The country has an equatorial humid climate with temperatures varying between
71 and 86 degrees F. There are four seasons: a long dry season, May to
September; a short rainy season, October to mid-December; a short dry
season, mid-December to mid-January; and a long rainy season of mid-
January to mid-May. The average rainfall at Libreville is 98 inches, increasing to the north, along the coast, and reaching 157.5 inches at Coco
Beach.

HISTORICAL SKETCH

The coastline was explored by European navigators as early as
1470. Following the outlawing of the slave trade in 1815, French vessels
guarded the coastline. From 1839 to 1841 treaties were signed with local
rulers whose authority extended over the southern and northern banks of
the Gabon River. In 1849 freed slaves were settled in what became Libreville. A period of exploration by numerous Frenchmen opened the in-

128

terior over the years 1855–1910. Gabon became a distinct administrative unit under French control in 1903 and it was joined to French Equatorial Africa. Under the 1946 French Constitution it became an overseas territory of the French Union with an elected territorial assembly and representatives in the French Parliament. In 1958 it became a member state of the new French Community and gained its independence on August 17, 1960. On September 20, 1960, it was admitted to the United Nations.

GOVERNMENT

Present Status

Independent republican state.

Constitution

Legislative power belongs to the National Assembly of 67 elected members. It may be dissolved by the President on the proposal of the government if two ministerial crises occur within a period of 26 months. The government is in the hands of the President who is also Prime Minister. He may ask for the revision of bills passed by the Assembly which must then be approved by a two-thirds majority. The Prime Minister and his Cabinet are forced to resign if the Assembly rejects a vote of confidence or adopts a motion of censure.

Franchise

Universal adult suffrage.

Local Government [3]

Local government units administered by elected councils are being established under the new constitution. Nine prefectures and 28 subprefectures have been created.

Political Parties [4]

Bloc Démocratique Gabonais (BDG), a local division of the RDA, led by Léon M'Ba who is both President and Prime Minister of the Republic.

Union Démocratique et Sociale Gabonaise (UDSG), led by Jean-Hilaire Aubame, Foreign Minister.

Parti de l'Unité Nationale Gabonaise (PUNGA).

POPULATION BREAKDOWN

Main Cities [5]
1958 estimate

Libreville	19,747
Port-Gentil	16,588

Urban-rural Distribution [6]
Of the total population some 9% live in towns of 5,000 or more inhabitants.

Ethnic Distribution [7]
1958 estimate

Non-African	4,976
African	407,700

There are five main tribal groups: The Eshira ± 120,000; Babinga ± 3,000; Fang, Omiene, and Bakota.

Religious Affiliation [8]

Christians	57%
Muslims	0.5%
Animists	42%

Languages
French is the official language. Main vernacular languages are unknown.

Sex Distribution [9]
1958 estimate

	Male	Female
African	192,300 (49.6%)	215,400 (50.4%)
Non-African	3,085 (66.5%)	1,891 (33.5%)

Age Distribution [10]
1958 estimate

	Under 18	18–60	61+
African	116,800	253,800	37,100
Non-African	1,236	3,623	1,891

SOCIAL DATA

Education [11]

As of January 1, 1958

TABLE I

	Enrollment	Public School Teachers
149 Public primary schools ⎱ 163 Private primary schools ⎰	39,763	413
3 Public secondary schools ⎱ 4 Private secondary schools ⎰	1,025	12
1 Public technical school ⎱ 1 Private technical school ⎰	131	21
103 Students studying abroad.		

In 1957, 66.8% of the children of school-going age were at school, of which 33.1% were girls. Educational expenditure represented 19.6% of the annual budget.

Health and Social Services

VITAL STATISTICS

Not available.

MAIN DISEASES

Sleeping sickness, leprosy, malaria, and blindness in children.

HEALTH SERVICES [12]

As of January 1, 1958

TABLE II

	Beds
3 Secondary hospitals	n.a.
20 Medical centers	n.a.
6 Private institutions	190
	323 (maternity)

There are 46 medical practitioners, 1 per 9,000; and 59 beds per 10,000 inhabitants.

SOCIAL WELFARE SERVICES [13]

Emphasis is placed on maternity and child welfare. Increasing attention is being paid to the education of women at special centers in rural areas. "Paysannat" programs assist in community development. In 1956 these covered some 65,000 persons.

ECONOMY

Gabon is predominantly a forest country whose economy is based on the lumbering industry. Its sizable surplus is due largely to lumber exports.

Transport and Communications

WATERWAYS

Most rivers in the Gabon are navigable and extensively used. The Lower Ogowe is navigable for 155 miles from N'Djole to the Atlantic. Other main waterways are the N'Gounie and Rombo N'Koni rivers.

PORTS

Libreville which handled 408,000 tons of freight in 1958 and Port-Gentil, 844,000 tons in the same year. Smaller ports are Owendo, Nyanga, and Banda.

ROADS

Gabon has 3,195 miles of roads, of which 2,590 are all-weather and 605 are seasonal roads. There is a 540-mile highway running from north to south.

RAILROADS

None.

AIRWAYS

There are international airports at Libreville and Port-Gentil linking the country with France and neighboring territories. In addition there are a number of secondary airports and landing fields for internal traffic. The Compagnie des Transports Aériens du Gabon runs flights to certain forest areas.

All main centers are equipped with postal and radio communications, but details are not available. All post offices are provided with telephone facilities and there are a number of private radio communication stations. Radio Brazzaville and Radio A.E.F. cover the whole region.

Resources and Trade

MAIN EXPORTS
Undressed and semifinished okoume wood (50% of exports), plywood, veneer, and other woods, and crude petroleum.

MAIN IMPORTS
Foodstuffs, fuel, and lubricants, manufactured goods, cement, iron and steel products, machinery and vehicles.

VALUE OF TRADE [14]
In millions of C.F.A. francs

	1956	1957	1958	1959	1960
Exports	4,850	6,300	8,369	10,927	11,826
Imports	4,400	7,750	7,282	7,000	7,838

LIVESTOCK
Not available.

Industry

MANUFACTURES
Most industrial activity is linked with the processing of lumber. One of the largest plywood factories in the world, the Compagnie Française du Gabon, is located at Port-Gentil. In addition there are a whale-oil-processing plant and rice and palm-oil mills. Plans are under way to develop the manufacture of cellulose and packing material, cement, and food.

MINING
Manganese is being mined at Moanda along with gold and diamonds. There are plans to mine potassium deposits.

POWER

Approximately 10 million kw. are generated at Libreville and Port-Gentil combined. Six oil fields have been developed since 1956.

Finance

CURRENCY

C.F.A. franc. 1 C.F.A. franc equals 2 old Metropolitan French francs.

BANKING [15]

Banque de l'Afrique Occidentale, Banque Commerciale Africaine, Banque Nationale pour le Commerce et l'Industrie, Société Générale, Crédit Lyonnais, and Banque Belge d'Afrique.

BUDGET [16]

In million C.F.A. francs

	1958
Revenue	1,983
Expenditure	1,983

DEVELOPMENT PLAN [17]

Gabon has a 5-year development plan with an estimated total expenditure of 1.562 million C.F.A. francs: 48% of which to be financed by the European Development Fund, 33% by the Aid and Cooperation Fund (FAC), 16% by local budgets and funds, and 3% by the post office. Allocations will go to increase and diversify production, encourage rural development, education, public health, and industrialization.

LABOR [18]

In 1957 the wage-earning population was estimated to be distributed as follows:

Public sector		
Civil service	2,000	
Non-Civil service	6,500	8,500
Private sector		
Agriculture, fishing, and forestry	12,940	
Mining and quarrying	6,230	
Industry	2,400	
Buildings and public works	3,840	
Commerce, banking, and professions	3,220	

Transport and storage	1,670	
Domestic service	2,800	33,100
TOTAL		41,600

In 1956 there were 242 trade unions throughout French Equatorial Africa. As of January 1, 1958 there were 1,130 employers contributing to the Family Equalization Fund, 4,055 workers were receiving allocations and 8,750 children benefiting.[19]

Preindependence legislaticn covered such matters as working hours, conditions of work, and accidents. Postindependence information not available.

THE GABON REPUBLIC NOTES

1 Unless otherwise stated, all information obtained from Ambassade de France, Service de Presse et d'Information, *The Gabon Republic*, New York, Feb. 1961.

2 Service des Statistiques d'Outre-Mer, *Outre-Mer 1958*, Paul Dupont, Paris, Nov. 1959, p. 792, Tables 1 and 2.

3 Librairie Générale de Droit et de Jurisprudence: *Revue Juridique et Politique d'Outre-Mer*, 15e année, No. 2, April–June 1961, Paris, p. 282; Communication received from the U.N. Mission Permanente de la République Gabonaise, New York, March 1962.

4 R. Segal, *Political Africa*, Stevens & Sons Ltd., London, 1961, pp. 331–33; *Africa Report*, Vol. 6, No. 10, Nov. 1961, Washington, D.C., p. 9.

5 *Outre-Mer 1958, op. cit.*, p. 793, Table 3.

6 Haut Commissariat de la République en Afrique Occidentale Française: *L'A.E.F. Economique et Sociale 1947–1958*, Edition Alains, Paris, May 1959, p. 8.

7 *Outre-Mer 1958, op. cit.*, p. 792, Tables 1 and 2.

8 *Ibid.*, p. 140, Table 1.

9 *Ibid.*, p. 792, Tables 1 and 2.

10 *Ibid.*

11 *Ibid.*, p. 793–94, Tables 6 and 7.

12 *Ibid.*, p. 793, Table 4.

13 U.N.: *Progress in the Non-Self-Governing Territories Under the Charter*, Territorial Surveys, Vol. 5, New York, 1960, p. 29.

14 *L'A.E.F. Economique et Sociale 1947–1958, op. cit.*, p. ix.

15 S. H. Steinberg (Ed.), *The Statesman's Yearbook 1959*, Macmillan & Co., Ltd., London, 1959, pp. 1018–1019.

16   *Ibid.*, p. 1017.
17   Communication received from the U.N. Mission Permanente de la République Gabonaise, *op. cit.*
18   *Outre-Mer 1958, op. cit.*, p. 209, Table 3.
19   *Ibid.*, p. 217, Table 15; U.N.: *Progress in the Non-Self-Governing Territories Under the Charter, op. cit.*, pp. 27 and 29.

Gambia[1]

AREA: *4,003 sq. m.*
(29 sq. m.—Colony
3,974 sq. m.—Protectorate)
POPULATION:[2] *294,900 (1959 estimate)*
Density: approx. 73 per sq. m.

GEOGRAPHY

Gambia, lying along the river of the same name, is Britain's most northerly dependency on the west coast of Africa. The colony consists mainly of the Island of St. Mary, on which Bathurst is situated, the adjoining division of Kombo St. Mary, at the mouth of the river, and MacCarthy Island in the middle river. The protectorate consists of a narrow strip of land, varying from 7 to 20 miles wide on each side of the river. The country is mainly flat. Sandy soil is found away from the river, while near its banks it is low-lying and swampy. The general range of temperature is 60 to 110 degrees F. The rainy season is from June to October, with an average rainfall of 40 inches on the coast, decreasing inland.

HISTORICAL SKETCH

Gambia is the oldest British African colony, dating from 1588 when British merchants were granted Royal Charters to operate in the colony area. For two centuries British interests in the area were largely limited to merchant enterprise. In 1821 Gambia was placed under the jurisdiction of the Sierra Leone Government, separated in 1843, reunited in 1866, and permanently separated in 1888. It was placed under its own Governor, Executive Council, and Legislative Council. Toward the end of the 19th century British interests spread into the interior under the protectorate system of administration. By 1902 the present boundaries of the territories had been established. In 1954 a new constitution was devised which for the first time provided for an elected majority in the Legislative Council and an unofficial majority in the Executive Council.

GOVERNMENT

Present Status
British colony and protectorate.

Constitution
The Constitution of April 1960 provides for a bicameral system: a House of Representatives (legislature), consisting of Governor as President, a Speaker, 4 official and 3 nominated unofficial members, and 27 elected members (7 representing the Colony and 20 the Protectorate). The Executive Council consists of the Governor, 4 official members, and not more than 6 members appointed from the House of Representatives.

Franchise
In the Colony the 7 House of Representative members are elected by persons over the age of 21, subject to certain residential qualifications. Of the 20 elected Protectorate members, 7 are elected by chiefs and 13 on the basis of universal adult suffrage.

Local Government
In the Colony, local government is in the hands of the Bathurst Town Council and the Kumbo Rural Authority, each with a majority of elected members. In the Protectorate, the 35 districts each have a native authority under a district head or head chief, and a native tribunal. Matters concerning the Protectorate as a whole are considered at an annual conference of chiefs.

Political Parties [3]
The Peoples Progressive Party (PPP), led by J. K. Jarawa, and supported by the self-elected chiefs in the House of Representatives.
The United Party, led by P. S. N'Jie.
The "national nonsectarian alliance" of the Gambia Muslim Congress, led by Mr. Farba-Jahumpa.
The Gambia Democratic Party, led by Rev. J. C. Faye.

POPULATION BREAKDOWN

Main City [4]
Bathurst (capital) 22,930.

Urban-rural Distribution
Not available.

Ethnic Distribution [5]

Non-African	European	269
	Syrian and Lebanese	201
	Other	74
African	Mandingo	104,000
	Fula	49,000
	Wollof	31,000
	Serahuli	24,000
	Jola	21,000
	Jombouko	7,000
	Lorobo	7,000
	Others	20,000

Religious Affiliation
Animism predominates throughout the protectorate. Both Christianity and Islam are practiced.

Language Distribution
Wollof is the most widely used vernacular language. English is the official language.

Sex Distribution
Not available.

Age Distribution
Not available.

SOCIAL DATA

Education [6]

TABLE I
1959

	Enroll-ment	Teachers
Colony:		
15 Infant and primary schools	4,340	139
4 Secondary schools	1,134	36

TABLE I—Continued

	Enroll-ment	Teachers
1 Government technical school	30	
1 Teachers' training college (Yundum)	48	

In addition the government maintains a domestic-science center and arts-and-crafts center for senior pupils of primary schools.

Protectorate:

36 Village schools	2,097	80
1 Secondary school	98	8

In 1958, 10.7% of children between the ages of 5 to 14 were at school.

In 1959 there were 24 Gambians with government scholarships and 15 with bursaries studying abroad.

Expenditure: £133,881 in 1959 (£27,694 in 1947).

Health and Social Services

VITAL STATISTICS [7]

Bathurst only, *per 1,000*

1959

Birth rate	Death rate	Infant Mortality rate
47.8	20.1	84.9

MAIN DISEASES

Malaria, trypanosomiasis, ascariasis (roundworms), yaws, bronchitis, leprosy, and eye infections.

HEALTH SERVICES [8]

TABLE II
1957

	Beds
2 General hospitals	245
1 Tuberculosis sanatorium	23
1 Mental hospital	24
1 Infirmary	20
1 Leprosarium	29 (patients)
7 Rural health centers	
37 Dispensaries and subdispensaries	

Maternity and child welfare clinics are held at 21 health centers and dispensaries throughout the country. A maternal and child-feeding program operates in Bathurst.

At the end of 1959 there were 11 doctors under the Director of Medical Services and only 1 private practitioner situated at Bathurst.

SOCIAL WELFARE SERVICES [9]
Both government and private agencies operate in the territory. A social welfare officer coordinates their activities and undertakes work connected with probation and juvenile delinquency, mainly in urban areas. There is a juvenile court and youth clubs and a center for youth activities run by the Central Council of Youth Clubs to be found in Bathurst.

ECONOMY

Gambia is a poor country. Its economy is almost entirely agricultural, with peanuts as the main cash crop. Rice is another important crop.

Transport and Communications

WATERWAYS
The Gambia River is navigable by ocean-going vessels 150 miles upstream to Kuntaur, and for vessels drawing not more than 6 feet to the village of Koina, 300 miles from the mouth. Two steamers provide a regular service as far as Basse, and ferries operate at a number of points.

PORTS
Bathurst is the main port. It handled 492,641 tons of freight in 1958. Ocean-going vessels dock at Kuntaur, Karur, and Balingho.

ROADS [10]
There are 42 miles of bituminous road in the vicinity of Bathurst, 185 miles of laterite all-season roads, and approximately 534 miles of dry-weather earth roads in the Protectorate. A new trans-Gambia road linking Senegal via Balingho and Yelitenda was opened in 1958. There were 1,558 licensed motor vehicles in 1958.

RAILROADS
None.

AIRWAYS
There is an airport at Yundum.

POSTS, TELECOMMUNICATIONS, AND BROADCASTING [11]

In 1958 there were 6 post offices. There is an automatic telephone system in the Bathurst area and telephonic lines to Senegal. Gambia does not have a broadcasting station.

Resources and Trade

MAIN EXPORTS [12]

Peanuts (82% of the total export value 1958/59), palm kernels, hides and skins, and beeswax.

MAIN IMPORTS

Machinery, metal manufactures, motor vehicles, cotton piece goods, artificial silk, clothing, rice, sugar, kola nuts, cigarettes, bags and sacks.

VALUE OF TRADE [13]

In £000's

	1955	1956	1957	1958	1959
Exports	2,634	2,553	4,243	4,351	2,956
Imports	3,710	3,730	4,762	3,668	2,979

Gambia's major trading partner is the United Kingdom.

MARKETING AND COOPERATIVE SOCIETIES [14]

The Gambia Oilseed Marketing Board, set up in 1949, handles the export of all peanuts and other oil seeds. A cattle marketing board was set up in 1955. A Registrar of Cooperative Societies, 3 inspectors, and an inspector-in-training have been appointed. Between 1955 and 1960 the number of registered societies grew from 4 with 74 members to 55 with 4,389 members, including 8 unregistered societies.

LIVESTOCK

Cattle	143,000
Sheep	50,500
Goats	75,500
Pigs	2,600
Horses	200
Donkeys	4,300
Poultry	227,100

Industry

MANUFACTURES

Peanut shelling is done in the territory. In addition Gambia encourages village industries based on local cotton, and there are small river-craft repair shops and building workshops.

MINING [15]

Gambia is at present prospecting for oil.

POWER

In 1957 about 3,580 million kw. were generated in Bathurst. There are small generating units in other towns.

Finance

CURRENCY

The West African Currency Board issues on a par with sterling.

BANKING [16]

There is one bank at Bathurst—The Bank of British West Africa Ltd.

BUDGET [17]

In £000's

	1960
Revenue	1,548
Expenditure	1,682

Customs receipts are the main source of revenue.

DEVELOPMENT PLAN [18]

1959–64

	£'000s
Total costs: £3,526,000	
Sources UKD&WD funds	1,782
Local resources	1,000
Loans	744

LABOR

Ninety percent of the population are peasant farmers. The estimated numbers in other occupations are

Government service	2,700	
Distributive trades	2,450	
Shipping	290	
Building	280	
Others	310	6,030

There are 3 registered trade unions. None has a membership of more than a few hundred.

Labor legislation covers such matters as minimum wages, arbitration, the registration of unemployed persons, the safety of workers, and workmen's compensation.

GAMBIA NOTES

1 Unless otherwise stated, information obtained from fact sheets on the United Kingdom Dependencies, Reference Division, U.K. Central Office of Information, No. R 4019, *The Gambia*, June 1960.

2 Communication received from the British Embassy, Washington, D.C., July 1961.

3 R. Segal, *Political Africa*, Stevens & Sons Ltd., London, 1961, pp. 333–34.

4 Communication from British Embassy, *op. cit.*

5 U.K.: *The Gambia 1958/59*, H.M.S.O., London, 1961, p. 7.

6 *Ibid.*, pp 30–34. Also, U.N. Economic Commission to Africa, UNESCO: *Final Report of the Conference of African States on the Development of Education in Africa*, Addis Ababa, May 15–25, 1961, "Outline of a Plan for African Educational Development," p. 7, Table I, UNESCO/ED/ 181.

7 U.K.: *The Gambia 1958/59*, *op. cit.*, p. 36.

8 *Ibid.*, pp. 37–38.

9 *Ibid.*, pp. 48–49.

10 S. H. Steinberg (Ed.), *The Statesman's Yearbook 1959*, Macmillan & Co., Ltd., London, 1959, p. 351.

11 U.K.: *The Gambia 1958/59*, *op. cit.*, pp. 65–66.

12 *Ibid.*, p. 16.

13 *Ibid.*, pp. 16–17, also; Colony of the Gambia: *Trade Report for the Year 1958*, Bathurst, Government Printer, 1959, p. 2.

14 *Annual Report of the Registrar of Co-operative Societies, Gambia, for the Year Ending March 31, 1960,* Government Printer, Bathurst, Sessional Paper No. 8/60, Table 9.

15 U.K.: *The Gambia 1958/59, op. cit.,* p. 29.

16 *Ibid.,* p. 15.

17 Colony of Gambia: *Estimates of Recurrent Revenue and Expenditure 1960,* Bathurst, Government Printer, 1959, p. i.

18 U.K.: Colonial Office, *The Colonial Territories 1960–1961,* H.M.S.O., London, *Cmnd. 1407,* June 1961, p. 120.

Ghana

AREA: [1] *91,843 sq. m.*

POPULATION: [2] *6,690,730 (provisional 1960 census results)*
Density: 72 per sq. m.

GEOGRAPHY [3]

Ghana consists of four main geographical regions: (a) a coastal plain, (b) a region of low hills never exceeding 2,000 feet, (c) a forest belt, and (d) a dry savanna region. It enjoys a tropical climate, with temperatures varying between 70–80 degrees F. It has two rainy seasons separated by a fairly dry spell in July and August and a longer one from December to February. Rainfall varies between 30–80 inches per annum.

HISTORICAL SKETCH [4]

Contact with Europe was first established in 1482 when the Portuguese built Elmina Castle as a permanent trading post. The first recorded English trading voyage to the coast was made by Thomas Windham in 1553, and in the course of the next three centuries the English, Dutch, Danes, and Germans all controlled various parts of the coastal area at different periods. In 1826 the United Kingdom took over control of the English private trading company operating in the Gold Coast settlement, and in 1844 the Fanti chiefs signed a bond recognizing Queen Victoria's jurisdiction over the area. From 1826 to 1900 the British fought a long series of campaigns against the Ashantis of the interior, and only in 1901 did they succeed in making Ashanti and the northern territory protectorates. The fourth territorial division eventually to form part of the nation, British Togoland, was taken from the Germans in 1922 and administered by the British as a League of Nations Mandate. In December 1956 it became a United Nations Trust Territory. In 1957, following

146

a plebiscite, the United Nations agreed to make it part of newly independent Ghana. On March 6 of that year the Gold Coast was the first of Britain's tropical African dependencies to gain its independence. Two days later it was admitted to the United Nations. On July 1, 1960, it became a Republic within the British Commonwealth of Nations.

GOVERNMENT

Present Status

Independent republican state.

Constitution [5]

The constitution provides for a President and a National Assembly, both elected every 5 years by popular vote. The National Assembly consists of a speaker and not less than 104 members. The President is both head of state and of government. He has power to veto legislation and to dissolve Parliament. The constitution provides for a Cabinet appointed by the President from among the members of the majority party in the National Assembly.

Franchise

Universal adult suffrage.

Local Government [6]

There are three municipal councils, 1 city council (Accra), and 56 local councils. The councilors are elected by popular vote and the number on each council will vary according to the size of the population of the area. Councils are empowered to impose general and special rates, and to levy fees.

Political Parties [7]

Convention People's Party (CPP), led by Kwame Nkrumah, President of the Republic.

United Party (UP), a merger of the National Liberation Movement, the Northern People's Party, Togoland Congress, and the Ghana Congress Party, led by Dr. K. Busia—now in exile.

POPULATION BREAKDOWN

Main Cities [8]
1960 census—provisional

Accra (capital)	338,000
Kumasi	190,000
Cape Coast	41,000
Takoradi	41,000
Tamale	40,000
Sekondi	35,000
Koforidua	28,000
Winneba	25,000

Urban-rural Distribution [9]

According to the provisional results of the 1960 census, about 17% of the population lives in towns of 10,000 or more.

Ethnic Distribution [10]
Mid-1955 estimate

European	11,110
Lebanese and Syrian	2,120
Asian	510
Other	340

African 3,405,962 (1948 census)—the main tribal groups are the Akan (Guan, Fanti, and Twi), Ewe, Ga, Adamgwe, and Krobo.

Religious Affiliation [11]

Muslims	300,000
Christians	750,000
Animists	3,498,000

Languages

Arabic, English (official language), and the local vernaculars, Akan (in Ashanti and the coastal regions), Ewe, Ga, Mole (chiefly in the northern territory), and Hausa.

Sex Distribution [12]
Mid-1955 estimate

	Male	Female
Non-African	9,180 (65.2%)	4,900 (34.8%)

1948 census

	Male	Female
African	1,709,415 (50.1%)	1,696,547 (49.9%)

Age Distribution [13]
Mid-1955 estimate

	Under 15	15+
Non-African	2,770	11,310

1948 census

	Under 16	16–44	45+
African	1,492,684	1,433,097	480,181

SOCIAL DATA

Education [14]

TABLE I

1959

		Enrollment
3,713	Primary schools	483,425
1,394	Middle schools	154,726
69	Secondary schools	15,317
38	Technical and trade institutions	4,563
30	Teacher-training colleges	4,274
	University College of Ghana	519
	Kumasi College of Technology	615

In 1961 Ghana had 15,546 teachers at the first level and 2,964 at the second level.

In 1959, 66.7% of children between the ages of 5–14 were at school.

Health and Social Services

VITAL STATISTICS [15]

Per 1,000

	1951	1955	1958
Birth rate	31.5	42.0	52.0
Death rate	19.3	21.8	21.0
Infant mortality rate	117.0	109.0	90.0

Yaws, chicken pox, scabies, skin deficiencies, eye and ear diseases, malaria, venereal disease, ascariasis, ankylostomiasis, dysentery, upper respiratory infections, bronchitis, chronic skin ulcers.

HEALTH SERVICES [17]

TABLE II

31 Government hospitals

17 Mission hospitals

6 Private hospitals

8 Mining hospitals

15 Government health centers

20 Clinics (mission)

2 Child-welfare clinics

148 Dispensaries and dressing stations

In 1955 there were 2,450 beds and cots in government hospitals.

SOCIAL WELFARE SERVICES [18]

Urban welfare: In 1958 there were 51 day nurseries serving 2,615 children. There are community and neighborhood centers for youths and 3 juvenile courts dealing with delinquents. Rural welfare: Much of rural welfare services fall under the Mass Education Section of the Department of Social Welfare and Community Development. Emphasis is placed on adult literacy and self-help activities.

ECONOMY

Ghana is primarily a one-crop agricultural export economy based on cocoa, which made up 61% of the value of exports in 1959.

Transport and Communications

WATERWAYS [19]

The Black and White Volta rivers are navigable for 280 miles from the sea to the Northern Region border only for shallow draughts, and to Akuse for launches. Fifty miles of the Ankobra River are navigable for many months of the year by surf boats and shallow-draught launches. The Tano River is navigable for 60 miles as far as Tamoso.

PORTS [20]

Takoradi is the largest port and handled 2,535,000 tons of cargo in 1959. Accra is next, handling 756,000 tons in 1959. A new port is being built at Tema and will be the largest port in Ghana. Other smaller ports handled some 84,000 tons of cargo in 1959.

ROADS [21]

There were 18,866 miles of roads in 1959, of which 1,947 miles were bituminized and 16,919 miles were gravel roads.

RAILROADS [22]

There was a total mileage of 591 miles of 3'6"-gauge track in 1959. The main line runs from Takoradi to Accra and Kumasi.

AIRWAYS [23]

Accra has an international airport. Other airfields are to be found at Takoradi, Kumasi, and Tamale. Internal lines link the various regions in the country.

POSTS, TELECOMMUNICATIONS, AND BROADCASTING [24]

There were 714 post offices and postal agencies in 1959. Ghana has telephone services in the major towns. In 1959 there were some 21,500 telephones in use. Radio Ghana broadcasts to all parts of Africa and provides programs in English, French, Portuguese, Hausa, Arabic, and Swahili.

Resources and Trade

MAIN EXPORTS [25]

Cocoa (representing 60.5% of the value of total exports for 1958/59) cocoa butter, wood and timber, bauxite, manganese, diamonds, and gold.

MAIN IMPORTS [26]

Textiles and other manufactured goods, machinery and transport vehicles, food, chemicals, mineral fuels, beverages, and tobacco.

VALUE OF TRADE [27]

In £'000's

	1956	1957	1958	1959	1960
Exports	7,217	7,633	8,713	9,446	9,666
Imports	7,410	8,057	7,049	9,419	10,776

The Ghana Cocoa Marketing Board purchases all cocoa produced for export. Its sales agents are located in London.

The Agricultural Development Corporation is a marketing board for the collection and sale of sheanuts.

In 1958/59 there were 408 produce marketing cooperatives with a membership of 43,003. The bulk of these were cocoa producers' cooperatives. There were also 20 primary cooperative societies with 383 members.

LIVESTOCK [29]

1960 estimate

Cattle	480,000
Sheep and goats	1,000,000
Horses	6,500
Pigs	49,000
Poultry	2,600,000

Industry

MANUFACTURES [30]

In 1958 manufacturing industries employed 7.3% of the total recorded employees of the country. The main manufacturing industries produce wood and cork products (except furniture). Other industries include printing, publishing, and allied industries, baker establishments, and repair shops.

MINING [31]

Mineral products represent about a quarter of Ghana's total export earnings, including gold, diamonds, bauxite, and manganese.

POWER [32]

In 1959 the total generating capacity of the country was 91,049 kw, of this 339 million kwh were consumed. By 1965 the Volta River hydroelectric project is expected to be completed. The whole project, which will consist of three stations, will have a generating capacity of 1,044,000 kw. The total cost of the project is expected to be £670,-642,000.

Finance

Ghana £ issued by the Bank of Ghana and maintained on a par with sterling.

BANKING [33]

The Central Bank of Ghana, Barclay's Bank D.C.O., Bank of West Africa Ltd., and Ghana Commercial Bank. In addition there is a post office savings bank.

BUDGET [34]

1960, in £'000's

Revenue	4,762
Expenditure	4,152

DEVELOPMENT PLAN [35]

1959/64 Total expenditure £G 242,000,000

Sources

	£G Millions
Sterling reserve (excluding currency reserves)	50
Cocoa Marketing Board reserves	25
General revenue	15

The following are the main expenditure heads: Communications, health, sanitation, and water supplies; education; agriculture and natural resources; industry and trade.

LABOR [36]

The following was the employment of the labor force in the money sector in 1959:

	Total	Government	Private	Others
Agriculture, fishing, and forestry	43,629	29,436	16,679	514
Mining and quarrying	32,996	—	32,942	54
Manufacturing	21,317	613	18,545	2,159
Construction	50,712	23,400	23,189	4,123
Electricity, water, and sanitation	9,574	4,529	201	4,844

	Total	Government	Private	Others
Transport, storage, and communications	28,996	18,913	8,417	1,666
Services	75,665	30,634	19,934	25,097
TOTAL	252,889			

In 1961 there were 16 trade unions with a total membership of over half a million, federated into the Trades Union Congress. All 16 are industrial/occupational unions.[37]

Labor legislation covers conditions of work, workmen's compensation, trade unions and regulations, trade disputes, and wages.

GHANA NOTES

1   U.K.: Central Office of Information, *The Making of Ghana*, H.M.S.O., London, 1957, p. 3.

2   Ghana: Central Bureau of Statistics, *Quarterly Digest of Statistics*, Accra, March 1961, p. 1. A communication received from the Ghana Census Office, Sept. 15, 1961, states that the final results of the March–April 1960 census will not be available for some time.

3   Ghana: Information Section, Ghana Embassy, *Fact Sheet*, Washington, D.C., p. 1; U.K.: *The Making of Ghana, op. cit.*, p. 3.

4   U.S.: Department of State, *The Newly Independent Nations: Ghana*, 7076 African Series 5, Dec. 1960.

5   Ghana: *Government Proposals for a Republican Constitution*, Government Printer, Accra, March 1960.

6   Communication received from Ministry of the Interior and Local Government (Local Government Division) Accra, Nov. 1961 (Ref. No. L 6, 102/8/147).

7   R. Segal, *Political Africa*, Stevens & Sons Ltd., London, 1961, pp. 335–39.

8   Ghana: *Quarterly Digest of Statistics, op. cit.*, p. 1.

9   *Ibid.* Computed from information on p. 1.

10   Ghana: *Report of the Ministry of Health 1955*, Government Printer, Accra, Appendix C, p. 54; U.K.: *The Making of Ghana, op. cit.*, pp. 4–5.

11   J. Spencer Trimingham, *Islam in West Africa*, O.U.P., 1959, p. 233, Appendix V.

12   Ghana: *Report of the Ministry of Health 1955, op. cit.*, Appendix C, p. 54, Table I; Gold Coast: Crown Agents for the Colonies, *Census of Population 1948*, London, 1950, p. 44, Table 7.

13 Ghana: *Report of the Ministry of Health 1955, op. cit.*, Appendix C, p. 54, Table 1; Gold Coast: *Census of the Population 1948, op. cit.*, p. 44, Table 7.

14 Ghana: *Education Statistics 1959*, Office of the Government Statistician, Dec. 1959, pp. 1–2, Table 1; U.N. Economic Commission for Africa, UNESCO: *Final Report of the Conference of African States on the Development of Education in Africa*, Addis Ababa, May 15–25, "Outline of a Plan for African Educational Development," p. 7, Table 1, UNESCO/ED/181; R. J. Smythe: "Problems of Teacher Supply and Demand in Africa South of the Sahara" in *The Journal of Negro Education*, Vol. XXX, No. 3, Howard University Press, 1961, p. 337, Table I.

15 Ghana: *Report of the Ministry of Health 1955, op. cit.*, p. 55, Table V (1955 figures); F. Lorimer, *Demographic Information on Tropical Africa*, Boston University Press, 1961, p. 96 (1958 figures).

16 Ghana: *Report of the Ministry of Health 1955, op. cit.*, Appendix J, pp. 72–75.

17 S. H. Steinberg (Ed.), *The Statesman's Yearbook 1961*, Macmillan & Co., Ltd., London, 1961, pp. 302–306; Ghana: *Report of the Ministry of Health 1955, op. cit.*, p. 64, Table XIX.

18 T. Peter Omar, "The Social Services in Ghana," *Journal of Human Relations*, Central State College, Wilberforce, Ohio, Vol. VIII, Nos. 3 and 4, pp. 689–92.

19 Ghana: Ministry of Trade and Industry, *Handbook of Commerce and Industry*, Accra, n.d.

20 Ghana: Government Statistician, *Economic Survey 1959*, Accra, 1959, pp. 53–55.

21 *Ibid.*, p. 51.

22 Ghana: *Handbook of Commerce and Industry, op. cit.*, p. 60.

23 S. H. Steinberg (Ed.), *op. cit.*, p. 301.

24 Ghana: *Economic Survey 1959, op. cit.*, pp. 56–57; External Service, Ghana Broadcasting System, *Radio Ghana Programs*, Accra, Nov. 1961.

25 Ghana: *Economic Survey 1959, op. cit.*, pp. 14–15.

26 *Ibid.*, Table IV, p. 11.

27 Ghana: *Quarterly Digest of Statistics, op. cit.*, p. 18.

28 Ghana: *Handbook of Commerce and Industry, op. cit.*, pp. 49–51; *Annual Report of the Department of Cooperation 1958/59*, Government Printer, Accra, 1960, Appendix II.

29 S. H. Steinberg (Ed.), *op. cit.*, p. 306.

30 Ghana: *Economic Survey 1959, op. cit.*, p. 41.

31 *Ibid.*, pp. 38–39.

32 *Ibid.*, p. 44, Table 31; *The Volta River Project*, Government Printer, Accra, 1961, pp. 9–10.

33 Ghana: *Economic Survey 1959, op. cit.*, p. 66, and *Quarterly Digest of Statistics, op. cit.*, p. 74.

34 Ghana: *Quarterly Digest of Statistics, op. cit.*, p. 44.

35 Ghana: *Second Development Plan 1959–1964;* Government Printer, Accra, n.d., pp. 1–2.
36 Ghana: Office of the Government Statistician, *Quarterly Digest of Statistics,* published in London, June 1960, p. 2, Table 3.
37 Communication received from the Director of Trades Union Congress, Accra, October 2, 1961.

The Republic of Guinea

AREA: [1] 95,935 sq. m.
POPULATION: [2] 2,529,000 (1958 estimate)
Density: [3] 28 per sq. m.

GEOGRAPHY [4]

Guinea consists of a coastal plain, the Fouta Djallon Mountain range on the coast, and the Guinea Highlands rising to 4,970 feet in the interior. It has a tropical climate with temperatures around 70 degrees F. throughout the year. Rainfall is highest along the coast and in the highlands, reaching 166 inches but dropping to 50 inches in the north.

HISTORICAL SKETCH [5]

The coast of Guinea was first visited by sailors from Dieppe in the middle of the 14th century. This traffic was never large. By the end of the 18th century trading with this area had increased considerably and the influence of the French was recognized.

From 1820 several expeditions were made into the Fouta Djallon and Upper Guinea. In 1882 French Guinea was formally constituted into a French colony. Under the 1946 constitution it was given considerable territorial autonomy which was extended under the Loi Cadre of 1956. On October 2, 1958 it proclaimed its independence following the referendum of September 2, 1958 when it decided to break with France. It became a member of the United Nations on December 12, 1958.

GOVERNMENT

Present Status
Independent republican state.

Constitution [6]

Executive power rests with the President, who is elected by popular vote for a period of 7 years. He selects the Cabinet of 5 secretaries and 9 ministers. The Cabinet shares with him the executive responsibility of government and is responsible solely to him. The President alone is responsible to the National Assembly, a unicameral legislature, of 60 members elected for 5 years. Members of the Cabinet may be heard either by the full assembly or by certain of its committees.

Franchise

Universal adult suffrage.

Local Government [7]

"Communes" and "circonscriptions" are being established under the new constitution. Details are not available.

Political Party [8]

Parti Démocratique de la Guinée (PDG) led by Sékou Touré, President of the Republic. Saifoulaye Diallo is the President of the National Assembly.

POPULATION BREAKDOWN

Main Cities [9]
January 1958

Conakry	78,388
Kankan	27,450
Kindia	18,432
Macenta	12,087
Labé	11,852
Siguiri	11,826
Mamou	9,951

Urban-rural Distribution [10]

About 6% of the total population lived in towns of 10,000 or more inhabitants in 1958.

Ethnic Distribution [11]
  1958 census

	Non-African	9,058

  1958 estimate

	African	2,520,000

  Main tribal groups
  Fulani (including Fula)   734,500
  Mande (including Malinke, Sussu, Djallube, etc.)   1,207,100
  Forest groups (including Guezze, Kissi,
    G'Bena, etc.)   465,900
  Other   161,700

Religious Affiliation [12]

Christians	1.5%
Muslims	62.0%
Animists	37.0%

Languages
  French is the official language. Mande and Fulani are the principal local vernacular languages.

Sex Distribution [13]
  In 1955, of the total population, 47.6% were males and 52.4% were females.

Age Distribution [14]
  In 1955, of the total population:

Under 14	15–54	55+
42.1%	50.3%	7.6%

SOCIAL DATA

Education [15]
  As of January 1958

TABLE I

	Enrollment	Public School Teachers
219 Public primary schools } 68 Private primary schools }	45,542	843

TABLE I—Continued

	Enrollment	Public School Teachers
16 Public secondary schools) 3 Private secondary schools)	2,171	41
6 Public technical schools) 3 Private technical schools)	675	21

There were 387 students studying abroad.

In 1957, 11.5% of the children of school-going age were at school, of which 21.8% were girls; educational expenditure amounted to 15.6% of the total budget.

Health and Social Services

VITAL STATISTICS [16]

Per 1,000

Birth rate	Death rate	Infant mortality rate	Net reproduction rate
62	40	205	1.58

MAIN DISEASES

Not available.

HEALTH SERVICES [17]

January 1, 1958

TABLE II

		Beds
1	Secondary hospital	426
28	Medical centers	1,009
15	Infirmaries	80
5	Private institutions	— (354 maternity beds)

There were 66 medical practitioners, 1 per 38,000 inhabitants; 6 beds per 10,000 inhabitants.

SOCIAL WELFARE SERVICES

Not available.

ECONOMY

Guinea is a poor country. Its economy is primarily based on three products: bananas, aluminum, and iron ore. The export of its banana crop has been diverted from France to the Soviet Bloc.

Transport and Communications

WATERWAYS [18]

The Niger River is navigable between Kouroussa and Bamako (Mali) from July to December.

PORTS [19]

Conakry is Guinea's main port. In 1958 it handled 1,187,000 tons of freight.

ROADS [20]

At the beginning of 1957 there were 7,600 km. of roads, of which 2,967 km. were federal roads, 2,145 km. local roads, and 2,500 km. trails.

RAILROADS [21]

At the beginning of 1957 there were 662 km. of railroads.

AIRWAYS [22]

There are two airports—at Conakry and Kankan.

POSTS, TELECOMMUNICATIONS, AND BROADCASTING [23]

In 1957 there were 26 post offices and 42 branches; 66 telegraph offices and 38 telephone offices. Guinea has its own broadcasting service. More powerful transmitters are being established.

Resources and Trade

MAIN EXPORTS [24]

Coffee (31.7% of the value of total exports 1959), bananas, palm kernels, iron, aluminum, and diamonds.

MAIN IMPORTS [25]

Machinery and transport equipment; food, beverages, and tobacco; metals; textiles; mineral fuels; chemicals; basic materials; other manufactures.

VALUE OF TRADE [26]

In millions U.S. $

	1958	1959
Exports f.o.b.	23.2	28.7
Imports c.i.f.	61.9	60.0

The Comptoir Guinéen du Commerce, which attempted to control all imports and exports, was abolished in 1961. The Minister of Commerce has taken over its functions and specialized state agencies have been set up which have to compete with private trade. Guinexport, which controls the buying and exporting of agricultural products, and Pharmaguinée, which has the sole rights of representing foreign pharmaceutical firms and opening chemist shops, are the only two state agencies with special monopolies.

LIVESTOCK [28]

1959 estimate

Cattle	1,364,000
Sheep and goats	700,000
Horses and donkeys	2,500
Pigs	7,000

Industry

MANUFACTURES [29]

Guinea produces soap and canned fruits.

MINING [30]

Diamonds are found in the Macenta district; iron ore in the Kaloum peninsula, and bauxite in the Lose Islands, Boke district, and Kindi-Telimele district.

POWER [31]

In 1958 consumption totaled 11,800,000 kwh.

Finance

CURRENCY [32]

Guinea franc is on a par with C.F.A. franc.

BANKING [33]

La Banque de la République de Guinée is the sole bank of issue. Information on other banks is not available.

BUDGET [34]

In millions of Guinea francs

1961

Revenue	8,745
Expenditure	8,745

DEVELOPMENT PLAN [35]

1960/63 Total estimated expenditure—38,912,000 Guinea francs.

Allocations—Public administration and transport	36.39%
Agricultural and industrial production	47.26%
Social services	15.96%
Reserve funds	0.38%

The plan is being financed by loans from both the eastern and western countries: Some of the loans are: Communist China, U.S.$25 million; U.S.S.R., U.S.$35 million; others contributing are Czechoslovakia, Israel, Western Germany, and Ghana.

LABOR

In 1957 the distribution of the wage-earning population was estimated to be as follows: [36]

Public Sector	15,600	
Private Sector		
Agriculture, fishing, and forestry	32,200	
Mining and quarrying	2,700	
Industry	3,900	
Building and public works	15,500	
Commerce, banking, and professions	11,000	
Transport and storage	9,500	
Domestic service	19,000	109,400

As of December 31, 1951, there were 14 employees' unions in the private sector with 4,290 members, and 26 employees' unions and 22 employers' unions in the private sector.[37] Later information is not available.

All labor matters were covered by the Labor Code of 1952 prior to independence. Postindependence information is not available.

THE REPUBLIC OF GUINEA NOTES

1 *The Negro Journal of Education,* Vol. XXX, No. 3, Howard University Press, 1961, p. 282.

2 Services des Statistiques d'Outre-Mer, *Outre-Mer 1958,* Paul Dupont, Paris, Nov. 1959, p. 832, Table 1.

3 *The Negro Journal of Education, op. cit.,* p. 282.

4 Headquarters Quartermaster Research and Engineering Company, U.S. Army, Technical Report EP-94, Canal Zone EP-93: Canal Zone Analogues IV: *Analogues of Canal Zone Climate in West Central Africa,* Natick, Mass., July 1958, pp. 1–2, and Figures 3, 5, and 8.

5 *French Guinea:* Ministère de la France d'Outre-Mer, Directions des Affaires Economiques, Paris, n.d., pages not numbered.

6 Librairie Générale de Droit et de Jurisprudence: *Revue Juridique et Politique d'Outre-Mer,* 15ᵉ année, No. 2, April–June 1961, Paris, pp. 295–98. République de Guinée: Institut National de Recherches et Documentation, Ministère de l'Intérieur, Secrétariat d'Etat et d'Information, *Recherches Africaines,* Nos. 1–4, January–December, 1959, p. 12.

7 *Revue Juridique et Politique d'Outre-Mer, op. cit.,* p. 295.

8 R. Segal, *Political Africa,* Stevens & Sons Ltd., London, 1961, pp. 340–42; *Africa Report,* Vol. 6, No. 10, Nov. 1961, Washington, D.C., p. 10.

9 *Outre-Mer 1958, op. cit.,* p. 833, Tables 2 and 3.

10 Computed from *ibid.,* pp. 832–33, Tables 1, 2 and 3.

11 *Ibid.,* p. 832, Table 1; also Haut Commissariat de L'A.O.F.: *Etude Démographique par Sondage en Guinée 1954–1955,* Résultats Définitifs, Administration Générale des Services de la France d'Outre-Mer, Services des Statistiques, p. 82, Table 2, 2, 1.

12 *Outre-Mer 1958, op. cit.,* p. 140, Table 1.

13 *Ibid.,* p. 93, Table 12; figures based on demographic survey conducted in Konkouré in 1955.

14 *Ibid.*

15 *Ibid.,* p. 835, Tables 7 and 8.

16 *Ibid.,* p. 834, Table 4.

17 *Ibid.,* p. 834, Table 5.

18 *The Columbia-Lippincott Gazetteer of the World,* Columbia University Press, New York, 1952, p. 1324.

19 *Outre-Mer 1958, op. cit.,* p. 836, Table 13.

20 *Ibid.,* p. 835, Table 9.

21 *Ibid.,* p. 836, Table 11.

22 *Ibid.,* p. 836, Table 14.

23 *Ibid.*, p. 837, Table 15: also *Marchés Tropicaux et Méditerranéens*, 17ᵉ année, No. 798, February 25, 1961, Paris, p. 483.

24 *Outre-Mer 1958, op. cit.*, p. 838, Table 19; also U.N.: *Economic Bulletin for Africa*, Vol. 1, No. 2, Addis Ababa, Ethiopia, June 1961, Annexe, p. 13.

25 *Ibid.*, Annexe, p. 17.

26 *Ibid.*, Annexe, pp. 4–5.

27 *West Africa*, July 29, 1961, Harrison & Sons, Ltd., London, p. 830.

28 République de Guinée: *Recherches Africaines, op. cit.*, p. 14.

29 *Outre-Mer 1958, op. cit.*, p. 837, Table 18.

30 S. H. Steinberg (Ed.), *The Statesman's Yearbook, 1961*, Macmillan & Co., Ltd., London, 1961, p. 1091.

31 *Outre-Mer 1958, op. cit.*, p. 837, Table 18.

32 S. H. Steinberg (Ed.), *op. cit.*, p. 1091.

33 *Ibid.*, p. 1092.

34 *Ibid.*, p. 1091.

35 République de Guinée: L'Action Politique du Parti Démocratique de la Guinée: *La Planification Economique*, Tome V, Année 1960, Imprimerie Nationale, Conakry, pp. 405–23, *African World*, Nov. 1961, African Publications Ltd., London, p. 12.

36 *Outre-Mer 1958, op. cit.*, p. 209, Table 3.

37 Haut Commissariat de L'A.O.F., *Annuaire Statistique de L'Afrique Occidentale française*, année 1950 à 1954, Vol. 5, Tome 2, Direction des Services de la Statistique Générale et de la Mécanographique, Paris, 1957, p. 133, Tables K-1-31, 32, and 33.

The Republic of the Ivory Coast[1]

AREA: *127,520 sq. m.*
POPULATION:[2] *3,222,600 (1958 estimate)*
Density: 25 per sq. m.

GEOGRAPHY

The land of the Ivory Coast rises gradually from the ocean to the north, until it reaches an altitude of over 1,300 feet. It is rolling country, broken only by a few isolated mountainous areas with peaks ranging from 3,000 to 5,000 feet. There are three main geographical areas: (a) a zone of lagoons extending for 185 miles from Fresco to the Ghana border with an equatorial climate of high temperatures between 76 and 83 degrees F., high humidity, and rainfall ranging from 79 to 123 inches per annum, falling mainly during the 140 days of rain; (b) a tropical forest zone immediately beyond the lagoons containing a stand of trees more than 80 feet tall and towering above them, trees of over 150 feet. Temperatures range from 57 to 103 degrees F., and rainfall ranges between 30 and 98 inches per annum; (c) a Sudanese zone with sparse vegetation in the north where the wooded savanna of the transitional zone is replaced by a grassy savanna and the harmattan (a dry, dusty wind). A north wind from the Sahara blows for a few weeks between December and February and brings cool, dry weather.

HISTORICAL SKETCH

French traders made contact with the Ivory Coast in the 15th century. They began to trade in ivory with the people of the region. French missionaries landed at Assinie in 1637, and in 1842 a treaty signed with the local chiefs placed the area under French protection. Between 1918 and 1938 the economy of the territory developed rapidly. In 1946 it became a territory under the Fourth Republic, with a local elected General Assembly and representation in the French Parliament. In 1952 members were elected to the Grand Council of French West Africa. In accordance with the Loi Cadre of 1956, the Ivory Coast was given its own Government Council, whose members were appointed by the Territorial Assembly, elected for the first time by universal adult suffrage on March 31, 1957. In 1959 the Ivory Coast became a member state of the French Community by unanimous vote. On August 7, 1960, it proclaimed its independence, and was admitted to the United Nations on September 20, 1960. It is a member of the Conseil de l'Entente.

GOVERNMENT

Present Status

Independent republican state.

Constitution

The constitution provides for a unicameral, presidential system of government. The President of the Republic, elected for a 5-year term by direct universal suffrage, exercises executive power. Mr. Houphouet-Boigny presently holds this office. He has power to issue regulations, controls the armed forces, and negotiates treaties. The 70-member National Assembly holds legislative power. It is elected at the same time as the President for a 5-year period.

Franchise

Universal adult suffrage.

Local Government

The country is divided into 4 departments where local affairs are managed by General Councils of 40 members elected for 5-year terms. The departments are, in turn, divided into 19 subprefectures.

Political Party [3]

Parti Démocratique de la Côte d'Ivoire (PDCI), an affiliate of the RDA, led by the President, Felix Houphouet-Boigny.

POPULATION BREAKDOWN

Main Cities [4]
1955 estimate

Abidjan (capital)	127,600
Bouake	41,400
Gagnoa	15,300
Agboville	13,100
Korhogo	13,000
Dalwa	12,500
Dimbroko	12,300
Barsam	11,500
Abengourou	8,000

Urban-rural Distribution [5]
About 8% of the total population lives in towns of 10,000 or more inhabitants.

Ethnic Distribution
1958 estimate

African	3,211,000

1956 census

Non-African	11,638

The African population is divided into the following tribes: Aqui, Ashanti, Baule, Kwa-Kwa and Krunen (including Bete and Bakue), Mande clan, Voltaic clan, Senufo clan, Dan, and Guro.

Religious Affiliation [6]

Christians	11%
Muslims	22%
Animists	67%

Languages
Baule, Senufo, Dan, and Guro are the principal vernacular languages spoken. French is the official language.

Sex Distribution [7]
African not available.
1956 census

	Male	Female
Non-African	6,567 (56.4%)	5,071 (43.6%)

Age Distribution
Available only for Abidjan.

SOCIAL DATA

Education [8]
As of January 1, 1958

TABLE I

	Enrollment	Public School Teachers
556 Public elementary schools ⎫ 412 Private elementary schools ⎭	125,727	2,766
23 Public secondary schools ⎫ 8 Private secondary schools ⎭	4,310	83
13 Public technical schools	794	33

1,131 students studying abroad.

In 1960, ±40% of children of school-going age were at school.

In 1957, 27.3% of the school-going age population attended school, of which 23.4% were girls; educational expenses in the same year represented 19% of the annual local budget.

Health and Social Services

VITAL STATISTICS [9]
Available for Bongouanou only.

Per 1,000

Birth rate	Death rate	Infant mortality rate	Net reproduction rate
50	25	157	1.7

MAIN DISEASES
Malaria, intestinal diseases (in the forest area), yellow fever, sleeping sickness, leprosy, yaws.

HEALTH SERVICES [10]
As of January 1, 1957

TABLE II

	Beds
2 Main hospitals	864
1 Secondary hospital	132
69 Medical centers	3,924

TABLE II—Continued

		Beds
10	Infirmaries	338
69	Dispensaries	—
31	Private institutions	500
52	Maternity centers	1,302

151 medical practitioners, 1 to every 20,500 of the population; 19 beds per 10,000 of the population.

SOCIAL WELFARE SERVICES

Not available.

ECONOMY

Ninety percent of the people of the Ivory Coast earn a living from agriculture, forestry, stock raising, or fishing, which furnish almost the entire income of the Republic. The chief cash crops are cocoa and coffee.

Transport and Communications

WATERWAYS

Although there are four major rivers in the Ivory Coast none of them is navigable for more than about 40 miles. Along with their tributaries they are used for the transportation of timber.

PORTS [11]

There is a deep-water port at Abidjan. This port handled 1,216 tons of freight in 1958. In addition there is a special fishing port west of Treichville Hospital.

ROADS [12]

In 1960 there were 520 miles of asphalt roads, 6,200 miles of surfaced roads, and 10,500 miles of tracks and trails.

RAILROADS

The Abidjan-Niger railroad to Ouagadougou, Upper Volta, includes 375 miles of track in the Ivory Coast.

AIRWAYS

Abidjan has an international airport capable of accommodating jet aircraft. In addition the Ivory Coast has 16 secondary airports and 4 more fields are now being completed.

POSTS, TELECOMMUNICATIONS, AND BROADCASTING [13]
There are 51 post offices and 22 postal agencies. There is an automatic interurban telephone system centered at Abidjan and 59 telephone offices throughout the country. The Abidjan radio station is capable of broadcasting to the world.

Resources and Trade

MAIN EXPORTS
Unroasted coffee, cocoa beans, wood, and bananas.

MAIN IMPORTS [14]
Textiles, metal products, cement, wine, motor fuels, and oils.

VALUE OF TRADE [15]
In millions of C.F.A. francs

	1956	1957	1958	1959	1960
Exports	26,340	24,426	31,492	33,821	33,329
Imports	18,417	19,512	22,827	28,287	29,611

The franc zone is the Ivory Coast's main trade client: in 1959 it took 64% of its exports, and in the same year 73% of its imports came from the franc zone.

LIVESTOCK [16]
1959 estimate

Cattle	270,000
Sheep and goats	710,000
Pigs	75,000
Horses	1,200
Donkeys	700

Industry

MANUFACTURES
Ivory Coast has some 50 industrial concerns, most of them concerned with agriculture: palm-oil mills, a flour mill, a margarine plant, fruit-canning factories, a tuna-fish canning factory, breweries, and soft-drink plants; and six coffee- and cocoa-bean-processing plants with a total capacity of more than 100,000 tons. Four instant-coffee plants are now being planned, which will be able to treat 22,000 tons of coffee annually.

MINING

Thirteen million tons of manganese were discovered at Grand Lahou and it is expected that 100,000 tons can be exported annually. In addition, gold is mined, but to a decreasing extent. Columbotantalite, diamonds, titanium, copper, chromite, and asphalt are known to exist.

POWER

In 1958 the Ivory Coast produced 31 million kwh. of electricity. Twelve steam plants were in service by 1960. An electric power plant with a capacity of 80 million kwh., at Ayame has just been opened, following the construction of a dam across the Bia River. Exploration of oil has just recently begun.

Finance

CURRENCY

C.F.A. franc. 1 C.F.A. franc equals 2 old Metropolitan French francs.

BANKING [17]

Banque de l'Afrique Occidentale, Banque Commerciale Africaine, Banque Nationale pour le Commerce et l'Industrie, Société Générale, Crédit Lyonnais.

BUDGET [18]

In millions of C.F.A. francs

	1960
Revenue	28,228
Expenditure	28,228

DEVELOPMENT PLAN [19]

1958/1962 Total estimated expenditure—27,052,000 C.F.A. francs.
It is hoped that about half the finances for the plan will come from current budgetary sources—territorial and local authority budgets; other sources are special accounts, public organizations, and foreign aid.

Allocations	
Research	1.47%
Production	37.33%
Infrastructure	30.29%
Social services	30.91%

LABOR

The wage-earning population was estimated to be distributed as follows in 1957: [20]

Public Sector

Civil service	6,000	
Non-Civil service	22,000	28,000

Private Sector

Agriculture, fishing, and forestry	90,000	
Mining and quarrying	2,000	
Industry	8,000	
Building and public works	11,000	
Commerce, banking, and professions	12,000	
Transport and storage	10,000	
Domestic service	10,000	143,000
TOTAL		171,000

In 1957 there were some 100,000 workers organized into trade unions, centered around 4 main central organizations: [21] Union Nationale des Travailleurs de la Côte d'Ivoire (U.N.T.C.I.); Confédération Africaine des Travailleurs Croyants (C.A.T.C.); Confédération Générale des Travailleurs (C.G.T.); Force Ouvrière (F.O.). In January 1960 in the Abidjan region alone there were about 100 trade unions with some 30,000 members.

Before independence, the Code du Travail of 1952 regulated all labor and covered such matters as minimum wages, disputes, trade union organization, etc.[22]

Postindependence information is not available.

THE REPUBLIC OF THE IVORY COAST
NOTES

1 Unless otherwise stated, information obtained from Ambassade de France, Service de Press et d'Information, *The Republic of the Ivory Coast*, New York, Nov. 1960.

2 Services des Statistiques d'Outre-Mer, *Outre-Mer 1958*, Paul Dupont, Paris, Nov. 1959, pp. 766–67, Tables 1 and 3.

3 R. Segal, *Political Africa*, Stevens & Sons Ltd., London, 1961, pp. 343–45.

4 *Outre-Mer 1958, op. cit.*, p. 768, Table 6.

5 *Ibid.*, pp. 766–68, Tables 1, 3, and 6. Population figures for the Africans were obtained in 1958, for Europeans in 1956, and those for the urban areas in 1955, so that the percentage given can only be regarded as a very crude estimate.

6 *Ibid.*, p. 140, Table 1.

7 *Ibid.*, p. 767, Table 3.

8 *Ibid.*, p. 769, Tables 10 and 11; also République de la Côte d'Ivoire: *Panorama de la Côte Ivoire*, Direction de l'Information, Part IV.

9 *Outre-Mer 1958, op. cit.*, p. 766, Table 2, figures for the Bongouanou area taken.

10 *Ibid.*, p. 768, Table 8.

11 *Ibid.*, p. 770, Table 16.

12 *Ibid.*, p. 770, Table 13.

13 *Ibid.*, p. 771, Table 18.

14 S. H. Steinberg (Ed.), *Stateman's Yearbook 1961*, Macmillan & Co., Ltd., London, 1961, p. 1028.

15 République de la Côte d'Ivoire: Ministère des Finances des Affaires Economiques et des Plans, *Bulletin de Statistique*, Abidjan, Jan. 1959, p. 6, and Feb. 1961, p. 9.

16 *Outre-Mer 1958, op. cit.*, p. 771, Table 22.

17 S. H. Steinberg (Ed.), *op. cit.*, p. 1009.

18 Ministère des Finances et des Affaires Economiques: Services des Statistiques, *Bulletin de Conjecture d'Outre-Mer*, No. 22, Feb. 1961, Tables 1 and 2, facing p. 134.

19 Territoire de la Côte d'Ivoire; 3eme *Plan Quadriennal de Dévelopement Economique et Social 1958–1962.* Imprimerie du Gouvernement Abidjan, 1958, pp. 106–107.

20 *Outre-Mer 1958, op. cit.*, p. 209, Table 3.

21 République de la Côte d'Ivoire: *Panorama de la Côte d'Ivoire*, Direction de l'Information, Part IV, n.d.

22 *Ibid.*

Kenya [1]

AREA: *224,960 sq. m.*
POPULATION: [2] *6,586,700 (1960 estimate)*
Density: [3] *24 per sq. m.*

GEOGRAPHY

Kenya consists of four major geographical areas: (a) an arid, thornbush-covered plain with a small nomadic population in the northeast; (b) low arid land including Lake Rudolf and a mountainous area in the northwest; (c) a dry, almost uninhabited stretch of land in the southeast; and (d) in the southwest, where 85% of the population and nearly all the economic production is concentrated, a plateau rising to 10,000 feet dominated by Mount Kenya (17,140 feet). This region is cut by the Great Rift Valley 30 to 40 miles wide and 2,000–3,000 feet lower than the land on either side. A 10-mile-wide coastal strip extending from the Tanganyika border to Kipini, together with the Lamu Archipelago, forms the Protectorate which comprises the mainland dominions of the Sultan of Zanzibar. The climate is cool except on the coast and immediate interior, where it is tropical. There are usually two rainy seasons—from April to June and from October to December, and no month is invariably dry. Mean annual rainfall varies from 10 inches inland to 40 inches on the coast and 70 inches near Lake Victoria.

HISTORICAL SKETCH

Arab traders are known to have been in contact with Kenya as early as A.D. 600. At the end of the 15th century, Portuguese traders replaced the Arabs and in turn were driven out by Arabs at the beginning of the 18th century. British contact was made in 1823, when the inhabitants of Mombasa asked to be placed under British protection. In 1887 the Imperial British East African Company was granted a concession over much of the mainland. In 1895 a Protectorate was declared over what is now Kenya and Uganda. Eleven years later the Protectorate was given Executive and Legislative Councils. In 1920 the territories outside the mainland dominions of the Sultan of Zanzibar were established as a colony. In 1948, when the East African High Commission was established, certain services came to be administered in common with those of Uganda and Tanganyika. Four years later, a state of emergency was declared as a result of Mau Mau terrorism. Since that time, various constitutional changes have been introduced which aim at creating an eventually independent state, but the multiracial aspects of the situation have made the issues complex and difficult.

GOVERNMENT

Present Status
Protectorate and colony.

Constitution [4]
The Council of Ministers, which is the executive authority, consists of 4 official and 8 nonofficial members (4 African, 3 European, and 1 Asian) with an Arab having the right of attendance. The Legislative Council consists of 69 or more members: 33 elected on a common roll (32 Africans and 1 Arab); 20 reserved seats (10 European, 5 Asian non-Muslim, 3 Asian Muslim, and 2 Arab); 12 national members (4 African, 4 European, 2 Asian non-Muslim, 1 Asian Muslim, 1 Arab) elected by the 53 constituency members sitting as an electoral college; and 4 officials. The Governor has the right to nominate further members.

Franchise [5]
Common-roll qualifications:
(a) Ability to read and write own language or over 40 years of age, or (b) an officeholder in a wide range of posts, or (c) income of £75 per annum.
Higher qualifications are required for the reserved seats' roll.

Local Government
There are 26 African district councils with powers similar to those of non-African local authorities. There are 7 county councils, partly

elected and partly nominated bodies, all of which include African and Asian councilors. Nairobi has a city council and there are 5 municipalities, most of which have councils with elected as well as nominated members, drawn from all the main communities.

Political Parties [6]

These are too numerous to list. Among the most important are the New Kenya Party, led by Michael Blundell; the Kenya African National Union (KANU), led by Jomo Kenyatta, Tom Mboya, and James Gichuru; and the Kenya African Democratic Union (KADU), led by Ronald Ngala and Masinde Mulira.

POPULATION BREAKDOWN

Although revisions of the 1948 census have been made, official publications still use the 1948 census for breakdowns.

Main Cities
1958 estimate

Nairobi (capital)	233,800

1957 estimate

Mombasa	127,020

1948 census

Nakuru	17,625
Kisumu	10,899
Eldoret	8,193
Kitale	6,339
Lamu	5,868

Urban-rural Distribution [7]

There are no official figures for urban-rural distribution, but the principal towns have a population totaling approximately half a million.

Ethnic Distribution [8]

	1948 census	1960 estimate
European	29,660	67,700
Asian	97,687	174,300
Arab	24,174	38,600
Other	3,325	6,100
African	5,251,120	6,264,000

According to the 1948 census the Africans were divided into

Kikuyu	19.5%
Luo	14.4%
Baluhya	12.5%
Kamba	11.7%
Meru	6.2%
Nyika	5.6%
Kisii	4.9%
Mandi	2.2%
Other	16.1%

Religious Affiliation [9]

Christian missionary societies have some 963,000 adherents among the Africans; the rest are pagan. Along the coast the Arabs are Muslims. The Asians are Hindu and Muslim, with the exception of the Goans, who are Roman Catholic.

Languages

English is the official language and Swahili the lingua franca of the Africans. Asians and Arabs speak Hindustani and Arabic, respectively.

Sex Distribution [10]

1948 census

	Male	Female
African	2,591,142 (49.3%)	2,659,978 (50.7%)
Non-African	86,916 (56.1%)	67,930 (43.9%)

Age Distribution [11]

1948 census

	Under 16	16–45	46+
African only	48.0%	43.2%	8.8%

SOCIAL DATA

Education [12]

TABLE I
1958

European		Enrollment
46	Primary and intermediate schools	8,497
14	Secondary schools	2,949

TABLE I—Continued

Enrollment

African

4,515	Primary and intermediate schools	603,113
30	Secondary schools	3,922

Asian

120	Primary and intermediate schools	39,365
34	Secondary schools	8,023

Arab

10	Primary and intermediate schools	2,482
2	Secondary schools	248
1	Interracial primary and intermediate school	68
42	African teacher-training colleges	3,545
1	Asian teacher-training college	262
25	African vocational schools	—
3	Arab and Asian vocational schools	—
	Royal Technical College of East Africa	148

In 1958, 52.1% of children between the ages of 5 and 14 were at school. In 1957 there were 10,339 teachers in Kenya.

In 1958, 1,385 Kenya students were studying abroad, mainly in the U.K., India, and Pakistan.

Expenditure 1958/59: £6,721,848 estimate (1935, £170,000).

Health and Social Services

VITAL STATISTICS

Registration of births and deaths has not been generally applied throughout Kenya and reliable data are not available.

MAIN DISEASES [13]

Tuberculosis, respiratory diseases, malaria, smallpox, gastroenteritis, helminthic (parasitic worms) diseases.

HEALTH SERVICES [14]

TABLE II
Hospital Beds, 1957

	European	*Asian*	*African*
Government hospitals			
General	18	173	4,076

TABLE II—Continued

	European	Asian	African
Infectious	23	69	1,035
Mental	32	51	481
Mission (estimate)	none	none	1,173
Private (estimate)	463	103	67

In 1957 there were 641 registered medical practitioners.

SOCIAL WELFARE SERVICES [15]

The Department of Community Development is principally concerned with rehabilitation work. In rural areas it organizes youth and adult activities, rural betterment schemes, work among women. A major aspect of its work is its program of social education through its two Jeanes Schools. The Federation of Social Services had 41 affiliated societies in 1959.

ECONOMY

Though still primarily an agricultural country, Kenya has an expanding industrial sector. Most of the industrial output is in the form of consumer goods.

Transport and Communications

WATERWAYS [16]

The EAR&H operate services on Lakes Victoria, Kyoga, Albert, and the River Nile in connection with the Kenya-Uganda Main Line, and on Lake Tanganyika in connection with the Tanganyika Central Line.

PORTS [17]

There is a deep-water port at Mombasa, which in 1957 handled 57,000 tons of cargo.

ROADS

In 1958, 24,694 miles of roads were maintained from Road Fund grants, including 8,956 miles of trunk and secondary roads (499 miles are bitumen-surfaced). In addition the Forest Department, National Parks Organization, and local resources maintain roads.

RAILROADS

The main line of 1,081 miles runs from Mombasa to Kasese in Uganda. In addition there are a number of smaller lines: Nakuru to Kisumu—131 miles; Voi to Kahe—94 miles; Nairobi to Nanyuki—145 miles; Gilgil to Thomson's Falls—48 miles; Kitale branch—41 miles; Solai branch—27 miles; Iksumu to Butere branch—43 miles; and Magadi branch—91 miles.

AIRWAYS

There is one international airport at Nairobi, and 13 main and 29 secondary airdromes. Internal and interterritorial services are operated by the East African Airways Corporation.

POSTS, TELECOMMUNICATIONS, AND BROADCASTING [18]

At the end of 1957 there were 18 post offices and 135 agencies, with a telegraph system throughout the territory. In 1958 there were 121 telephone exchanges, of which 48 were automatic. Kenya Broadcasting Service broadcasts programs in Arabic, Swahili, Kikuyu, other African languages, English, and Hindustani. A commission has been set up to examine the possibilities of television development.

Resources and Trade

MAIN EXPORTS

Coffee (representing some 38% of the total export value for 1955/ 59), sisal, tea, wattle-bark extract, hides and skins, sodium carbonate.

MAIN IMPORTS [19]

Machinery, transport equipment, mineral fuels, lubricants, food, chemicals, and textiles.

VALUE OF TRADE [20]

In £'000's

	1955	1956	1957	1958	1959
Domestic exports	25,667	28,983	26,361	29,300	33,306
Reexports	2,350	4,051	4,887	3,924	5,079
Net imports	71,523	69,823	72,003	60,869	61,508

MARKETING AND COOPERATIVE SOCIETIES

African producers are assisted by the African Livestock Marketing Organization, The Nyanza Province Marketing Board, the Maize Controller, and other similar organizations.[21]

In 1958 registered societies numbered 512, of which 487 were all-African; of these latter 455 were producer societies including 156 farmers' societies, 101 coffee, and 55 dairy societies.

LIVESTOCK

1957 estimate

Cattle	7,036,000
Sheep	7,499,000

Industry

MANUFACTURES

There are about a hundred manufacturing and industrial concerns producing such goods as foodstuffs, metal goods, cement, cigarettes, clothing, footwear, and furniture.

MINING

The principal minerals are cement, soda ash, copper, salt, lime, gold, and diatomite. The total value of minerals produced in 1958 was £4.1 million.

POWER

In 1957 the total generating capacity was 85,000 kw. In 1958 the country began receiving additional electricity supplies from the Owen Falls hydroelectric scheme in Uganda, and these will eventually amount to 45,000 kw.

Finance

CURRENCY

East African shilling (20 sh equal £1 sterling) issued by the East African Currency Board.

BANKING [22]

Among the banks in Kenya are the Standard Bank of South Africa Ltd.; Nederlandsche Handel-Maatschappij N.V.; Bank of India Ltd.;

Bank of Basoda Ltd.; Ottoman Bank; the Land and Agricultural Bank of Kenya. Also, there is a savings bank.

BUDGET

In £'000's

1958/59

Revenue	36,824
Expenditure	40,063

DEVELOPMENT PLAN [23]

1960/63

Total gross expenditure £27,144,275.

Main sources	Loans	£16,500,000
	CD&W funds	£4,699,541
	IBRD loan	£2,000,000

Main allocations: Agriculture (27%), communications (15%), and government works (11%).

The U.K. Development Corporation operates 8 projects in Kenya, for which a total capital of nearly £10 million has been approved as of 1959.

LABOR

Most of the African population is engaged in peasant farming, a lesser number being pastoralists. In 1958 there were 534,733 Africans, 35,849 Asians, and 22,588 Europeans in wage-earning employment. Among the non-Africans, the largest numbers are employed in the public service, commerce, and manufacturing; and among Africans, in agriculture and forestry—247,000; the public service—137,900; and manufacturing—46,000.

At the end of 1958 there were 42 registered trade unions, 9 of them employers' unions.

Legislation covers such matters as collective bargaining, working conditions, workmen's compensation, etc.

KENYA NOTES

1   Unless otherwise stated all information obtained from Fact Sheets of the U.K. Dependencies, Reference Division, U.K. Central Office of Information, No. R 4232, *Kenya*, Sept. 1959.

2 Communication received from the British Embassy, Washington, D.C., July 1961.

3 Colony and Protectorate of Kenya: East Africa Statistical Department, Kenya Unit, *Statistical Abstract 1960*, Government Printer, Nairobi, 1960, p. 15.

4 British Embassy communication, *op. cit.*

5 *Ibid.*

6 *Ibid.*, R. Segal, *Political Africa*, Stevens & Sons Ltd., London, 1961, pp. 346–52; *Africa Report*, Vol. 6, No. 10, Nov. 1961, Washington, D.C., p. 11.

7 British Embassy communication, *op. cit.*

8 Colony and Protectorate of Kenya: *Statistical Abstract 1958*, Government Printer, Nairobi, 1958, p. 11, Table 13, and p. 16, Table 16; The East Africa Statistical Department: *Quarterly Economic and Statistical Bulletin, No. 50, Dec. 1960*, E. A. Printers (Boyds) Ltd., Nairobi, 1960, p. 3, Table A2.

9 S. H. Steinberg (Ed.), *The Statesman's Yearbook 1961*, Macmillan & Co., Ltd., London, 1961, p. 332.

10 Colony and Protectorate of Kenya: *Statistical Abstract 1958, op. cit.*, p. 11, Table 13.

11 British Embassy communication, *op. cit.*

12 U.K.: *Kenya 1958*, Government Printer, Nairobi, 1959, pp. 56, 124–26. Also U.N. Economic Commission for Africa, UNESCO: *Final Report of Conference of African States on the Development of Education in Africa*, Addis Ababa, May 15–25, 1961, "Outline of a Plan for African Educational Development," p. 7, Table I, UNESCO/ED/181.

13 U.N.: *Progress of Non-Self-Governing Territories Under the Charter*, Territorial Surveys, Vol. 5, New York, 1960, p. 67.

14 *Statistical Abstract 1958, op. cit.*, p. 125, Table 180.

15 U.K.: *Kenya 1957*, Government Printer, Nairobi, 1958, pp. 88–90.

16 Colony and Protectorate of Kenya: Ministry of Commerce and Industry, *Commerce and Industry in Kenya, 1960*, Nairobi, p. 4.

17 *Statistical Abstract 1958, op. cit.*, p. 53, Table 74.

18 U.K.: *Kenya 1958, op. cit.*, p. 85; U.K.: *Kenya 1957, op. cit.*, p. 112.

19 *Statistical Abstract 1960, op. cit.*, p. 29.

20 *Ibid.*, p. 28.

21 U.K.: *Kenya 1959*, Government Printer, Nairobi, 1960, pp. 38–41.

22 U.K.: *Kenya 1957, op. cit.*, pp. 29–30.

23 Colony and Protectorate of Kenya: Sessional Paper No. 4, 1959/60, *The Development Program 1960/63*, Government Printer, Nairobi, 1960, pp. 17 and 22.

Liberia

AREA:[1] *43,000 sq. m.*
POPULATION:[2] *2,500,000 (1961 estimate)*
Density: About 55 per sq. m.

GEOGRAPHY [3]

Liberia rises from a marshy, lagoon-studded shore line (370 miles long), in a series of ill-defined plateaus toward the inland border, which ranges in height from 4,000 to 6,000 feet.

There are two principal seasons—a dry season when temperatures vary between 50 and 60 degrees F. by night and 80 to 90 degrees F. by day; and a rainy season from May to October with yearly rainfalls of 120 to 130 inches along the coast, and decreasing to ±70 inches inland.

HISTORICAL SKETCH [4]

Relationships between Liberia and the United States have been close ever since the establishment in 1822 by the American Colonization Society of a small colony of freed slaves near the present site of Monrovia. It survived its early hardships mainly because of the efforts of Jehudi Ashmun and Ralph Gurely. A free and independent republic was proclaimed in 1847, its government and constitution patterned on that of the United States. Throughout the later 19th century and early 20th century, the aegis of the United States protected Liberia from encroachments by France and Great Britain. Financial hardships resulting in bankruptcy placed Liberia under virtual United States protection in 1909. The 99-year lease over 1 million acres was granted the Firestone Company in 1926 and marked the beginning of economic development. Liberia was one of the original signatories to the United Nations Charter in 1946, in San Francisco.

GOVERNMENT

Present Status
Independent republican state.

Constitution [5]
The Legislature consists of two houses: the Senate of 10 members elected for 6 years, and the House of Representatives of 35 members, 12 of whom represent tribal elements, elected for a period of 4 years. The President heads the executive. He and the Vice-President are elected by popular vote for 8 years. The President appoints the Cabinet, which is then confirmed by the Senate.

Franchise
Universal adult suffrage.

Local Government [6]
The coastal region is divided into 4 counties and 1 territory under a government superintendent, and Monturado is subdivided into 2 districts, each under a superintendent. Monrovia is administered by a Municipal Council appointed by the President. The hinterland is divided into 3 provinces, subdivided into 9 districts administered by commissioners appointed by the President.

Political Party [7]
The True Whig Party, led by President Tubman.

POPULATION BREAKDOWN

Main City [8]

Monrovia	41,391

Urban-rural Distribution
Not available.

Ethnic Distribution [9]

Americo-Liberian	12–20,000
British Negro	2,000
European	1,000

African: 6 principal groups are Mandingo, Vai, Gola, Kwepsi, Kru and allies, and Greboes.

Religious Affiliation [10]

Animists	1,200,000
Muslims	100,000 (6.6%)
Christians	200,000

Languages

English is the official language. There are no main African vernacular languages. Some 28 dialects are spoken in the country.

Sex Distribution [11]

	Male	Female
For Monrovia only	23,309 (56.3%)	18,082 (43.7%)

Age Distribution [12]

	Under 20	20–44	45+
For Monrovia only	18,116	19,985	3,290

SOCIAL DATA

Education [13]

TABLE I
1959/60

		Enrollment	Teachers
40	Government kindergartens	3,342	105
3	Mission kindergartens	1,245	7
360	Government elementary schools	38,332	1,086
154	Mission elementary schools	12,468	530
53	Private elementary schools	3,630	130
10	Government secondary schools	1,328	124
14	Mission secondary schools	1,263	102
1	Private secondary school	215	8
10	Elementary tribal schools	596	11
	Vocational schools	394	6
5	Home arts schools	192	6
	University of Liberia	n.a.	n.a.
366	students on foreign scholarships		

In 1959/60, 22.4% of the children between the ages of 5 to 14 were at school. Expenditure totaled $2,441,254.

Health and Social Services

VITAL STATISTICS

Not available.

MAIN DISEASES

Not available.

HEALTH SERVICES [14]

TABLE II
1957

		Beds
23	Hospitals	1,200
8	Leprosaria	
106	Clinics	
1	Tuberculosis sanatorium	50
1	Mobile dental van	

In 1957 these were manned by a total of 82 doctors.

A program of health education is conducted in the hinterland by the Bureau of Public Health and Sanitation assisted by the W.H.O.

SOCIAL WELFARE SERVICES [15]

The bulk of social welfare work is conducted by volunteer organizations, such as the Red Cross, Young Christian Association, and Girl Guides and Boy Scouts. The Bureau of Fundamental Education and Community Development (a division of the Department of Public Instruction) is developing a government agency responsible for social welfare activities, particularly in the rural areas.

ECONOMY

The bulk of the population is still engaged in subsistence activities. Apart from the rubber industry, conducted primarily by Firestone, and the mining of iron deposits, the mineral resources of Liberia are comparatively undeveloped.

Transport and Communications [16]

WATERWAYS

The River St. Paul is navigable for 25 miles for small craft. The Cavella River is navigable for 50 miles.

PORTS [17]

Monrovia is a free port. In 1960, 3,514,771 tons of cargo were handled. Liberia has its own merchant navy of over 11 million gross tonnage.

ROADS

About 1,000 miles of state roads and private roads in the rubber plantations are fit for motor traffic.

RAILROADS

There is a light-railway line of 40 miles linking Monrovia with the Bomi Hills iron ore mines, built in 1951. A line from Nimba to Bassa (170 miles) is under construction.

AIRWAYS

There is an airport at Robertsfield, 50 miles from Monrovia, built by the United States Army during World War II, and an airstrip at James Spriggs Payne Airfield, 5 miles from Monrovia.

POSTS, TELECOMMUNICATIONS, AND BROADCASTING

Postal agencies have been organized throughout the interior. There is cable communication with Europe and America. Monrovia has a radio station. Telephone services exist at Monrovia, Robertsfield, and the Firestone plantations. A commercial broadcasting station opened in December 1959.

Resources and Trade

MAIN EXPORTS [18]

Rubber (representing 51.5% of the total value of exports in 1959), iron ore, palm kernels, and diamonds.

MAIN IMPORTS

Classified manufactures, machinery, and transport equipment, miscellaneous manufactures, foodstuffs.

VALUE OF TRADE [19]

In $'000's

	1956	1957	1958	1959	1960
Exports	44,537.8	40,362.2	53,768.3	66,892.8	82,609.2
Imports	26,799.2	38,255.6	38,482.4	42,908.5	69,190.4

The United States is Liberia's chief trade partner.

MARKETING AND COOPERATIVE SOCIETIES

Not available.

LIVESTOCK

Not available.

Industry

MANUFACTURES [20]

Rubber is Liberia's chief product. The Firestone Plantation Co., which employs 35,000 workers, produced 83.8 million lbs. of rubber in 1958. In 1958 other companies produced a combined total of 11 million lbs. Goodrich and Co. were granted an 80-year concession in 1954. Other locally produced goods are rum, brick, tile, and soap.

MINING [21]

Iron ore deposits are being mined at Bomi Hills and Putu. Gold from alluvial diggings is also being mined. Diamonds are of increasing importance.

POWER [22]

The total generating capacity of electricity is 28,000 kw., of which 24,000 kw. are produced by 5 main installations. In addition there are some 320 small units throughout the country. Two new installations of 40,000 kw. and 30,000 kw., respectively, are under construction.

Finance

CURRENCY

Dollar on a par with U.S.$.

BANKING [23]

Bank of Liberia, The First National City Bank of New York, and Tradevco Bank.

BUDGET [24]

In millions U.S.$

1959

Revenue	17,802
Expenditure	22,718

DEVELOPMENT PLAN

Not available.

LABOR [25]

Labor distribution figures are not available. Liberia has two labor organizations: The Labor Congress of Liberia, established in 1954; and the older Labor Union of Liberia, established in 1949.

A minimum-wage law has been enacted, and a Labor Commission —a government agency—arbitrates in strikes and complaints from workers and employers.[26]

LIBERIA NOTES

1   Liberia: Liberian Information Service, *Invest, Trade and Prosper with Liberia*, Consolidated Productions Co., Ltd., London, 1959, p. 5.
2   Liberia: Liberian Information Service, *Liberia—Land of Promise*, A. Brown & Sons Ltd., London, Nov. 1961, p. 14. According to information received from Monrovia, the first scientifically conducted census is being planned for 1962. The only other census ever taken was limited to Monrovia done in 1956. See footnote 8.
3   *The Columbia Lippincott Gazetteer of the World*, Columbia University Press, New York, 1952, p. 1042; *Invest, Trade and Prosper with Liberia, op. cit.*, p. 5.
4   *The Columbia Lippincott Gazetteer of the World, op. cit.*, p. 1042.
5   *Invest, Trade and Prosper with Liberia, op. cit.*, p. 5.
6   S. H. Steinberg (Ed.), *The Statesman's Yearbook 1959*, Macmillan & Co., Ltd., p. 1205.
7   R. Segal, *Political Africa*, Stevens & Sons Ltd., London, 1961, p. 353.

8   Republic of Liberia: Department of Agriculture and Commerce, *Census of the Population of Monrovia*, C. P. Report No. 1—1956, Monrovia, Dec. 1956, p. 1.

9   S. H. Steinberg (Ed.), *op. cit.*, p. 1205.

10 J. S. Trimingham, *Islam and West Africa*, Clarendon Press, Oxford, 1959, p. 233, Appendix V.

11 Republic of Liberia: *Census of the Population of Monrovia, op. cit.*, p. 4.

12 *Ibid.*, p. 3.

13 Liberian Information Service: *Annual Report: Department of Public Information, October 1959–September 1960*, Monrovia, Oct. 1960, Appendix VII, Tables 1, 3, 5, and 14; p. 91, Appendix VIII; also United Nations Economic Commission for Africa, UNESCO: *Final Report of the Conference of African States on the Development of Education in Africa*, Addis Ababa, May 15–25, 1961, "Outline of a Plan for African Educational Development," p. 7, Table 1, UNESCO/ED/181.

14 *Liberia: Story of Progress*: Liberian Information Service, Monrovia, 1960, pp. 33–35.

15 *Ibid.*, pp. 60–61.

16 S. H. Steinberg (Ed.), 1961, *op. cit.*, pp. 1216–17 for all transport and communication data, unless otherwise indicated.

17 *Liberia—Land of Promise, op. cit.*, p. 9.

18 Republic of Liberia: *Foreign Trade Supplement for 1959*, F.T. Report No. 1—1960, Bureau of Economic Research, Division of Statistics, p. 7.

19 *Ibid.*, p. 3–6; and *Liberia—Land of Promise, op. cit.*, p. 32.

20 S. H. Steinberg (Ed.), 1961, *op. cit.*, p. 1215.

21 *Ibid.*

22 *"Feature"* received from Monrovia, Dec. 1961.

23 S. H. Steinberg (Ed.), 1959, *op. cit.*, p. 1208.

24 *Ibid.*, 1961, p. 1214.

25 International Labor Office, *African Labor Survey*, Geneva, 1958, p. 237.

26 *Liberia—Land of Promise, op. cit.*, p. 23.

The United Kingdom of Libya

AREA:[1] *1,760,000 sq. m.*
POPULATION:[2] *1.2 million (1959 estimate)*
Density: 1 per sq. km.

GEOGRAPHY [3]

From its coastline Libya extends deep into the Sahara. The climate is arid and torrid throughout the country. There is a string of coastal oases where rainfall reaches about 15 inches annually.

HISTORICAL SKETCH [4]

The history of Libya dates back to the Phoenicians who first colonized Tripolitania, and the Greeks who colonized Cyrenaica. Both became part of the Roman Empire in the first century B.C. The collapse of the Roman Empire in North Africa was marked first by the repeated incursion of Berber tribes from the south and later by the invasion of the Vandals from Spain. The first Arab invasion came in the middle of the 7th century A.D. The caravan centers which the Arabs established for trade with Europe, other parts of Africa, and the Middle East made possible the continued importance of coastal cities as commercial centers. Tripoli was occupied at different times by the Arabs, Sicilians, the Spaniards, the Knights of St. John, and the Turks. Under the Caramanli dynasty, which ruled the city from 1711 to 1835, it became a stronghold of the Barbary pirates. Nominally part of Turkey from the 16th century, it was placed under direct Turkish rule in 1835. The Italians began their occupation of Libya in 1911 but, because their occupation was so bitterly contested, they did not succeed in finally pacifying the country until 1932. During World War II much of the North African campaign was fought across the country. When the Germans and Italians were expelled in 1942, Tripolitania and Cyrenaica came under British military rule, and the Fezzan under the

French. In 1949 the British recognized the Amir Muhammed Idris as-Sanussi as Amir of Cyrenaica. In that same year the United Nations decided to unite the three territories into a single sovereign country. On December 24, 1951, the United Kingdom of Libya came into being and in 1956 was admitted to the United Nations.

GOVERNMENT

Present Status
Indepedent monarchy.

Constitution [5]
Libya is a constitutional monarchy with a bicameral legislature. The monarchy is hereditary, with a federal, representative form of government composed of three provinces of Cyrenaica, Tripolitania, and Fezzan. The Senate consists of 24 members, 8 from each province. The King nominates half of the members; the other half are nominated by the 3 provincial legislative councils. Members serve for 8 years, half of the total being nominated every four years. The House of Representatives is elected on the basis of one deputy to every 20,000 inhabitants. In 1961 there were 55 deputies.

Franchise
Universal adult suffrage.

Local Government [6]
Each province is headed by a Wali (Governor) assisted by an executive and a legislative council, three-quarters of whose members must be elected. The Wali is appointed by the King, whom he represents, on the advice of the Prime Minister, but executive authority is vested in the President of the Executive Council, who is appointed by the King in consultation with the Wali. Each member (Nazir) of the Executive Council is responsible for a department.

Political Parties [7]
There are no legal political parties in Libya, although a party known as the National Congress opposed government-supported candidates in the 1952 elections. The party was banned after the disturbances

following the elections. The leader, Bashir Bey Sa'dawi, was exiled to Egypt.

POPULATION BREAKDOWN

Main Cities [8]

1960 estimate

Tripoli (capital of Tripolitania)	184,000
Bengasi (capital of Cyrenaica)	80,000

1958 estimate

Sebha (capital of Fezzan)	7,193

Urban-rural Distribution [9]

The urban population is estimated roughly at 25–30% of the total population.

Ethnic Distribution [10]

The main ethnic groups are Arab, Berber, Italian, Greek, Maltese, and Jew.

Religious Affiliation [11]

Islam is declared the state religion, but the rights of others to practice their religion is provided for.

Languages [12]

Arabic is the official language. English is used in government publications and is fairly widely spoken among the people. Italian is also spoken.

Sex Distribution [13]

1954 census

	Male	Female
Libyans only	516,100 (52.0%)	477,100 (48.0%)

Age Distribution [14]

1954 census

	Under 14	15–34	35–54	55+
Libyans only	38.4%	31.8%	17.9%	11.7%

SOCIAL DATA

Education [15]

TABLE I

	Enrollment	Teachers
Kindergarten—		
20 Libyan schools (1959/60)	2,637	90
25 Foreign schools (1956/57)	2,010	94
Primary—		
495 Libyan schools (1959/60)	139,569	4,214
69 Foreign schools (1956/57)	7,205	328
Preparatory—		
58 Libyan schools (1959/60)	7,392	393
Secondary—		
15 Libyan schools (1959/60)	1,771	238
8 Foreign schools (1956/57)	1,615	167
Vocational and technical (1959/60)—		
6 Male teachers' colleges	1,605	115
2 Female teachers' colleges	297	40
2 Agricultural schools	201	36
2 Commercial schools	344	48
4 Technical schools	311	41
1 Fundamental education center	100	10

Higher education—
> University of Libya 800; and 340 Libyan students at foreign universities.

In 1961 approximately 70% of Libyan children between the ages of 6 and 12 were at school.

1958/59 expenditure—£2,504,000, 1960—£3,220,000.

Health and Social Services

VITAL STATISTICS [16]

No study has been made of the measurement of levels of health of the Libyan people, and in the absence of accurate health records in all areas an assessment of the health of the people cannot be supported by statistics.

MAIN DISEASES [17]

Infantile gastroenteritis, trachoma, and tuberculosis.

HEALTH SERVICES [18]

TABLE II
1959

Cyrenaica

		Beds
1	Central hospital	453
4	General hospitals	555
3	Smaller hospitals	100
2	Tuberculosis hospitals	—
1	Mental hospital	—

Tripolitania

1	General hospital	1,267
3	District hospitals	352
1	Tuberculosis hospital	166
1	Mental hospital	—

Fezzan

5	General hospitals	161
1	Tuberculosis wing at Sebha	20

There is also a network of dispensaries throughout the country. There are 152 doctors in Libya and in 1959 there were 47 Libyans studying medicine abroad.

ECONOMY

Libya's economy is primarily agricultural and extremely poor as a result of the vast desert areas. Most of the population is concentrated on the coastal strip.

Transport and Communications

WATERWAYS

None.

PORTS [19]

Tripoli, Libya's largest port, handles about 75% of her foreign trade and in 1958 handled 404,414 tons of cargo. Bengasi, handling about

20% of the country's foreign trade, handled 80,691 tons in 1958. Derna and Tobruk are lesser ports, and there are nine minor harbors of smaller size.

ROADS [20]

There are some 10,600 km. of roads in Libya; of these, 3,303 km. are black-topped and 342 km. are macadamized. The federal government is responsible for 3,200 km. of these, while the provinces are responsible for the rest.

RAILROADS [21]

There are 2 small single-track 95-centimeter-gauge railways in Libya. The Tripolitanian railroad of 178 miles links Zaura to Ezizza. The Cyrenaican railroad of 164 miles links Solluk to Barce via Bengasi.

AIRWAYS [22]

There are two major airports—one at Idris that will handle smaller jet aircraft, and one at Benina.

POSTS, TELECOMMUNICATIONS, AND BROADCASTING [23]

Information on postal services is not available. In 1956 there were 7,000 telephones in use in Libya. Tripoli and Bengasi were linked by radio-telephone. Two radio stations were recently constructed and broadcast services started.

Resources and Trade

MAIN EXPORTS [24]

Peanuts, live animals, olive oil, and esparto grass represent about 60% of the total value of exports from 1954 to 1958.

MAIN IMPORTS [25]

Food and beverages, machinery and transport equipment, textiles, base metals and manufactures, building and other materials, fertilizers, other chemicals, and rubber tires.

VALUE OF TRADE [26]

In £ millions

	1954	1955	1956	1957	1958
Exports	3.5	4.3	4.0	5.2	4.8
Imports	11.3	14.3	16.5	22.8	23.9

Italy is Libya's chief trading partner; for the years 1954–1958 Italy took an average of 40.5% of its exports. The U.K. accounted for about 20.2% during the same period.

MARKETING AND COOPERATIVE SOCIETIES [27]

All agricultural products exported are handled by private enterprise with the exception of esparto grass and tobacco. Esparto grass is collected, baled, and shipped by a government-owned corporation; and tobacco exports are organized by the government monopoly in Tripolitania.

By 1959 there were over 30 general agricultural cooperative societies with a total membership of some 6,000. They are mainly savings and credit societies, but some are expanding into the agricultural sector.

LIVESTOCK [28]

1958 estimates

Cattle	111,000
Sheep and goats	2,708,000
Camels	172,000

Industry

MANUFACTURES [29]

Libya's main industries include food, textiles, footwear, furniture, printing, light engineering, and beverage enterprises.

MINING [30]

Although iron deposits are found in Fezzan there are no facilities, such as transport, that allow for exploration. There are gypsum deposits in Tripolitania which are being explored. Other known minerals include potash, alum, natron, celestite, and building stone.

POWER [31]

At the beginning of 1959 the country had an installed electrical capacity of 29,943 kw. By the beginning of 1960 oil had been struck in more than 20 places but the commercial sales are not expected to begin for another year or two.

Finance

CURRENCY [32]

Libyan pound equals £1 sterling.

BANKING [33]

The National Bank of Libya, established in 1956, possesses the sole right of currency issuance. Other banks include a National Agriculture Bank, five branches of Barclay's Bank D.C.O., the British Bank of the Middle East, the Banco d'Italia, Banco di Sicilia, Banque Misr, etc.

BUDGET [34]

In £'000's

	1958/59
Revenue	23,094
Expenditure	19,179

About 20% of the revenue comes from external assistance from the United Kingdom and the United States of America.

DEVELOPMENT PLAN [35]

A six-year plan was approved in 1956, but never put into effect, although many of its projects have been completed or provided for from funds supplied by the U.S. Projects are concerned largely with land use, public utilities, and health.

LABOR [36]

In 1956 the wage-earning labor force was distributed as follows:

Agriculture and fishing	80
Petroleum prospecting and quarrying	703
Manufacturing and repairs	14,504
Construction	2,751
Electricity, gas, water, and sanitation	1,118
Commerce	12,986
Transport, storage, and communications	4,009
Services	31,553
TOTAL	67,704

The Libyan General Workers' Union claims 30,000 "followers"; only a fraction of these are dues-paying members. The Port Workers'

Union of Tripoli has between 450 and 700 members. There are also several small independent unions in Tripolitania. In Cyrenaica the General Assembly of Cyrenaican Labor Unions has a total membership of about 3,000. The Petroleum Workers' Union was organized in 1958.[37]

The Libyan Government passed a labor law in 1958 covering such matters as holidays, length of work week (48 hours), and child and female employment. Labor disputes may be settled by the Provincial Labor Commissioner's office and are governed by provincial legislation. A Social Insurance Act was passed at the end of 1958 establishing an unemployment insurance scheme.[38]

THE UNITED KINGDOM OF LIBYA NOTES

1   International Bank for Reconstruction and Development (I.B.R.D.): *The Economic Development of Libya*, I.B.R.D., Washington, D.C., 1960, p. 24.

2   *Ibid.* According to the I.B.R.D., the total could well be an underestimate; United Kingdom of Libya: Ministry of National Economy, Census Department, *General Population Census 1954*, Report and Tables, Tripoli, 1959, p. vii.

3   *The Columbia Lippincott Gazetteer of the World*, Columbia University Press, New York, 1952, p. 1050.

4   J. D. Stamp, *Africa: Study in Tropical Development*, John Wiley & Sons, Inc., New York, pp. 265–66; I.B.R.D., *op. cit.*, pp. 21–23.

5   S. H. Steinberg (Ed.), *The Statesman's Yearbook 1961*, Macmillan & Co., Ltd., London, 1961, p. 1219.

6   *Ibid.*

7   R. Segal, *Political Africa*, Stevens & Sons Ltd., London, 1961, pp. 354–56.

8   S. H. Steinberg (Ed.), *op. cit.*, p. 1219; and S. H. Steinberg (Ed.), 1959, p. 1210.

9   I.B.R.D., *op. cit.*, p. 23.

10   S. H. Steinberg (Ed.), 1961, *op. cit.*, p. 1219.

11   *Ibid.*

12   *Basic facts on the United Kingdom of Libya*; distributed by the Embassy of Libya, Washington, D.C., p. 1.

13   United Kingdom of Libya: *General Population Census, 1954, op. cit.*, Table facing p. xii.

14   *Ibid.*

15 Libya: *Libyan Cultural Newsletter,* Cultural Office, Embassy of Libya, Washington, D.C., Issue No. 1, July 1961, pp. 4–7.

16 I.B.R.D., *op. cit.,* p. 253.

17 *Ibid.*

18 *Ibid.,* pp. 254–60 and 465–68.

19 *Ibid.,* pp. 217, 239, 460–62.

20 *Ibid.,* p. 452.

21 *Ibid.,* p. 210.

22 *Ibid.,* pp. 225 and 463.

23 *Ibid.,* p. 247.

24 *Ibid.,* p. 333.

25 *Ibid.,* p. 334.

26 *Ibid.,* p. 332.

27 *Ibid.,* pp. 124–25.

28 *Ibid.,* p. 334.

29 *Ibid.,* p. 164.

30 *Ibid.,* pp. 356–63.

31 *Ibid.,* pp. 52 and 441.

32 *Ibid.,* p. vi.

33 S. H. Steinberg (Ed.), *op. cit.,* p. 1222; I.B.R.D., *op. cit.,* p. 291.

34 I.B.R.D., *op. cit.,* p. 323.

35 *Oxford Regional Economic Atlas:* "The Middle East and North Africa," prepared by the Economist Intelligence Unit Limited and the Cartographic Department of the Clarendon Press, O.U.P., London, 1960, p. 110.

36 U.S.: Department of Labor, Bureau of Labor Statistics, *Summary of the Labor Situation in Libya,* Washington, D.C., June 1958, p. 3.

37 *Ibid.,* p. 537.

38 *Ibid.,* pp. 8–9 and 290–91.

The Malagasy Republic
(MADAGASCAR)[1]

AREA: *228,000 sq. m.*
POPULATION:[2] *5,298,298 (1960 census)*
Density: 22 per sq. m.

GEOGRAPHY

The island of Madagascar has six major geographical regions: (a) the northern region of fertile valleys and volcanic soil, cut away from the rest of the island by Mount Tsaratanana, which reaches an altitude of 9,450 feet; (b) the northwest region, consisting of a series of extremely fertile valleys; (c) the west, watered by three major rivers—the Manambolo, Tsiribihina, and Mangoky; (d) the south, a very arid region rich in minerals; (e) the central plateau, with a cool climate; and (f) the east coast, a narrow strip of about 750 miles with a warm, humid climate. Rainfall is lowest on the west coast, averaging 20 inches in some places, and increases eastward, reaching a high average rainfall of over 100 inches on the east coast.

HISTORICAL SKETCH

Studies have established a definite kinship between the Malagasy people and the populations of the Indonesian world, suggesting successive immigrations from the Sunda Isles (now Indonesia). Beginning in the 7th century and continuing throughout the Middle Ages, Arabs from the Persian Gulf traded along its coastlines and established trading posts. During the 16th, 17th, and 18th centuries, Madagascar saw the rise and fall of numerous kingdoms. The Portuguese were the first to discover the island in the 17th century and were followed by the Dutch and the English. In 1642 the French founded Port Dauphin, but no European control was established over the island until 1895, when the Merian monarchy collapsed and the French intervened. The revolt of 1947 was a clear demonstration of the extent of political unrest on the island. The Loi Cadre of 1956 provided for universal adult suffrage and greater local participation in government and paved the way for the proclamation of the Malagasy Republic on October 14, 1958. It became independent on June 26, 1960 and was admitted to the United Nations on September 20, 1960.

GOVERNMENT

Present Status
Independent republican state.

Constitution
The President is head of the government. He is elected by an electoral college which includes, in addition to the members of Parliament and of the General Councils of the Provinces, delegates from the municipal and rural assemblies. He issues regulations, promulgates laws and may request reconsideration of a law, ensures the maintenance of law and order, makes state appointments, proclaims the Council of Ministers and the dissolution of the Assembly on the advice of the Senate and after consultation with the President of the National Assembly. Parliament consists of the National Assembly of 107 elected members, and a Senate of 54 members, two-thirds elected by the provinces and local territorial units and one-third by the government. The High Council of Institutions is responsible for seeing that laws and regulations are constitutional.

Franchise
Universal adult suffrage.

Local Government [3]
The 6 provinces, under the supervision of a specially delegated secretary of state, are subdivided into districts, the districts are further divided into cantons. Each canton comprises a number of communes which correspond to the traditional fokonolona.

Political Parties [4]
Parti Social Démocrate de Madagascar et des Comores (PSD), led by Philibert Tsiranana, President of the Republic—75 seats.
Antokon'ny   Kongresin'ny   Faheleovantenana'i   Madagasikara (AKFM), led by Abbé Ricard Andriamanjato—3 seats.

Union Démocratique Socialiste de Madagascar (UDSM), led by Norbert Zafimahova—1 seat.

Rassemblement Chrétien de Madagascar (RCM)—6 seats.

Mouvement National pour l'Indépendance de Madagascar (MONIMA), led by Manja Gaona.

Communist Party—banned 1947, reemerged in 1960 as a small illegal party.

POPULATION BREAKDOWN

Main Cities [5]
1960 *census*

Tananarive (capital)	247,917
Majunga	34,119
Tamatave	39,627
Tulear	33,850
Diego-Suarez	28,772
Fianarantsoa	36,819
Antsibare	18,909
Mananjary	13,582
Fort Dauphin	11,847
Ambositra	10,677

Urban-rural Distribution [6]
About 9% of the population lives in towns of 10,000 or more inhabitants.

Ethnic Distribution [7]
1960 *census*

French	89,829
Indian	12,064
Chinese	8,032
Antaimoro	197,391
Antaisaka	291,455
Antandroy	262,861
Antanosy	152,893
Bara	213,873
Bestileo	658,456
Betsimisakara	817,479

Merina	1,330,879
Sakalava	300,022
Sihanaka	115,188
Tanala	220,319
Tsimihety	357,498
Other	260,000

Religious Affiliation [8]

Christians	38%
Muslims	5%
Animists	57%

Languages

Malagasy and French. French is the official language.

Sex Distribution [9]

1960 census

	Male	*Female*
African	2,572,588 (49.7%)	2,610,379 (50.3%)
Non-African	66,411 (47.6%)	48,920 (42.4%)

Age Distribution [10]

	Under 15	*15+*
African	2,263,864	2,919,103
Non-African	47,487	67,744

SOCIAL DATA

Education [11]

As of January 1, 1958

TABLE I

	Enrollment	Public School Teachers
1,522 Public primary schools } 832 Private primary schools	321,518	3,281
31 Public secondary schools } 126 Private secondary schools	17,053	102
127 Public technical schools } 36 Private technical schools	6,314	336
1 Higher education institute	459	2

There were 1,063 students studying abroad in 1958.

In 1957, 46.5% of the school-going age population attended school, of which 41.8% were girls. Educational expenditure amounted to 9.7% of the budget for that year.

Health and Social Services

VITAL STATISTICS [12]

> per 1,000

Birth rate	Death rate	Infant mortality rate
36.6 (1956)	13.1 (1955)	78.0 (1954)

MAIN DISEASES

Malaria, leprosy, tuberculosis, venereal disease.

HEALTH SERVICES [13]

> As of January 1, 1958

TABLE II

		Beds
2	General hospitals	1,346
5	Secondary hospitals	1,978
163	Medical centers	5,877
244	Infirmaries	2,501
99	Dispensaries	—
23	Private institutions	924
326	Maternity and specialized services	5,236

618 medical practitioners, 1 to every 8,200 of the population; 25 beds per every 10,000 inhabitants.

SOCIAL WELFARE SERVICES [14]

Free medical services are given to the indigenous population. Private and public welfare services are coordinated and concentrate on relief work. Community-development schemes are to be found in rural areas. Agricultural workers and domestic servants are covered by family, antenatal, and maternity-allowance schemes.

ECONOMY

Malagasy is an agricultural country. Its population is chiefly rural; 90% of the Malagasy are farmers, craftsmen, or shopkeepers, while

10% are wage earners. Unlike most African countries, Malagasy's economy is agriculturally diversified.

Transport and Communications

The island is so mountainous that airplanes are used more than any other means of transportation.

WATERWAYS

The island has a total of 1,550 miles of navigable waterways. The longest of these is situated on the west coast: the Magoky River is navigable for 151, the Onilahy for 134 in the rainy season, the Netsiboka for 128, the Mahvavy for 126, the Anambolo for 102, and the Tsiribihina for 86 miles. In addition, the Pangalanes Canal, formed of lagoons, is 403 miles long, and the sandy and rocky bars which at present block it along the route are being cut through to permit the passage of larger barges.

PORTS

There are 18 ports in all. Tamatave, the largest, handled 452,000 tons in 1958, and apart from Diego-Suarez it is the only point on the island where large ships can dock.

ROADS

There are over 20,000 miles of roadways, but only 5,000 are passable in all weather.

RAILROADS

There are four main lines which total 532 miles of track: a trunk line from Tananarive to Tamatave (229 miles) with two branches (one 98 miles long, ending at Antsibare; and the other, 104 miles long, connecting Mormanga with Lake Alaotra); the fourth line, 101 miles long, links Fianarantsoa with the east coast and ends at Mankara.

AIRWAYS

Madagascar has over 100 airfields. There is an international airport at Arivonimano and 3 major airports at Ivato, Tamatave, and Tulear.

POSTS, TELECOMMUNICATIONS, AND BROADCASTING [15]

At the beginning of 1958 there were 228 post offices and agencies, 248 telegraph offices, 6,285 telephone subscribers, and 5,127 branch-line services. Radio Tananarive has two stations broadcasting a total of 117 hours per week.

Resources and Trade

MAIN EXPORTS [16]

Coffee (representing about 32% of the total value of exports for 1960), processed foodstuffs, sugar, and vanilla.

MAIN IMPORTS [17]

Transportation equipment, textiles, steel and steel products, industrial chemicals, mineral products, and processed foodstuffs.

VALUE OF TRADE [18]

In millions of C.F.A. francs

	1956	1957	1958	1959	1960
Exports	16,300	16,234	20,248	18,649	18,485
Imports	23,094	26,158	26,564	29,506	27,593

France is the Republic's chief trading partner.

LIVESTOCK [19]

1956 estimate

Cattle	6,343,000
Sheep and goats	477,000
Pigs	291,000
Horses	2,600

Industry

MANUFACTURES

Malagasy has a number of rice mills, starch plants, sugar refineries, rum distilleries, peanut oil mills, and aleurite-processing mills.

MINING

The most profitably mined resource is high-quality graphite, and the island is one of the world's largest graphite producers (12,000 tons in 1958). Mica is another important mineral resource. There are also small quantities of quartz, industrial beryl, precious stones, gold, and nickel.

POWER

Coal mining was begun several years ago in the Tulear province. Oil exploration is being carried on all over the island, and thorium deposits are being exploited in the southern part of the island. Dams have been built on the Mandraka and Tsiazompaniry rivers. In 1957 22 steam and 8 hydroelectric plants furnished a total of 85 million kw.

Finance

CURRENCY [20]

C.F.A. franc. 1 C.F.A. franc equals 2 old Metropolitan French francs.

BANKING [21]

The Bank of Madagascar and the Comores is the issuing bank and has branches all over the island. Other banks are the Comptoir National d'Escompte de Paris, the Banque Nationale pour le Commerce et l'Industrie, and the Franco-Chinese Bank.

BUDGET [22]

In millions of C.F.A. francs

	1960
Revenue	8,059
Expenditure	16,488 (estimate)

DEVELOPMENT PLAN

See Appendix III.

LABOR [23]

The distribution of the wage-earning population in 1957 was:

Public Sector

Civil service	10,000	
Non-Civil service	40,200	50,200

Private Sector

Agriculture, fishing, and forestry	72,000	
Mining and quarrying	5,000	
Industry	18,000	
Building and public works	18,000	
Commerce, banking, and professions	29,000	
Transport and storage	14,000	
Domestic service	37,000	193,000
TOTAL		243,200

In 1957 there were 74 employers' unions with 2,590 members and 309 workers' unions with a membership of 27,600. At the beginning of 1958, 6,700 employers were contributing to the Family Equalization Fund and 12,100 workers were receiving allocations.

Preindependence labor legislation covered such matters as hours of work, holidays, minimum wages, trade unions, disputes, and employment of women and children.[24] Postindependence information is not available.

THE MALAGASY REPUBLIC NOTES

1 Unless otherwise stated, information obtained from Ambassade de France, Service de Presse et d'Information, *The Malagasy Republic*, New York, Sept. 1960.

2 République Malgache: Service des Statistiques, Ministère des Finances, *Population de Madagascar*, 1960, p. 2.

3 S. H. Steinberg (Ed.), *The Statesman's Yearbook 1961*, Macmillan & Co., Ltd., 1961, London, p. 1032.

4 R. Segal, *Political Africa*, Stevens & Sons Ltd., London, 1961, pp. 357–60.

5 *Population de Madagascar, op. cit.*, p. 10.

6 *Ibid.*, pp. 2 and 10.

7 *Ibid.*, pp. 8–9.

8 Service des Statistiques d'Outre-Mer, *Outre-Mer 1958*, Paul Dupont, Paris, Nov. 1959, p. 140, Table 1.

9 *Population de Madagascar, op. cit.*, pp. 8–9.

10 *Ibid.*

11 *Outre-Mer 1958, op. cit.*, pp. 806–807, Tables 6 and 7.

12 U.N.: *Progress of Non-Self-Governing Territories Under the Charter*, Territorial Surveys, Vol. 5, New York, 1960, p. 128.

13 *Outre-Mer 1958, op. cit.*, p. 805, Table 4.

14 U.N.: *Progress of Non-Self-Governing Territories Under the Charter*, *op. cit.*, pp. 138–39.

15 *Outre-Mer 1958, op. cit.*, p. 808, Tables 15 and 16.

16 République de Malgache: Service des Statistiques, Ministère des Finances, *Statistiques du Commerce Extérieur de Madagascar*, 1960, pp. VII–X.

17 *Ibid.*

18 *Ibid.*, p. II.

19 *Outre-Mer 1958, op. cit.*, p. 809, Table 18.

20   S. H. Steinberg (Ed.), *op. cit.*, p. 1034.
21   *Ibid.*
22   République de Malgache: Service de la Statistique et des Etudes Socio-Economiques, *Note sur la Situation Economique au début de 1961*, 1961, pp. 54–55.
23   *Outre-Mer 1958, op. cit.*, p. 209, Table 3.
24   *Ibid.*, p. 207, Table 1, and p. 217, Table 15; U.N.: *op. cit.*, pp. 137–38.

The Republic of Mali

AREA: [1] *464,873 sq. m.*
POPULATION: [2] *3,708,000 (1957 estimate)*
Density: [3] *9+ per sq. m.*

GEOGRAPHY [4]

Mali falls mainly in the relatively depressed zone extending north of the Guinea highlands. The only mountainous range is that of the Adrar des Moras on the Algerian border in the north, west of which lie the extremely dry deserts of Tanezrouft and El Djouf. Mali has a hot tropical climate. Temperatures range between 70 degrees F. in the cool months to 90 degrees F. in the hot months, and rainfall ranges between 3 and 5 inches in the north to never more than 3 inches in the southwest. The vegetation is arid, with scrub and desert plants in the north, progressing to tall grass and savannas in the south.

HISTORICAL SKETCH [5]

The French conquest of the region began under Faidherbe in 1885, but was not completed until the end of the century. Timbuktu was occupied in 1893. The area designated as French Sudan then became part of French West Africa. In 1946 it was granted a degree of autonomy under the constitution of the Fourth Republic. In 1958 it became a member of the French Community. From January 1959 to September 22, 1960, it joined together with Senegal to form the Federation of Mali. It became an independent Republic in September of that year and withdrew from the Federation. Mali was admitted to the United Nations on September 29, 1960.

GOVERNMENT

Present Status

Independent republican state.

Constitution [6]

Government is in the hands of the President who is elected for five years. He is both head of government and head of state. He appoints the Vice-President and Ministers, but is responsible to the legislature (the National Assembly). He is responsible for the promulgation of the laws 15 days after submission by the Assembly and may call for a review within that period. Members of the Assembly are elected for a period of 5 years.

Franchise

Universal adult suffrage.

Local Government [7]

Under the new constitution the country is to be divided into regions, "cercles," "arrondissements," communes, villages, nomadic tribes, and fractions, each administered by an elected council. Details are not available.

Political Party [8]

Union Soudanaise (U.S.), led by Modibo Keita, President of the Republic. Other important political personalities are Jean-Marie Kone, Minister of State, and Madeira Keith, Minister of the Interior.

POPULATION BREAKDOWN

Main Cities [9]

1955 census

Bamako (capital)	62,879
Kayes	19,587
Ségou	17,466
Sikasso	13,570
Mopti	12,678
San	7,766

Urban-rural Distribution [10]

Of the total population in 1955, some 3% lived in towns of 10,000 or more inhabitants; this was made up of 3% of the African population and 64% of the non-African population.

Ethnic Distribution [11]

1956 census

Non-African	7,113

1955 estimate

African	3,636,000

Consisting of the following main tribal groups:

Bambara	820,000
Fulani	450,000
Marka	211,000
Songhai	196,000
Malinke	190,000
Tuareg	176,000
Minianka	155,000
Senufo	132,000
Dogu	130,000

Religious Affiliation [12]

Christians	1%
Muslims	63%
Animists	36%

Languages

French is the official language. Many local African vernaculars are spoken. Mande is the most widely used.

Sex Distribution [13]

1955 estimate

	Male	Female
African	1,842,000 (50.6%)	1,794,000 (49.4%)

1956 census

	Male	Female
Non-African	4,178 (58.7%)	2,935 (41.3%)

Age Distribution [14]

Of the total population

	1957	
Under 15	15–54	55+
36.4%	52.6%	11.0%

SOCIAL DATA

Education [15]
As of January 1, 1958

TABLE I

	Enrollment	Public School Teachers
247 Public primary schools } 30 Private primary schools }	42,052	925
7 Public secondary schools } 3 Private secondary schools }	1,790	52
8 Public technical schools } 3 Private technical schools }	959	93

337 students studying abroad.

In 1957, 8.2% of the children of school-going age were at school, of which 22.5% were girls. Education expenditure amounted to 24.6% of the annual local budget.

Health and Social Services

VITAL STATISTICS [16]
per 1,000

Birth rate	Death rate	Infant mortality rate	Net reproduction rate
53	41	293	0.9

MAIN DISEASES [17]

Sleeping sickness, trypanosomiasis, and leprosy.

HEALTH SERVICES [18]
As of January 1, 1958

TABLE II

	Beds
1 General hospital	650
2 Secondary hospitals	192
32 Medical centers	1,501
137 Dispensaries	—
30 Private institutions	—
35 Maternity and specialized services	700 (maternity)

79 medical practitioners, 1 per 46,000 inhabitants; 6 beds per 10,000 inhabitants.

SOCIAL WELFARE SERVICES [19]

Social welfare services are little developed and the population is being assisted primarily through the health services. There are some specialized centers for abandoned children.

ECONOMY [20]

The economy depends primarily on the export of peanuts. Agriculture and stock raising are nearly the only economic activities.

Transport and Communications

WATERWAYS [21]

The Niger River is navigable for 1,782 km. in Mali, from Kouroussa (Guinea) to Bamako (July–December), Koulikoro to Mopti (August–November), Mopti to Timbuktu (August–December), and Timbuktu to Asongo (October–March). The Senegal River is navigable from July to October up to Kayes.

PORTS

None.

ROADS [22]

At the beginning of 1957 there were a total of 11,200 km. of roads: 2,641 km. of federal roads, 3,521 km. of local roads, and 5,000 km. of trails.

RAILROADS [23]

In 1959 there were 1,677 km. of principal lines and 208 km. of branch or secondary lines.

AIRWAYS [24]

Mali has three airports, situated at Bamako, Mopti, and Ségou.

POSTS, TELECOMMUNICATIONS, AND BROADCASTING [25]

In 1957 there were 45 post offices and 13 postal agencies, 74 telegraph offices, and 56 telephone offices. There were 48 hours of radio broadcasting service per week.

Resources and Trade

MAIN EXPORTS [26]

Peanuts and their products (representing 85% of the total value of exports for Senegal, Mali, and Mauritania from 1954 to 1959); livestock, dried smoked fish, hides and skins, and cotton.

MAIN IMPORTS [27]

Textiles and thread, vehicles and parts, sugar and sugar derivatives, petroleum products, precision instruments, electrical equipment.

VALUE OF TRADE

See under SENEGAL: VALUE OF TRADE.

LIVESTOCK [28]

January 1, 1956

Cattle	2,900,000
Sheep and goats	6,500,000
Horses	80,000
Donkeys	230,000
Camels	95,000
Pigs	5,000

Industry

MANUFACTURES [29]

Little industrial development exists in Mali. Processing industries produce peanut oil and soap.

MINING [30]

Mali mines phosphates and titanium in small quantities. A small amount of titanium is exported.

POWER [31]

In 1957 Mali produced 8.4 million kwh.

Finance

CURRENCY [32]

C.F.A. franc: 1 C.F.A. franc equals 2 old Metropolitan French francs.

BANKING [33]

Banque de l'Afrique Occidentale, Banque Commerciale Africaine, Banque Nationale pour le Commerce et l'Industrie, Société Générale and Crédit Lyonnais.

BUDGET [34]

In millions of C.F.A. francs

1958

Revenue	5,818
Expenditure	5,818

DEVELOPMENT PLAN [35]

1961/65

Total estimated expenditure—64 million C.F.A. francs.

Sources (1961 only) Local—4 million C.F.A. francs

Foreign aid—7 million C.F.A. francs

Loans—3,362,956,508 C.F.A. francs

Fonds d'Aide et de Coopération—1,508,441,000 C.F.A. francs

Fonds Européens—676,825,000 also I.C.A.

ALLOCATIONS

Development of agricultural and livestock production; research of mining and petroleum resources, hydroelectric development, and production of raw materials; transport, education, health, administration, and social services; formation of cadres.

LABOR

In 1957 employment of the wage-earning labor was estimated to be as follows: [36]

Public Sector		
Civil service	5,700	
Non-Civil service	9,860	15,560
Private Sector		
Agriculture, fishing, and forestry	7,380	
Mining and quarrying } Industry	3,840	
Building and public works	5,470	
Commerce, banking, and professions	3,940	
Transport and storage	3,420	
Domestic service	2,200	26,250
TOTAL		41,810

In 1953 Mali had a total of some 5,300 trade-union members, 5,000 of whom were affiliated with the Confédération Générale du Travail and 300 with the Force Ouvrière.[37] Later information is not available.

Preindependence labor legislation covered such matters as trade unions, collective agreements, conditions of work, contracts of apprenticeship, hours of work, employment of children, etc.[38] Postindependence information is not available.

THE REPUBLIC OF MALI NOTES

1 *The Journal of Negro Education*, Vol. XXX, No. 3, 1961, Howard University Press, p. 282.

2 Service des Statistiques d'Outre-Mer, *Outre-Mer 1958*, Paul Dupont, Paris, Nov. 1959, p. 78, Table 1.

3 *The Journal of Negro Education*, *op. cit.*, p. 282.

4 Headquarters of the Quartermaster Research and Engineering Command, U.S. Army: Technical Report EP-93 Canal Zone Analogs iv, *Analogs of Canal Zone Climate in West Central Africa*, Natick, Mass., July 1958, p. 2, and figures 2, 3, 5, and 8; *The Columbia Lippincott Gazetteer of the World*, Columbia University Press, New York, 1952, p. 1837.

5 *The Columbia Lippincott Gazetteer of the World*, *op. cit.*, p. 643; S. H. Steinberg (Ed.), *The Statesman's Yearbook 1961*, Macmillan and Co., Ltd., London, 1961, p. 1035.

6 Librairie Générale de Droit et de Jurisprudence: *Revue Juridique et Politique d'Outre-Mer*, 15e année, No. 2, April–June 1961, Paris, pp. 326–31.

7 *Ibid.*, pp. 331–32.

8 R. Segal, *Political Africa*, Stevens & Sons Ltd., London, 1961, pp. 361–63; *Africa Report*, Vol. 6, No. 10, Nov. 1961, Washington, D.C., p. 13.

9 *Outre-Mer 1958*, *op. cit.*, p. 734, Table 3.

10 Figures computed from *Ibid.*, p. 734, Tables 1 and 3.

11 *Ibid.*, p. 734, Tables 1 and 2: l'Annuaire Vert, *Annuaire Economique 1958*, Editions C.E.P., Publicité, Casablanca (Morocco), p. 268.

12 *Outre-Mer 1958*, *op. cit.*, p. 140, Table 1.

13 *Ibid.*, p. 734, Tables 1 and 2.

14 *Ibid.*, p. 94, Table 14. Based on demographic survey carried out in the Office du Niger Region, in 1957.

15 *Ibid.*, pp. 735–36, Tables 7 and 8.

16 *Ibid.*, p. 735, Table 4.

17 *Annuaire Economique, 1958*, *op. cit.*, p. 270.

18 *Outre-Mer 1958, op. cit.*, p. 735, Table 5.

19 *Ibid.*

20 *Ibid.*

21 S. H. Steinberg (Ed.), *The Statesman's Yearbook 1959*, Macmillan & Co., Ltd., London, 1959, p. 1011; also *The Columbia Lippincott Gazetteer of the World, op. cit.*, p. 1324.

22 *Outre-Mer 1958, op. cit.*, p. 736, Table 9.

23 Fédération du Mali: *Compte Rendu de Gestion pour l'Exercise, 1959*, Régie Fédérale des Chemins de fer, Réseau Dakar–Niger.

24 *Outre-Mer 1958, op. cit.*, p. 736, Table 11.

25 *Ibid.*, p. 737, Tables 12 and 13.

26 République du Mali: *Bulletin Statistique Mensuel*, No. 5, May 1961, Ministère de l'Economie Rurale et du Plan, Service Statistique, p. 18, Fédération du Mali, *Bulletin Mensuel Statistique et Economique*, Dakar, January–February–March 1960, p. 8.

27 République du Mali: *Bulletin Statistique Mensuel, op. cit.*, pp. 14–16.

28 *Outre-Mer 1958, op. cit.*, p. 738, Table 16.

29 *Ibid.*, p. 738, Table 17.

30 Fédération du Mali: *Bulletin Mensuel Statistique et Economique, op. cit.*, p. 20.

31 *Outre-Mer 1958, op. cit.*, p. 738, Table 17.

32 S. H. Steinberg (Ed.), 1959, *op. cit.*, p. 1009.

33 *Ibid.*

34 *Ibid.*, p. 1011.

35 Guinée: *Etude Sommaire du Plan Quinquennial Mali 1961–1965*, Chambre de Commerce, d'Agriculture et d'Industrie de Bamako, Sept. 1961, Bamako.

36 *Outre-Mer 1958, op. cit.*, p. 209, Table 3.

37 International Labor Office, *African Labor Survey*, Geneva, 1958, p. 236, Table XII.

38 *Ibid.*

The Islamic Republic of Mauritania [1]

AREA: 418,810 sq. m.

POPULATION: [2] 625,600 (1955 estimate)

Density: 1.5 per sq. m.

GEOGRAPHY [3]

The Chemama region, which lies along the southern section of Mauritania, consists of a valley of alluvial soil, watered regularly by the flooding Senegal River and the rains which fall from July to October. North of this lies the Sahelian plain, its surface broken by grassy dunes and gum trees which retain the annual rainfall of about 4 inches. Toward the northeast the dunes give way to the foothills of the Adrar plateau, with its steep cliffs. The mountainous region of Adrar, Tagant, and Affole consists of vast palm groves and has an abundant rainfall. To the north lies the dry, Saharan region. There is only one harbor on the coastline at the Baie du Levrier where Port-Etienne was constructed. The climate throughout is hot and dry, temperatures ranging from 70 to 97 degrees F.

HISTORICAL SKETCH

The Moors and Touareg are able to trace their history back to the 10th century A.D., when they were brought back to the orthodox Muslim faith by Emir Yahya Ibrahim upon his return from Mecca. Then followed the "Almoravid Epic," marked by the founding of Marakech in 1062, the destruction of the Ghana Empire in 1076, and the conquest of Fez in Morocco. Its influence spread sometimes as far as Algiers, and even into Andalusia after the defeat of the King of Spain. This expansion, imposing a way of life foreign to the Moors, did not satisfy them and they returned to their native domain. As early as the 15th century the Moors had contact with Europe, first with the Portuguese, then with the Dutch and the French. In the 16th century the Maqils, Arabs from the east, came and settled in Mauritania and intermarried with the local inhabitants. France's presence in this country dates back to the middle of the 19th century. Faidherbe and later Cappolani were its first agents. Gradually administrative unity was achieved under French control. As in other French territories Mauritania was granted a large measure of self-government under the Loi Cadre of 1956, paving the way for even greater autonomy under the 1958 Constitution of the Fifth Republic and eventual independence on November 28, 1960. Mauritania was admitted to the United Nations on October 27, 1961.

GOVERNMENT

Present Status
Independent republican state.

Constitution
Executive power lies in the hands of the Prime Minister, elected by the National Assembly by an absolute majority on the first two ballots, and a relative majority on the third ballot. He determines and conducts the policy of the state, sees that laws are carried out, makes appointments to state posts, and appoints members of the government and terminates their functions. Legislative power rests with the elected National Assembly of 34 members. The Prime Minister and his ministers are jointly responsible to the Assembly and can be forced to resign either by a motion of censure or a vote of no confidence.

Franchise
Universal adult suffrage.

Local Government
The local administrative units are the circle and commune. The circles are administered by local councils, which are an expression of the traditional local collectives. The communes are administered by elected councils. The territory is divided into 11 circles, each composed of one or more subdivisions.

Political Parties [4]
Union National Mauritanienne (merger of Nanda Party and the Parti du Regroupement Mauritanien [PRM], led by Moktar Ould Daddah, the Prime Minister.

L'Union des Socialistes Musulmans Mauritaniens (USMM), centered around Adrar chiefs dissatisfied with the government party.

POPULATION BREAKDOWN

Main Cities [5]

Nouakchott (new capital) to accommodate 6,000.

Kaedi	8,834
Tidjikdja	6,006
Atar	5,299
Rosso	2,520

Urban-rural Distribution [6]

Some 2% of the total population lives in towns of 5,000 or more inhabitants (1955–1956).

Ethnic Distribution [7]

European	599
Other (non-European)	341
African	556,000

Of which the main ethnic groups are:

Moor	452,000
Fulani	28,500
Bambara	1,100

Religious Affiliation [8]

Muslims	100%
Christians	—
Animists	—

Languages

The national language is Arabic and the official language is French.

Sex Distribution [9]

	Male	Female
African	315,000 (51.3%)	299,000 (48.7%)
Non-African	1,161 (71.8%)	455 (28.2%)

Age Distribution [10]

	Under 20	20+	Unknown
Non-African	397	1,217	2
African	Not available		

SOCIAL DATA

Education

Until very recently education was left in the hands of the Muslim scholars and the present government is anxious to preserve this spiritual heritage. A Department of Arab Education has been set up. The Institute of Islamic Studies at Boutilimit, founded in 1955, has 300 students, and plans are under way to provide for a total of 1,000 students. Attempts are also being made to introduce a modern system of education.

As of January 1, 1958, the position was as follows: [11]

TABLE I

	Enrollment	Teachers
95 Elementary schools	6,493	200
2 Secondary schools	291	6

31 students were studying in Dakar and France.
In 1957, 7.2% of the school-going age population was at school, of which 7.8% were girls. Education expenditure amounted to 15% of the budget for that year.

Health and Social Services

VITAL STATISTICS

Not available.

MAIN DISEASES

Not available.

HEALTH SERVICES [12]

As of January 1, 1958

TABLE II

	Beds
10 Medical centers	123
18 Dispensaries	—
10 Infirmaries	—
1 Private institution	—
	57 maternity beds

15 medical practitioners, 1 per every 41,000 of the population; 2 beds per every 10,000 of the population.

SOCIAL WELFARE SERVICES

Not available.

ECONOMY

Mauritania's economy is still limited to subsistence farming, pastoral life in central and northern regions, and agriculture along the Senegal River.

Transport and Communications

WATERWAYS

The Senegal River is navigable and regular steamship services are run between its river ports of Boghe, Rosso, and Kaedi.

PORTS

A harbor is under construction at Port-Etienne, and until it is completed Mauritania continues to be served by Dakar.

RAILROADS

A railroad is under construction to link Port-Etienne with Akjoujt and Fort-Gouraud.

ROADS [13]

Mauritania has about 3,700 km. of roads. The main route between Nouakchott and Fort-Gouraud of 850 miles is passable in all weather.

AIRWAYS

There are 8 class B airports, and each regional capital has a class C airport. Regular flights link Mauritania with Dakar.

POSTS, TELECOMMUNICATIONS, AND BROADCASTING [14]

In 1957 there were 23 post offices and agencies, 24 telegraph offices, and 14 telephone offices. Mauritania has a radio station providing a 22¾ hours-per-week service.

Resources and Trade

MAIN EXPORTS [15]

Shelled peanuts (42.8% of the total export value of 1959), crude and refined peanut oil, oilseed cake.

MAIN IMPORTS [16]

Food, beverages, and tobacco; machinery and transport equipment, textiles, metals, mineral fuels; chemicals; basic materials, and other manufactures.

VALUE OF TRADE

See under SENEGAL: VALUE OF TRADE.

LIVESTOCK [17]

1956 estimate

Cattle	750,000
Sheep and goats	3,200,000
Camels	200,000
Horses and donkeys	170,000

Industry

MANUFACTURES

A fish-processing industry is being developed at Port-Etienne. Mauritania has no other processing industries.

MINING

Mining activities have not yet started. The mineral resources include iron ore in the Kedia d'Idjill Mountains to be mined by Société des

Mines de Fer de Mauritanie (MIFERMA), with a capital of $53.2 million; and copper known as the Guelb-Moghrein deposits, some 180 miles northeast of the capital, to be mined by Société des Mines de Cuivre de Mauritanie (MICUMA), with a capital of $6.1 million.

POWER [18]

In 1953 the total generating capacity was 80 kw. and consumption 44,000 kwh. At present three companies have received permits to explore the possibilities of developing an oil industry.

Finance

CURRENCY

C.F.A. franc. 1 C.F.A. franc equals 2 old Metropolitan French francs.

BANKING [19]

Banque de l'Afrique Occidentale, Banque Commerciale Africaine, Banque Nationale pour le Commerce et l'Industrie, Société Générale and Crédit Lyonnais.

BUDGET

In millions U.S.$

1960

Revenue	4,320
Expenditure	11,972

It is estimated that by 1965 revenue will have increased to $14.8 based on the anticipated activity of mining enterprises.

DEVELOPMENT PLAN [20]

1961/65

Total estimated expenditure of 69,670 million C.F.A. francs to be given by France, mainly to mine Fort-Gouraud iron-ore deposits, copper ore at Akjoujt, and to prospect for petroleum along the coast between St. Louis and Port-Etienne. Also the building of a new capital at Nouakchott.

LABOR

In 1959 there were only between 5,000 and 6,000 wage earners in the country. With the development of mining enterprises a labor shortage is anticipated and an Office of Manpower has been created to train the necessary skilled workers. A Vocational Training Center is being opened at Port-Etienne for the training of artisans.

In 1957 the wage-earning population was estimated to be distributed as follows: [21]

Public Sector

Civil service	1,200	
Non-Civil service	1,850	3,050

Private Sector

Agriculture, fishing, and forestry	130	
Mining and quarrying	210	
Industry	20	
Building and public works	590	
Commerce, banking, and professions	200	
Transport and storage	200	
Domestic service	400	1,750
TOTAL		4,800

In 1953 Mauritania had 300 trade-union members; 200 affiliated with the Confédération Générale des Travailleurs and 100 with the Force Ouvrière.[22]

A Labor and Social Laws Inspection Board has been set up to enforce the Labor Code of 1952. An Equalization Fund for Family Allowances was created in 1956 and already has some 2,000 workers listed, with 5,000 children benefiting.

THE ISLAMIC REPUBLIC OF MAURITANIA NOTES

1   Unless otherwise stated, all information obtained from: Ambassade de France, Service de Presse et d'Information, *The Republic of Mauritania*, New York, Nov. 1960.

2   Service des Statistiques d'Outre-Mer, *Outre-Mer 1958*, Paul Dupont, Nov. 1959, Paris, p. 754, Table 1.

3   Headquarters Quartermasters Research and Engineering Command, U.S. Army, Technical Report EP-93: Canal Zone Analogs iv, *Analogs of Canal Zone Climate in West Central Africa*, Natick, Mass., July 1958, figures 3, 5, and 8.

4   R. Segal, *Political Africa*, Stevens & Sons Ltd., London, 1961, pp. 364–65; *Africa Report*, Vol. 6, No. 10, Nov. 1961, Washington, D.C., p. 11.

5   *Outre-Mer 1958, op. cit.*, p. 754, Table 3.
6   *Ibid.*, percentage computed from p. 754, Tables 1 and 3.
7   Agence de Distribution de Presse: *Guide de l'A.O.F.*, 1957–1958, Dakar, n.d., p. 215.
8   *Outre-Mer 1958, op. cit.*, p. 140, Table 1.
9   *Ibid.*, p. 754, Tables 1 and 2.
10 *Ibid.*, Table 2.
11 *Ibid.*, p. 755, Tables 6 and 7.
12 *Ibid.*, p. 754, Table 4.
13 *Ibid.*, p. 756, Table 8.
14 *Ibid.*, Tables 11 and 12.
15 U.N.: *Economic Bulletin for Africa*, Vol. 1, No. 2, Addis Ababa, Ethiopia, June 1961, Annexe, p. 13. Exports listed are those for Mali, Senegal, and Mauritania combined.
16 *Ibid.*, Annexe, p. 17. Imports listed are those for Mali, Senegal, and Mauritania combined.
17 *Outre-Mer 1958, op. cit.*, p. 757, Table 13.
18 Haut Commissariat de l'A.O.F.: *Annuaire Statistique de l'Afrique Occidentale Française*, Années 1950–1954, Vol. 5, Tome 1, Imprimerie Servant-Crouzet, Paris, 1956, p. 253, Table G-3-21.
19 S. H. Steinberg (Ed.), *The Statesman's Yearbook 1959*, Macmillan & Co., Ltd., London, 1959, p. 1004.
20 *African World*, March 1961, African Publications Ltd., London, pp. 9–10.
21 *Outre-Mer 1958, op. cit.*, p. 209, Table 3.
22 International Labor Office, *African Labor Survey*, Geneva, 1958, p. 236, Table XII.

The Kingdom of Morocco

AREA: [1] *450,000 sq. km. (estimate)*
POPULATION: [2] *11,626,470 (1960 census)*
Density: Former French zone: 22 per sq. km.
Former Spanish zone: 52 per sq. km.
Tangier: 501 per sq. km.

GEOGRAPHY [3]

Morocco is divided into two main zones: (a) the humid zone on the Atlantic coast, the most heavily populated region of the country, and (b) the thinly populated, arid zone of the interior consisting of steppes or desert. There are four mountain ranges: the Rif, Middle Atlas, High Atlas, and anti-Atlas. Morocco has a Mediterranean climate with dry, hot summers and cold, rainy winters. The heaviest rainfall is found in the northwest region (1,000 mm. per annum) and the lowest in the southern desert region (0–200 mm. per annum).

HISTORICAL SKETCH [4]

Morocco's known history dates back to prehistoric times. The earliest known inhabitants were the Berbers. The Phoenicians were the first to discover Morocco. Later the Carthaginians established commercial trading posts in the region, but their presence did not have the influence it had farther east. Part of the area fell under Roman control in 40 A.D. and so it remained until the third century A.D.

In the 5th century A.D., the region was ravaged by Vandals. From the time of the Arab invasions, starting in the 7th century, the region was governed by numerous dynasties, among them the Almoravids, Saadian, and Alaouites. The Alaouites date back to 1660 and still rule today. Contact with the United Kingdom dates from Elizabethan times. From 1912 to March 2, 1956, when Morocco gained its independence, the largest part of the country was a French Protectorate, two smaller zones were

Spanish Protectorates, and Tangier was an international city. It was admitted to United Nations membership on November 2, 1956.

GOVERNMENT

Present Status
Independent monarchy.

Constitution [5]
Since May 1960, Morocco has had a democratic constitution. Executive power is vested in a Cabinet consisting of the King as Premier, his son the Crown Prince as Vice-Premier, and 14 appointed Ministers. At the moment a Constitutional Council of 78 appointed members is acting as a constituent assembly until the new constitution is completed. Its completion is anticipated at the end of 1962.

Franchise
To depend on arrangements under the new constitution.

Local Government [6]
There are 19 provinces, 5 urban prefectures, and more than 800 councils at the village and rural levels.

Political Parties [7]
The Istiqlal, led by Allal al-Fassi and Ahmed Balafrej.
Union Nationale des Forces Populaires (UNFP), led by Mehdi Ben Barka.
The Communist Party is illegal, but claims a membership of some 12,000.

POPULATION BREAKDOWN

Main Cities [8]

Rabat (capital)	227,443
Casablanca	975,277
Marrakech	243,134
Fès	216,133
Meknès	175,943
Tangier	141,714

Urban-rural Distribution [9]
29.3% of the population is urban.

Ethnic Distribution [10]
1952 census

Moroccan		
	Muslim	7,442,110
	Jew	199,160
Foreigner		
	Other	357,038

Religious Affiliation [11]
The majority of the population are Sunni Muslims of the Malekite school. French and Spanish settlers are Roman Catholic.

Languages
Arabic is the official language and that spoken by the majority of the people. French is also spoken.

Sex Distribution [12]
1952 census

	Male	*Female*
Muslims	3,691,180 (49.5%)	3,750,930 (51.5%)
Jews	97,500 (49.0%)	101,660 (51.0%)
Others	179,268 (50.2%)	177,770 (48.8%)

Age Distribution [13]
1955—Muslim population only

Under 15	*15–49*	*50+*
3,810,000	4,335,000	1,035,000

SOCIAL DATA

Education [14]

TABLE I

	Enrollment	Teachers
2,835 Primary government schools including technical schools (1957)	579,683	13,690
2,853 Secondary government schools including technical schools	47,394	1,583

TABLE I—Continued

	Enrollment	Teachers
Private—Primary and secondary traditional		
Islamic schools (1957/58)	11,400	N.A.
Primary and secondary modern		
Islamic schools (1957/58)	±70,000	N.A.
European schools (1957/58)	10,000	N.A.
Moroccan University (1957/58)		
Law faculty	1,049	
Science faculty	451	

In 1957/58, 30% of the children of school-going age attended school.

In addition the Mission Culturelle Française runs schools which serve mainly the French community. In 1957/58 it had 30,919 pupils in primary schools, 537 in primary technical schools, 8,289 in secondary schools, and 1,420 in secondary technical schools.

In 1952 educational expenditure was estimated at 18.7% of the budget; in 1947 it was estimated at 9.68% of the total budget.

Health and Social Services

VITAL STATISTICS [15]

Per 100

Birth rate	Death rate	Reproduction rate
45	20–25	2–2.5

MAIN DISEASES [16]

Dysentery, tuberculosis, malaria, venereal disease, trachoma, eye diseases of infants, and malnutrition.

HEALTH SERVICES [17]

As of January 1958

TABLE II

40 Hospitals
100 Infirmaries and rural hospitals
56 Urban health centers and dispensaries
34 Maternal and infant-protection centers
16 Rural dispensaries
19 Mobile sanitation units
49 Private clinics

In 1951 there were 8,300 beds; there was 1 doctor per 10,000 inhabitants.

SOCIAL WELFARE SERVICES [18]

In 1951 the Public Health Department employed 120 social workers and provided services for mothers and infants, free hospitalization, relief for the aged and incurables, child-welfare services, subsidies to benevolent societies, day nurseries, holiday camps, and children's homes.

ECONOMY

Agriculture and phosphate quarrying are the most important activities in the southern zone, while mining is the basis for the northern zone's economy.

Transport and Communications

WATERWAYS [19]

Although Morocco has numerous rivers, they are not navigable, but are used for irrigation purposes.

PORTS [20]

The principal ports are Casablanca, which handled 8,059,000 tons of cargo in 1957; Kenitra (549,000 tons, 1957); Fedala (404,000 tons, 1957); Safi (1,425,000 tons, 1957); and Agadir (171,000 tons, 1957).

ROADS [21]

In 1957 there were about 15,000 km. of asphalt or bituminized roads in the country. In the northern zone, 6,076 km. of principal roads, 4,851 km. of secondary roads, and 6,627 km. of tertiary roads. In the southern zone, 832 km. of rough roads, 1,015 km. of bituminized roads, and 606 km. of asphalt roads.

RAILROADS [22]

In 1957 there were 1,894 km. of railroads—1,645 in the southern zone, and 249 in the Province of Tangier and the northern zone, of which 706 were electric. There is a main line from Casablanca to the Algerian border on the east; a line from Tangier to Petit-Jean; another from Casablanca to Marrakech with two branches, one to the phosphate mines to the east, and the other from Ben Guerir to Port Safi.

AIRWAYS [23]

Morocco has 4 major civil airports, 3 secondary civil airports, 13 air-strips, 9 civil and military airports, and 5 military airports. Royal Air Maroc monopolizes the internal air services and uses some of the international airlines.

POSTS, TELECOMMUNICATIONS, AND BROADCASTING [24]

In 1957 there were 396 post offices and agencies; 103,430 km. of urban and 193,336 km. of inter-urban telephone lines, and 9 broadcasting stations.

Resources and Trade

MAIN EXPORTS [25]

1952–1958

Raw materials and semifinished products (representing 53% of the value of total exports, of which phosphates were the most important); finished products (3% of which oil, canned fish, sugar, hides, and skins are the most important); foodstuffs (44% including cereals, eggs, etc.).

MAIN IMPORTS [26]

1952–1958

Primary and semifinished products (23%), machinery (15%), food-stuffs (23%), other consumer goods (32%).

VALUE OF TRADE [27]

In millions of francs

	1956	1957	1958	1959
Exports	118.9	117.9	139.3	144.2
Imports	160.7	149.1	164.9	144.8

The bulk of Morocco's trade is with France, which buys about 60% of its exports and supplies about 50% of its imports.

MARKETING AND COOPERATIVE SOCIETIES

Information not available.

LIVESTOCK [28]

1957 estimate

Cattle	2,541,000
Sheep and goats	15,587,000
Pigs	43,000
Others	1,746,000

Industry

MANUFACTURES [29]

Most of the locally extracted minerals are exported unprocessed. There is 1 lead foundry, 1 superphosphate and hyperphosphate factory, 1 petroleum refinery, and 2 factories producing a combination of manganese and coal. Also, household goods, building materials, chemicals, foodstuffs, tobacco, and leather goods are produced on a limited scale.

MINING [30]

Mining activities are situated mainly in the southern zone. The most important minerals, representing about half the total value of mined products, are phosphate, followed by manganese, lead iron, zinc, cobalt, and coal.

POWER [31]

Local net production of electricity in 1958 totaled 948.4 million kwh. and consumption, 873 million kwh. In the same year Morocco produced 510,000 tons of coal.

Finance

CURRENCY [32]

1 Dirham equals 100 old Metropolitan French francs.

BANKING [33]

Banque du Maroc (issuing bank); and some 20 private banks (1952) as well as six popular banks (operated under state supervision) providing credit facilities.

BUDGET [34]

In millions of francs

1960

Revenue	148.3
Expenditure	148.3

The main source of revenue comes from indirect and direct taxation and customs.

DEVELOPMENT PLAN [35]

1960/64

Estimated total expenditure: 660,074 million francs.

Sources	Million francs
Government	258,967
Collectives	39,498
Semipublic sector	15,825
Private sector	345,784

The main heads of expenditure are agriculture, industry, technical training, electricity, transportation and communications, education and health services, administration.

LABOR

According to the 1951/52 census, the wage-earning population was employed as follows: [36]

Agriculture, fishing, and forestry	2,073,724	
Mining and quarrying	18,338	
Industry	252,969	
Building and public works	98,386	
Transport and storage	254,422	
Commerce	134,221	
Health and social services	82,149	
Administration and professions	100,455	
Defense forces	36,626	
Unstated	27,609	3,088,899

In December of 1957 Morocco had some 880,000 trade-union members, all affiliated with the International Confederation of Trade Unions.[37]

Labor legislation covers such matters as hours of work and overtime, leave, maternity and sick benefits, workmen's compensation, wages, etc.[38]

THE KINGDOM OF MOROCCO NOTES

1   S. H. Steinberg (Ed.), *The Statesman's Yearbook 1961*, London, Macmillan & Co., Ltd., 1961, p. 1243. No exact figure can be given for the area of Morocco since the eastern and southern boundaries have never been finally fixed.

2   Royaume du Maroc: Recensement Démographique (June 1960), Minis-
    tère de l'Economie Nationale, *Population Légale du Maroc*, Imprimerie
    Areissala, Rabat, 1961, p. 35; also *Oxford Regional Economic Atlas*,
    "The Middle East and North Africa," prepared by the Economist Intelli-
    gence Unit Limited, and the Cartographic Department of the Clarendon
    Press, London, O.U.P., 1960, p. 106 for density figures.

3   Royaume du Maroc: Ministère de l'Economie Nationale, Division de la
    Coordination Economique du Plan, Service Central des Statistiques,
    Tableaux Economiques du Maroc 1915–1959, Rabat, 1960, p. 13.

4   Maroc: Ministère des Affaires Etrangères, *Faits et Actes*, Rabat, 1961,
    pages not numbered.

5   *Ibid.*; also *Statements and Documents*, Vol. II, No. 10 issued by the
    Press and Information of the Moroccan Embassy, Washington, D.C.,
    May 31, 1960, pp. 2–4.

6   Maroc: *Faits et Actes, op. cit.*; also S. H. Steinberg (Ed.), *op. cit.*, p.
    1243.

7   R. Segal: *Political Africa*, Stevens & Sons Ltd., London, 1961, pp. 367–
    69; also *Africa Report*, Vol. 6, No. 10, Nov. 1961, Washington, D.C., p.
    15.

8   *Statements and Documents*, Vol. III, No. 5, July 1961, *op. cit.*, p. 4.

9   Maroc: *Faits et Actes, op. cit.*

10 Maroc: *Tableaux Economiques du Maroc 1915–1959, op. cit.*, p. 28,
    Table 5.

11 S. H. Steinberg (Ed.), *op. cit.*, p. 1244.

12 Maroc: *Tableaux Economiques du Maroc 1915–1959, op. cit.*, p. 28,
    Table 5.

13 *Ibid.*, p. 27.

14 *Ibid.*, pp. 31–38; also *Morocco Today*; Editions Africaines, Perceval,
    n.d., Rabat, p. 36.

15 Maroc: *Tableaux Economiques du Maroc 1915–1959, op. cit.*, p. 19.

16 *Ibid.*, p. 39; also Maroc: Société d'Etudes Economiques, Sociales et Statis-
    tiques, *Bulletin Economique et Social du Maroc*, Vol. XXIV, Nos. 86
    and 87, Rabat, Feb. 1961, p. 393.

17 Maroc: *Tableaux Economiques du Maroc 1915–1959, op. cit.*, pp. 39–40;
    also *Morocco Today, op. cit.*, p. 14.

18 *Morocco Today, op. cit.*, pp. 12–14.

19 *Columbia Lippincott Gazetteer of the World*, Columbia University Press,
    New York, 1952, pp. 1246–47.

20 Maroc: *Tableaux Economiques du Maroc 1915–1959, op. cit.*, p. 157;
    also Royaume du Maroc: Ministère de l'Economie Nationale, Division de
    la Coordination Economique et du Plan, *L'Evolution du Maroc dans le
    cadre du deuxième plan quadriennal* (1954–1957), June 1959, p. 182.

21 Maroc: *Tableaux Economiques du Maroc 1915–1959, op. cit.*, p. 159.

22 *Ibid.*, p. 164; also S. H. Steinberg (Ed.), *The Statesman's Yearbook
    1959, op. cit.*, p. 1236.

23   Royaume du Maroc: Ministère de l'Economie Nationale, *Plan Quin-quennal 1960–1964*, Rabat, Nov. 1960, p. 250; also Maroc: *Tableaux Economiques du Maroc 1915–1959*, *op. cit.*, p. 158.

24   Maroc: *Tableaux Economiques du Maroc 1915–1959*, *op. cit.*, p. 169, Table 13. Also Royaume du Maroc: *L'Evolution Economique du Maroc*, *op. cit.*, p. 192.

25   Maroc: *Tableaux Economiques du Maroc 1915–1959*, *op. cit.*, pp. 178 and 201.

26   *Ibid.*, pp. 178 and 199.

27   *Ibid.*, pp. 185 and 203; also Morocco: *Economic News from Morocco*, Vol. II, No. 4, May 1960, p. 21, and Vol. III, No. 6, June 1961, p. 7; also Maroc: *Faits et Actes*, *op. cit.*

28   Maroc: *Tableaux Economiques du Maroc 1915–1959*, *op. cit.*, p. 65, Table 8.

29   *Ibid.*, pp. 81 and 116–26.

30   *Ibid.*, pp. 81 and 86.

31   *Ibid.*, pp. 104 and 107.

32   *Ibid.*, p. 243.

33   *Ibid.*, pp. 244–45; also *Morocco Today*, *op. cit.*, p. 102.

34   Royaume du Maroc: Ministère de l'Economie Nationale et des Finances, Division de la Coordination Economique et du Plan, *La Situation Economique du Maroc en 1959*, Rabat, June 1960, p. 64. Also S. H. Steinberg (Ed.), *The Statesman's Yearbook 1961*, *op. cit.*, p. 1244.

35   Maroc: *Plan Quinquennal 1960–1964*, *op. cit.*, pp. 30–34.

36   *Tableaux Economiques du Maroc 1915–1959*, *op. cit.*, p. 28, Table 5.

37   U.S.: Department of Labor, Office of International Labor Affairs, *Directory of Labor Organizations, Africa*, Feb. 1958, p. x, Table 1.

38   U.S.: Office of Labor Affairs, *Summary of Labor Situation in Morocco*, I.C.A., June 1959, pp. 18–20.

Mozambique [1]

AREA: *297,731 sq. m.*
POPULATION: *6,592,994 (1960 census)*
Density: ±21 per sq. m.

GEOGRAPHY [2]

Mozambique has a 1,700-mile-long coastline and varies in width from 120 to 400 miles. The major part of the country is a flat lowland (one of the largest coastal plains in Africa) merging gradually in the west with an undulating plateau 800 to 1,200 feet high. Higher elevations are limited to the northwest frontier and in the north to the rim of the Great Rift Valley. Several isolated mountain groups rise abruptly from the north-central lowland. There are several rivers, the largest of which is the Zambezi, and short coastal streams. The plain has a tropical savanna climate. In the north and center the average annual temperature is 77 degrees F., and rainfall averages 40–60 inches, falling mainly from December to April. In the south a cooler and drier climate prevails.

HISTORICAL SKETCH [3]

Vasco da Gama reached the coast of Mozambique in 1498. The first Portuguese settlements were made at Sofala in 1505 and Sena and Tete, on the Zambezi River, in 1531. In 1544 other settlements were made near Quelimane and Lourenço Marques. The frontier with British Central and South Africa was fixed in 1891.

GOVERNMENT

Present Status
Province of Portugal.

Constitution [4]

The province is governed by a council composed of officials and elected representatives of commercial, industrial, and agricultural interests, and an executive council.

Franchise

Qualified adult suffrage: literacy in Portuguese, a tax qualification, or head of a family.

Local Government [5]

The province is divided into nine administrative districts.

Political Parties [6]

Mozambique African National Union (MANU).
União Democratica Nacional de Mozambique (UDENAMO), led by Adeline Gwambe.

POPULATION BREAKDOWN

Main Cities [7]

Lourenço Marques (capital)	93,516 (1950)
Mozambique	12,510 (1950)
Quelimane	4,451 (1940)
Beira	2,897 (1940)
Tete	2,733 (1940)

Urban-rural Distribution

Not available.

Ethnic Distribution [8]

1958 census

Non-African	112,851

Of which

White	65,798
Yellow	1,945
Indian	15,235
Colored	29,873
African	5,651,511

Of which 4,554 "civilized" and 5,646,957 "noncivilized."

The African group consists of some 80 tribes divided into 9 main groups: Mhanja-Wo, Ma-Konde, Macwa-Loume, Marewi, Karanga-Shona, Chopi-Batonga, Nguni-Swazi, Thonga-Shangaan, and the "Zambezi complex."

Religious Affiliation
Not available.

Languages
Portuguese is the official language. Shangaan, Thonga, Chopi, Shona, and Karanga are the principal vernacular languages spoken.

Sex Distribution [9]
1958 census

	Male	*Female*
African	2,695,379 (48.0%)	2,956,132 (52.0%)
Non-African	61,455 (54.4%)	51,396 (44.6%)

Age Distribution
Not available.

SOCIAL DATA

Education [10]

TABLE I
1961

	Enrollment	*Teachers*
Elementary schools	911,509	3,339
Secondary schools	20,095	551

Some 1,500 students from all overseas territories are attending universities in Portugal.

Health and Social Services

VITAL STATISTICS
Not available.

MAIN DISEASES
Not available.

HEALTH SERVICES [11]

In 1961 there were 48 hospitals, 61 regional nursing wards, 80 medical stations, 177 maternity services, 476 first-aid stations, 39 children's clinics, 12 prenatal clinics, 7 psychiatric hospitals, 7 leprosaria, and 3 tuberculosis clinics.

In 1958 there were 162 medical practitioners.

SOCIAL WELFARE SERVICES [12]

Social welfare services include assistance to scholars, pension schemes, and children's homes.

ECONOMY

Mozambique's economy is primarily agricultural. There are some mining activities.

Transport and Communications

WATERWAYS [13]

Large-scale commercial navigation on the Zambezi River is impossible, but steamboats are able to go up to Tete.

PORTS [14]

There are three main ports: Lourenço Marques, which handled 6,-184,625 tons in 1959; Beira (4,219,873 tons in 1959), and Mozambique (1,026,129 tons in 1959).

ROADS [15]

In 1955 there were 15,477 miles of roads: 2,667 first-class roads, of which 200 miles were tarred; 4,435 second class, and 8,375 third class.

RAILROADS [16]

There are 12 separate lines, varying in length from about 25 to 350 miles and totaling approximately 1,500 miles. All lines run inland from ports and are not interlinked.

AIRWAYS [17]

There are three major airports at Lourenço Marques, Beira, and Lumbo, and two small ones at Tete and Quelimane.

POSTS, TELECOMMUNICATIONS, AND BROADCASTING [18]

In 1958 there were 286 post offices, 220 telegraph offices, and 9,973 telephones. Radio Clube de Mozambique, with 11 transmitters, provides daily services in Portuguese (7½ hours), and English (17 hours).

Resources and Trade

MAIN EXPORTS [19]

Raw cotton (28.4% of the value of total exports in 1959), raw sugar, copra, cashew nuts, sisal, and tea.

MAIN IMPORTS [20]

Cotton goods, agricultural and industrial machinery, motor vehicles, railway material, common wines, and mineral oils.

VALUE OF TRADE

In U.S.$ millions

	1956	1957	1958	1959	1960
Exports	52.7	65.1	70.5	66.2	73.0
Imports	95.1	104.2	114.9	120.6	126.8

MARKETING AND COOPERATIVE SOCIETIES

Not available.

LIVESTOCK [21]

1959 census

Cattle	999,968
Sheep and goats	475,159
Pigs	90,196
Asses	11,921

Industry

MANUFACTURES [22]

Sugar refining; cotton ginning, spinning, and weaving; production of cement, soap and oils, rubber, jute bags and sisal fiber are among the local processing industries.

MINING [23]

Mozambique has a variety of mineral deposits, but exploitation is limited to coal, near Tete, gold dredging, and mica mining.

POWER [24]

In 1953 the Revué and Movené rivers scheme was being developed with a combined potential of 207 million kwh per annum. Other information is not available.

Finance

CURRENCY

Escudo. 1 escudo equals about U.S.$ 1.035.

BANKING [25]

The Banco Nacional with headquarters in Portugal is the issuing bank and has several branches in Mozambique. Others are the Standard Bank of South Africa Ltd., and Barclay's Bank D.C.O., with branches in Lourenço Marques and Beira.

BUDGET

In million U.S.$

	1960
Revenue	159.9
Expenditure	160.9

DEVELOPMENT PLAN

Not available.

LABOR

Detailed labor figures are not available. It is estimated that in all at least 200,000 male Africans work outside Mozambique each year. More than 100,000 of these work in the mines of the Transvaal and Rhodesia and remain there from 1 year to 18 month.[26]

There were five national trade unions with a membership of 23,-000 in December 1957. Europeans, Asians, and "assimilados" only may be members. Affiliation with foreign labor groups or federations is expressly forbidden by law.[27]

The 1928 "Labor Code for the Natives in Portuguese Colonies" and subsequent amendments provide for safeguards against the exploitation of African labor and cover such matters as conditions of work, recruiting, accidents, and compensation.[28]

MOZAMBIQUE NOTES

1 Unless otherwise stated, all information obtained from the Portuguese Embassy, Washington, D.C., January 1962.

2 *The Columbia Lippincott Gazetteer of the World*, Columbia University Press, New York, 1952, p. 1258.

3 S. H. Steinberg (Ed.), *The Statesman's Yearbook 1961*, Macmillan & Co., Ltd., London, 1961, pp. 1358–59.

4 *Ibid.*, p. 1359.

5 *Ibid.*

6 R. Segal, *Political Africa*, Stevens & Sons Ltd., London, 1961, p. 366.

7 *The Columbia Lippincott Gazetteer of the World, op. cit.*, pp. 185, 1087, 1258, 1542, and 1899.

8 Provincia de Mozambique: *Annuaro Estatistico*, Anno XXXI, 1958, Imprensa Nacional de Mozambique, Lourenço Marques, pp. 26–27, Table 8.

9 *Ibid.*

10 All information from Portuguese Embassy, Washington, D.C., except number of teachers: Raymond J. Smythe: "Problems of Teacher Supply and Demand in Africa South of the Sahara," in *Journal of Negro Education*, Vol. XXX, No. 3, Howard University Press, 1961, p. 337.

11 Provincia de Mozambique: *Annuaro Estatistico, op. cit.*, p. 59.

12 *Ibid.*, pp. 106–13.

13 *The Columbia Lippincott Gazetteer of the World, op. cit.*, p. 2136.

14 S. H. Steinberg (Ed.), *op. cit.*, p. 1359.

15 Overseas Economic Surveys: *Portuguese East Africa (Mozambique)*, H.M.S.O., London, 1955, p. 31.

16 *Ibid.*, p. 30.

17 *Ibid.*, p. 35.

18 Provincia de Mozambique: *Annuaro Estatistico, op. cit.*, pp. 492–93, 503–504, and 509; Overseas Economic Surveys, *op. cit.*, p. 36.

19 U.N.: *Economic Bulletin for Africa*, Vol. I, No. 2, June 1961, Addis Ababa, Annexe, p. 14.

20 Overseas Economic Surveys, *op. cit.*, pp. 51–52, Appendix IV and V.

21 S. H. Steinberg (Ed.), *op. cit.*, p. 1359.

22 Overseas Economic Surveys, *op. cit.*, pp. 27–29.

23 *The Columbia Lippincott Gazetteer of the World, op. cit.*, p. 1258.

24   Overseas Economic Surveys, *op. cit.*, pp. 29–40.
25   *Ibid.*, p. 7.
26   *Ibid.*, p. 43.
27   U.S. Department of Labor, Office of International Labor Affairs, *Directory of Labor Organizations, Africa*, Feb. 1958, p. x, Table I, and p. 20.1.
28   Overseas Economic Surveys, *op. cit.*, p. 44.

The Republic of the Niger[1]

AREA: *490,000 sq. m.*
POPULATION:[2] *2,414,800 (1957 estimate)*
Density: 5 per sq. m.

GEOGRAPHY [3]

The country is divided into two geographical areas: the semiarid, scrub-covered steppes stretching from Lake Chad to Niamey in the south and the desert region to the north. There are two climatic seasons: a dry season from October to May and a rainy season from June to September. Only 8% of the land has an annual rainfall of over 21 inches; 48% receives less than 4 inches.

HISTORICAL SKETCH

The history of parts of this territory dates back to Roman times when expeditions to the Air Massif were recorded. From the 7th to the 18th century the area was ruled by a series of kingdoms, starting with the Songhai Empire and ending with the Kingdom of Sokoto. At various times, different populations asserted their ascendancy over the area and now form the basis of Niger's population. The explorer Mungo Park was the first European to penetrate this area, at the beginning of the 19th century. The region was further explored by Germans followed by the French in the 1890's. The first French outpost was established at Talibia in 1896. Until 1921, when a system of civil administration was introduced and the Niger Colony was formally constituted, the area was under military rule. During the next 20 years various realignments of the districts of the region occupied the French administration, until 1947 when the districts of Fada N'Gourma and Dor were separated and joined to Upper Volta. In 1946 Niger set up its own elected Territorial Assembly and began sending its representatives to the Metropolitan Parliament. Ten

249

years later, under the Loi Cadre of 1956, the territory was given a large measure of self-government. Its independence was attained on August 8, 1960. It was admitted to United Nations' membership on September 20 that same year. It is a member of the Conseil de l'Entente.

GOVERNMENT

Present Status

Independent republican state.

Constitution

Executive power belongs to the President of the Council, who is invested by the Legislative Assembly after each general election. A presidential system of government reform under review would make the President head of the state, elected by direct suffrage. The Legislative Assembly is made up of 60 elected members. The government may be forced to resign and the Assembly dissolved by a motion of censure by a two-thirds majority of the Assembly. Such a step may not be taken until three years after the investiture of the President of the Council.

Franchise

Universal adult suffrage.

Local Government [4]

Preindependence Niger was divided into 10 administrative "cercles" and 21 subdivisions, under the control of administrators assisted by "Conseils de Notables." At the village level, chiefs were used by the administration. Postindependence information is not available.

Political Parties [5]

Union pour la Communauté Franco-Africaine (UCFA) branch of the ex-Parti Progressiste Nigérien (PPN), led by Hamani Diori, President of the Republic.

Sawaba, ex-Union Démocratique Nigérienne (UDN), led by Djibo Bakary.

POPULATION BREAKDOWN

Main Cities [6]
  1956 estimate

Niamey (capital)	17,207
Sinder	13,310
Tahoua	12,415
Maradi	10,205
Agadis	4,769

Urban-rural Distribution [7]
About 2% of the total population lives in towns of 10,000 or more inhabitants.

Ethnic Distribution [8]
  1957 estimate

Non-African	3,040
African	2,411,800

Divided into the following main tribal groups (to the nearest '000): Hausa, 1,125,000; Djerma-Songhai, 544,000; Fulani, 414,000; Tuareg, 250,000.

Religious Affiliation [9]

Christians	0.2%
Muslims	85.0%
Animists	14.0%

Languages
Arabic and French, the official language.

Sex Distribution [10]
  1957 estimate

	Male	*Female*
African	1,216,000 (50.4%)	1,195,800 (49.6%)
Non-African	Not available	

Age Distribution
Not available.

SOCIAL DATA

Education [11]

TABLE I
1960

		Enrollment 1960	Public School Teachers 1958
192	Elementary schools	21,054	376
8	Secondary schools	1,040	11
1	School of classical modern studies	n.a.	n.a.
3	Normal schools training assistant teachers	n.a.	n.a.
4	Continuation-class institutions	n.a.	n.a.
1	Technical and vocational school	73	3

In 1958 there were 60 students studying abroad.

In 1945, 1% of the school-going age population was at school; by 1960 this had increased to 5%. In 1957 educational expenditure amounted to 12.3% of the local budget.

Health and Social Services

VITAL STATISTICS

Not available.

MAIN DISEASES

Malaria, smallpox, yellow fever, sleeping sickness, venereal disease, and leprosy.

HEALTH SERVICES [12]

TABLE II
1959

		Beds
2	Hospitals	360
21	Medical centers	505
22	Maternity wards	272
35	Dispensaries	—
1	Tuberculosis sanatorium	—
6	Private institutions	100

At the beginning of 1958 there were 40 medical practitioners, 1 to every 60,000 of the population; 4 beds per 10,000 of the population.

In addition, mobile health and prophylaxis units and health teams tour the countryside to combat yellow fever, smallpox, venereal disease, and leprosy. In 1959 a school for nurses and technicians was opened in Niamey.

SOCIAL WELFARE SERVICES

Not available.

ECONOMY

Niger is a poor country. Over 90% of its population earn their income from a subsistence agriculture and stock raising and are at the mercy of the weather, which is particularly harsh. Adequate rainfall is limited to a quarter of the country's total area, and production is concentrated in this zone.

Transport and Communications

WATERWAYS [13]

The Niger River is navigable between Bassa (Nigeria) and Say from July to October.

PORTS

None.

ROADS [14]

There are two main roads: one linking Niamey with N'Guimy through Zinder, and the other linking Zinder northward to Tamanrasset in the Republic of Mali. Branch roads lead to Tahoua, Goure, and Bilma. At the beginning of 1957 total mileage was 3,504 km.

RAILROADS

None.

AIRWAYS

There are airports at Niamey, Zinder, and Agades.

POSTS, TELECOMMUNICATIONS, AND BROADCASTING [15]

In 1957 there were 35 post offices and agencies, 30 telegraph and 27 telephone offices; also two radio stations providing 30 hours' service per week.

Resources and Trade

MAIN EXPORTS

Shelled peanuts, and oil (representing about 80% of the total value of exports in 1958), livestock on the hoof, tin, and hides.

MAIN IMPORTS

Consumer goods, fuel, energy, raw materials and semifinished articles, capital goods.

VALUE OF TRADE [16]

In millions of C.F.A. francs

	1956	1957	1958	1959
Exports	3,426	2,601	3,818	2,851
Imports	1,566	1,872	2,298	1,787

France and the other countries of the franc area take four-fifths of Niger's exports and furnish about three-fifths of its imports.

LIVESTOCK [17]

1956 estimate

Cattle	2,100,000
Sheep and goats	5,700,000
Camels	251,000
Horses	86,000
Donkeys	300,000

Industry

MANUFACTURES

Processing industries have been introduced recently. There are three oil mills and one cotton ginnery.

MINING

Mining is relatively unimportant. Small quantities of tungsten and tin are mined in the Air Massif.

POWER [18]

In 1958 Niger produced 4.8 million kwh.

Finance

CURRENCY

C.F.A. franc. 1 C.F.A. franc equals 2 old Metropolitan French francs.

BANKING [19]

Banque de l'Afrique Occidentale, the Banque Commerciale Africaine; Banque Nationale pour le Commerce et l'Industrie, Société Générale, and Crédit Lyonnais.

BUDGET [20]

In millions of C.F.A. francs

	1958
Revenue	3,232
Expenditure	3,232

DEVELOPMENT PLAN

See Appendix III.

LABOR

In 1957 the wage-earning population was estimated to be employed as follows: [21]

Public Sector

Civil service ⎱ Non-Civil service ⎰	6,375	

Private Sector

Agriculture, fishing, and forestry	190	
Mining and quarrying	120	
Industry	500	
Building and public works	3,860	
Commerce, banking, and professions	1,180	
Transport and storage	410	
Domestic service	940	7,200
TOTAL		13,575

In 1953 Niger had some 600 trade-union members, all affiliated with the Confédération Générale de Travailleurs.[22]

The government is working on its own Labor Code, based on the general principles of the 1952 Labor Code of the French Republic. Since 1957 the Equalization Fund for Family Allowances has been in operation and makes it possible for wage earners in both the public and private sectors of the economy to receive family benefits.

THE REPUBLIC OF THE NIGER NOTES

1 Unless otherwise stated, information obtained from Ambassade de France, Service de Presse et d'Information, *The Republic of the Niger*, New York, October 1960.

2 Service des Statistiques d'Outre-Mer, *Outre-Mer 1958*, Paul Dupont, Nov. 1959, Paris, p. 760, Table 1.

3 Edmond Sere de Rivières, *Le Niger*, Société d'Editions Géographiques, Maritimes et Coloniales, Paris, (V_e), 1952, pp. 9–16.

4 L'Annuaire Vert, *Annuaire Economique 1958*, Editions C.E.P. Publicité, Casablanca, Morocco, p. 448.

5 R. Segal, *Political Africa*, Stevens & Sons Ltd., London, 1961, pp. 370–71.

6 *Outre-Mer 1958, op. cit.*, p. 760, Table 2.

7 Percentage computed from *Ibid.*, p. 760, Tables 1 and 2.

8 *Outre-Mer 1958, op. cit.*, p. 760, Table 1.

9 *Ibid.*, p. 140, Table 1.

10 *Ibid.*, p. 760, Table 1.

11 *Ibid.*, p. 761, Tables 5 and 6.

12 *Ibid.*, p. 760, Table 3.

13 *The Columbia Lippincott Gazetteer of the World*, Columbia University Press, New York, 1952, p. 1324.

14 *Outre-Mer 1958, op. cit.*, pp. 761–62, Tables 7 and 8.

15 *Ibid.*, p. 762, Tables 10 and 11.

16 *Ibid.*, p. 763, Table 14; also S. H. Steinberg (Ed.), *The Statesman's Yearbook 1959*, Macmillan & Co., Ltd., London, 1959, p. 1008; and France: Service des Statistiques, *Bulletin de Conjecture d'Outre-Mer*, No. 21, Paris, Aug. 1960, p. 22.

17 *Outre-Mer 1958, op. cit.*, p. 762, Table 12.

18 *Ibid.*, p. 763, Table 13.

19 S. H. Steinberg (Ed.), *op. cit.*, p. 1009.

20 *Ibid.*, 1961, p. 1037.

21 *Outre-Mer 1958, op. cit.*, p. 209, Table 3.

22 International Labor Office, *African Labor Survey*, Geneva, 1958, p. 236, Table XII.

Nigeria[1]

AREA:[2] *356,669 sq. m.*
Northern Region 281,782
Eastern Region 29,484
Western Region 45,376
Lagos 27

POPULATION:[3] *35,105,800 (1960 estimate)*
Density: 93 per sq. m.

GEOGRAPHY

Although Nigeria lies wholly within the tropics and has a hot climate, the sandy country in the north is dry, while the low-lying swampy coastal areas in the south are damp and enervating. The rainy season extends from April to October in the north, with rainfall ranging between 25 and 60 inches; the rainy season in the south is between March and November, with rainfall between 60 and 160 inches. The annual average temperature is about 80 degrees F. There are four main geographic areas in Nigeria: (1) an almost impenetrable swamp and mangrove forest area in the south; (2) an inland tropical forest ranging between 50 and 100 miles in depth; (3) an area of open woodland and grass savanna beyond the tropical forest of about 100 miles; and (4) a northern area of open land with an elevation of about 2,000 feet. The most prominent physical feature of Nigeria is the River Niger with its main tributary, the Benue; a great difference between high and low water—sometimes as much as 35 ft.—makes navigation of these rivers impossible.

HISTORICAL SKETCH

The Portuguese, in the 15th century, were the first Europeans to reach Nigeria; the first English ships reached the Bight of Benin in 1553. The area was known as the "Slave Coast."

It was the antislavery movement in England, coupled with the commercial interests of the British trading companies, that resulted in British penetration and administrative control of the interior. The protective role of the British was recognized at the Berlin Conference in 1885, and in

1914 Lagos and the interior protectorates were amalgamated as the Colony and Protectorate of Nigeria. In 1922 a strip of the former German Cameroon was attached administratively to Nigeria, first as a mandated territory under the League of Nations, and later as a United Nations Trust Territory. Nigeria became a Federation in 1955 and an independent nation on October 30, 1960, at which time it became a full member of the British Commonwealth and the United Nations. In June 1961 Northern Cameroons joined the Northern Region, Southern Cameroons joined the French-speaking Cameroon Republic on October 1, 1961.

GOVERNMENT

Present Status

Independent federal state.

Constitution

Nigeria has a federal constitution, under which the respective powers of the central and the three regional legislatures are clearly defined. The titular head of state at the federal level is the Governor General, and Governors head each region.

The bicameral Federal Parliament consists of a House of Representatives and a Senate. The Federal Cabinet forms the principal instrument of policy. The House of Representatives consists of a Speaker and 311 members elected in single-member constituencies, on a population basis of approximately one number for each 100,000 persons, giving the Northern Region (including Northern Cameroons) 175 members, the Western Region 61, the Eastern Region 73, and the federal territory of Lagos 3. The Senate has revisionary powers and consists of 12 members from each Region nominated by their governments and approved by their legislatures; in addition, there are 4 members from Lagos and 4 special members nominated by the Governor General. The Federal Cabinet consists of a Prime Minister and 18 other ministers.

At the regional level each legislature consists of two houses: a House of Assembly and a House of Chiefs. The House of Chiefs usually consists of first-class chiefs, there by traditional right, and other chiefs variously selected. All members to the House of Assembly are elected, except for 5 special members in the Northern Region appointed by the Governor. Each region has an Executive Council consisting of the leader of the majority party as Premier and ministers appointed by the Governor on his advice.

Franchise

Northern Region, adult male suffrage; adult universal suffrage in the rest of the Federation.

Local Government

Northern Region: The birthplace of Lugard's system of "indirect rule," whereby traditional rulers and their councils were used as units of local government, called Native Authorities. In recent times these have broadened their membership and been given greater representation through elections. Provincial Councils and Native Authority Committees are being established to coordinate the work of Native Authorities.

Western Region: Divisional district and local Councils with elected majorities form the units of local government. In each case, provision is made for the appointment of traditional members, who are not to exceed a quarter of the membership.

Eastern Region: The system of local government is based, wherever possible, on modern democratic lines and suited to local needs and varying degrees of social and political development. At the local level the franchise is restricted to taxpayers and, in certain urban areas, to rate payers. It is intended to introduce universal adult suffrage in time. Lagos has a wholly elected City Council.

Political Parties

There are three main parties, largely regionally based:

The Northern Peoples' Congress (NPC), exclusively of the Northern Region, led by Alhaji Sir Ahmadu Bellow, Sardauna of Sokoto, which, together with its allied groups in the other Regions, holds 149 seats in the House of Representatives.

The Action Group (AG), predominantly of the Western Region, led by Chief Awolowo. Together with its allied groups, it holds 72 seats in the House of Representatives.

The National Council of Nigeria and the Cameroons (NCNC), predominantly of the Eastern Region, led by Dr. Michael Okpara. Together with the Northern Elements Progressive Union (NEPU), it holds 90 seats in the House of Representatives.

There is one Independent member for the Northern Region.[4]

Alhaji Sir Abubakar Balewa, parliamentary leader of the NPC in the Federal House of Representatives, is the Prime Minister. Dr. Nnamdi Azikiwe is the Governor General of the Federation.

POPULATION BREAKDOWN

Main Cities [5]

1960 estimate

Lagos (Federal capital)	364,000
Kaduna (N. Region capital)	51,000
Ibadan (W. Region capital)	500,000
Enugu (E. Region capital)	63,000

Urban-rural Distribution [6]

Six million (19% live in 350 towns of 5,000 or more). Apart from Lagos, urbanization is greatest in the Western Region and least in the Northern Region.

Ethnic Distribution [7]

Non-African   14,800 (1952/53 census)

The following major African groupings make up about 58% of the total population (1959 estimate):

Hausa-Fulani	9,500,000
Ibo	6,000,000
Yoruba	5,500,000

Religious Affiliation [8]

Western Region:

1952	
Christians	2,201,000
Muslims	1,971,000
Animists	1,913,000

Eastern Region:

1953	
Christians	3,612,000
Muslims	23,000
Animists	3,580,000

Northern Region:

	1952
Christians	558,000
Muslims	11,661,000
Animists	4,616,000

Lagos:

	1952
Christians	146,000
Muslims	112,000
Animists	9,000

Languages

The main African languages are Hausa, Ibo, Yoruba, Fulani, Jukun, Tiv, Idoma, and Ibibio. English is the official language.

Sex Distribution [9]

	Male	Female
African	14,861,000 (48.9%)	15,541,000 (51.1%)
Non-African	9,196 (62.5%)	5,524 (37.5%)

Age Distribution [10]

	Under 14	15 and over
African	13,455,500	16,943,500
Non-African	Not available	

SOCIAL DATA

Education [11]

TABLE I

		Enrollment (1959)	Teachers (1958)
16,047	Primary schools	2,840,014	79,761
420	Modern secondary schools	64,209 ⎫	4,378
284	Secondary grammar schools	48,243 ⎬	
320	Teacher-training schools	27,172	1,917
44	Technical and vocational schools	7,692	—
	University College, Ibadan	1,024	—
	Nigerian College of Technology	1,088	—
	University of Nigeria, Nsukka	200	—

The percentage of children between the ages of 5 and 14 who were in school in 1958 was 42.9%: 85.4% in Lagos; 7.4% in the Northern Region; 100% in the Western Region, and 78.3% in the Eastern Region.

Expenditure: 1959   £1,801,393.

Health and Social Services

VITAL STATISTICS [12]

For Lagos only, not available for the rest of the Federation.

Crude birth rate	49.1
Crude death rate	14.2
Infant mortality rate	80.2

Estimated population increment at 4% per year: 12,990.

MAIN DISEASES

Malaria, yellow fever, trypanosomiasis, cerebrospinal meningitis, pneumonia, smallpox, leprosy, yaws, tuberculosis, dysentery, venereal disease, intestinal parasites, filariasis, onchocerciasis (blinding filaria), elephantiasis, and tropical ulcers.

HEALTH SERVICES

TABLE II
1957

		Beds
188	Hospitals	13,000
479	Maternity centers	—
6	Rural health centers	—
+1,000	Dispensaries	—
819	Qualified physicians	
1	Teaching hospital, Ibadan	510

Special provisions are made for lepers (of whom there are estimated to be 500,000) in separate villages, and for a sleeping-sickness service.

There is free medical service in schools in the Western Region for children under 18 years of age, and school medical services operate in certain areas. Mobile field units carry out mass vaccinations and deal with outbreaks of infectious diseases.

SOCIAL WELFARE SERVICES

The Federal Department of Social Welfare in Lagos operates Boys' and Girls' clubs, a Family Welfare Center, a Juvenile Welfare Center, two remand homes, and three approved schools for young delinquents.

In Northern Nigeria, government social welfare staff concentrate their efforts on urban centers with mixed Nigerian populations. Youth clubs, remand homes, and reformatories are provided.

Social welfare work in the Western and Eastern Regions follows much the same pattern as in Lagos. Community development project work is well established in the Eastern Region. In the Western Region, community centers provide recreational and educational activities for all age groups.

ECONOMY

Agriculture, by far the most important sector of the economy, occupies most of the male working population and provides 85% of the country's exports. However, 80% of total agricultural production is devoted to products consumed locally.

Transport and Communications

WATERWAYS

The Niger River is navigable from the coast to Onitsha (232 miles) throughout the year, and to Jebba (537 miles) from August to March. The Benue is navigable as far as Garua in the French Cameroons (972 miles from the sea and 547 miles from its confluence with the Niger at Lokoja) during August and September, and to Yola and Makurdi from July to October. The operation of river fleets is handicapped by the restricted access to the delta ports, and by navigational difficulties on both rivers.

PORTS [13]

The ports of Lagos and Harcourt between them serve the whole country and handle over three-quarters of Nigeria's overseas trade. Warri, Sapele, and Burutu on the Niger delta in the Western Region, and Calabar and Degema in the Eastern Region, also handle foreign trade. Total tonnage handled in 1958 was 4,940,000 tons.

ROADS

There are a total 41,944 miles of road, of which more than 4,800 are bituminized, the remainder being gravel or dirt.[14]

There are three classes of roads: (1) trunk A roads (5,799 miles) which link the Federal and Regional capitals, and these to larger towns, ports, and important centers of neighboring foreign territories; (2) trunk B roads (6,745 miles) connecting provincial and divisional headquarters and other large towns with the trunk A system and points on the railway; and (3) other roads (24,433 miles), which accommodate local traffic and act as feeders to the trunk systems.

RAILROADS [15]

In 1934 route mileage was 1,900 miles of 3 ft. 6 in. track. There are two main single track lines with branch lines. The western line runs from Lagos through Ibadan and Kaduna to Kano. The eastern line runs from Port Harcourt to Enugu and Kaduna.

AIRWAYS [16]

Eight international airlines operate scheduled services to and from Lagos and Kano both of which have Grade I (international) airports. In addition to operating air services within Nigeria which link the Federal and Regional capitals and other important towns, Nigerian Airways operates services between London and Lagos, and between Lagos and Accra and Dakar. In March 1960 Nigeria had 3,986 miles of unduplicated airways.

POSTS, TELECOMMUNICATIONS, AND BROADCASTING

There are 48,000 telephones in use (1961/62 estimate) and about 75% of these are operated under an automatic exchange system. The Nigerian Broadcasting Corporation operates transmitting stations at Lagos, Ibadan, Kaduna, and Enugu. A wire service is operated in the Northern and Eastern Regions. Programs are broadcast in English and in 15 vernacular languages. The first television network in Africa south of the Sahara was inaugurated in the Western Region in 1959.

Resources and Trade

MAIN EXPORTS

Palm kernels (about 27% of the value of export 1956/58) (the world's largest producer), palm oil (world's largest producer), peanuts (world's largest producer), cocoa (ranks third only to Ghana and Brazil), cotton, tin ore, columbite ore, timber (logs and sawn), bananas, hides and skins, rubber, coffee, and ginger.

MAIN IMPORTS

(in order of importance)

Machinery and transport equipment, manufactured goods, piece goods and synthetic fibers, and cotton piece goods.

VALUE OF TRADE [17]

In millions of £'s

	1955	1956	1957	1958
Exports	132	135	127	136
Imports	136	153	152	167

Nigeria's principal customers (export and import trade) are the United Kingdom (purchased 51.5% of Nigeria's exports in 1959), the Netherlands (purchased 16.2% of Nigeria's exports in 1959), West Germany, Japan, the U.S., and Italy.

MARKETING AND COOPERATIVE SOCIETIES [18]

Most of Nigeria's agricultural exports are handled by Regional marketing boards. These boards purchase the goods and are responsible for their delivery to port. The Nigerian Produce Marketing Company Ltd. takes over export produce from the boards at ports of shipment and is responsible for shipment and overseas sales of all marketing board produce.

The produce which the marketing boards' agents are alone authorized to export are cocoa, palm oil, palm kernels, peanuts, cotton, sesame seed, soya beans, and, in the Western Region, citrus fruits. The Western Region is planning to develop cooperative settlements in units of 1,500 acres to begin with, but they will be expandable to 5,000 or 6,000 acres containing 200 settlers and their families. Each unit will have a central pool of machinery and facilities for credit. There are also cooperative societies in other export industries, printing and publishing, banking, and transport.

LIVESTOCK [19]

1959 estimate

	Cattle	Goats	Sheep	Pigs
		(thousands)		
N. Region	6,000	11,000	3,000	150
W. Region	70	650	300	110
E. Region	160	1,370	800	20
TOTALS	6,230	13,020	4,100	280

Industry

MANUFACTURES

Mills to extract oil from palm kernels have been organized since the end of the war. There is some factory weaving and other minor industries. The governments of Nigeria have attempted to encourage foreign investment by providing import-duty relief and income-tax relief.

MINING [20]

Although several minerals are found in Nigeria, the output of the whole industry is quite small. All minerals are controlled and mined by the federal government. They include tin and columbite in the Northern Region, and oil in the Eastern Region. Nigeria is the only country in equatorial West Africa at present producing coal. Large lead and zinc deposits are also found in the Eastern Region, but they have yet to be exploited.

POWER [21]

In 1952/53 there was an installed electricity capacity of 34,290 kw.

In 1958/59 installed capacity had been increased to 102,420 kw. and 242 million were sold.

Finance

CURRENCY

Nigeria is a member of the sterling area and maintains its currency at par with British sterling.

BANKING [22]

The Central Bank of Nigeria was established in 1958 and has sole right to issue currency. Twelve banks now operate in Nigeria; they include 8 Nigerian, 3 British, and 1 French bank. Nigerian sterling assets held in London were at £263.1 million in 1955 and £243.1 and £222.1 million in 1957 and 1959, respectively.

BUDGET [23]

In £'000's

	1961
Revenue	95,955
Expenditure	94,354

Customs duties are the major source of revenue, accounting for about 66% of 1961 estimated receipts.

DEVELOPMENT PLAN [24]

For Plan 1955–62

	£ million
Total cost	275.8
Sources of finance—	
internal	202.8
external loans	25.0
Colonial development and welfare grants	19.4
Other grants	1.7
TOTAL	248.9

Two-thirds of the expenditures of the 1955–62 plan are on the following items in order of their magnitude: roads, railways, administration and general services, education, housing, social welfare, and waterways and harbors.

LABOR [25]

Most Nigerians are peasant farmers who produce food crops for themselves or for local sale and contributing to certain important export crops. The numbers employed in the principal wage-earning occupations in 1958, in undertakings employing 10 or more persons, were:

Government services	122,789
Construction	123,846
Commerce	45,698
Mining and quarrying	49,506
Transport and communications	48,656
Agriculture, forestry, and fishing	45,416
Manufacturing	29,693
TOTAL	465,604

In 1946 there were 100 labor unions with a membership of 52,747, a number which had grown by the end of 1957 to 232,953, involving 297 trade unions. A new central labor organization, the Trades Union Congress of Nigeria, was formed in 1959 to replace the two such former organizations. Legislation covers such matters as conditions of employment, health, welfare, and other conditions of labor.

NIGERIA NOTES

1   Unless otherwise stated, all information obtained from: British Information Services, I.D., *Nigeria: The Making of a Nation*, June 1960.

2   Federation of Nigeria: Federal Ministry of Commerce and Industry,
Handbook of Commerce and Industry in Nigeria, Lagos, 1960, p. 1.
(Figures for Southern Cameroons excluded.)

3   Federation of Nigeria: Federal Office of Statistics, *Digest of Statistics*,
Vol. IX, No. 4, Lagos, October 1960, p. 3; the 1952/53 census was obtained from a single enumeration and therefore did not allow "for the
systematic evaluation of its reliability"—F. Lorimer, *Demographic Information on Tropical Africa*, Boston University Press, 1961, p. 111.

4   *Independent Nigeria*, Pacific Printers, Lagos, 1960, pp. 56–63. Figures
compiled from the list of members of the House of Representatives.

5   Federation of Nigeria: *Digest of Statistics, Vol. IX, No. 4, op. cit.*, p. 3.

6   Federation of Nigeria: *Economic Survey of Nigeria*, 1959, Federal Government Printer, Lagos, 1959, p. 13 (1952/53 census).

7   Federation of Nigeria: *Digest of Statistics, Vol. IX, No. 4, op. cit.*, p. 3.
Also *Economic Survey of Nigeria*, 1959, *op. cit.*, p. 12.

8   S. H. Steinberg (Ed.), *The Statesman's Yearbook 1961*, Macmillan &
Co., Ltd., London, 1961, p. 312.

9   Federation of Nigeria: *Economic Survey of Nigeria, 1959, op. cit.*, pp.
104–105 (excluding figures for Southern Cameroons).

10   *Ibid.*

11   Federation of Nigeria: Ministry of Education, *Digest of Statistics 1959*,
Lagos, pp. 3–5, Tables 1, 2, and 3; *One Hundred Facts About Nigeria*,
F.I.S., Lagos, p. 16; U.N. Economic Commission for Africa, UNESCO:
*Final Report of the Conference of African States on the Development
of Education*, Addis Ababa, May 15–25, 1961, "Outline of a Plan for
African Educational Development," p. 7, Table 1, UNESCO/ED/181,
and Federation of Nigeria: *Annual Report of the Department of Educa-
tion for the Year 1959*; Federal Government Printer, Lagos, 1961,
Table V.

12   Federation of Nigeria: *Annual Report on the Medical Services of the
Federal Territory of Lagos for the Year 1957*, Federal Government
Printer, Lagos, 1958, p. 23.

13   Federation of Nigeria: *Digest of Statistics, Vol. IX, No. 4, op. cit.*, p. 54;
Federation of Nigeria: *Economic Survey of Nigeria 1959, op. cit.*, p. 71.

14   Federation of Nigeria: *Digest of Statistics, Vol. IX, No. 4, op. cit.*, p. 63.

15   *Ibid.*, p. 66.

16   *Ibid.*, p. 60.

17   Chemical Bank of New York Trust Co.: *International Economic Survey*,
No. 134, June 1961, p. 4; Nigeria Consulate General, Trade Investment

Division, New York: *Facts About Nigeria*, p. 6; Federation of Nigeria: *Economic Survey of Nigeria 1959, op. cit.*, p. 100.

18 Federation of Nigeria: *Handbook of Commerce and Industry in Nigeria*, *op. cit.*, pp. 121–24.

19 Federation of Nigeria: *Economic Survey of Nigeria 1959, op. cit.*, p. 45.

20 *Ibid.*, pp. 51 and 53.

21 *Ibid.*, p. 55.

22 Federation of Nigeria: *Handbook of Commerce and Industry in Nigeria*, *op. cit.*, pp. 170–72; Federation of Nigeria: *Digest of Statistics, Vol. IX, No. 4, op. cit.*, p. 16.

23 Federation of Nigeria: *Digest of Statistics, Vol. IX, No. 4, op. cit.*, pp. 6–7.

24 Federation of Nigeria: *Economic Survey of 1959, op. cit.*, pp. 88–89.

25 Federation of Nigeria: *Digest of Statistics, Vol. IX, No. 4, op. cit.*, p. 81.

Portuguese Territories[1]

PORTUGUESE GUINEA

AREA: *13,948 sq. m.*
POPULATION: *510,777 (1950 census)*
Density: ±36 per sq. m.

GEOGRAPHY, HISTORY, AND GOVERNMENT

Portuguese Guinea was discovered in 1446 by Nuna Tristao. It includes the adjacent archipelago of Bijagos. It is governed by a Governor General.

POPULATION BREAKDOWN AND SOCIAL DATA

Bissau is the main city and capital of the territory.
According to the 1950 census, the population was divided as follows:

European	2,263
Half-caste	4,458
Negro	503,935
Indian	11

Education

164 Elementary schools with 11,142 pupils in 1957
21 Technical schools with 861 pupils in 1958
1 Secondary school with 243 pupils in 1958

ECONOMY

The chief commercial products of the territory are rice, palm oil, seeds, and hides.
The 1958 budget
In escudos '000's

Revenue	144,386
Expenditure	150,857

The trade value in 1958
In escudos '000's

Exports	200,259
Imports	244,018

There are three ports—Bissau, Bolama, and Cacheu. There were 3,289 km. of roads in 1958.

PRINCIPE AND SÃO TOME

AREA: *964 sq. m.*
POPULATION: *60,159 (1950 census)*
Density: ±62 per sq. m.

HISTORY, GEOGRAPHY, AND GOVERNMENT

The islands of Principe and São Tome, off the east coast of Africa opposite Rio Muni and Gabon, respectively, were discovered in 1471 by Pedro Escoba and Joso Gomes. Since 1522 they have been a province of Portugal, ruled by a Governor.

POPULATION BREAKDOWN AND SOCIAL DATA

According to the 1950 census the population was divided as follows:

European	1,152
Half-caste	4,300
Negro	54,697
Other	10

Education

1959
20 Elementary schools with 2,802 pupils
1 Technical school with 95 pupils
1 Secondary school with 171 pupils

ECONOMY

The chief commercial products of these islands are cocoa, coffee, coconut and copra, palm oil, and cinchona. The livestock was estimated to be 2,223 oxen, 5,239 sheep and goats, and 5,976 pigs in 1959.
Budget 1959
In escudos '000's

Revenue	83,139
Expenditure	74,754

Trade Value 1959
In escudos '000's

Exports	186,589
Imports	158,904

Transport and Communications

In 1959 there were 278 km. of roads; one radio station; 600 km. of telephone lines, and 14 telephone exchanges.

NOTE

1   All information obtained from S. H. Steinberg (Ed.), *The Statesman's Yearbook 1961*, Macmillan and Co., Ltd., London, 1961, pp. 1356–57.

The Federation of Rhodesia and Nyasaland [1]

HISTORICAL SKETCH

In 1953 the Federation was endorsed by the legislatures of Northern and Southern Rhodesia and Nyasaland and by the United Kingdom Parliament, and was inaugurated in September of that year. Lord Llewellin became its first Governor General and Sir Godfrey Huggins (later Lord Malvern) its first Prime Minister. At the first federal elections held in December 1953, the Federal Party was elected to power.

The creation of the Federation was the end result of a series of discussions and conferences dating back to 1938, when a Royal Commission was appointed to inquire into the possibility of closer cooperation or association between the three territories. The Commission's Report took the view that any such attempts were unlikely to succeed because of the wide disparity among the three territories. They nevertheless recommended that a Council be set up to survey the possibilities of coordinating government services and to investigate the economic needs of the whole area. A Central African Council was established immediately following World War II to coordinate policy and action among the three governments. It was not until 1950 that the question of closer political association was again examined. An official conference in London at the beginning of 1951 recognized that African opposition in the Northern Protectorates was still a serious obstacle to closer association. In a September 1951 Ministerial Conference at Victoria Falls, African representatives of the two Northern Territories made it clear that they were unable to accept any scheme in which the white-controlled self-governing colony of Southern Rhodesia was closely associated with Northern Rhodesia and Nyasaland. To meet African objections, the Conference recommended that, in any further considerations of any proposals for federation, the Protectorate status of

273

the two Northern Territories be accepted and preserved; the land question and the political advancement of the peoples of these two territories remain the responsibility of the territorial governments and Whitehall. Far from accepting the proposals, the Africans from the two Northern Territories refused to participate in the meetings convened in London at the beginning of 1952 and the following year in January. At the latter Conference a final scheme was drawn up, reiterating the assurances given at the Victoria Falls Conference, and this scheme became the federal constitution passed as the Rhodesia and Nyasaland Federation Act of August 1, 1953.

African resistance in the two Northern Territories took on a more and more vocal form, culminating in the outbreak of riots in 1958 and 1959 and the declaration of a state of emergency in both Northern Rhodesia and Nyasaland in 1959. In July of the same year, the British Government announced the appointment of a Commission under the chairmanship of Lord Monckton to review the constitution of the Federation. It reported in 1960, and its constitutional recommendations are to be considered in 1962.[2]

GOVERNMENT

Present Status

Self-governing federal state.

Constitution [3]

The legislature consists of Her Majesty and a Federal Assembly of Speaker and 59 members: 44 of unspecified race are elected from a system of direct election (24 from Southern Rhodesia, 14 from Northern Rhodesia, and 6 from Nyasaland); 8 Africans elected on a system of direct election on a considerably wider franchise than the 44 members of unspecified race (4 from Southern Rhodesia, 4 from Northern Rhodesia, and 2 from Nyasaland); 4 Africans (2 from Northern Rhodesia and 2 from Nyasaland) elected in each territory by a body designated by the Governor as "representative of Africans"; and 3 Europeans charged with special responsibilities for African interests (1 elected from Southern Rhodesia and 1 each from Northern Rhodesia and Nyasaland appointed by their respective Governors). Executive power is vested in the Prime Minister and his Cabinet.

To safeguard African interests, a standing committee of the Federal Assembly, the African Affairs Board—consisting of 3 Europeans and 1 of the elected African members from each territory—is set up. The Chairman is appointed by the Governor General from among the members.

The Federal Assembly has exclusive legislative power on the following subjects: external affairs, defense, immigration, banking, external trade, fiscal matters, main roads, railways, posts and telegraphs, European agriculture in Southern and Northern Rhodesia, federal courts, and education (excluding primary and secondary education for Africans).

There is a "joint list" of subjects on which both the federal and territorial assemblies may legislate; these include development of industries, electricity, scientific and industrial research, health, town-planning, census, and statistics.

Franchise [4]

Qualified franchise—There are two rolls, general and special. Common to both rolls are the following:

Twenty-one years of age and over.

Citizen of Rhodesia and Nyasaland or a British protected person.

Two years residence in the Federation.

Oath of allegiance to the Queen.

Literacy in English and ability to complete the application enrollment form.

A wife is deemed to have the qualifications of her husband. In the case of a polygamous marriage, this applies only to the first wife.

General-roll qualifications

Income of £720 per annum or immovable property to the value of £1,500; or

Income of £480 per annum or immovable property to the value of £1,000 and primary education; or

Income of £300 per annum or immovable property to the value of £500 and 4 years of secondary education; or

Ministers of religion who have had certain prescribed periods of training and service.

Special-roll qualifications

Income of £150 per annum or immovable property to the value of £500; or

Income of £120 and 2 years of secondary education.

Special voters can never be more than 20% of the total of ordinary voters. Once a person is on a roll, he cannot be removed if income or material prosperity subsequently fall below the requirements.

It has been estimated that in Southern Rhodesia the number of Africans qualifying for the general roll is some 3,000 and for the special roll 10,000 to 11,000.

Political Parties [5]

United Federal Party (UFP), a merger of the Federal and United Rhodesia Parties, led by Sir Roy Welensky—the present government party holding 44 of the 59 seats.

Federal Dominion Party (FDP), led by Winston Field, a merger of the Southern Rhodesia Dominion and Northern Rhodesia Commonwealth parties. It is the principal opposition party and has 7 seats.

SOCIAL DATA

Education [6]

The federal government is responsible for all European, Asian, and Colored education. For details see territorial sections. It is also responsible for all higher education.

The University College of Rhodesia and Nyasaland was incorporated by Royal Charter on February 10, 1955. It is located in Salisbury and is open to members of all races. It has two faculties: that of arts and that of science. By 1959 there were 166 full-time and 22 part-time students and a staff of 63.

Health Services [7]

Health services are controlled by the Federal Ministry of Health. A Secretary for Health as head of the department, and three Directors of Medical Services, one for each territory, as his regional representatives.

In general Europeans and other non-Africans are required to contribute toward the cost of government medical and health services, while Africans are generally exempt from all payment.

For figures relating to hospitals, number of beds, medical practitioners, and the like, see under relevant section in each territory.

ECONOMY

MAIN EXPORTS [8]

Copper (about 58% of the total value of exports in 1960); tobacco, tea, chrome ore, copper concentrates, zinc, apparel, cobalt, peanuts, meats (fresh, frozen, and chilled), hides, lead, radio parts, wattle extracts, ferrochrome, and maize.

MAIN IMPORTS [9]

Metals, machinery, and vehicles; consumers' goods; fuel and lubricants.

VALUE OF TRADE [10]

In £ millions

	1956	1957	1958	1959	1960
Exports	181.8	156.1	135.8	187.0	205.9
Imports	159.3	177.5	157.6	150.2	156.8

MARKETING [11]

There are five statutory boards under federal-government control.

The Tobacco Marketing Board: Legislation provides for the registration of all growers, graders, and buyers of tobacco, the licensing of auction floors, the control of selling charges, the regulation of procedure on auction floors, the control of the sale and export of specific types and varieties of tobacco that may be sold in, or exported from, the Rhodesias.

The Federal Grain Marketing Board and Maize Price Guarantees: A market for maize, peanuts, kaffir corn, munga, and rupoko is guaranteed by the board. It is also responsible for the storage of grain, including the maintenance of a six-month reserve of maize stocks in accordance with government policy. The board's buying prices for maize and other controlled products are determined by the federal government.

The Cold-Storage Commission: It guarantees markets for cattle, sheep, pigs, and goats within a 50-mile radius from Limbe, Blantyre, and Zomba. It also operates a hide-purchasing scheme throughout Nyasaland. The commission acts in the capacity of a residual buyer. It is obliged to accept all slaughtered cattle offered it at prices laid down by government. Thereafter it sells the products either internally or on the export market at wholesale prices.

The Dairy Marketing Board: It operates only in Southern Rhodesia. It purchases milk for resale either through its retail delivery organization or on a wholesale basis to independent retailers. The board's selling and buying prices are controlled by the government. It is in a position of a residual buyer, producers being free to make other arrangements for the distribution of their milk.

Cotton Industries Board: A price is fixed by the Minister of Commerce and Industry, with the agreement of the Minister of Agriculture. Owners of Southern Rhodesian and Northern Rhodesian seed cotton may require the board to buy at that price, and owners of lint derived from federal seed cotton are required to offer it for sale to the board, which is obliged to buy it.

DEVELOPMENT PLAN [12]

1959/63

Total cost: £76,764,000
Main sources:

Federal Power Board	£25,387,000
Special-project finance	5,086,000
Loan recoveries	4,675,000
Borrowing	36,682,000

Major expenditure heads—power, railways, roads, and bridges.
For territorial development plans, see under territorial sections.

Finance

BANKING [13]

Barclay's Bank (D.C.O.), National & Grindlay's Bank Ltd., Ottoman Bank, the Netherlands Bank of S.A. Ltd., Standard Bank of South Africa Ltd., Merchant Bank of Central Africa Ltd.

THE FEDERATION OF RHODESIA AND NYASALAND NOTES

1   *Handbook on the Federation of Rhodesia and Nyasaland,* Government Printer, Salisbury, 1960, p. 778.
2   U.K.: Report of the Advisory Commission on the Review of the Constitution of Rhodesia and Nyasaland, London, H.M.S.O., *Cmnd. 1148,* pp. 12–15.

3 U.K.: *The Commonwealth Relations Office List 1961*, H.M.S.O., London, 1961, pp. 287–88.

4 Federation of Rhodesia and Nyasaland: *The Franchise for Federal Elections in Rhodesia and Nyasaland*: C. Fed. 72, Government Printer, Salisbury, 1957, pp. 5–12; Chatham House Memoranda: Department of Race Relations, *The Franchise in Rhodesia and Nyasaland*, Occasional Papers, No. 1, July 1957, distributed by O.U.P. for R.I.I.A., pp. 13–15.

5 R. Segal, *Political Africa*, Stevens & Sons Ltd., London, 1961, pp. 382–85.

6 U.K.: Advisory Commission on the Review of the Federation of Rhodesia and Nyasaland Report, Appendix VI, Survey of Developments since 1953, H.M.S.O., *Cmnd. 1149*, London, 1960, pp. 161–64.

7 *Ibid.*, pp. 132–35.

8 Federation of Rhodesia and Nyasaland: *Monthly Digest of Statistics*, No. 1, April 1961, Central Statistical Office, Salisbury, pp. 34–37, Table 26.

9 *Ibid.*, p. 38, Table 27.

10 *Ibid.*, p. 21, Table 17.

11 U.K.: *Cmnd. 1149, op. cit.*, pp. 389–94.

12 Federation of Rhodesia and Nyasaland, *Development Plan 1959–1963*, Government Printer, Salisbury, C. Fed. 122, 1959, Schedules A and B.

13 Federation of Rhodesia and Nyasaland: Office for Rhodesia and Nyasaland Affairs, *Basic Information for the Potential Investor*, Washington, D.C., June 1960, p. 40.

Nyasaland[1]

AREA: *46,066 sq. m., of which 9,380 are water*
POPULATION:[2] *2,860,000 (1960 estimate)*
Density:[3] *73 per sq. m.*

GEOGRAPHY

Nyasaland is about 520 miles long and varies in width from 50 to 100 miles. Its main geographical feature is the deep depression forming part of the Great Rift Valley which traverses it from end to end. The greater part of this depression is occupied by Lake Nyasa, about 1,500 feet above sea level. There are plateaus on either side, mainly 3,300 to 4,400 feet high. The southern highlands are dominated by the Mlanje Mountains, which rise to nearly 10,000 feet. The lake shore has a humid climate; temperatures seldom rise above 100 degrees F. Elsewhere the climate varies with the altitude. The dry season lasts from May to October and the wet season from November to April. Depending upon the zones, rainfall ranges from 30 to over 70 inches per annum.

HISTORICAL SKETCH

Lake Nyasa was discovered in 1859 by Livingstone. Since 1874 missionaries have been active in the area. In 1891 the area was placed under British protection "with the consent and desire of the Chiefs and people." By 1896 the British Administration had completed the work of extinguishing the slave trade. Eight years later the British extended their administration to the Northern Province, and in 1907 the area was designated the Nyasaland Protectorate with its own Executive and Legislative Councils. The territory continued to be ruled with little local participation in governmental affairs until 1949 when, for the first time, African and Asian members were nominated to the Legislative Council. The indigenous population was given increasingly more and more of a share in the Legislature and Executive until, in 1961, a new constitution was drawn up introducing an elected unofficial majority in the Legislative Council and equal representation for unofficial members on the Executive Council. In 1953 Nyasaland joined the Federation of Rhodesia and Nyasaland.

GOVERNMENT

Present Status
British protectorate.

Constitution
The 1961 Legislative Council consisted of 28 elected unofficial members, 3 ex-officio, and 2 nominated official members of the Executive Council. Twenty of the 28 unofficial members are elected by B (lower) roll constituencies, and the rest by A (upper) roll constituencies. The Governor has the power to appoint additional members to the Legislative Council on the advice of Her Majesty. The Executive Council consists of 5 unofficial (elected) and 5 official members, the Chief Secretary, the Attorney General, the Financial Secretary, and 2 nominated officials, who are ex-officio members. Of the 5 elected members, 3 are elected by the B roll and 2 by the A roll.

Franchise [4]
Qualifications for both rolls are: citizenship of the U.K. and Colonies, residency in Nyasaland, and 21 years of age. For the B roll one of the following is required in addition: income of £120 per annum or ownership of not less than £250 and literacy in English; or payment of taxes for the past 10 years and literacy in English or common Nyasaland dialect; or chiefs, members of Native Authorities, past and present members of District Councils and group or village headmen; or master farmer or pensioners or ex-servicemen. Qualifications for the A roll are the same as those for the A roll in Northern Rhodesia.

Local Government
Nyasaland is divided into 18 districts, each containing one or more Native Authorities of varying sizes, depending generally upon the degree of tribal homogeneity in each area. There are 132 Native Authorities in all. Some of them have been taken over by District Councils, which were first established in 1953. These Councils, which have been

set up in 11 of the 18 districts, are multiracial in composition. In addition, each of the three Provinces has an African Provincial Council.

Political Parties [5]

Malawi Congress Party, led by Dr. Hastings Banda.

Congress Liberation Movement, breakaway from the MCP, led by T. D. T. Banda.

Christian Social-Democratic Party (CSDP), led by Chester Katsonga.

Asian Convention, led by A. Sattar Socranie, an Indian association which cooperates with the Malawi Congress.

POPULATION BREAKDOWN

Main Cities [6]

Blantyre/Limbe	29,560
Lilonkwe	4,670
Zomba	4,670

Urban-rural Distribution [7]

See footnote.

Ethnic Distribution [8]

December 1960 estimate

European	9,500
Asian and Colored	13,200
African	2,840,000

Of the last named, the Chewa represented 28%, Nguru 19%, Nyanja 15%, Yao 14%, and Ngoni 9%.

Religious Affiliation

The African population is about evenly divided between Christians and Muslims.

Languages

Myanja is the language of education and a lingua franc throughout the country. Tumbula and Yao are also recognized as media in the areas where they are spoken. English is the official language.

Sex Distribution
Total data not available. See footnote 7.

Age Distribution
Total data not available. See footnote 7.

SOCIAL DATA

Education [9]
African

TABLE I
1960

	Schools	Enrollment	Teachers
Junior primary			
Government	10	3,301	32
Aided	843	128,153	3,064
Unaided	2,064	130,300	3,156
Senior primary			
Government	2	204	5
Aided	235	21,639	591
Unaided	27	1,566	148
Secondary			
Government	3	285	19
Aided	16	991	58
Unaided	5	225	19
Vocational and technical			
Government	7	114	12
Aided	16	188	11
Unaided	14	162	39
Teachers' training			
Government	4	138	12
Aided	18	519	61
Unaided	1	27	3

In 1958, 50.5% of children between the ages of 5 and 14 were at school.

Expenditure 1960—£1,018,417 (1952—£246,000).

Health and Social Services

VITAL STATISTICS [10]

Available only for Europeans per 1,000

1958

Birth rate	37.3
Death rate	4.1
Infant mortality rate	21.5

MAIN DISEASES

Malaria, bilharziasis, hookworm, and relapsing fever.

HEALTH SERVICES

For the administration of the services see under Federal Section.

TABLE II
1959

	Beds
3 Government hospitals for Europeans	51
19 Government hospitals for Africans	1,383
At various government hospitals for Asian and Colored	39
1 Mental hospital	208
1 Leprosarium	296
Mission hospitals (number unknown)	1,351
96 Rural government dispensaries	
7 Health units	

SOCIAL WELFARE SERVICES

There are 4 Social Development Officers and 1 Social Development Assistant to coordinate the activities of government and voluntary organizations in welfare work. The latter are represented on the Nyasaland Council of Social Service. The Nyasaland Society for the Blind runs a rural training center at Mlanje.

ECONOMY

Nyasaland is extremely underdeveloped. It is almost entirely an agricultural country. Tobacco, tea, and tung are grown in elevated areas and food crops and cotton in the low-lying areas. The production of commercial crops is in the hands of European farmers, but Africans produce most of the cotton and fire-cured tobacco. Some secondary industry has appeared since the war, mainly in the Blantyre area, but is still on a small scale.

Transport and Communications

WATERWAYS

Steamship services are run on Lake Nyasa.

PORTS

There are no sizable ports on the Lake.

ROADS

Total road mileage is 5,152, of which just over 100 miles are bituminized.

RAILWAYS

The railroads are run by Nyasaland Railways Ltd. and its associated companies, which are all private undertakings. The only line runs south, from Salima on Lake Nyasa to the Portuguese port of Beira, where connection is made with rail services to Rhodesia. There are 289 miles of permanent way within the territory.

AIRWAYS

Airfields are at Blantyre and Lilongwe, and air services run to the Rhodesias and to East Africa. There are 12 minor airfields; at 8 of these Central African Airways operates an internal schedule service.

POSTS, TELECOMMUNICATIONS, AND BROADCASTING [11]

In 1959 Nyasaland had 57 post offices and 113 postal agencies. In the same year there were 4,736 telephones. Nyasaland is served by the Federal Broadcasting Corporation, which has stations in Lusaka and Salisbury.

Resources and Trade

MAIN EXPORTS   MAIN IMPORTS   VALUE OF TRADE

See under Federal Section.

MARKETING COOPERATIVE SOCIETIES

For marketing see under Federal Section. At the end of 1958 there were some 88 cooperative societies with a total membership of 7,700. The majority were producer societies for dairy produce, coffee, and rice.

LIVESTOCK

1958 estimate

Cattle	343,000
Sheep and goats	475,000
Pigs	83,000

Some meat and nearly all butter and cheese are imported.

Industry

MANUFACTURES

Soap, cigarettes, furniture, cement, clothing, and other articles are manufactured in Nyasaland. Brickmaking is a well-established industry.

MINING

In 1958 the mining and export of iron ore from deposits near Blantyre was begun. Steps are being taken to exploit limestone. The Geological Survey Department has discovered asbestos, copper, and mica.

POWER

There is a small thermal station in Blantyre. Installed capacity on June 30, 1958, was 8 mw.

Finance

CURRENCY

Federal currency is maintained on a par with the £ sterling and is issued by the Bank of Rhodesia and Nyasaland.

BANKING

See under Federal Section.

BUDGET [12]

In £ millions   1960/61
                          Revenue   6.3
                          Expenditure   6.3

A considerable amount of the revenue is received from the federal government as the Nyasaland share of federal income tax collected throughout the Federation, and also from a territorial surcharge of 20% on the federal income tax which is chargeable on incomes earned in Nyasaland.

DEVELOPMENT PLAN [13]

For Federal Plan see under Federal Section.
Capital Development Plan 1957/61, over £12 million.

Main sources	C. W. & D. grants	£1,386,000
	Loans	£7,420,000
	Local sources	£2,566,000

Allocations: Development of natural resources, housing, roads, and bridges.

LABOR

The Nyasaland labor force is continually moving between the cash and subsistent sectors of the economy. After a short period of work for employers, either in Nyasaland or outside the territory, most Nyasas return to cultivate their own land. At times of peak employment in the money sector, the labor force is estimated at 160,000, the majority being employed in agriculture. Migrant laborers (mainly males), seek work outside the territory in Southern and Northern Rhodesia and South Africa. In 1958 it was estimated that about 160,-000 were absent.

Labor is organized only in the relatively few nonagricultural undertakings. In 1958 there were 9 unions with a total membership of 1,000.

Labor legislation covers such matters as movement of migrant laborers, supervision of contracts, conditions of employment, workmen's compensation, and wage rates.

NYASALAND NOTES

1   Unless otherwise stated, information obtained from Fact Sheets on the U.K. Dependencies, Reference Division, U.K. Central Office of Information No. R 4250, *Nyasaland*, August 1959.

2   Federation of Rhodesia and Nyasaland: Central Statistical Office, *Monthly Digest of Statistics*, Salisbury, March 1961, p. 1.

3   U.K.: Advisory Commission on the Review of the Constitution of the Federation of Rhodesia and Nyasaland Report: Appendix VI: *Survey of Developments Since 1953*, H.M.S.O., *Cmnd. 1149*, London, 1960, p. 330.

4   U.K.: Cultural Office, *Report of the Nyasaland Constitutional Conference*, H.M.S.O., *Cmnd. 1132*, London, August 1960.

5   R. Segal, *Political Africa*, Stevens & Sons Ltd., London, 1961, pp. 389–93.

6   U.K.: *Nyasaland 1959* (annual report) H.M.S.O., London, 1959, p. 147.

7   Breakdown figures for the African population cannot be used for computations of this kind since they either limit themselves to taxpayers or only those in employment. See for example Federation of Rhodesia and Nyasaland, *Report of an Economic Survey of Nyasaland 1958/59*, Government Publication, pp. 46–49, or U.K.: *Cmnd.*, *1149*, *op. cit.*, p. 330, Table 31.

8   Federation of Rhodesia and Nyasaland: *Monthly Digest of Statistics*, *op. cit.*, p. 1.

9   Nyasaland Protectorate: *Annual Report of the Education Department for the Year Ended December 31, 1960*, Government Printer, Zomba, 1961, p. 37; Table 1, p. 38; Table 2, p. 43; Table VII; also U.N. Economic Commission for Africa, UNESCO: *Final Report of the Conference of African States on the Development of Education in Africa*, Addis Ababa, May 15–25, 1961, "Outline of a Plan for African Educational Development," p. 7, Table 1; UNESCO/ED/181.

10 Federation of Rhodesia and Nyasaland: *Annual Report on the Public Health of the Federation of Rhodesia and Nyasaland for the Year 1958*, Government Printer, Salisbury, 1959, pp. 4–5 for the 1948 and 1958 figures.

11 U.K.: *Cmnd. 1149*, *op. cit.*, pp. 467–69.

12 Nyasaland Protectorate: *Estimates 1960/61*, Government Printer, 1960, p. i.

13 U.K.: Colonial Office, *The Colonial Territories 1960–1961*, H.M.S.O., *Cmnd. 1407*, London, 1961, p. 120.

Northern Rhodesia[1]

AREA: *208,130 sq. m.*

POPULATION:[2] *2,460,000 (1960 estimate)*

Density:[3] *8 per sq. m.*

GEOGRAPHY

The greater part of Northern Rhodesia is flat or undulating, with elevations varying from 3,000 to 5,000 feet above sea level. In the northeast, the Muchinga Mountains rise to about 8,000 feet. Lake Bangweulu and the swamps at its southern end cover an area of 3,800 miles, and there are many other lakes. There are three seasons—a cool, dry season from May to August; a hot, dry season from September to November; and a wet, warm season from December to April. Temperatures vary from 60 to 80 degrees F. in the cool season, and from 80 to 90 degrees F. in the hot season. Rainfall is heaviest in the north, where about 50 inches fall annually. This amount decreases to 20–30 inches in the south.

HISTORICAL SKETCH

The earliest known contacts with Europe occurred in 1798, when a Portuguese expedition explored as far as the shores of Lake Mweru. In 1855 Dr. Livingstone discovered the Victoria Falls, and in 1889 the British South Africa Company was granted a royal charter over the area. Toward the end of the century, the company's administration of the territories north of the Zambezi was consolidated, and in 1911 they were amalgamated under the designation of Northern Rhodesia. In 1924 the British Crown assumed the administration of the area; a Governor was appointed and Legislative and Executive Councils were established. In 1953 the territory joined the Federation of Rhodesia and Nyasaland.

GOVERNMENT

Present Status
British protectorate.

Constitution
1961

The Legislative Council consists of a Speaker and 30 members, of whom 6 are officials and 2 nominated by the Governor. The remaining 22 are elected—12 by "ordinary" constituencies with a predominantly European electorate, 6 by "special" constituencies with a predominantly African electorate, 2 by the regrouped "ordinary" constituencies and reserved for Africans, and 2 by the regrouped "special" constituencies and reserved for Europeans. The Executive Council consists of 4 official members and 6 unofficial members (2 Africans) nominated by the Governor after consultation with the member of the Legislative Council most likely to command the support of the majority of elected members.

Franchise [4]

B (lower) roll—open to voters of all races. Qualifications: citizenship of the U.K. and Colonies, 21 years of age, resident in the Federation, having either property to the value of £250 or income of £120 for 1 year before enrollment, and literacy qualifications in English or the ability to complete, in the vernacular, the enrollment application form; or ability to complete in the vernacular the enrollment application form and a member of *one* of the following categories: Hereditary Councilors, Departmental Councilors to Native Authorities, and other members of Native Authorities, members of Native Courts, headmen of registered villages, pensioners, ex-servicemen, registered peasants or improved farmers, and the wives of persons so qualified. In 1961 it was estimated that the number of eligible Africans was about 70,000.

A (upper) roll—ability to write English, 21 years of age, citizen of the U.K. and Colonies, resident of the Federation for 2 years, and either 4 years secondary education and income of £300 per annum or property of £500; or primary education and income of £480 per annum or property of £1,000; or income of £720 per annum or property of £1,500.

Local Government
There are Native Authorities in African areas. In the towns there are 3 municipal councils, 13 management boards, and 8 mine-townships management boards. In addition there are 6 townships occupied only by Africans under African management boards. The major local authorities have a majority of elected members.

Political Parties [5]
United Federal Party (UFP), led by John Roberts.
Central African Party.
Dominican Party.
Northern Rhodesia African National Congress, led by H. Nkumbula.
United National Independence Party (UNIP), led by Kenneth Kaunda.
Northern Rhodesia Liberal Party, led by Sir John Moffat.
The Rhodesia Reformed Party, led by John Gaunt.

POPULATION BREAKDOWN

Main Cities [6]
1958 estimate (Europeans and Africans only)

Lusaka (capital)	72,000
Kitwe	81,300
Livingstone	23,900
Luanshya-Roan	50,980
Broken Hill	29,400
Chingola	26,218
Mufilara	51,100
Ndola	83,800

Urban-rural Distribution [7]
In 1958 over 19% of the total African and European population lived in towns of 10,000 or more inhabitants; over 17% of the African population and over 77% of the European population.

Ethnic Distribution [8]

Dec. 31, 1960, estimate

European	77,000
Asian	8,400
Colored	2,200
African	2,135,647

of which the main tribal groups were:

Bemba	179,756
Chewa	126,027
Nsenga	96,402
Tonga	242,866
Ngoni	87,878

Religious Affiliation

Not available.

Languages

Bemba, Lozi, Luvale, Tonga, and Nyanja are the main languages used for educational and administrative purposes. English is the official language.

Sex Distribution [9]

1951 census

	Male	Female
European	20,076 (54.1%)	17,003 (45.9%)
Colored	579 (52.0%)	533 (48.0%)
Asian	1,672 (66.2%)	852 (33.8%)
African (1960 figures)	1,078,741 (50.5%)	1,056,906 (49.5%)

Age Distribution [10]

1951 census

	Unknown	Under 19	20–49	50+
European	71	13,289	20,195	3,524

According to figures obtained in 1960, the African population was made up of 1,220,349 children and 915,298 adults.

SOCIAL DATA

Education [11]

TABLE I

1960

African	Enrollment	Teachers
1,543 Primary schools	233,667 }	5,694
460 Upper primary schools	53,869 }	
26 Secondary schools	2,599	143
13 Teacher-training colleges	1,156	106
39 Technical and vocational schools	1,445	136

In 1959/60 about 60% of the children of primary-school age in rural areas were attending school. In 1958 there were 32 students studying in the U.K. and at the Rhodesian University. Expenditure, £2,733,-400 (£33,000 in 1938).

1958

European

     53 Government schools

      2 Government-aided schools

      8 Private schools

Indian

     12 Government schools

Colored

      3 Government schools

Technical education is provided by the Copper Belt Technical Foundation and the Federal Government. For higher education see under Federal Section.

Health and Social Services

VITAL STATISTICS [12]

Available for the European population only (*per 1000*).

	1958	1960
Birth rate	37.2	30.0
Crude death rate	4.2	4.0
Infant mortality rate	20.8	—

MAIN DISEASES

Smallpox, poliomyelitis, malaria, tuberculosis, leprosy, bilharziasis, trypanosomiasis, and venereal disease.

HEALTH SERVICES [13]

For the administration of the services, see under Federal Section.

TABLE II

		Beds
12	European hospitals	500
16	Government African hospitals	2,501
68	Medical missions	2,034
6	Mine hospitals	1,553
134	Rural health centers	—
42	Urban health clinics	—

There were 295 medical practitioners by the end of 1958.

SOCIAL WELFARE SERVICES

The Northern Rhodesia Council of Social Services coordinates the efforts of government, local authorities, and voluntary organizations in social welfare work. The Department of Welfare and Probation Services, serving all communities, is concerned with the care of the aged, relief of distress, care and protection of minors, the treatment of delinquents, and the care and assistance of handicapped persons, particularly the blind.

ECONOMY

The prosperity of Northern Rhodesia is largely dependent upon its modern copper-mining industry, which supplies over 90% of the territory's exports and the greater part of the government revenue. Since World War II there has been some development of secondary industry and agricultural production.

Transport and Communications

WATERWAYS

The Zambezi River Transport Service Board of Control operates a passenger-and-goods service (by road and river) along the Zambezi from Livingstone to Mongu.

PORTS

The small port of Mpulungu on Lake Tanganyika serves the extreme north of the territory.

ROADS

There are 22,210 miles of roads, of which 545 are bituminized.

RAILROADS

A main line runs from Livingstone to Ndola, with branch lines from the latter to the copper belt. Total permanent way within the territory is 655 miles.

AIRWAYS

There is an international airport at Livingstone and national airports are found at Lusaka, Ndola, and Kasama. Subsidiary airports serve most of the outlying districts.

POSTS, TELECOMMUNICATIONS, AND BROADCASTING [14]

In 1959 Northern Rhodesia had 49 post offices and 71 postal agencies; a direct telegraph connection exists with Lourenço Marques. In the same year it had 18,828 telephones and direct services to Cape Town, Durban, and Elizabethville.

The Central African Broadcasting Service became a statutory corporation in 1958 with headquarters in Lusaka. It runs two stations weekly. It provides 88 hours of service to Africans each week in 8 vernaculars and English. It is estimated that 100,000 Africans own radio sets and some 40,000 tune in to Lusaka at peak hours.

Resources and Trade

MAIN EXPORTS   MAIN IMPORTS   VALUE OF TRADE

See under Federal Section.

MARKETING AND COOPERATIVE SOCIETIES

For marketing, see under Federal Section.

In 1957 there were 21 European cooperative societies and 180 African societies, with a total membership of 27,000. The African movement is expanding, and 36 new agricultural producers' societies were registered in 1957. Thrift societies are becoming increasingly important in the urban areas.

LIVESTOCK

The cattle are mostly African-owned.

1958 estimate

Cattle	1,084,000
Sheep and goats	172,000
Pigs	63,000

Industry

MANUFACTURES

Apart from these those industries connected with the production and processing of copper, there are firms engaged in iron and steel production, saw milling, wood and joinery manufacturing, tire-retreading, food-and-drink processing, the manufacture of cement and cement products. A government Industrial Loans Board assists industrial development.

MINING

Mining, the main industry of the country, employs about 8,000 Europeans and 47,000 Africans. The copper belt is the fourth largest source of copper in the world. Of the 6 mines, 3 are controlled by British and American interests and 3 by South African interests—the Rhodesian Selection Trust Group and the Anglo-American group, respectively. The industry is a manufacturing as well as a mining industry, with smelter and electrolytic refineries at several mine centers. Cobalt is produced in association with copper at certain copper belt mines. Zinc and lead are produced at Broken Hill.

POWER [15]

In 1960 installed capacity was 278.46 million mw. (See Southern Rhodesia for power from Kariba dam.)

Finance

CURRENCY

Federal currency is maintained on a par with £ sterling.

BANKING

See under Federal Section.

BUDGET [16]

1960/61 estimate in £'000's

Revenue	18,240
Expenditure	18,638

The main sources of revenue come from federal government imcome, tax collections, and the territorial surcharge on company-income-tax assessment.

DEVELOPMENT PLAN [17]

For federal plan, see under Federal Section.
 1959/63   Total costs £33,800,000.
  Main sources

U.K. C. D. & W. grants	£1,540,000
Loans	13,220,000
Local sources	16,040,000

  Main allocations

Loan to local authorities	£9,052,000
Law, order, and administration	4,550,000
Loans for housing	3,810,000
Public works	2,687,000
Rural development	3,218,000

LABOR

Most of the Africans are farmers producing crops for local consumption or export. About 267,400 men and women were in paid employment in 1958. The main occupations are as follows:

Mining and quarrying	42,000
Agriculture	48,000
Building and civil engineering	57,500

Trade unions may be mixed racially. There were 1 Asian, 11 European, and 11 African trade unions or associations in 1958.

Industrial relations are regulated by the Trade Union and Trade Disputes Ordinance and the Industrial Conciliation Ordinance. Legislation covers settlement of disputes, wages and conditions of service, workmen's compensation, employment of women and children, and the like.

NORTHERN RHODESIA NOTES

1   Unless otherwise stated, all information obtained from Fact Sheets on U.K. Dependencies, Reference Division, U.K. Central Office of Information, No. R. 4248, *Northern Rhodesia*, Nov. 1959.

2   Federation of Rhodesia and Nyasaland: Central Statistical Office, *Monthly Digest of Statistics*, No. 1, Salisbury, April 1961, p. 1.

3   U.K.: Advisory Commission on the Review of the Constitution of the Federation of Rhodesia and Nyasaland Report, Appendix VI; *Survey of Developments Since 1953*, H.M.S.O., Cmnd. 1149, London, Oct. 1960, p. 330.

4   All information for this section obtained from Fact Sheets on the U.K. Dependencies, British Information Services, *Northern Rhodesia*, New York, October 1961, and *Federation of Rhodesia and Nyasaland Newsletter*, # 26/61, pp. 1–1a and 10.

5   R. Segal, *Political Africa*, Stevens & Sons Ltd., London, 1961, pp. 385–89.

6   U.K.: *Cmnd. 1149, op. cit.*, p. 329.

7   *Ibid.*, figures computed from Tables 25, 28, and 29, pp. 327–29.

8   Federation of Rhodesia and Nyasaland: *Monthly Digest of Statistics*, No. 1, *op. cit.*, p. 1; Communication received from Northern Rhodesia, Information Department, Lusaka, Sept. 1961, Annexure A.

9   Northern Rhodesia: *Report on the Census of Population, 1951*, Government Printer, Lusaka, 1954, p. 44, Table 1; Communication received from Northern Rhodesia, Information Department, *op. cit.*, Annexure B.

10   Northern Rhodesia: *Report on the Census Population, 1951, op. cit.*, p. 45, Table III; Communication received from Northern Rhodesia, Information Department, *op. cit.*, Annexure B.

11   Northern Rhodesia: Ministry of African Education, *Triennial Survey*, Government Printer, Lusaka, 1961, p. 19; p. 36, Table 1; p. 37, Table II; and p. 42, Table V.

12   Federation of Rhodesia and Nyasaland: *Annual Report on the Public Health of the Federation of Rhodesia and Nyasaland for the Year 1958*, Government Printer, Salisbury, 1959, pp. 4–5; Federation of Rhodesia and Nyasaland; *Monthly Digest of Statistics, March 1961*, Central African Statistical Office, p. 2.

13   Federation of Rhodesia and Nyasaland: *Annual Report on the Federation of Rhodesia and Nyasaland for the Year 1958, op. cit.*, p. 23.

14   U.K.: *Cmnd. 1149, op. cit.*, pp. 467–69.

15   Federation of Rhodesia and Nyasaland: *Monthly Digest of Statistics*, No. 1, *op. cit.*, pp. 13–14.

16   Northern Rhodesia: *Estimates of Revenue and Expenditure Including Capital Expenditure for the Year, July 1, 1960 to June 30, 1961*, Government Printer, Lusaka, 1960, p. 5; *The Colonial Office List 1961*, H.M.S.O., London, 1961, p. 134.

17   U.K.: Colonial Office, *The Colonial Territories 1960–1961*, H.M.S.O., Cmnd. 1407, London, 1961, p. 120.

Southern Rhodesia

AREA:[1] *150,333 sq. m.*
POPULATION:[2] *3,110,000 (1960 estimate)*
Density:[3] 17 per sq. m.

GEOGRAPHY [4]

Southern Rhodesia is relatively high, with 21% of the land over 4,000 feet above sea level. The low veld region, below 2,000 feet, follows a narrow strip along the Zambezi Valley and broadens in the basins of the Limpopo and Sabio rivers. Along the eastern border lies a mountainous region consisting of plateaus in the north some 7,000 feet high and the Vumba Mountains to the south. Between them lies the Umtali gap. The mean annual rainfall is 26.1 inches and temperatures range between 50 and 70 degrees F.

HISTORICAL SKETCH [5]

European contact was first made in the 16th century when Portuguese explorers reached the area. For some 300 years there was no further white contact until the coming of the great missionary-explorers, hunters, traders, and gold-seekers. In 1830 the Mashona were invaded by the off-shoots of the Zulu pressing northward, more particularly the Matabele, who eventually settled in Matabeleland. It was here that Robert Moffat, of the London Missionary Society, established his famous station in 1861. In 1888, Loben Gula, chief of the Matabele, granted the Rudd Concession over the minerals in his country, which led to the formation of the British South Africa Company in 1889. The subsequent settlement of the area by whites was resisted by the Mashona and Matabele, and final peace was not established until 1897. The territory was given its present name in 1895 and was administered by the British South Africa Company from 1890 until the grant of responsible government in 1923. A referendum was held in 1922 to decide between self-government or inclusion into the

Union of South Africa as a fifth province. By a large majority the local white settlers chose self-government. Thirty years later, again by referendum decision, Southern Rhodesia decided to join the Federation of Rhodesia and Nyasaland.

GOVERNMENT

Present Status

Self-governing colony within the British Commonwealth.

Constitution [6]

The present constitution provides for a Legislative Assembly of 65 members: 50 elected by 50 constituencies and 15 by electoral districts. The Speaker and Deputy Speaker are elected by the Assembly. A Constitutional Council, consisting of a Chairman and 11 members elected by a specially assembled electoral college, reviews all legislation passed, with the right of referring it back to the Assembly. Its membership must include at least 2 Europeans, 2 Africans, 1 Asian, 1 Colored, and 2 advocates, or attorneys, of the High Court of not less than 10 years' standing. The electoral college consists of present and past members of the Council, present and past judges of the High Court, and the President of the Council of Chiefs. A Declaration of Rights sets out 12 basic freedoms enforceable by the Constitutional Council. Executive power is vested in the Governor assisted by a Governor's Council (Cabinet) consisting of the Prime Minister and twelve ministers.

Franchise [7]

There are two rolls (A and B) for each constituency. For both rolls the following qualifications apply: citizenship, over 21 years of age, 2 years' residency in the country, literarcy in English. In addition, those on the A roll must have an income of £720 or property to the value of £1,500; or an income of £480 or property to the value of £1,000 and primary education; or an income of £300 or property to the value of £500 and 4 years secondary education; or be persons holding responsible public office, such as chiefs and headmen. B roll: either an income of £240 or an income of £120 and 2 years of secondary education unless over 30 years of age, earning £15 per month, and able to speak English.

Local Government [8]

Local government in European communities is in the hands of the elected Village Management, Town Management Boards, or Municipal Councils. In urban African areas, Native Advisory Boards operate. African rural areas are governed by Native Councils of elected and appointed members.

Political Parties [9]

United Federal Party (UFP), led by Sir Edgar Whitehead, Prime Minister.

The Dominion Party, led by W. J. Harper.

National Democratic Party (NDP), formed in January 1960 as a care-taker party for the banned African National Congress (ANC), led by Joshua Nkomo.

Central African Party (CAP), led by Garfield Todd.

In addition there are a number of minority parties such as the Confederate Party, led by Stanley Gurland, the Republican Party of Rhodesia, the Rhodesian Citizens Party, and others.

POPULATION BREAKDOWN[10]

Main Cities [11]

December 1958 estimate

Salisbury	257,000
Bulawayo	189,000
Umtali	33,000
Gwelo	30,700
Gatooma	10,000
Que Que	11,200
Fort Victoria	10,700

Urban-rural Distribution [12]

In 1958, 20% of the total African and European population lived in towns of 10,000 or more inhabitants; 15% of the total African population and 73% of the total European population. (Asian figures are not included.)

Ethnic Distribution [13]
1960 estimate

European	225,000
Colored	10,500
Asian	6,200
African	2,870,000

The two main tribal divisions are the Shona and Ndebele.

Religious Affiliation [14]
Not available for Africans.

Languages [15]
English is the official language. There are two main African language groups: those speaking dialects of Sindebele (21%), and those speaking dialects of Chishona (79%).

Age Distribution [16]

	Under 1 year	1 year to puberty	Over puberty
African only	3.9%	43.2%	52.9%

Sex Distribution [17]

	Male	Female
European (1956 census)	91,020 (53.3%)	85,280 (46.7%)
African (1953/55 demographic sample surveys)	49.9%	50.1%

SOCIAL DATA

Education [18]
For higher education, see Federal Section.

TABLE I

1959	Enrollment (1958)	Teachers
154 (127 primary, 27 secondary) European government schools	40,898	1,738
18 Asian and Colored government schools	3,882	—
37 Private European schools	6,291	—
6 Private Asian and Colored schools	1,359	—

TABLE I—Continued

	Enrollment (1959)	Teachers
Salisbury Polytechnic	1,629	
Bulawayo Technical College	752	

African education (responsibility of territorial government)

		(1960 estimate)
2,700	Primary aided schools	446,000
50	Government primary schools	33,800
	Upper primary aided schools	43,000
	Upper government aided school	9,800

		(1959)
18	Aided secondary schools	2,386
5	Government secondary schools	914
9	Aided technical and vocational schools	510
4	Government technical and vocational schools	896

There are a number of teacher-training institutions, the majority of which are run by missionary societies.

Teachers 1959	African	European
Mission schools	10,461	389
Government schools	873	103
Other schools	464	7

In 1959, 83.5% of the African children between the ages of 5–14 were at school.

Expenditure on African education, 1959: £2,807,000.

Health and Social Services

VITAL STATISTICS [19]
Per 1,000

	1958
European only	
Birth rate	26.5
Crude death rate	6.2
Infant mortality rate	22.6

MAIN DISEASES

Smallpox, malaria, bilharziasis, poliomyelitis, tuberculosis, leprosy, trypanosomiasis, relapsing fever, disease of the eye, and venereal disease.

HEALTH SERVICES [20]

For general administration see Federal Section.

TABLE II
1959

Government-maintained
All races

		Beds
42	General hospitals	3,146
15	Maternity hospitals	435
4	Mental hospitals	760

Europeans only

1	Hospital for nervous disorders	23
1	Home for retarded children	80

Africans only

2	Leprosaria	1,294
2	Tuberculosis hospitals	321
92	Clinics	4,256

In addition there are 56 missionary institutions.
In 1960 there were 698 medical practitioners in the country.

SOCIAL WELFARE SERVICES [21]

The Department of Social Welfare concerns itself with social welfare for all races, covering such services as: relief of distress, grants to institutions, treatment of inebriates, remand homes, and probation hostels. Numerous voluntary organizations, clubs, municipal organizations, and employers organizations promote social welfare services of various kinds.

ECONOMY[22]

The economy is diversified.

Most of Southern Rhodesia's domestic output in the money economy is contributed by secondary industry.

Transport and Communications

WATERWAYS

The construction of the Kariba Dam created the second largest man-made lake in the world.

PORTS

None.

ROADS [23]

There are 1,384 miles of road which are the responsibility of the federal government. In addition, Southern Rhodesia has 3,234 miles of main roads for which the territorial government is responsible, and 13,146 miles of native area roads for which the Native Affairs department is responsible.

RAILROADS [24]

The two Rhodesias are served by the Rhodesia Railways, which connect with the South African Railways at Mafeking. In 1957 the total mileage was 2,735. In 1955 an important 400-mile-long line was opened, linking the Midlands of Southern Rhodesia with Lourenço Marques in Mozambique.

AIRWAYS [25]

The Central African Airways Corporation operates a system of air services within the Federation, with links to South Africa, East Africa, Mozambique, and London. There is an international airport at Salisbury.

POSTS, TELECOMMUNICATIONS, AND BROADCASTING [26]

The federal government is responsible for postal, telegraph, telephone, radio, and post office savings bank services. In 1959 there were 198 post offices and agencies in Southern Rhodesia and 66,438 telephones. The Federal Broadcasting Corporation serves Europeans throughout the Federation from Salisbury and provides radio services in the vernaculars for Africans from Lusaka. Commercial broadcasting was introduced in 1959, television in 1960.

Resources and Trade

MAIN EXPORTS
MAIN IMPORTS
VALUE OF TRADE
    See under Federal Section.

MARKETING AND COOPERATIVE SOCIETIES [27]
    For marketing, see under Federal Section.
    In 1959 there were 12 African agricultural cooperatives with a membership of 765.

1959 African-owned

Cattle	2,039,401
Sheep	154,484
Goats	402,788
Pigs	47,142

Industry

MANUFACTURES [29]
    The manufacturing industry makes the most important contribution to domestic product. The main manufacturing groups are iron and steel, metal products, textiles, chemicals, and food preparations. In addition, pulp, board, and wattle extracts, a copper-smelting refinery, fruit-canning, and ferrochrome industries are being developed.

MINING [30]
    The following minerals are mined: gold, asbestos, chrome, coal, copper, beryl, tungsten, lithium, tin concentrate, and tin metal. Several companies have been granted exclusive prospecting rights to explore for gold, copper, nickel, and other minerals.

POWER [31]
    The Kariba Dam, opened in 1960, has a capacity at present of 100,-000 kw. (estimated capacity is 12,000 mw.). The total installed capacity in the country in December 1960 was 801.38 mw. The consumption was 1,647.6 kwh.

Finance

CURRENCY

Federal currency is issued by the Bank of Rhodesia and Nyasaland and maintained at par with sterling.

BANKING

See under Federal Section.

BUDGET [32]

1960/61 estimate in £'000's

Revenue	21,853
Expenditure	22,338

The main sources of revenue are income-tax receipts and customs duties.

DEVELOPMENT PLAN [33]

1957/61—Total cost—£36,834,000

Sources	£'000's
Revenue account	7,164
Revenue contributions to loan account	5,800
Loan recoveries	7,200
Balance to be borrowed	16,670

The development plan was revised in 1958 and total expenditure lowered to £34,974,000.

Allocations are being made to local authorities, housing, roads, and bridges, agriculture and land husbandry, water development and irrigation, forestry, Kariba bush clearing, African education, administrative buildings, and equipment for the public works department.[34]

LABOR

The following were the estimated employment figures in 1958:[35]

	European	African
Agriculture and forestry	4,600	230,000
Mining and quarrying	2,800	53,000
Manufacturing	14,600	81,000
Construction	9,100	60,000
Electricity and water	1,300	5,000
Commerce	21,500	31,000
Transport and communications	9,500	14,000

Domestic service	—		71,578⎫	
Other services	18,000	139,000	46,818⎬	1956
Other activities	1,200		4,000	
TOTAL	82,600		617,000	

The total number of registered trade unions at the end of 1960 was 32, with a membership of 25,565. Membership is nonracial.[36]

Legislation covers such matters as registration and regulation of trade unions, prevention and settlement of disputes, regulation of conditions of employment, apprenticeship, health and safety, workmen's compensation, and wages.[37]

SOUTHERN RHODESIA NOTES

1   U.K.: *The Commonwealth Relations Office List 1959*, H.M.S.O., London, 1959, p. 197.

2   Federation of Rhodesia and Nyasaland (F.R.N.): Central Statistical Office, *Monthly Digest of Statistics*, No. 1, Salisbury, April 1961, p. 1, Table 1.

3   U.K.: Advisory Commission on the Review of the Federation of Rhodesia and Nyasaland Report, Appendix VI, *Survey of Developments Since 1953*, H.M.S.O., Cmnd. 1149, London, 1960, p. 330.

4   *Ibid.*, p. 368; *The Commonwealth Relations Office List 1959*, *op. cit.*, p. 197; Headquarters Quartermaster Research and Engineering Command, U.S. Army Technical Report EP-94, Canal Zone Analogs v: *Analog of Canal Zone Climate in South Central Africa and Madagascar*, Natick, Mass., July 1958, Figures 3 and 5.

5   U.K.: *Cmnd. 1149, op. cit.*, pp. 197–99.

6   Secretary of State for Commonwealth Relations: *Southern Rhodesia Constitution*, H.M.S.O., Cmnd. 1400, London, June 1961, pp. 4–21; *Federation of Rhodesia and Nyasaland Newsletter*, No. 24/61, p. 1.

7   U.K.: *Cmnd. 1400, op. cit.*, pp. 27–29; U.K.: *Cmnd. 1149, op. cit.*, pp. 33–36; *Federation of Rhodesia and Nyasaland Newsletter*, *op. cit.*, p. 1.

8   U.K.: *Cmnd. 1149, op. cit.*, pp. 94–99.

9   R. Segal, *Political Africa*, Stevens & Sons Ltd., London, 1961, pp. 393–98.

10   Official demographic information in Southern Rhodesia is scientifically collected and considered reliable. *Vide* F. Lorimer, *Demographic Information on Tropical Africa*, Boston University Press, 1961, pp. 174–81.

11   U.K.: *Cmnd. 1149, op. cit.*, p. 328.

12   *Ibid.*, percentages computed from pp. 327 and 328, Tables 25, 26, and 27.

13 F.R.N.: *Monthly Digest of Statistics, op. cit.*, p. 1, Table 1; Communication received from the Central Statistical Office, Rhodesia and Nyasaland, Salisbury, Sept. 1961.

14 Communication received from the Central Statistical Office, *op. cit.*

15 *Ibid.*

16 *Ibid.*, distribution as found in the 1953–1955 Demographic Sample Surveys of the Central Statistical Office, Rhodesia and Nyasaland.

17 S. H. Steinberg (Ed.), *The Statesman's Yearbook 1961*, Macmillan & Co., Ltd., London, 1961, p. 294; Communication received from the Central Statistical Office, *op. cit.*

18 U.K.: *Cmnd. 1149, op. cit.* pp. 168–81; also U.N. Economic Commission for Africa, UNESCO: *Final Report of the Conference of African States on the Development of Education in Africa*, Addis Ababa, May 15–25, 1961, "Outline of a Plan for African Educational Development," p. 7, Table I, UNESCO/ED/181; also, U.K.: *Cmnd. 1149, op. cit.*, pp. 151–56.

19 F.R.N.: *Annual Report on the Public Health of the Federation of Rhodesia and Nyasaland for the Year 1958*, Government Printer, Salisbury, 1959, pp. 4–5.

20 Federation of Rhodesia and Nyasaland: *Handbook to the Federation of Rhodesia and Nyasaland*, Government Printer, Salisbury, 1960, p. 778; also communication received from Office for Rhodesia and Nyasaland, Washington, D.C., August 1961.

21 U.K.: *Cmnd. 1149, op. cit.*, pp. 263–66.

22 *Ibid.*, pp. 306, para. 13, 330, and 444, Table 89.

23 *Ibid.*, p. 453.

24 S. H. Steinberg, 1959, *op. cit.*, p. 286.

25 *Ibid.*

26 *Ibid.*; U.K.: *Cmnd. 1149, op. cit.*, pp. 467–68.

27 U.K.: *Cmnd. 1149, op. cit.*, p. 402, para. 156.

28 S. H. Steinberg, 1961, *op. cit.*, p. 297.

29 U.K.: *Cmnd. 1149, op. cit.*, pp. 444–45.

30 *Ibid.*, pp. 430–31.

31 F.R.N.: *Monthly Digest of Statistics, op. cit.*, p. 13, Table 12; p. 14, Table 13.

32 *Ibid.*, p. 53.

33 Southern Rhodesia: Southern Rhodesia Treasury, *Development Plan 1957/61*, June 1957, p. 9, Table 1; p. 11, Table 2.

34 F.R.N.: *The Handbook to the Federation of Rhodesia and Nyasaland, op. cit.*, 1950, p. 864.

35 U.K.: *Cmnd. 1149, op. cit.*, pp. 338–39, Tables 39 and 40.

36 Communication received from the Department of Labor, Salisbury, Southern Rhodesia, Dec. 21, 1961.

37 U.K.: *Cmnd. 1149, op. cit.*, pp. 340–43.

Rwanda and Burundi
(*Formerly* RUANDA-URUNDI)

AREA:[1] *54,172 sq. km.*
POPULATION:[2] *4,425,500 (1956 estimate)*
Density: ±81.5 per sq. km.

GEOGRAPHY [3]

Rwanda and Burundi are divided in a north-south direction by the Nile-Congo mountain watershed, with a volcanic range in Rwanda. The highest peaks reach 2,600 meters in Burundi and 3,000 meters in Rwanda. In its southern region this mountain range is separated from Lake Tanganyika by an alluvial plain, the Tanganyika Plain, whose average width is 3 km. Farther north this plain widens to an average width of 20 km. where it is known as the Ruzizi Plain. Rwanda and Burundi have a Sudanese climate characterized by a dryness varying according to altitude and latitude. The two plains have a tropical climate with an average temperature of 70 degrees F. and little rain.

HISTORICAL SKETCH [4]

The area, known as Ruanda-Urundi until the granting of independence in 1962, was opened up to European penetration toward the second half of the 19th century, when Stanley and Livingstone sought the source of the Ruzizi River in 1871. They were followed by a number of German and English explorers who opened up Urandi and the region around Lake Kivu. The White Fathers were the first to settle permanently in the area in the 1890's. German interests began with the establishment of a post at Usumbura in 1899. Until World War I the area was administered as part of German East Africa. Under a League of Nations mandate, Ruanda-Urundi was placed under Belgian control; in 1946 it was placed under the Trusteeship system of the United Nations. Ruanda-Urundi received its independence in 1962.

GOVERNMENT

Present Status

Ruanda-Urundi was transformed into two independent states on July 1, 1962: Rwanda, a republic, and the Kingdom of Burundi. Both were admitted to United Nations membership on July 27, 1962.

Constitution [5]

On January 1, 1962 the Belgian Government granted separate transitional constitutions to Ruanda and Urundi, allowing a large measure of internal autonomy, but reserved control over foreign affairs, security, and finance. Ruanda was constituted a republic; it has an elected President-Premier and a legislative assembly—the Territorial House—consisting of 44 elected members. Urundi was established as a constitutional monarchy, with the Mwami as Head of State. Its Territorial House is composed of 64 elected members. Upon the granting of independence, the powers reserved by the Belgian Government were transferred to Rwanda and Burundi, both of which retained the constitutional structure given them during the transitional period.

The President-Premier of Rwanda is Grégoire Kayibanda; Burundi's monarch is Mwami Mwumbutsa IV and her Prime Minister is André Muhirwa.

Franchise

Universal adult franchise in both nations.

Local Government [6]

In the preindependence period, each territory was divided into a number of circumscriptions called "prefectures" in Urundi and "provinces" in Ruanda. The "sous chefferies" and "centres coutumiers" were being transformed into municipalities. Postindependence information on local government is not available.

Political Parties [7]

Rwanda has four major parties:

Parmehutu (Republican Democratic Movement), led by the President and holding 35 of the 44 seats in the legislative assembly; Aprosoma (The Association for the Advancement of the Masses), which holds 2; UNARA (The National Rwanda Union), which hold 7 seats; and RADER, which was unable to secure any seats.

Burundi has 24 parties; however, Uprona (Union and National Progress of Burundi), with 58 out of 64 seats in the Territorial House, is clearly the most important. The remaining 6 seats are held by the Front Commun (United Front), led by the Parti Démocrate Chrétien (P.D.C.).

POPULATION BREAKDOWN

Main Cities [8]

Usumbura	47,327
Kigali	4,055
Kitega	3,212
Astrida	2,972

Urban-rural Distribution

Usumbura is the only city with a population of 10,000 or more inhabitants. One percent of the total population live in urban areas.

Ethnic Distribution [9]

1956	
European (73% Belgian)	6,486
Asian (41% Arab)	2,491
Mixed blood	967
African	4,415,595
Of which	
Batwa	1.32%
Bahutu	83.73%
Batutsi	14.95%

Religious Affiliation [10]

Of the African population, 2,231,662 are Christians.

Languages [11]

The Twa, Hutu, and Tutsi speak the same agglutinative Bantu language; English; and French, which is the official language.

Sex Distribution [12]

	Male	Female
African	2,032,221 (46.1%)	2,383,374 (53.9%)
European	3,597 (55.4%)	2,889 (44.6%)
Asian	1,414 (56.8%)	1,077 (43.2%)
Mixed blood	477 (49.4%)	490 (50.6%)

Age Distribution [13]

	Children	Adult	Aged
African	48.93%	42.21%	8.86%

	Under 15	15–45	45+
European	1,974	3,405	1,107

The age-breakdown figures for Asians and mixed bloods are not available.

SOCIAL DATA

Education [14]

TABLE I

African		Enrollment
10	Primary government schools	2,490
2,684	State-aided private primary schools	233,625
1	Secondary government school	271
8	Private schools for apprentices	391
1	Government school for tutors	61
15	Private schools for tutors	1,515
1	Government teacher-training college	36
3	Government specialized schools	392
29	Private specialized schools	1,469
13	Technical and vocational schools	±500
	Metropolitan	
9	Government schools	525
6	Private schools	604

These are predominantly attended by Europeans, though Africans do attend in small numbers.

In 1958, 35.5% of children between the ages of 5 and 14 were at school. There were 33 students studying abroad. In 1959 there was a total of 7,001 teachers in the territory.

In 1959 the expenditure on education was $6.62 million, 23% of the ordinary budget.

Health and Social Services

VITAL STATISTICS [15]

Only the birth rate for the African population is available and stood at 51.5% in 1956 for both Rwanda and Burundi.

MAIN DISEASES [16]

Malaria, dysentery, ankylostomiasis.

HEALTH SERVICES [17]

TABLE II

		Beds
18	Government hospitals	2,266
15	Mission hospitals	962
3	Company hospitals	245
87	Government dispensaries	671
25	Mission dispensaries	222
4	Company dispensaries	104
9	Private dispensaries	—
132	Maternity and child protection centers	1,073
2	Tuberculosis sanatoria	300
1	Leprosarium	807

There are 443 doctors, i.e., 1 doctor per ±10,000 inhabitants.

SOCIAL WELFARE SERVICES [18]

Employees of government, local authorities, industrial, and agricultural enterprises are covered by a system of old age, invalid, and pension schemes, accident and illness compensation, maternity allowances, and family indemnities. Government, local authorities, and private organizations provide assistance to indigents. In addition, 3 social centers, situated at Usumbura, Astrida, and Nyundo, provide activities for women; and a Social and Educational Center at Usumbura provides activities for adults and youth.

ECONOMY [19]

Stock raising and agriculture are the principal economic activities of Rwanda and Burundi. There are a number of small mining undertakings.

Transport and Communications

WATERWAYS [20]

There are no navigable rivers. Lakes Kivu and Tanganyika are used for transport purposes.

PORTS [21]

Usumbura is the only port and is situated on Lake Tanganyika. In 1956 it handled a total of 268,739 tons of freight.

ROADS [22]

In 1956 there were 345.3 km. of principal asphalt roads, 2,274.2 km. of secondary roads, 6,118.5 km. of rough roads often impassable during the rainy season, 195.2 km. of private roads, and 2,188 km. of tracks.

RAILROADS [23]

None.

AIRWAYS [24]

There are airfields at Usumbura, Kigali, Astrida, and Kitega. The principal airport at Usumbura can accommodate DC4's and DC3's. In 1955, 39 airfields for helicopters were built throughout the countries.

POSTS, TELECOMMUNICATIONS, AND BROADCASTING [25]

In 1956 there were 5 main post offices and 11 postal agencies, with 15 telegraph offices. There is an automatic telephone exchange in Usumbura and a manual exchange at Kisenyi. There were 996 telephones in 1956. Neither country has a radio station.

Resources and Trade

MAIN EXPORTS [26]

Coffee (represented about 70% of the value of export in 1958), minerals, cotton, hides and skins.

MAIN IMPORTS [27]

Steel, vehicles, fuels, iron and lead products, machines, textiles and clothing, and electric products.

VALUE OF TRADE [28]
In millions of Congolese francs

	1952	1953	1954	1955	1956
Exports and reexports	1,352.0	1,440.4	1,613.1	2,006.1	1,931.7
Imports	1,648.6	1,525.0	1,838.0	2,005.7	2,303.8

MARKETING AND COOPERATIVE SOCIETIES [29]

All products are marketed privately. In 1956 there were 1 commercial cooperative with 29 members; 3 consumer cooperatives with 1,345 members; 2 agricultural cooperatives with 7,659 members, and 4 coffee growers' cooperatives with 21,965 members.

LIVESTOCK [30]

1956

Cattle	930,024
Sheep and goats	2,097,516
Pigs	61,483

Industry

MANUFACTURES [31]

Processing industries are little developed and provide solely for local needs. Among these are oil mills, a cement factory, brick and tile factories, clothing factories, 2 aluminum factories, confectioner, soft drink factories, and a brewery.

MINING [32]

Among the minerals extracted are lead, zinc, gold and silver, columbite, and tungsten.

POWER [33]

There are no local combustible resources. There are 7 electric plants —3 hydroelectric and 4 thermal.

Finance

CURRENCY [34]

Congolese franc—50.43 equal £1 sterling; 141.05 equal $1 U.S.

BANKING [35]

Among the banks in Rwanda and Burundi are the Banque Centrale du Congo Belge, Banque Belge d'Afrique, Crédit Congolais, Krediet-bank-Congo, Banque de Paris et des Pays-Bas. The savings bank is the Caisse d'Epargne du Congo Belge et du Ruanda-Urundi.

BUDGET [36]

In millions of Congolese francs

1959

Revenue	1,011
Expenditure	841

DEVELOPMENT PLAN

1949/59 estimated total cost: 3,091.2 million francs. By December 31, 1958, 2,298 million francs had been spent, allocated as follows: [37]

Agriculture and stock raising	42%
Scientific equipment and public services	20%
Education, health, and sanitation and housing	23%
Public works and urban development	15%

LABOR

In 1956 the wage-earning population was distributed as follows: [38]

	Average
Agriculture, fishing, and forestry	25,594
Mining	20,546
Industry	5,610
Construction	14,390
Electricity, gas, water, and sanitary services	3,301
Commerce	10,982
Transport and communications	15,514
Services	22,979
Other activities	3,984
TOTAL	122,400

There are five local branches of trade-union federations linked with parent bodies in Belgium: A.F.A.C., A.P.I.C., C.G.S.L.B., C.S.C., F.G.T.B.[39]

Labor legislation sets up employers' and workers' councils and covers such matters as trade unions, conditions of work, and settlement of disputes.[40]

RWANDA AND BURUNDI NOTES

1   *Rapport sur l'Administration du Ruanda-Urundi 1956*, Imprimerie Fr. van Muysewinkel, Brussels, 1957, p. 1.

2   *Ibid.*, pp. 299, 310–12.

3   *Ibid.*, pp. 2–3.

4   *Ibid.*, p. 9.

5   Communication received from the Belgian Embassy, Washington, D.C., March 8, 1962.

6   *Ibid.*

7   *West Africa*, Harrison & Sons Ltd., London, # 2311, Sept. 16, 1961, p. 1015; # 2317, Oct. 28, 1961, p. 1191.

8   *Rapport sur l'Administration du Ruanda-Urundi 1956*, *op. cit.*, p. 4.

9   *Ibid.*, pp. 4, 7, 299, 310–12.

10   *Ibid.*, p. 171.

11   *Ibid.*, pp. 4–8; *Ruanda-Urundi*, No. 9, Sept. 1961, INFOR, Ministry for Foreign Affairs and External Trade, Brussels, p. 3.

12   *Rapport sur l'Administration du Ruanda-Urundi 1956*, *op. cit.*, pp. 301, 311–12.

13   *Ibid.*, pp. 302, 310–11.

14   *Ibid.*, pp. 479–82; *Ruanda-Urundi*, INFOR, Brussels, 1959, pp. 317–18; communication received from Belgian Embassy, Washington, D.C., Oct. 1961.

15   *Rapport* . . . *1956*, *op. cit.*, p. 307.

16   *Ibid.*, p. 230.

17   *Ibid.*, pp. 220–34, 468–69. Also, Congo Belge *Rapport Annuel de la Direction Générale des Services Médicaux du Congo Belge*, Services Médicaux, 1958, p. 2.

18   *Rapport* . . . *1956*, *op. cit.*, pp. 204–11, 464–65.

19   *Ibid.*, p. 60.

20   *Ibid.*, p. 442.

21   *Ibid.*

22   *Ibid.*, pp. 158 and 440–41.

23   *Ruanda-Urundi*, 1959, *op. cit.*, p. 277.

24   *Ibid.*, pp. 275–77.

25   *Rapport* . . . *1956*, *op. cit.*, pp. 155–56, 440.

26   *Ruanda-Urundi*, 1959, *op. cit.*, p. 253.

27   *Ibid.*, p. 252.

28   *Rapport* . . . *1956*, *op. cit.*, p. 397.

29   *Ibid.*, p. 437.

30 *Ibid.*, p. 421.

31 *Ibid.*, pp. 150–51.

32 *Ibid.*, pp. 149, 429–30.

33 *Ibid.*, pp. 154–55.

34 *Ibid.*, p. 57; also S. H. Steinberg (Ed.), *Statesman's Yearbook 1959*, Macmillan and Co., Ltd., London, 1959, p. 836.

35 S. H. Steinberg, *op. cit.*, p. 836.

36 Royaume de Belgique: Ministère des Affaires Africaines, Direction Des Etudes Economiques, *La Situation Economique du Congo Belge et du Ruanda-Urundi en 1959*, 1960, p. 138.

37 *Ruanda-Urundi, 1959, op. cit.*, pp. 297–98; also Royaume de Belgique: *La Situation Economique du Congo Belge et du Ruanda-Urundi en 1959, op. cit.*, p. 197.

38 *Rapport . . . 1956, op. cit.*, p. 453.

39 *Ruanda-Urundi, 1959, op. cit.*, pp. 169–70.

40 *Rapport . . . 1956, op. cit.*, pp. 201–204.

Senegal[1]

AREA: *76,000 sq. m.*
POPULATION:[2] *2,257,000 (1956 estimate)*
Density: 30 per sq. m.

GEOGRAPHY

Sengal is mostly a region of plains with an altitude of less than 650 feet, drained by the Senegal, Saloum, Gambia, and Casamance rivers. In the southeast, plateaus with a maximum altitude of 1,640 feet form the foothills of the Fouta-Djalon Mountains. North of Cape Verde, the coast forms an almost straight line. Farther south, it is indented by many estuaries and is often marshy. Two well-defined seasons, one dry (November to July) and the other rainy, are the result of the alternating winds from the northeast in the winter and from the southwest in the summer. During the humid months the temperature varies between 81 and 84 degrees F. Rainfall averages about 20 inches per annum.

HISTORICAL SKETCH

In the 17th century Cardinal Richelieu encouraged the French to settle at the mouth of the Senegal River. The interior was subsequently opened by several expeditions. In 1854 Faidherbe was able to establish peace along the Senegal River and to protect the people from the raiding Moors. He opened the way to Sudan by subduing the Tukulor Conqueror, El Hadj Omar.

In 1902 Dakar became the headquarters of French West Africa. French citizenship, which was granted in 1916 to the four communes of Saint-Louis, Dakar, Gorée, and Rufisque, was extended to all Senegalese under the 1946 Constitution. The General Council, which had been established in the 19th century, was transformed into the Territorial Assembly in 1952. The Loi Cadre of 1956 considerably increased the powers of the local assembly, and in 1957 it was elected by universal adult suffrage for the first time. In 1958 the Senegalese chose to remain part of the French Community and proclaimed a Republic at the end of that year. In January 1959 a new constitution was adopted, after union with the Sudanese Republic, creating the Federation of Mali. The independence of the Mali Federation was proclaimed June 20, 1960. In August of that year, following serious disagreement with the Sudanese Republic on the implementation of the constitution, the Republic of Senegal withdrew from the Mali Federation and proclaimed its independence. A new constitution was adopted in September 1960. The Republic of Senegal was admitted to the United Nations on September 28, 1960.

GOVERNMENT

Present Status
Independent republican state.

Constitution
Senegal has a unicameral system of government. The constitution provides for a President, elected every 7 years by a special electoral college meeting in congress, which includes, in addition to the members of the National Assembly, one from each regional assembly and one from each municipal council. Executive power is exercised by the President of the Council of Ministers, who is appointed by the President of the Republic and invested, after he has outlined his program, by an absolute majority of the National Assembly. The President of the Council may choose his ministers from National Assembly deputies or from outside. He may issue regulations, and is in charge of administration and defense. Legislative power is exercised by the National Assembly, elected for 5 years. It may force the government to resign by a vote of no confidence or by a motion of censure. The National Assembly may be dissolved if two ministerial crises occur within a period of 36 months.

Franchise
Universal adult suffrage.

Local Government
Senegal is divided into 6 regions which have elected local assemblies, and 13 territorial circumscriptions, headed by officials appointed in

the Council of Ministers. There are 25 communes, or townships, with elected municipal councils.

Political Parties [3]

Union Progressiste Sénégalaise (UPS), led by Léopold Senghor, President of the Republic, and Mamadou Dia, Prime Minister.

Parti du Regroupement Africain-Sénégal (PRA-Sénégal), led by Abdoulaye Ly.

Parti Africain de l'Indépendance (PAI), led by Mahjmout Dip and Oumar Diallo.

Bloc des Masses Africains, led by Sheikh Auta Diop.

POPULATION BREAKDOWN

Main Cities [4]

	1956
Dakar (capital)	214,464
Saint-Louis	47,195
Kaoloack	46,470
Thies	39,603
Rufisque	37,142
Ziquinchor	23,107
Diourbel	18,555
Louga	14,966

Urban-rural Distribution [5]

About 19% of the total population lives in towns of 10,000 inhabitants or more.

Ethnic Distribution

Non-African (1956)	45,500 [6]
Moors	25,000
African	
Wolof	709,000
Fulani	323,000
Serer	304,000
Tukulor	246,000
Diola	111,000
Malinke	84,000
Sarakile	31,000

Religious Affiliation [7]

Muslims	79%
Animists	16%
Christians	5%

Languages

Two vernacular tongues are considered dominant: Wolof and Pular, the language of the Tukulor and Fulani. The official language is French.

Sex Distribution [8]

	Male	*Female*
1956 estimate		
African	1,057,000 (51.1%)	990,700 (48.9%)
1956 census		
Non-African	25,499 (54.8%)	21,030 (45.2%)

Age Distribution [9]

	Under 14	*14–60*	*60+*
African	583,700	1,236,300	72,700

	Under 20	*20+*	*Unknown*
Non-African	17,007	28,444	88

SOCIAL DATA

Education [10]

As of January 1, 1958

TABLE I

	Enrollment	Public School Teachers
365 Public elementary schools ⎫ 64 Private elementary schools ⎬	80,473	2,587
10 Public secondary schools ⎫ 5 Private secondary schools ⎬	5,066	233
4 Public technical schools ⎫ 4 Private technical schools ⎬	646	105

The University of Dakar has a School of Medicine and Pharmacy, a Faculty of Science, a Faculty of Law, and a Faculty of Liberal Arts.

In 1958/59 the enrollment was 1,315, of which just under half were registered in the Law Faculty.

In 1957, 25% of the children of school-going age were attending school, of which 30% were girls; educational expenses represented 12% of the annual local budget.

Health and Social Services

VITAL STATISTICS [11]

Per 1,000

1957

Birth rate	Death rate	Infant mortality rate	Net reproduction rate
50	26	167	1.6

MAIN DISEASES [12]

Trypanosomiasis, leprosy, bilharziasis, malaria.

HEALTH SERVICES [13]

As of January 1, 1958

TABLE II

		Beds
2	Main hospitals	1,379
28	Medical centers	1,435
137	Dispensaries	—
5	Infirmaries	39
39	Specialized institutions	694

There are a tuberculosis sanatorium and a stomalogical center in Dakar; 135 medical practitioners, 1 to every 11,700 inhabitants; 13 beds per 10,000 of the population.

SOCIAL WELFARE SERVICES

Not available.

ECONOMY

Despite a growing processing industry, centered in Dakar, and the development of a mining industry, the economy of Senegal remains essentially agrarian, with peanuts as the main cash crop.

Transport and Communications

WATERWAYS

The Senegal River is navigable for more than 155 miles at all times, and twice that distance during high-water periods; the Saloum is navigable as far as Kaolack, about 75 miles; and the Casamance about 43 miles to Ziguinchor.

PORTS

Dakar, the main port, is situated on Cape Verde and is one of the leading ports of Africa. In 1959 it handled about 3,700,000 tons of cargo. The harbor covers an area almost one square mile, one-third of which accommodates ships drawing 40 feet of water.

ROADS

There were 6,950 miles of roads in 1958: 450 miles of asphalt roads, 2,000 miles of all-weather roads, and 4,500 miles of other kinds of roads.

RAILROADS

In 1958 there were over 700 miles of tracks. The main Dakar-Niger line is 446 miles, Dakar–St. Louis trunk line 161 miles, and the Louga-Linguère line 123 miles.

AIRWAYS

There are 15 airports, including the Yoff International Airport at Dakar which can handle the largest intercontinental jets. There is an extensive network of domestic airways linking major cities with remote villages and towns.

POSTS, TELECOMMUNICATIONS, AND BROADCASTING [14]

Dakar has a well-developed system of communication: 67 main post offices and 20 postal agencies, 90 telegraph and 98 telephone offices. It has a telex system and cable service to France and Latin America, with a large sending and receiving station at Cape Verde. Two radio stations situated at Dakar provide a service of 142 hours per week.

Resources and Trade

MAIN EXPORTS

Peanuts, peanut oil, other oleaginous products, gum arabic, fish, livestock, hides, and mineral products.

MAIN IMPORTS

Food, beverages, tobacco, and other consumer goods; fuel, raw materials, and semifinished products; capital goods.

VALUE OF TRADE [15]

In million C.F.A. francs (figures combined for Senegal, Mali, and Mauritania).

	1958	1959	1960
Exports	28,774	26,677	27,878
Imports	43,774	44,037	42,479

Separate trade figures given for Senegal only for 1959 and 1960 suggest that Senegal contributes about 80% of the total value of trade of the three countries combined.

LIVESTOCK [16]

1957 estimate

Cattle	1,385,000
Sheep and goats	909,000
Donkeys	84,000
Pigs	31,000
Camels	5,500

Industry

MANUFACTURES

Processing industries producing oil, soap, vinegar, biscuits, chocolate, canned fish, beer and sparkling water, sisal, leather, and textiles are among the most important. There are numerous chemical industries producing such products as liquid gas, potassium, chloride water, dyes, bleaches, paints, and explosives. Dakar has ship repair and construction industries. Cement and brick are produced for the local building trade. The hotel industry is also important.

MINING

The Taiba Phosphates Company began mining phosphate deposits in 1957 and the expected rate of production for 1960 was 600,000 tons. Alumina phosphate—the only deposits of this mineral in the world—is being mined at Pallo. In addition, Senegal produces limestone, ilmenite, rutile, and zirconium.

POWER

Three companies have been exploring the petroleum potential since 1952.

Finance

CURRENCY

One C.F.A. franc equals 2 old Metropolitan French francs.

BANKING [17]

Banque de l'Afrique Occidentale, Banque Commerciale Africaine, Banque Nationale pour le Commerce et l'Industrie, Crédit Lyonnais, Société Générale.

BUDGET [18]

In millions of C.F.A. francs

	1960
Revenue	19,134
Expenditure	19,134

Taxation is the main source of revenue, representing about 55% of the total.

DEVELOPMENT PLAN

A 4-year plan for the years 1961–1964 is being revised.

LABOR

In 1957 the wage-earning population was estimated to be distributed as follows: [19]

Private Sector		
Civil service	5,550	
Non-Civil service	15,200	20,750
Public Sector		
Agriculture, fishing, and forestry	4,650	
Mining and quarrying	1,000	
Industry	12,550	
Building and public works	11,600	
Commerce, banking, and professions	20,750	
Transport and storage	17,500	
Domestic service	11,500	79,550
TOTAL		100,300

In 1953 there were 23,900 trade-union members, of whom 12,000 were members of unions affiliated with the Confédération Générale du Travail; 5,700 were members of unions affiliated with the Force Ouvrière; 2,100 were members of unions affiliated with the Confédération des Travailleurs Chrétiens; and 4,100 were members of independent unions.[20]

Preindependence labor legislation dealt with such matters as leave, trade-union wages, accidents and illness, contracts, and family allowances. Postindependence information is not available.[21]

SENEGAL NOTES

1   Unless otherwise stated, information obtained from Ambassade de France, Service de Presse et d'Information, *The Republic of Senegal*, New York, Dec. 1960.

2   Service des Statistiques d'Outre-Mer: *Outre-Mer 1958*, Paul Dupont, Paris, Nov. 1959, pp. 726–27, Tables 1 and 2.

3   R. Segal, *Political Africa*, Stevens & Sons Ltd., London, 1961, pp. 405–407; *African Report*, Vol. 6, No. 10, Nov. 1961, Washington, D.C., p. 18.

4   *Outre-Mer 1958, op. cit.*, p. 727, Table 3.

5   *Ibid.*, pp. 726–27, Tables 1, 2, and 3.

6   *Ibid.*, p. 727, Table 2.

7   *Ibid.*, p. 140, Table 1.

8   *Ibid.*, pp. 726–27, Tables 1 and 2.

9   *Ibid.*, see footnote to Table 1, p. 726.

10   *Ibid.*, p. 729, Tables 7 and 9.

11   *Ibid.*, p. 728, Table 4. Limited to a study conducted in the lower valley of the Senegal River.

12   République du Sénégal: Ministère de l'Information de la Radiodiffusion et de la Presse, *Le Sénégal en Marche*, March 1961, pp. 173–76.

13   *Outre-Mer 1958, op. cit.*, p. 728, Table 5.

14   *Ibid.*, p. 731, Tables 16 and 17.

15   République du Sénégal: Service de la Statistique et de la Mécanographie, *Bulletin Statistisque Economique Mensuel*, No. 5, Dakar, 1961, pp. 22–23; Chambre de Commerce, d'Agriculture et d'Industrie de Dakar: *L'Economie du Sénégal*, Dakar, April 1961, p. 182; France: Service des Statistiques, *Bulletin de Conjecture d'Outre-Mer*, Paris, Aug. 1960, p. 25.

16   *Outre-Mer 1958, op. cit.*, p. 732, Table 19.

17   République du Sénégal: *L'Economie du Sénégal, op. cit.*, p. 169.

18 Ministère des Finances et des Affaires Economiques: Service des Statistiques, *Bulletin de Conjecture d'Outre-Mer*, No. 22, Feb. 1961, Tables 1 and 2, opposite p. 134.

19 *Outre-Mer 1958, op. cit.*, p. 209, Table 3.

20 International Labor Office: *African Labor Survey*, Geneva, 1958, p. 236, Table XII.

21 *Ibid.*, p. 654.

Sierra Leone[1]

AREA: *27,925 sq. m.*

POPULATION: *2,400,000 (1959 estimate)*
Density:[2] *550 per sq. m. ex-Colony area*
4 per sq. m. ex-Protectorate

GEOGRAPHY [3]

Sierra Leone has a 210-mile coastline. The country includes a flat, low-lying coastal strip backed by extensive mangrove swamps; rolling wooded country and hills in the west and south; an upland plateau some 1,500 feet high which rises to nearly 3,000 feet in the north and east; and, near the Guinea border, Bintimani Peak and the summits of the Tingi Range, rising to over 6,000 feet. The country is well watered by a network of rivers and streams. There are two distinct seasons—the dry season from November to April and the rainy season for the rest of the year. Rain is heaviest on the coast. Rainfall is about 115 inches annually in the north, 153 inches in Freetown, and 177 inches in the south; the period of heaviest rain is from July to September. The mean temperature is about 80 degrees F.

HISTORICAL SKETCH

The Colony was founded in 1787 by British philanthropists eager to find a home for emancipated slaves. In 1791 it was put under the jurisdiction of the Sierra Leone Company and transferred to the British Crown in 1808. By 1861 British interests had been extended into the interior through various treaties with local chiefs. In 1863, Legislative and Executive Councils were established. In 1896 a British Protectorate was declared over the hinterland and administered separately from the Colony until 1924, when the two were united. In 1951 a new constitution introduced an unofficial majority in the Legislative Council for the first time.

330

Subsequent changes in its franchise arrangements and constitution paved the way to eventual independence on April 27, 1961. It remained within the British Commonwealth and was admitted to the United Nations on September 28, 1961.

GOVERNMENT

Present Status

Independent state.

Constitution [4]

The new constitution is unicameral. Executive power is vested in a Cabinet consisting of the Prime Minister, as President, and not less than 7 ministers appointed from among the elected members of the House of Representatives. Legislative power is vested in the House of Representatives, comprising 54 members: the Speaker, 51 elected members, and 2 nominated members with no voting power.

Franchise

Universal adult suffrage.

Local Government

In the Colony, local government is in the hands of the Freetown City Council, the Sherbro Urban District Council, and a three-tier system of rural authorities. The Protectorate is divided into 145 chiefdoms (1959) organized as native authorities. In addition, each of the 12 districts has a District Council, of which some are elected members. There is one elected town council at Bo.

Political Parties [5]

Sierra Leone Peoples Party (SLPP), led by Sir Milton Morgai, Prime Minister and President.
People National Party (PNP), led by Albert Margai.
All Peoples Congress (APC), led by Siaka Stevens.
National Council of Sierra Leone (NCSL), led by Wallace Johnson.
United Peoples Party (UPP), led by Cyril Rogers-White.

POPULATION BREAKDOWN

Main Cities

Freetown (capital)	88,000
Bo	20,000
Makeni	9,000
Kenema	7,500

Urban-rural Distribution [6]

About 5% of the total population lives in towns of 9,000 or more inhabitants.

Ethnic Distribution [7]

European	±2,000
Asian	±3,000

African—The balance are divided into two main groups: the Mende, representing about 30% of the total population, and the Temne.

Religious Affiliation [8]

Christians	70,000
Muslims	588,000
Animists	1,692,000

Languages

The lingua franca is Creole (Krio) which is fairly widespread. Mende is spoken in the south and Temne in the north. English is the official language.

Sex Distribution

Not available.

Age Distribution

Not available.

SOCIAL DATA

Education [9]

TABLE I
1959

		Enrollment	Teachers
550	Primary schools	74,481	2,168
28	Secondary schools	6,808	353
2	Technical schools	265 full time	
		872 part time	
6	Teacher-training colleges	600	
	University College, Sierra Leone	328 (1959/60)	
	(formerly Fourah Bay College)		

In 1959, 21% of all children between the ages 5–14 were at school. Expenditure: 1960/61 £1.7 million (1950 £185,000).

Health and Social Services

VITAL STATISTICS
   Not available.

MAIN DISEASES
   Malaria, venereal diseases, ascariasis, dysentery, colitis, leprosy, sleeping sickness, eye diseases, tuberculosis, respiratory diseases, and smallpox.

HEALTH SERVICES [10]

TABLE II
1958

		Beds
23	Government hospitals	1,336
6	Mission hospitals	
13	Dispensaries	
2	Mining hospitals	472
1	Military hospital	

There were 35 nongovernment medical practitioners at the end of 1958.

SOCIAL WELFARE SERVICES [11]

There are 3 main fields of activity: in social welfare, in juvenile delinquency, and in community development, all falling under one department. Among the services provided are: marriage and family guidance services, community centers, youth clubs, a school for blind children, a juvenile court, an approved school and remand home, and women's institutes.

ECONOMY

Sierra Leone has an agricultural export economy. Rice is the main subsistence crop. Of recent years, however, the development of diamond mining and urban wage-earning employment have adversely affected agricultural output.

Transport and Communications

WATERWAYS

There are nearly 500 miles of launch routes, some of which are navigable for only three months of the year. Much local produce is carried to Freetown down the Great and Little Scaries rivers and from the Bouthe area.

PORTS [12]

Freetown is a natural harbor with anchorage room for more than 200 ships. In 1954 a 1,250-foot-long, deep-water dock was built which made the berthing of ships possible. In 1958, 443,100 tons of materials were handled.

ROADS

There are 3,442 miles of roads. The Public Works Department maintains 1,642 miles, including 150 miles of bituminized roads, and about 200 miles are maintained by private companies. In 1958 there were 7,562 commercial and private motor vehicles.

RAILROADS

There are 310 miles of railroads, consisting of a main line from Freetown to Pendembua and a branch line from Banya Junction to Makeni in the Northern Province.

AIRWAYS

There is an international airport at Lungi. The government operates an internal air service between Lungi and Hastings, Hastings and Bo, Kenema and Daru, Maghuraka and Port Loko.

POSTS, TELECOMMUNICATIONS, AND BROADCASTING [13]

In 1958 there were 116 post offices and postal agencies. In that same year there were 1,815 direct telephone-exchange lines and 1,300 extensions in service. A broadcasting department was established in 1958 with 4,030 subscribers and 2,860 radio license holders.

Resources and Trade

MAIN EXPORTS [14]

Diamonds (averaging 33% of the annual value of exports from 1956 to 1958), iron ore and concentrates, palm kernels, raw coffee, cocoa, piassava, kola nuts, ginger, and chrome ore.

MAIN IMPORTS

Food, beer, wine, cotton and other fabrics, clothing and footwear, motor vehicles, steel, electrical machinery and appliances, tobacco, medical and pharmaceutical products.

VALUE OF TRADE

In £'000's

	1955	1956	1957	1958
Exports	9,930	12,132	15,008	16,541
Imports	17,115	23,093	28,250	23,903

MARKETING AND COOPERATIVE SOCIETIES

The Sierra Leone Marketing Board, established in 1949, controls the export of palm kernels, cocoa, palm oil, peanuts, sesame seed, and copra.

The 29 societies in existence in 1950 had increased to 390 with a total membership of some 24,000 by the end of 1959. The most important group are the coffee and cocoa marketing societies.

LIVESTOCK

1959 estimate

Cattle	150–200,000
Sheep and goats	55,000
Pigs	5,500

Industry

MANUFACTURES

Sierra Leone processes such primary products as iron ore, palm kernels, and rice; but there is as yet little secondary industry. The Forest Industries Board of the Forestry Department runs a sawmill and timber-utilization operation at Kenema. The Road Transport Department operates vehicle repair shops and there is a machine engineering works.

MINING

Mining has become the main source of government revenue and yielded about £2.5 million in revenue in 1959. The main mineral products are diamonds, iron and chrome ore, and platinum.

POWER

In 1959, 20 million kw. were generated in Freetown. Facilities are being gradually extended to villages around Freetown and to towns in the provinces.

Finance

CURRENCY

The West African Currency Board issues the currency, which is interchangeable with £ sterling at par.

BANKING [15]

Bank of West Africa Ltd. in Freetown and 6 branch offices in the provinces; Barclay's Bank D.C.O. in Freetown with 4 branches in the provinces. There is a government post office savings bank.

BUDGET [16]

In £'000's

	1960
Revenue	11,494
Expenditure	11,696

DEVELOPMENT PLAN [17]

1956/59 £'000's   Total: £10,500

Sources—Colonial development welfare grants		2,481
Loan funds		4,958
Local resources		3,061

1961/62 development estimates: £4 millions, to be allocated to improvements to Lungi airport runway, inland waterways, electricity supplies, provincial water supplies, roads, and bridges.

LABOR

In recent years there has been an increasing migration of young men to urban areas. In 1958 it was estimated that there were between 75,-000 and 80,000 wage earners in towns. The following table gives the number of workers in undertakings employing 6 or more workers:

Building and construction	7,556
Mining	6,596
Transportation	6,964
Public administration offices	5,666
Private and commercial undertakings	5,568
Maritime and waterfront workers	2,048
Others	9,931
TOTAL	44,329

By the end of 1958 there were 11 registered workers' unions and 3 employers' unions, with a total membership of over 27,000.

Labor legislation covers such matters as minimum wages, conditions of employment, employment of women and children, safety of workers, and workers' compensation.

SIERRA LEONE NOTES

1 Unless otherwise stated, all information is obtained from British Information Service, I.D., *Sierra Leone, Making of a Nation,* Nov. 1960.

2 Sierra Leone: *Economic Survey of Sierra Leone,* Government Printing Department, Sierra Leone, 1958, p. 3.

3 U.K.: *Sierra Leone 1958* (annual report), H.M.S.O., London, 1960, p. 99.

4 Communication received from the British Embassy, Washington, D.C., July 1961.

5 R. Segal, *Political Africa*, Stevens & Sons Ltd., London, 1961, pp. 408–10.

6 Estimate based on a computation of population of cities of 9,000 or more to total population. Since it is not known whether the figures of the urban population refer to the same year as the total population figure (1959), this can only be taken as a very crude estimate.

7 S. H. Steinberg (Ed.), *Statesman's Yearbook 1961*, Macmillan & Co., Ltd., London, 1961, p. 358; also U.K.: *Sierra Leone 1958, op. cit.*, p. 11. A census is to be conducted shortly.

8 J. Spencer Trimingham, *Islam in West Africa*, O.U.P., 1959, p. 233, Appendix V.

9 Sierra Leone: *Education Statistics 1959*, pp. 5–6; U.N. Economic Commission for Africa, UNESCO, *Final Report of the Conference of African States on the Development of Education in Africa*, Addis Ababa, May 15–25, 1961, "Outline of a Plan for African Education Development," p. 7, Table 1: UNESCO/ED/181.

10 Communication received from the British Embassy, *op. cit.*; also U.K.: *Sierra Leone 1958, op. cit.*, p. 68.

11 U.K.: *Sierra Leone 1958, op. cit.*, pp. 71–72.

12 *Ibid.*, p. 86.

13 *Ibid.*, pp. 91–93.

14 *Ibid.*, p. 31.

15 U.K.: Colonial Office, *The Colonial Territories 1960–1961*, H.M.S.O., Cmnd. 1407, London, 1961, p. 121.

16 *Assistance from the United Kingdom for Overseas Development*, Cmnd. 974, 1960, p. 17.

17 *The Sierra Leone Trade Journal*, Vol. I, No. 1, 1961, Sierra Leone, pp. 8–9.

The Somali Republic

AREA: [1] *246,000 sq. m.*
Somalia, 178,000, formerly Italian
Northern region, 68,000, formerly British
POPULATION: [2] *About 2,000,000*
Density: Somalia, 3 per sq. m.
Northern region, 4 per sq. m.

GEOGRAPHY [3]

The country, forming a right angle on the Horn of Africa, varies in width from 95 to 250 miles. Somalia has a mountainous northern region, of which Mount Bakai, at 7,200 feet, is the highest peak. The southeastern section is an extensive flat area, less than 325 feet above sea level. Average altitude is 600 feet. The country is traversed by the Giuba River in the south and the Uebi Scebeli River in the center. The climate is tropical, with an average annual temperature of 80 degrees F. Rainfall average 4 inches annually in the north and 16 inches in the south. There are 4 seasons, determined by the direction of the winds: one hot and dry, one cold and dry, and two hot and humid seasons.

HISTORICAL SKETCH [4]
(FORMER ITALIAN SOMALILAND)

Prior to the arrival of the Portuguese in the 16th century, the area was inhabited by various Hamitic groups intermingled with Arab traders, particularly along the coast. For some time the Portuguese ruled some towns in the coastal area which later fell under the control of the Sultan of Zanzibar. It was from Somali tribes, and later by agreement with these tribes, that Italy acquired the land as a colony in 1884, and leased it to a company for exploitation in 1893. In 1905 the Italian Government took the area back from the company, but it was not before the Fascist administration in the 1920's that it took a deep interest in the colony. The British took over Italian Somaliland during World War II, and from 1941 until 1950 they administered the area. It was then placed under the

United Nations Trusteeship system, with Italy as administering authority assisted by a U.N. Advisory Committee. The first elected Legislative Assembly was constituted in 1956, together with an all-Somali Council of Ministers. In July 1960 it attained its independence, and was united with the British Protectorate of Somaliland.

(FORMER BRITISH SOMALILAND)

The protectorate was acquired by the British upon its abandonment by the Egyptians in 1884, primarily to protect the trade route through the Red Sea. British Somaliland, was originally administered as part of the Indian Empire, and progress toward self-government was slow. In February 1960, for the first time, a Legislative Council with an elected Somali majority took office. In July 1960 it joined with Somalia to form the Somali Republic.

GOVERNMENT

Present Status

Independent republican state.

Constitution [5]

The legislature consists of a National Assembly of 123 elected deputies—90 from Somalia and 33 from the Northern Region (formerly British)—from whose numbers the Assembly elects its President and one or more Vice-Presidents. The President appoints the Prime Minister who, in turn, selects a Cabinet. The President has the power to vote in the Assembly and certain other powers which place him in a position between that of a titular head of state and leader of a presidential form of government.

Franchise

Universal adult suffrage.

Local Government

There are 8 regions—6 in Somali and 2 in the Northern Region, each headed by a Governor. These are subdivided into districts headed by a District Commissioner. Governors and District Commissioners are appointed by the Minister of the Interior. Elected Municipal Councils exist in the larger towns of Somali, and local government councils in those of the Northern Region.

Political Parties

Somali Youth League (SYL), which holds most of the 90 Somali seats.

Somali National League–United Somali Party (SNL–USP), holding 32 of the 33 Northern Region seats. Together they form the coalition government. The President is Aden Abdullah Oswan, and the Prime Minister is Abdi Rashid Shermurka.

POPULATION BREAKDOWN

Main Cities [6]

Mogadiscio (capital)	86,600
Merca	61,400
Margherita	20,000
Bosaso	6,500

Urban-rural Distribution

Not available.

Ethnic Distribution [7]

	1953
Somali	90%
Italian	5,000
Arabi	30,000
Indian and Pakistani	1,000

There are four major tribal groups: the Daret ($\pm$450,000), the Hawiya (+300,000), the Rahanwein ($\pm$350,000), and the Ishaak.

Religious Affiliation [8]

Somalia only: Muslims $\pm$90%

Languages

Somali, English, Italian, and Arabic.

Sex Distribution [9]
1959 estimate

	Male	Female
Somalia only	384,873 (69.2%)	184,400 (30.8%)

Age Distribution [10]
Limited to 35 municipal areas in Somalia

Under 20	20–59	60+
45.5%	49.1%	5.4%

SOCIAL DATA

Education [11]

TABLE I

Somalia: 1958/59	Enrollment	Teachers
181 Primary schools for children	22,879	
166 Primary schools for adults	25,929	905
18 Primary schools for Italians and Pakistanis	1,763	84
18 Secondary lower schools ⎫		
Secondary upper schools ⎬	1,504	139
Normal college ⎭		
4 Vocational and technical schools	423	49
Institute of Law and Economics	81	11

10.2% of children between the ages of 5–14 were at school in 1958/59.

Northern Region: 1958		
25 Government elementary schools	961	70
13 Local-authority elementary schools	1,006	N.A.
13 Government intermediate schools	914	54
1 Government secondary school	81	6
1 Teacher-training college	22	6
1 Technical and vocational school	71	4

1958 expenditure: £268,115.

Health and Social Services

VITAL STATISTICS
Not available.

MAIN DISEASES [12]

Malaria, venereal disease, and eye diseases.

HEALTH SERVICES [13]

TABLE II

Somalia: 1959

		Beds
11 Hospitals	⎫	
20 Infirmaries	⎬	2,411
141 Infirmaries	⎭	
67 Doctors		

Northern Region: 1957

7 Hospitals	570
1 Tuberculosis hospital	145
1 Mental hospital	65
12 Rural dispensaries	
1 Town dispensary	
14 Doctors	

SOCIAL WELFARE SERVICES [14]

In Somalia, insurance schemes exist for pensions, accidents, and sickness.

ECONOMY

The economies of the two areas have not yet been integrated. Each continues to have different budgets, sources of revenue, fiscal years, currencies, commercial policies, and patterns of trade. The majority of the inhabitants make their living from stock raising and agricultural activities. There is little industrial or mining development.

Transport and Communications

WATERWAYS

A part of the Juba River is navigable for small crafts.

PORTS [15]

Mogadiscio (by far the most developed), Merca, Chicimaio, and Bosaso which, combined, handled 238,745 metric tons in 1959. Berbera is the only notable port in the Northern Region.

ROADS [16]

In Somalia there are approximately 5,490 miles of roads, of which 2,300 are trails only and 390 are bituminized. In the Northern Region there were about 2,660 miles of roads in 1957—190 miles of main roads, 2,470 of district roads.

RAILROADS

None.

AIRWAYS [17]

There is an international airport at Mogadiscio. In addition there are some 20 cleared runways throughout the country.

POSTS, TELECOMMUNICATIONS, AND BROADCASTING [18]

Somalia has 10 post offices and 24 postal agencies; 22 radio telegraph offices and telephone exchanges, mostly manually operated, at Mogadiscio and 7 other urban centers. There is one radio station at Mogadiscio. The Northern Region has 8 post offices and 11 postal agencies. There are manually operated telephone exchanges at Berbera and Burao.

Resources and Trade

MAIN EXPORTS [19]

Foodstuffs, of which bananas are the most important (representing 58.7% of the value of Somalia exports in 1959), hides and skins, and livestock.

MAIN IMPORTS [20]

Textile goods and cotton goods, machinery and transport equipment, and food.

VALUE OF TRADE [21]

In million of Somalos—Somalia only:

	1955	1956	1957	1958	1959
Exports	103,327.9	117,789.2	119,970.9	101,959.6	134,335.5
Imports	74,048.6	65,191.3	76,954.8	95,869.1	106,019.7

Italy is Somalia's chief trading partner.

MARKETING AND COOPERATIVE SOCIETIES [22]

Products are marketed privately in Somalia. The cooperatives that exist in Somalia are limited-liability companies. At the end of 1956 there were 25 cooperatives, 17 of which were active.

LIVESTOCK [23]

Somalia

Cattle	1,000,000
Camels	1,300,000
Sheep and goats	4,400,000
Donkeys	20,000
Horses	300

Industry

MANUFACTURES [24]

Somalia has few industries, including a sugar refinery, tuna canneries, beef canneries, and combined shoe and leather factories.

MINING [25]

Four companies are exploring for oil. In the Northern Region columbite, tantalite, and beryl are mined in small quantities.

POWER [26]

In Somalia the combined capacity generated by 8 electrical generating groups totals 6,942 kw. In 1959, 8,832,551 kwh. were produced.

Finance

CURRENCY [27]

Somalia—a somalo equals 1 East African shilling (U.S.$ 0.14).

BANKING [28]

Somalia—Banco di Roma, Credito Somalo, Banco di Napoli, Banco Nazionale Somala. Northern Region—branches of National Overseas and Grindlay's Bank Ltd.

BUDGET [29]

	Somalia— in 000's somalos 1959	Northern Region— in £'000's 1956/57
Revenue	103,554.3	1,693.9
Expenditure	112,876.0	1,715.7

DEVELOPMENT PLAN [30]

Somalia 1954/60	Somalos
Total expediture	124,281,142

Allocations

Agriculture	30,509,714
Livestock	24,071,428
Communications	30,580,000
Urban development	7,000,000
Industrial development	24,120,000
Commerce	2,100,000
Credit	50,900,000

LABOR

In Somalia the economically active male population totaled 319,000 in 1955.[31] The breakdown of labor figures is not available.

In Somalia there are 15 trade unions combined into two major federations: Confédération Somalie des Travailleurs and Fédération des Syndicats des Travailleurs Unis.[32]

A Labor Code in Somalia regulates disputes and contracts, and family-alowance schemes cover accidents and illness. In the Northern Region labor legislation covers contracts, wages, trade unions and disputes, compensation, and the employment of women and children.[33]

THE SOMALI REPUBLIC NOTES

1   "Somali Republic—Basic Country Data," mimeograph handout prepared by the American Embassy, Mogadiscio, Somali Republic, n.d., p. 1.

2   Ibid. Also Oxford Regional Economic Atlas, "The Middle East and North Africa," prepared by the Economist Intelligence Unit Limited and the Cartographic Department of the Clarendon Press, London, O.U.P., 1960, p. 106 for the density figures.

3   World Trade Information Service: Economic Reports, Basic Data on the Economy of the Somalia (Somali) Republic, Part I, No. 61–5, U.S. Department of Commerce, U.S. Government Printing Office, 1961, pp. 1 and 2.

4   "Somali Republic—Basic Country Data," op. cit., pp. 1 and 2.

5   Ibid., p. 2.

6 World Trade Information Service, *op. cit.*, p. 2.

7 International Bank for Reconstruction and Development: *The Economy of the Trust Territory of Somaliland*, Washington, I.B.R.D., 1957, p. 5. Also, "Somali Republic—Basic Country Data," *op. cit.*, p. 1. Also, *Asia and Africa Review*, Vol. 1, No. 3, March 1961, Independent Publishing Co., London, p. 14.

8 I.B.R.D., *op. cit.*, p. 5.

9 *Rapport du Gouvernement Italien à l'Assemblée Générale des Nations Unies sur l'Administration de Tutelle de la Somalie 1959*, Ministère des Affaires Etrangères, Rome, 1960, p. 214.

10 *Ibid.*

11 *Ibid.*, pp. 309–24. Also, U.N. Economic Commission for Africa, UNESCO: *Final Report of the Conference of African States on the Development of Education in Africa*, Addis Ababa, May 15–25, 1961, "Outline of a Plan for African Educational Development," p. 7, Table 1 UNESCO/ED/181; also Somaliland Protectorate: Education Department, *Annual Report* (summary) 1958, n.d.; mimeograph, p. 6, Table 1; p. 7, Table II A; p. 12, Table V.

12 *Rapport du Gouvernement Italien . . .* , 1959, *op. cit.*, p. 286. Also U.K.: *Somaliland Protectorate 1956 and 1957*, London, H.M.S.O., 1959, pp. 26–27.

13 *Rapport du Gouvernement Italien . . .* , 1959, *op. cit.*, p. 236.

14 United Nations Advisory Council for the Trust Territory of Somaliland, *Report 1958*, pp. 88–89.

15 World Trade Information Service, *op. cit.*, pp. 12–13.

16 *Ibid.*, p. 11. Also U.K.: *Somaliland Protectorate 1956 and 1957*, *op. cit.*, p. 39.

17 World Trade Information Service, *op. cit.*, p. 12. Also U.K.: *Somaliland Protectorate 1956 and 1957*, *op. cit.*, p. 17.

18 World Trade Information Service, *op. cit.*, p. 13. Also, U.K.: *Somaliland Protectorate 1956 and 1957*, *op. cit.*, pp. 40–41.

19 *Rapport du Gouvernement Italien . . .* , 1959, *op. cit.*, pp. 250–59. Also U.K.: *Somaliland Protectorate 1956 and 1957*, *op. cit.*, p. 17.

20 *Rapport du Gouvernement Italien . . .* , 1959, *op. cit.*, pp. 246–49. Also U.K.: *Somaliland Protectorate 1956 and 1957*, *op. cit.*, p. 15.

21 *Rapport du Gouvernement Italien . . .* , 1959, *op. cit.*, pp. 234–37.

22 International Labor Office: *African Labor Survey*, Geneva,, 1958, pp. 456–57.

23 World Trade Information Service, *op. cit.*, p. 5.

24 *Ibid.*, p. 10.

25 *Ibid.*, p. 7. Also U.K.: *Somaliland Protectorate 1956 and 1957*, *op. cit.*, p. 21.

26 World Trade Information Service, *op. cit.*, p. 11.

27 *Ibid.*, p. 14. Also U.K.: *Somaliland Protectorate 1956 and 1957*, *op. cit.*, p. 14.

28 World Trade Information Service, *op. cit.*, p. 14.

29 *Rapport du Gouvernement Italien* . . . , 1959, *op. cit.*, p. 225 and 227. Also U.K.: *Somaliland Protectorate 1956 and 1957*, *op. cit.*, pp. 11 and 12.

30 *Rapport du Gouvernement Italien* . . . , 1959, *op. cit.*, p. 53.

31 I.L.O.: *African Labor Survey*, *op. cit.*, p. 666, Table 2.

32 *Rapport du Gouvernement Italien* . . . , 1959, *op. cit.*, p. 118.

33 *Ibid.*, pp. 117, 281, and 282. Also U.K.: *Somaliland Protectorate 1956 and 1957*, *op. cit.*, p. 10.

The Republic of South Africa

AREA: [1] *472,359 sq. m.*

POPULATION: [2] *15,851,128 (1960 estimate)*

Density: [3] *26.8 per sq. m.*

GEOGRAPHY [4]

South Africa has vast interior plateaus, largely flat or undulating, with local ridges varying in altitude from 2,000 to 6,000 feet and generally rising toward the north. Among the more arid tablelands of the west are the Little and Great Karoos. The elevated grasslands, mainly in the Orange Free State and the Transvaal, are called the Veld: the Low Veld (500–2,000 feet), the Middle Veld (2,000–4,000 feet), and the High Veld (4,000–6,000 feet). Within the High Veld lies the Witwatersrand, one of the world's richest gold-bearing reefs. Escarpments bound the plateaus and fall to the coastal strip along the even and rocky shore line. These escarpments, winding in a wide curve, rise to over 11,000 feet in the Drakensberg range, beginning in the eastern Transvaal and rising between Basutoland and Natal; other ranges are the Sneeuwberg and Swartberg of the Cape Province. There are two main rivers, the Vaal and Orange. The climate is generally mild and remarkably uniform because of the equalizing effect of the high plateaus. Cape Town's mean temperature is 62.5 degrees F., and Pretoria's is 64.5 degrees F. The southern part of the Cape Province has winter rains (April–October), whereas summer rains predominate elsewhere. Rainfall averages about 25 inches per year in Cape Town and 30 inches per year in Johannesburg.

HISTORICAL SKETCH [5]

Europeans first landed at the Cape of Good Hope in 1652. Thereafter, for more than a century and a half, the southwestern portion of the present Republic was the possession of Holland. It was occupied by Britain during the Napoleonic Wars. The interior was opened up by the Great Trek of the 1830's and 1840's. Natal came under British control in 1843 and the independence of the two Boer republics—the Orange Free State and South African Republic (now Transvaal)—was recognized by Britain in the 1850's. Following the Anglo-Boer War of 1899–1902, the two Boer republics became British colonies. In 1910 the four colonies united into the Union of South Africa and became a Dominion within the British Empire. The independence of the Dominion was given legal status in 1931 under the Statute of Westminster. In 1948 the Nationalist Party was elected to power. It introduced and has since followed the segregation policy of "Apartheid." In 1961, South Africa became a Republic by national referendum and subsequently withdrew from membership in the British Commonwealth of Nations.

GOVERNMENT

Present Status
Independent republican state.

Constitution [6]
Pursuant to the South African Act, 1909, South Africa is a unitary state of four provinces. The State President, following the declaration of the Republic in 1961, is the titular head of the state. The bicameral Parliament consists of the House of Assembly and the Senate. The Cabinet, consisting of the Prime Minister and 16 other ministers, is the principal policy-making body. The House of Assembly consists of 160 members elected in single-member constituencies, one of whom is elected Speaker. Four M.P.'s. are elected by colored voters in the Cape Province, in special constituencies. The Senate consists of 43 senators elected indirectly and 11 senators nominated by the government.

Provincial government is exercised within each province by a unicameral Provincial Council, a 4-man executive committee elected by the Council and a Provincial Administrator appointed by the Senate President upon the advice of the Cabinet. The scope of provincial legislation and administration is established by Parliament.

Franchise
Universal adult suffrage (18 years of age) for whites; adult male suffrage for colored possessing certain educational and property qualifications in the Cape province, voting on a separate roll.

Local Government

Local government is in the hands of elected city councils, town councils, village councils, or local boards. These bodies fall under the legislative control of their respective Provincial Council.

Political Parties [7]

Four parties are represented in Parliament:

The Nationalist Party, the governing party, led by Dr. H. Verwoerd, Prime Minister—105 seats.

The United Party, the official opposition, led by Sir de Villiers Graaf —49 seats.

The Progressive Party, led by Dr. J. Steytler—1 seat.

The National Union Party, led by J. Basson—1 seat.

C. R. Swart is the State President.

POPULATION BREAKDOWN

Main Cities [8]

Preliminary results of the 1960 census:

Johannesburg	1,096,541
Cape Town	718,189
Durban	655,370
Pretoria	420,053
Port Elizabeth	270,815
Germiston	204,605
Bloemfontein	140,924

Urban-rural Distribution [9]

On the basis of towns of 10,000 or more, the urban distribution according to the 1951 census was approximately as follows:

All races	33%
White	62%
Nonwhite	25%

Ethnic Distribution [10]

	1960
White	3,067,638
Colored	1,488,267
Asian	477,414
African	10,807,809

African tribal groups

Xhosa	2,486,164
Zulu	2,205,878
South-Sotho	916,890
Sepedi	941,343
Tswana	703,083

Religious Affiliation [11]

Christians—8,616,508

White	2,503,591
African	5,078,910
Asian	22,883
Colored	1,011,124

Muslims—146,629

African	4,626
Asian	78,787
Colored	63,216

Hindus	246,234
Jews	108,497
Confucians	1,689
Buddhists	539

It can be assumed that the balance of the Africans are pagan.

Languages

The main languages spoken in South Africa are English and Afrikaans (both official languages). Vernaculars include Xhosa, Zulu, South-Sotho, and Sepedi. Tamil and Hindu are the two principal Asian languages.

Sex Distribution [12]

1951 census

	Male	Female
White	1,322,754 (50.1%)	1,318,935 (49.9%)
African	4,369,157 (51.0%)	4,190,926 (49.0%)
Asian	189,595 (51.0%)	177,069 (49.0%)
Colored	550,579 (50.0%)	552,437 (50.0%)

Age Distribution [13]

1951 census

	Under 15	15–49	50+
White	31.7%	50.4%	17.9%
African	39.1%	50.1%	10.8%
Asian	47.7%	45.2%	7.1%
Colored	43.0%	46.5%	10.5%

SOCIAL DATA

Education [14]

TABLE I
1958

	Number	Enrollment	Teachers
Public primary and secondary schools			
White	2,547	614,178	25,960
African	6,223	1,243,088 }	36,312 *
Asian and Colored	1,842	381,190 }	
Private primary and secondary schools			
White	237	45,762	2,286
African	716	95,335 }	2,406
Asian and Colored	50	6,872 }	
Teacher-training colleges			
White	14	6,389	
African	54	6,330	
Asian and Colored	14	2,168	
Universities—white			
University of Cape town		4,430	
University of Natal		3,123	
University of the Orange Free State		1,709	
Potchefstrom University		1,474	
Rhodes University		1,144	
University of Pretoria		6,461	
University of Stellenbosch		3,694	
University of Witwatersrand		4,984	
University of South Africa (correspondence)		8,128	

* This total includes teachers in teacher-training colleges.

TABLE I—Continued

Nonwhite

	Enrollment
The University College of the North	Not available
The University College of Zululand	Not available
The University College of Fort Hare	438

Total public expenditure on education, 1958: £68,815,000.

Health and Social Services

VITAL STATISTICS [15]

Per 1,000

1959

	Birth rate	Crude death rate	Infant mortality rate (1958)
White	25.4	8.6	29.4
African		Not available	
Asiatic	33.0	8.9	65.1
Colored	47.9	15.6	132.3

MAIN DISEASES [16]

Bilharziasis, diphtheria, dysentery, typhoid fever, malaria, measles, pellagra, venereal disease, poliomyelitis, influenza, epidemic cerebrospinal meningitis, scarlet fever, and tuberculosis.

HEALTH SERVICES [17]

TABLE II
1958

				Beds	
Institution	White	Nonwhite	Mixed	White	Nonwhite
Public hospitals	13	11	135	11,547	12,255
Infectious disease hospitals	6	63	13	2,118	10,067
Private nursing homes	111	9	39	5,568	1,434
Maternity homes	79	14	7	1,804	856
Mission hospitals	—	52	25	158	8,960
Mine and industrial hospitals	3	67	11	340	11,171

There were 13 mental institutions in 1958.

There were 7,549 registered physicians in 1958.

Responsibility for health services is divided between central and provincial administrations. The central government has executive and advisory duties and is responsible for preventive and health-promotion services. The provinces are responsible for the preventive services— they administer general hospitals, school medical inspections, and supervise the health functions of local authorities.

SOCIAL WELFARE SERVICES [18]

South Africa has an extensive social welfare program undertaken for all races by both voluntary and official bodies. The Department of Social Welfare is the principal official agency.

ECONOMY

South Africa's economy is a rapidly growing one and has a large industrial sector. Agricultural production and mining are important segments of the economy, while manufacturing is now the main contributor to the national income and the largest employer of labor. Much of South Africa's capital equipment and luxury goods are imported, but industries producing import substitutes are on the rise.

Transport and Communications

WATERWAYS

There are no navigable rivers in South Africa.

PORTS [19]

The main ports of the country are Durban, Cape Town, Port Elizabeth, and East London. In 1958, tonnage handled by these ports was distributed as follows:

	Overseas cargo	Coastwise cargo
Durban	7,522	813
Cape Town	4,363	587
Port Elizabeth	2,215	307
East London	1,226	150

ROADS [20]

South Africa has the most developed and extensive network of roads on the African continent. In 1959 there were 112,012 miles of roads, of which 9,947 were bituminized.

RAILROADS [21]

The railway network of the country is run by the South African Railways and Harbor Administration. In 1959 there were 13,439 miles of 3-foot 6-inch-gauge tracks; 961 miles of which were electric.

AIRWAYS [22]

The South African Airways is government-owned and handles all domestic air travel. International air service is provided by the S.A.A. as well as nine foreign airlines. The Jan Smuts airport at Johannesburg handles most of the international flights. There are national airports at Cape Town, Durban, and Bloemfontein, and intermediate airports at Port Elizabeth, East London, Kimberley and, Windhoek (S.W.A.). There are also a number of local airports and landstrips throughout the country.

POSTS, TELECOMMUNICATIONS, AND BROADCASTING [23]

In 1951 there were 3,326 post offices and 3,462 telegraph offices; 1,867 telephone exchanges and 775,274 telephones in use.

The South African Broadcasting Corporation maintains three national networks, one in English, one in Afrikaans, and one which is leased to a private company for commercial purposes. Programs are offered in the vernacular languages for a limited part of every day.

Resources and Trade

MAIN EXPORTS [24]

South Africa is the world's largest producer of gold. In 1958 gold exports represented 39% of the total export value and an average of 36% from 1954 to 1958. Other exports: wool (7% of total export value in 1958), atomic energy material, foodstuffs.

MAIN IMPORTS [25]

Motor vehicles and parts, other machinery, and metals represented 50% of the total import value of 1958. Other goods imported: textiles, oils, waxes, paints, varnishes, resins, drugs, chemicals, and fertilizers.

VALUE OF TRADE [26]

In £'000's (excluding ships, stores, and gold)

	1954	1955	1956	1957	1958
Exports	263,509	327,904	365,000	397,949	353,661
Imports	434,387	480,990	494,884	549,819	555,464
Gold Exports	155,848	178,141	193,205	216,893	221,869

Marketing boards control many commodities, including corn, wheat, oats, barley, rye, citrus fruits, milk and other dairy products, and tobacco. In 1959 there were 311 agricultural cooperatives with a combined membership of 281,121 and 150 trading (consumers') societies with a combined membership of 115,938.

LIVESTOCK [28]

	1957
Cattle	12,042,000
Sheep and goats	43,672,000

	1955
Pigs	1,127,000
Donkeys	518,000
Horses	558,000
Mules	75,000

Industry

MANUFACTURES [29]

Gross industrial output in 1957/58 was £182,529,000; of this the food industry represented about 24%, chemicals and chemical products ±10%, metal products ±10%, and wearing apparel ±9%. South Africa also has a sizable construction industry.

MINING [30]

Gold mining is the most important of the mining industries. Other minerals and metals mined are uranium, coal, diamonds, salt, silica, limestone, asbestos, iron ore, manganese, and copper.

POWER [31]

Total generated electrical power in 1958 was 22,308 million kwh.

Finance

CURRENCY [32]

South Africa adopted the decimal system in 1961. The new unit of currency is the rand. 2R equal £1 sterling.

BANKING [33]

The South African Reserve Bank is the central bank and has the sole right of note issuance. Other banks include: Barclay's Bank, D.C.O., the Standard Bank of South Africa, Nederlandsche Bank van Suid Afrika Bpk., Volkskas Bpk., French Bank of Southern Africa Ltd., South African Bank of Athens Ltd., First National City Bank of New York, Chase Manhattan Bank. In addition there are 50 noncommercial banks and post office savings banks.

BUDGET [34]

1961/62 estimate in rands

Revenue	725,300,000
Expenditure	688,136,200

DEVELOPMENT PLANS [35]

Official South African racial policy calls for the "separate development" of the Bantu reserves. To promote industrial development of these areas and to create developmental and financial institutions among the Bantu in the reserves, the government created in 1958 the Bantu Investment Corporation, whose initial capital is £500,000.

LABOR

The distribution of the wage-earning population was as follows: [36]

	White	Colored and Asiatic	African
Agriculture (1957)	11,071	124,971	827,580
Mining (1959)	64,690	3,781	518,018
Quarrying (1959)	1,529	*	*
Private industry (1955/56)	192,837	130,130	429,562
Retail (1952)	69,714	21,571	68,055
Wholesale (1952)	41,813	8,651	42,940
Service (1952)	24,819	15,859	49,189
South African Railways (1959)	113,684	10,493	101,303

* The combined figure for the Colored and Asian and African populations is 14,990.

In 1960 there were a total of 134 trade unions; of these 91 were white, 35 colored, and 58 racially mixed (excluding Africans) trade unions. Africans are legally barred from forming trade unions.[37]

Labor legislation covers such matters as conditions of employment, reservation of certain kinds of employment to particular racial groups, government-operated arbitration, and wages.[38]

The Native Labor (Settlement of Disputes) Act sets up special machinery for the settling of disputes between employers and African employees.

THE REPUBLIC OF SOUTH AFRICA
NOTES

1 Union of South Africa (U. of S.A.): *Official Yearbook of the Union and of Basutoland, Bechuanaland Protectorate and Swaziland,* No. 30–1960, Bureau of Census and Statistics, The Government Printer, Pretoria, p. 10.

2 *South African Scope,* Vol. 4, No. 1, Jan.–Feb. 1961, p. 11.

3 *State of the Union Yearbook for South Africa 1961,* Da Gama Publications, Johannesburg, n.d., p. 68.

4 *The Columbia Lippincott Gazetteer of the World,* Columbia University Press, New York, 1952, p. 1800.

5 *Vide* C. W. de Kiewiet; *A History of South Africa, Social and Economic,* O.U.P., London, 1957.

6 U. of S.A.: *Official Yearbook,* No. 30–1960, *op. cit.,* Chapter II.

7 R. Segal, *Political Africa,* Stevens & Sons Ltd., London, 1961, pp. 415–38.

8 *State of the Union Yearbook for South Africa 1961, op. cit.,* pp. 67–68.

9 U. of S.A.: Bureau of Census and Statistics, *Union Statistics for Fifty Years,* The Government Printer, Pretoria, 1961, pp. A–8 and A–12. In order to make the South African figures comparable to other urban figures in the handbook, the percentages were computed from all towns of 10,000 or more inhabitants. Official South African figures are differently computed, *vide* U. of S.A.: *Population Census, May 8, 1951,* Vol. I, The Government Printer, Pretoria, pp. V–VI.

10 *State of the Union Yearbook for South Africa 1961, op. cit.,* p. 66; U. of S.A.: *Union Statistics for Fifty Years, op. cit.,* pp. 8–19.

11 U. of S.A.: *Union Statistics for Fifty Years, op. cit.,* pp. A–26 to A–29.

12 *Ibid.,* pp. A–3, A–4, and A–5.

13 *Ibid.,* p. A–14.

14 *Ibid.,* Table E; *State of the Union Yearbook for South Africa 1961, op. cit.,* pp. 88–90.

15 U. of S.A.: *Union Statistics for Fifty Years, op. cit.,* pp. B–30 and B–31; *State of the Union Yearbook for South Africa 1961, op. cit.,* p. 68.

16 U. of S.A.: *Official Yearbook,* No. 30–1960, *op. cit.,* pp. 131–34.

17 U. of S.A.: *Union Statistics for Fifty Years, op. cit.,* pp. D–2, D–4 to D–8 and D–11; U. of S.A.: *Official Yearbook,* No. 30–1960, *op. cit.,* pp. 127–29.

18 U. of S.A.: *Official Yearbook,* No. 30–1960, *op. cit.,* Chapter V.

19   U. of S.A.: *Union Statistics for Fifty Years, op. cit.*, pp. O–12 and 1–13.

20   *Ibid.*, p. O–17.

21   *Ibid.*, p. O–6.

22   U. of S.A.: *Official Yearbook*, No. 30–1960, *op. cit.*, pp. 356–57.

23   *Ibid.*, p. 374: U. of S.A.: *Union Statistics for Fifty Years, op. cit.*, p. P–2.

24   U. of S.A.: *Union Statistics for Fifty Years, op. cit.*, pp. N–4 and N–5.

25   *Ibid.*, pp. N–2 and N–3.

26   *Ibid.*, pp. N–2 to N–4.

27   U. of S.A.: *Official Yearbook*, No. 30–1960, *op. cit.*, p. 438; *State of the Union Yearbook for South Africa 1961, op. cit.*, p. 203.

28   U. of S.A.: *Union Statistics for Fifty Years, op. cit.*, pp. I–4 through I–9.

29   *Ibid.*, pp. L–6 to L–34.

30   U. of S.A.: *Official Yearbook*, No. 30–1960, *op. cit.*, Chapter XVIII.

31   U. of S.A.: *Union Statistics for Fifty Years, op. cit.*, p. L–34.

32   U. of S.A.: *Official Yearbook*, No. 30–1960, *op. cit.*, p. 459.

33   *Ibid.*, pp. 463–68.

34   U. of S.A.: *Estimates of the Revenue to be Received During the Year Ending March 31, 1961*, Pretoria, Cape Times Ltd., 1961, p. 6 (this figure excludes revenue from the Provincial and the Railways and Harbor Administrations); *Estimates of the Expenditure to be Defrayed from Revenue Account for the Year Ending March 31, 1962*, Pretoria, Cape Times Ltd., 1961, p. XIV.

35   *State of the Union Yearbook for South Africa 1961, op. cit.*, p. 113.

36   U. of S.A.: *Union Statistics for Fifty Years, op. cit.*, pp. G–6 to G–15.

37   *State of the Union Yearbook for South Africa 1961, op. cit.*, p. 384.

38   U. of S.A.: *Official Yearbook*, No. 30–1960, *op. cit.*, pp. 205–12.

South-West Africa[1]

AREA: *318,099 sq. m.*
POPULATION: *572,000 (1960 estimate)*
Density: 1.8 per sq. m.

GEOGRAPHY

South-West Africa consists of three regions; a coastal strip of 50–80 miles in width, which is dry and mostly uninhabited; an interior plateau 3,600 feet high where most of the population is to be found, which is a continuation of the South African plateau; and the Kalahari Desert on the east. Except for the coast with only one inch of rain per annum, avearge rainfall is 22 inches per year in the north, 6 inches in the south. Severe droughts alternate with periods of excessive rainfall. The territory is hot throughout the year. There are three rivers: the Kunene, Okavango, and Orange.

HISTORICAL SKETCH

Portuguese sailors were the first Europeans to establish contact with the area in the 15th century. The first European settlers, mostly German, came in 1840 under the auspices of the London Missionary Society. In 1884, Germany proclaimed the territory a Protectorate. In 1915 the country was occupied by South African troops and in 1920 the League of Nations gave South Africa a Class C Mandate over the territory. Following World War II the South African government did not place the country under the United Nations' Trusteeship system and continues to run it as a Mandate. It was given representation in the Parliament of the Union (now Republic) in 1949.

361

GOVERNMENT

Present Status
Class C Mandate of the League of Nations administered by the Republic of South Africa.

Constitution
The Parliament of South Africa is the supreme legislative authority, and the Republic government the supreme executive authority. The State President of the Republic of South Africa appoints the chief administrative officer of the territory—the Administrator. He is assisted locally by an Executive of four members selected by the Legislative Assembly, a body of 18 elected members. Six Members of Parliament and four Senators from South-West Africa now sit in the Republic's Parliament in Cape Town. The territory of Walvis Bay, while technically part of the Cape Province of South Africa, is administered as part of South-West Africa.

Franchise
Universal adult suffrage for whites only.

Local Government
Local government is conducted by municipal or village management boards under the supervision of the Legislative Assembly.

Political Parties [2]
National Party of South-West Africa and United National South-West Party.

POPULATION BREAKDOWN

Main Cities [3]
1951 census

Windhoek	20,598
Keetmanshoop	5,245
Tsumeb	5,821

Urban-rural Distribution [4]

In 1951 a total of 53,059 persons, or approximately 9% of the total population, lived in towns of 2,000 or more inhabitants.

Ethnic Distribution

June 1960 estimate

European	73,000
Colored	22,000
African	477,000
Ovambo	200,000
Okabango	30,000
Herero	32,000
Nama	30,000
Rehobother	8,900
Damara	25–30,000
Bushmen	10–15,000

Religious Affiliation

Not available.

Languages

Afrikaans	66.3% (of the European population)
German	23.9%
English	8.3%
Other	1.5%

The Colored population speaks both Afrikaans and English. Africans speak the language of their tribal grouping, and Ovambo is the most widespread.

Sex Distribution [5]

1951 census

	Male	Female
European	26,130 (52.3%)	23,800 (47.7%)
African and Colored	192,427 (50.09%)	191,720 (49.91%)

Age Distribution

Not available.

SOCIAL DATA

Education [6]

TABLE I
1958/59

Primary and secondary schools

	Enrollment	Teachers
European		
54 Public schools	12,740	487
7 Private schools	1,732	79
Colored		
40 Schools	3,705	N.A.
African		
254 Schools	29,130	N.A.

For the fiscal year 1958–1959 the total public expenditure on education amounted to £1,372,982, of which £1,121,585 was spent on European education.

Health and Social Services

VITAL STATISTICS [7]

1956

	Birth rate	Death rate	Infant mortality rate
Europeans only	2,044	411	65

MAIN DISEASES [8]

Anthrax, malaria, tuberculosis, typhus fever, scarlet fever, Malta fever, typhoid fever, and leprosy.

HEALTH SERVICES [9]

TABLE II

	Beds
14 State-aided hospitals (12 for Europeans only) (patients) (1959)	5,882
11 State-owned African hospitals	984
6 Mission hospitals for Europeans	
3 Mission hospital for Europeans and nonwhites	222
5 Mission hospitals for nonwhites	
91 Registered medical practitioners	

In addition to these services, mining firms maintain hospitals for their employees.

SOCIAL WELFARE SERVICES

Not available.

ECONOMY

The economy of South-West Africa rests principally on mining and stock-raising activities. There is little agricultural production and virtually no manufacturing.

Transport and Communications

WATERWAYS

None.

PORTS [10]

Walvis Bay is the principal port. Total tonnage handled in 1958 was 915,611 tons, most of which was handled through Walvis Bay.

ROADS

There are more than 21,000 miles of public roads.

RAILROADS

The railways of South-West Africa have been incorporated into the railway system of South Africa. There are 1,462 miles of railroad of which 1,110 are 3-foot 6-inch gauge and the remainder 2-foot gauge.

AIRWAYS

South African Airways operates services between Windhoek and Johannesburg, Cape Town and Livingston. There are 35 licensed private airfields in the territory.

POSTS, TELECOMMUNICATIONS, AND BROADCASTING [11]

Postal, telegraph, telephone, and radio services within South-West Africa are linked with the appropriate facilities in South Africa.

Resources and Trade

MAIN EXPORTS

Minerals (diamonds and lead represent over 80% of the value of South-West Africa's exports), fish, dairy products, canned and chilled meat, and karakul pelts.

MAIN IMPORTS [12]

The territory imports almost all its consumption and capital goods. Capital goods, foodstuffs, and textiles predominate.

VALUE OF TRADE
  In £'000's

	1956	1957	1958	1959
Exports	23,215	20,548	17,714	20,114
Imports	6,380	6,557	8,408	6,749

MARKETING AND COOPERATIVE SOCIETIES [13]

In 1960 there were 10 agricultural cooperative societies.

LIVESTOCK

	1958
Cattle	3,221,681
Sheep	3,123,924
Horses	95,838
Mules	3,199
Donkeys	81,281
Pigs (1950)	19,867 [14]

Industry

MANUFACTURES [15]

A lack of water and coal has impeded the development of manufacturing in the territory. Meat and fish packing, paint production, and two breweries are the principal manufacturing undertakings. These, however, are very small enterprises.

MINING [16]

Mining is the main economic activity in the territory. In 1959 mineral sales amounted to over £25 million. Diamonds, lead, copper, and zinc are mined.

POWER

There are virtually no domestic sources and demand is satisfied by imports.

Finance

CURRENCY

South-West Africa changed its currency with South Africa in 1961 from the S.A.£ to the S.A.rand (2R equals £1 sterling).

BANKING

Barclay's Bank D.C.O., Standard Bank of South Africa, Volkskas Bpk., and the Netherlands Bank of South Africa.

BUDGET

	1955/1956	1960/1961
Revenue	£12,034,000	£13,490,000
Expenditure	10,720,000	n.a.

DEVELOPMENT PLAN

Since 1952 all capital expenditure has been included in ordinary expenditure.

LABOR

Labor figures for South-West Africa are not provided separately but are included in those for South Africa.

As of 1958 there were 3 trade unions with a combined membership of 700 and 3 employers organizations with a membership of 190.[17]

The Wage and Industrial Conciliation Ordinance of 1952 created machinery for wage determinations, the registration and control of trade unions and employers' organizations, the settlement of disputes, and voluntary and compulsory arbitration.[18]

SOUTH-WEST AFRICA NOTES

1   Unless otherwise stated, all information obtained from *State of the Union Yearbook for South Africa 1961*, Da Gama Publications, Johannesburg, 1961, pp. 499–509.

2   R. Segal, *Political Africa*, Stevens & Sons Ltd., London, 1961, p. 439.

3   Union of South Africa (U. of S.A.): *Official Yearbook*, No. 29—1956–1957, The Government Printer, Pretoria, 1958, p. 767.

4   *Ibid.*

5   U. of S.A.: *Official Yearbook*, No. 29–1956–1957, *op. cit.*, p. 767.

6   U. of S.A.: *Official Yearbook*, No. 30–1960, The Government Printer, Pretoria, 1961, p. 604.

7   U. of S.A.: *Official Yearbook*, No. 29—1956–1957, *op. cit.*, p. 767.

8   U. of S.A.: *Official Yearbook*, No. 16—1933–1934, The Government Printer, Pretoria, 1934, pp. 1004–1005.

9   U. of S.A.: *Official Yearbook*, No. 30—1960, *op. cit.*, pp. 598–602.

10   *Ibid.*, p. 622.

11   *Ibid.*, pp. 624–25.

12   U. of S.A.: *Official Yearbook*, No. 29—1956–1957, *op. cit.*, p. 785.

13   U. of S.A.: *Official Yearbook*, No. 30—1960, *op. cit.*, p. 628.

14   U. of S.A.: *Official Yearbook*, No. 29—1956–1957, *op. cit.*, p. 785.

15   U. of S.A.: *Official Yearbook*, No. 30—1960, *op. cit.*, p. 627.

16   U. of S.A.: *Official Yearbook*, No. 29—1956–1957, *op. cit.*, p. 801.

17   U. of S.A.: *Official Yearbook*, No. 30—1960, *op. cit.*, p. 625.

18   *Ibid.*, p. 619.

Spanish Territories[1]

SPANISH SAHARA AND IFNI

AREA: *106,271 sq. m.*

POPULATION: *193,224 (1950 estimate)*

GOVERNMENT

The two areas are each provinces of Spain, governed by a Governor General.

Main Cities
Sidi Ifni (capital of Ifni)
Villa Cisnero (Spanish Sahara)
Smara (Spanish Sahara)

FERNANDO PO AND RIO MUNI

AREA: *10,852 sq. m.*

POPULATION: *214,271 (1950 estimate)*

GOVERNMENT

Present Status
Provinces of Spain.

Constitution
The two provinces are governed by a Governor General at Santa Isabel, assisted by two subgovernors at Bata and Elobey.

Local Government
Fernando Po is divided into 2 districts and Río Muni into 11 districts, each under a territorial administrator who has at his disposal the colonial guard.

POPULATION AND SOCIAL DATA

Main Cities
Bata (Río Muni)
Santa Isabel (Island of Fernando Po)

Ethnic Distribution
Bubis (Fernando Po)
Fang (Río Muni)
Benga

Education

	1959	
	Enrollment	*Teachers*
119 Primary schools	19,678	208
3 Secondary schools	239	13

ECONOMY

Fernando Po and Río Muni produce cocoa, coffee, fruits, vegetables, and wood, all of which are exported principally to Spain.

NOTE

1   All information obtained from S. H. Steinberg (Ed.), *The Statesman's Yearbook 1961*, Macmillan and Co., Ltd., London, 1961, pp. 1389–91.

Sudan[1]

AREA:[2] *967,500 sq. m.*
POPULATION: *10,262,536 (1955/6 census)*
Density:[3] 4 per sq. m.

GEOGRAPHY

The Sudan is an immense country divided into several major zones: (a) the northern desert area; (b) the mountainous eastern area; (c) the western area consisting of desert, semidesert, and volcanic mountains; (d) the clay plains of the Central and Southern Sudan; and (e) the plateau of the southwest. In the northern region rain is extremely rare. The main portion of the Sudan, excluding the Red Sea coast, is dominated by the movement between the dry northerly winds in winter and the moist southerly winds in the summer. On the seacoast the climate is profoundly influenced by the Red Sea and most of the rain falls during the winter. Annual rainfall varies from about 40 inches in the extreme south to 4 inches in the north. Temperatures range between 60 to over 100 degrees F.

HISTORICAL SKETCH

The first known settlement of this region was between the 5th and 4th centuries B.C., but it is only when the area now known as the Sudan became linked with Egyptian recorded history that reliable information became available. Raiding of the northern regions and trading between it and Egypt are known to have taken place between 2800 and 2000 B.C. About this time Egypt started colonizing the Sudan as far as the 4th cataract on the Nile and established a Governor at Kerma. Egyptian control of the area, varying in degree, seems to have lasted until 750 B.C., when a Sudanese Kingdom arose at Napapta (near modern Meroe) and itself conquered Egypt to become the 25th dynasty of Egypt. About a century later the Sudanese were driven out of Egypt and consolidated their position at Meroe to establish the Meroe Kingdom, which reached the height of its prosperity at about the beginning of the Christian era. The Meroe Kingdom collapsed and for some 500 years the Sudan was ruled by a number of small independent kingdoms. The conversion of Sudan to Christianity began in the mid-6th century when Justinian sent two missionaries into the area. By the 7th century A.D. the Coptic Church had established its dominance over the area, which was divided into the two political kingdoms of Dongola in the north and Alwa in the south. The conquest of Egypt by Muslims was followed by sporadic attacks on the Dongola Kingdom, leading to its eventual collapse in 1340 and the gradual extension of Islam over the northern two-thirds of present-day Sudan. The overthrow of the Alwa Kingdom came in 1504. It was super-seded by the Muslim Kingdom of the Funj, which lasted some 300 years. In 1821 and after, the country gradually came under the control of the Pashas of Egypt. During this period a system of administration was intro-duced, the country was divided into provinces and regions under Turko-Egyptian administrators. European explorers and administrators were also employed, among them General Gordon. In 1882 a religious rebellion led by Muhammed Ahmad (the Madhi) successfully culminated in the over-throw of Egyptian control and the capture of Khartoum in 1885, when Gordon was killed. The British in the meantime had occupied Egypt and advised the withdrawal of Turko-Egyptian control over the area. Sudan thus remained independent until 1898, when the British, partially out of fear of the establishment of French influence over the Upper Nile, sent an army under Kitchener to conquer Sudan. It was victorious, and Kitchener was made Governor General. The 1899 Condominium Agree-ment separated the administration of Sudan from Egypt, and it remained under British control until 1953. During that period a process of "Sudani-zation" took place, first at the local administrative level, later at the cen-tral government level, when Sudanese replaced British officials. In 1953 Egypt dropped its demand for the reincorporation of the Sudan on the understanding that at the end of three years the Sudanese were to decide on the future of their country. Before the period was up, Sudan became an independent state in January 1956.

GOVERNMENT

Present Status
Independent republican state.

Constitution

The highest constitutional authority is the Supreme Council of the Armed Forces, consisting of a President and 6 members, assisted by a Council of Ministere of 12 members. All legislative, judicial, and executive powers, and command of the armed forces, are delegated to the President of the Supreme Council.

Franchise

There are no elections to the central government, and franchise at the local level is unknown.

Local Government

The country is divided into 9 provinces, each of which is governed by a Province Council of some 12–20 members representing local authorities; other members are nominated by the Governor. The country is further subdivided into 52 districts, many of which are still in the charge of a district commissioner responsible to the Governor or Commissioner concerned. In certain districts local government councils have started to replace the district commissioners. Local authorities are being established, three-quarters of the membership of which are elected and the remainder nominated by the Governor. In 1960 there were 18 urban and 56 rural units of this kind.

Political Parties [4]

National Unionist Party (N.U.P.), led by Ismail El Azhari.
Umna (Independent) Party, led by Siddik El Mahdi.
Peoples Democratic Party (P.D.P.), led by Ali Abdel-Rahman.
Liberal Party, led by Saturnino Lohure.
Socialist Republican Party (S.R.P.).
General Ibrahim Abhoud is President of the Republic.

POPULATION BREAKDOWN

Main Cities

Khartoum (capital)	93,103
Omdurman	113,686
Wad Medani	46,677
El Obeid	52,372

Kassala	40,612
El Fasher	26,161
Juba	10,660
Malkal	9,680

Urban-rural Distribution

About 6% of the total population lives in towns of 10,000 or more inhabitants.

Ethnic Distribution [5]

Arab	39%
Nuba	6%
Beja	6%
Nubiyin	3%
Central southerners (mainly Nilotic)	20%
Eastern southerners (mainly Nilo-Hamitic)	5%
Western southerners (mainly Sudanic)	5%
Westerners	13%
Foreigners	2%
Miscellaneous	1%

Religious Affiliation

No census of religious affiliations has yet been taken. The population of the northern region is almost entirely Muslim, apart from very small areas of pagan and Christian communities in the towns. In the southern region there are a certain number of Christians and Muslims, but the majority are pagan.

Languages [6]

Arabic (51.4%), Nilotic languages (17.7%), Nilo-Hamitic languages (4.9%), Sudanic languages (4.7%), Darfurian (5.6%), other African languages (3.5%), European languages (0.1%), non-Arabic languages in north and central Sudan (12.1%).

Sex Distribution [7]

1955/6 census

Male	Female
5,186,126 (50.5%)	5,076,410 (49.5%)

Age Distribution [8]

1955/6 census

Under 5	5–under puberty	Over puberty
2,042,936	2,371,779	5,847,821

SOCIAL DATA

Education [9]

TABLE I

Schools	Government	Enrollment	Nongovernment	Enrollment
Sub-grades	1,244	107,460	19	2,402
Elementary	848	151,497	85	12,416
Intermediate	144	20,851	105	16,515
Secondary	37	4,976	28	6,834
Technical and vocational	18	1,659	10	1,267
Cairo University (Khartoum branch)		1,068		
Khartoum Technical Institute		4,309		

In 1961 there were 7,307 teachers at the first level of teaching and 3,154 at the second level. In 1959/60 it was estimated that 12.8% of the children aged 5–14 were at school.

Expenditure on education between 1953/56 was £4.5 million, 12.0% of the total expenditure of government.

Health and Social Services

VITAL STATISTICS [10]

Per 1,000

Crude birth rate	Crude death rate	Crude infant mortality rate
51.7	18.5	93.6

MAIN DISEASES

Malaria, yellow fever, dysentery, typhoid fever, eye diseases, sleeping sickness, rabies, cerebrospinal meningitis.

HEALTH SERVICES

In 1959/60 there were 60 hospitals, 890 dispensaries and dressing stations, and 270 doctors. In addition each province has a preventive hygiene service, and the rural areas are served by a home midwifery service.

The new Khartoum hospital has 362 beds and the old Khartoum hospital 251 beds.

SOCIAL WELFARE SERVICES

Not available.

ECONOMY [11]

The economy of the Sudan still depends largely on agricultural and pastoral pursuits. It has traditionally relied on its exports of cotton, gum arabic (85% of the world supply), and livestock. Secondary industries, mainly in the processing of local products, are gradually expanding.

Transport and Communications

WATERWAYS

There are 3,744 km. of navigable waterways in the Sudan. The Nile is navigable at almost all seasons from Alexandria to Wadi Halfa and again from Khartoum to Juba. Its tributaries, the Atbara, Rahad, and Dinda rivers, have been navigated in the flood season, but are not normally navigable. The Sobat River is navigable as far as Johau, and its tributary, the Pibor, as far as Akobo for parts of the year. The Baro River is navigable, only by small craft, as far as Abu Zaid. The Jur River is navigable to Wau from July to October and Lake Ambodi from July to March.

PORTS

Port Sudan, some 490 miles from Khartoum, is Sudan's largest port and can anchor 9 large vessels at a time, and one medium-sized vessel. Suakin is used by small craft. Flamingo Bay Harbor is used almost exclusively by sambuks, as is Trinkitat. Total tonnage handled in 1958/59 was 1,688,000 tons.

ROADS [12]

Roads in Northern Sudan, and other town roads, are only cleared tracks, mostly impassable directly after rain. In the Upper Nile Province, motor traffic is limited mostly to the drier months (January–May). In Equatoria and Bahr El Ghazal provinces there are a number of good graveled roads which can be used all year round, though minor roads are impassable after rain.

RAILROADS

In 1958/59 there were 4,789 km. of railroads.

AIRWAYS

The government of Sudan runs its own airline with internal services as well as services to Europe and other parts of Africa. There is an international airport at Khartoum and 10 other airfields throughout the country.

POSTS, TELECOMMUNICATIONS, AND BROADCASTING

Sudan has extensive postal and telegraph facilities. Larger towns have automatic telephone systems, and manual services are provided in the smaller towns. Radio Ondurman has 2 transmitters and Feteihab Radio has 2. Programs are given daily in Arabic, English, and southern Sudanese languages.

Resources and Trade

MAIN EXPORTS [13]

Cotton (56.8% of the total value of exports for 1956/58), gum arabic, peanuts, and sesame.

MAIN IMPORTS

Base metals and manufactures, vehicles and transport equipment, cotton piece goods, petroleum products, machinery, refined sugar.

VALUE OF TRADE [14]

In £S'000's

	1956	1957	1958	1959	1960
Exports	66,789	51,423	43,429	66,770	63,374
Imports	25,258	67,557	59,491	57,055	62,998

The United Kingdom is Sudan's chief trading partner.

There are 560 cooperatives in the Sudan, of which 418 are formally registered; of these 115 are marketing and credit societies, 83 agricultural pumping schemes; 30 general-purpose societies, 165 consumer cooperative societies, 10 cooperative flour mills, and 15 other cooperatives.

The entire Gezira cotton production scheme is under the control of the Sudan Gezira Board (see Development Plan).

LIVESTOCK

1960 estimate

Cattle	6,907,000
Sheep	6,946,000
Goats	7,748,000
Camels	2,000,000

Industry

MANUFACTURES
The following are produced locally: cement, beer, aluminum, cigarettes, oil, soap, perfume, shoes, knitwear, confectionery, pulp and paper, hides and skins, pharmaceuticals, sugar, and petroleum products.

MINING
Mineral resources do not exist in any quantity. At present, gold, iron ore, iron, manganese ore, mica, limestone, copper ores, and lead-zinc ores are being exploited.

POWER
Electricity is supplied by the Central Electricity and Water Administration at Khartoum, Ondurman, Khartoum North, and Wad Medani, while the Ministry of Works supplies electricity at 11 other smaller centers.

Petroleum resources are being explored by a number of licensed prospecting companies, mainly along the Red Sea coast.

Finance

CURRENCY
One pound Sudanese (£S) equals £1.0.6.15 sterling.

BANKING

Barclay's Bank D.C.O., National Bank of Egypt, Ottoman Bank, Crédit Lyonnais, Bank Misr, Bank El Arabi, the State Bank of Ethiopia, Agricultural Bank of Sudan, and the Sudan Commercial Bank.

BUDGET

In £S'000's

1958/59

Revenue	41,983
Expenditure	41,409

The main sources of revenue are indirect taxation through customs, duties on imported goods, and royalties on produce exported.

DEVELOPMENT PLAN [15]

Sources

1958/63 *in £S millions*—total expenditure £S137

Budget	36
World Bank Loan	39
I.C.A.	30.6

Main areas of development expenditure

Managil extension and proposed Roseires dam	42
Railway construction	35
Other transport and communications	15
Health and education	12

The Gezira cotton production scheme, started in 1925, continues to progress under the Managil Extension. It is run under a triple partnership of government, tenant-cultivator, and the Sudan Gezira Board. The basic shares of these partners are 42% for government, 42% for tenant-cultivators, 10% for the Sudan Gezira Board; and 2% for social development, 2% to local government in the Gezira, and 2% for tenant reserve fund. There are about 55,000 tenants.

LABOR [16]

Of the 10.3 million people (1956), some 3 million (or 30%) over the age of puberty were economically active. The nonagricultural labor force numbered only about 470,000 (about 15% of the labor force), of whom some 125,000 were employed either directly or indirectly by the government.

Distribution of the economically active adult labor force for 1955/56 was:

Agricultural and pastoral

Farmers, hunters, fishermen	2,091,000	
Animal owners and nomads	151,665	
Farm and forestry laborers	39,593	
Shepherds	284,936	
Others	235	2,567,435

Nonagricultural

Professional	3,986	
Semiprofessional	48,652	
Clerical	24,344	
Personal services	98,422	
Others	292,365	467,769
TOTAL		3,035,204

(These figures are based on data collected on primary occupations only.)

In 1955 there were 132 trade unions of workers and three of employers. It is estimated that the membership of workers' unions was between 100,000 and 150,000.[17]

Labor legislation deals with such matters as trade unions, regulation of disputes, workmen's compensation, wages, conditions of work, and the like.

SUDAN NOTES

1   Unless otherwise stated, all information obtained from The Republic of the Sudan: *Sudan Almanac 1960*, an official handbook, McCorquedale & Co. (Sudan) Ltd., Khartoum, 1960.

2   S. H. Steinberg (Ed.), *The Statesman's Yearbook 1961*, Macmillan & Co., Ltd., London, 1961, p. 1392.

3   Embassy, Republic of the Sudan, *This Is the Sudan*, Washington, D.C.

4   R. Segal, *Political Africa*, Stevens & Son Ltd., London, 1961, pp. 443–49, *Africa Report*, Vol. 6, No. 10, Nov. 1961, Washington, D.C., p. 21.

5   Republic of the Sudan: *21 Facts About the Sudanese*, prepared by Karol Jozef Krótki, Ministry for Social Affairs, Population Census Office, 1958, p. 23.

6 Republic of the Sudan: *First Population Census of Sudan 1955/1956,* Last (9th) Interim Report, Ministry for Social Affairs, Khartoum, May 1958, p. 7, Table 4.

7 *Ibid.,* p. 4, Tables 1 and 2.

8 *Ibid.,* pp. 4–5, Table 1.

9 U.N. Economic Commission for Africa, UNESCO: *Final Report of the Conference of African States on the Development of Education in Africa,* Addis Ababa, May 15–25, 1961, "Outline of a Plan for African Educational Development, p. 7, Table 1, UNESCO/ED/181. Also, Raymond J. Smythe: "Problems of Teacher Supply and Demand in Africa South of the Sahara," in *The Journal of Negro Education,* Vol. XXX, No. 3, Howard University Press, p. 337, Table I; The Republic of the Sudan: "This Is Our Way to Build a Strong Nation" series; *Education,* n.d., p. 12.

10 Republic of the Sudan: *First Population Census of Sudan 1955/1956,* op. *cit.,* p. 57, Table 12.

11 *This Is the Sudan, op. cit.;* also Embassy, Republic of the Sudan, *The Economy of the Republic of the Sudan,* Washington, D.C.

12 S. H. Steinberg (Ed.), *op. cit.,* p. 1396.

13 The Republic of the Sudan: *Economic Survey 1960;* Research and Statistical Section, Economic Branch, Ministry of Finance and Economics, Khartoum, May 1961, p. 74.

14 *Ibid.,* pp. 74 and 84.

15 *Oxford Regional Economic Atlas,* "The Middle East and North Africa," prepared by the Economist Intelligence Unit Limited, and the Cartographic Department of the Clarendon Press, London, O.U.P., 1960, p. 109.

16 U.S.: Department of Labor, Bureau of Labor Statistics, in cooperation with I.C.A., *Labor in the Sudan,* Washington, D.C., February 1961, pp. 6 and 7.

17 International Labor Office, *African Labor Survey,* Geneva, 1958, p. 239

Swaziland[1]

AREA: *6,704 sq. m.*
POPULATION:[2] *237,041 (1956 census)*
Density: ±35 per sq. m.

GEOGRAPHY

Swaziland is divided into three well-defined regions running from north to south: (a) the mountainous high veld on the west rises from 3,500 feet to over 5,000 feet, where the country is rugged and broken. The slopes are often too steep for cultivation and grazing is poor, but they are now being used for afforestation; (b) the middle veld, averaging 2,000 feet, where the soil has deteriorated but the rainfall is plentiful; and (c) the low veld on the east, known as the plateau of the Lebombo Mountains, traversed by the gorges of the Ingwavuma, the Great Usutu, and the Black Umbulusi rivers, which, together with the Komati River in the northwest, are the most important rivers. Rainfall varies considerably and tends to be concentrated in a few violent storms. The average rainfall is 56.6 inches in the high veld, 36.8 inches in the middle veld, and 26.5 inches in the low veld. Temperatures vary between 52 and 84 degrees F.

HISTORICAL SKETCH

The Swazis settled in present-day Swaziland in about 1750 and applied to the British Agent General in Natal a century later for protection against the warring Zulus. Peace was introduced in the area, thus encouraging white settlement. By the 1880's such an excessive number of concessions had been made to the whites by Mbandzeni, the Swazi Paramount Chief, that some form of control became necessary. Until 1906, when the British finally assumed control over Swaziland, the territory was alternately controlled by the Transvaal Republic and the British

Government. In 1907 the Swazis were handed back part of the concessions and given protection on white lands until 1914. In 1921 an elected European Advisory Council was constituted. In 1944 the Paramount Chief and Council were recognized as the Native Authority, and six years later the terms of recognition were revised and a Swazi National Treasury was set up.

GOVERNMENT

Present Status
British Colony.

Constitution
The territory is governed by a Resident Commissioner under the direction of the High Commissioner for Basutoland, Bechuanaland Protectorate, and Swaziland, in whom legislative power is vested.

The sole Native Authority follows the traditional system of government of a Paramount Chief acting in conjunction with a council consisting of chiefs and leading men, in the discussions of which any adult male Swazi may take part. It is known as the Swaziland National Council.

Franchise
Not applicable.

Local Government
See Native Authority, above.

Political Party [3]
Swaziland Progressive Party (SPP), led by J. J. Nquku.

POPULATION BREAKDOWN

Main Cities [4]

Mbabane (capital)	3,428
Stegi	612

Urban-rural Distribution [5]
In 1956 there were 3,219 Africans, 371 Eurafricans, and 2,848 Europeans living in urban and village areas.

Ethnic Distribution [6]
1956 census

European	5,919
Swazi	229,744
Colored	1,378

Religious Affiliations [7]

	African	European	Colored
Christians	137,566	5,764	1,330
Animists	92,178	—	—
Others	—	155	48

Languages
English, Afrikaans, and Swazi.

Sex Distribution [8]
1956 census

	Male	Female
European	3,190 (53.7%)	2,729 (46.3%)
African	110,055 (48.0%)	119,689 (52.0%)
Colored	699 (50.7%)	679 (49.3%)

Age Distribution [9]
1956 census

	Under 18	18–49	50+
European	1,260	1,371	559
African	121,578	88,373	19,693
Colored	409	235	55

SOCIAL DATA

Education [10]

TABLE I
1959

African Education	Enrollment	
280 Primary schools	30,412	
14 Secondary schools	805	943 teachers
2 Technical and vocational schools	75	
3 Teacher-training colleges	73	

In 1959 between 55% and 58% of the children of school-going age were at school. There were 15 students studying abroad: 4 at Roma in Basutoland, 1 in South Africa, 2 in Southern Rhodesia, and 4 in the United Kingdom.

Expenditure in 1959 was £163,778 (1946/47—£24,115).

European Education	Enrollment
9 Primary schools	1,066
3 Secondary schools	223

Expenditure in 1959: £124,021.

Eurafrican Education	
5 Primary schools	529
3 Secondary schools	50
2 Technical and vocational schools	6

Expenditure in 1959 was £9,015.

98% of European children and 85% of Eurafrican children of school-going age attend school.

Health and Social Services

VITAL STATISTICS [11]

Available for Europeans only

	1959
Birth rate	123
Death rate	31
Deaths of infants under 1 year of age	1

MAIN DISEASES [12]

Tuberculosis, bilharziasis, influenza, enteric fever, infectious diseases, dysentery, venereal disease, tapeworm, and nutritional diseases.

HEALTH SERVICES [13]

TABLE II
1959

	Government	Mission
Hospitals	4 (326 beds)	3 (293 beds)
Clinics	11 (64,513 attendances)	11 (30,385 attendances)

In addition a private company operates a hospital and other companies provide clinics. The Swazi National Treasury maintains and staffs three clinics.

SOCIAL WELFARE SERVICES [14]

Community development is carried out by the District Commissioners in conjunction with the Swazi National Council. Social welfare work is done mainly by voluntary organizations such as the British Red Cross, Child Welfare Society, etc. There are two funds supervised by the government, the Swaziland Soldiers' Benefit Fund, and Pauper Relief. The Girl Guide and Boy Scout movements are both active in the territory.

ECONOMY

The territory's economy is highly underdeveloped and based on the exploitation of minerals, of which asbestos is by far the most important. There are prospects of further mineral developments. Swaziland possesses good soil, a good climate, and an abundant supply of water. In African areas (over half the total area), the predominant activities are animal husbandry and peasant farming, with an increasing emphasis on cash crops like cotton, tobacco, rice, and vegetables.

Transport and Communications

WATERWAYS

There are no navigable rivers in Swaziland.

PORTS

None.

ROADS

Swaziland has 1,200 miles of graveled or earth roads.

RAILROADS

None. Goods and passengers are transported by road to railheads in neighboring territories.

AIRWAYS [15]

There are no regular services within the territory, but a number of unlicensed land strips are in regular use.

POSTS, TELECOMMUNICATIONS, AND BROADCASTING [16]

There were 1,750 telephones in 1959 and a number of private extensions. There is an automatic exchange at Bremersdorp. There is no internal system of broadcasting. There were 30 post offices and agencies in 1957.

Resources and Trade

MAIN EXPORTS [17]

Asbestos (representing 47% of the total value of exports in 1959), sugar, cotton, tobacco (30% in 1959), livestock, and forestry products.

MAIN IMPORTS

Consumer goods, motor vehicles and spares, timber, building materials, sugar, and mining stores.

VALUE OF TRADE [18]

In £'000's

	1955	1956	1957	1958	1959
Exports	3,306	3,603	4,116	3,891	4,384
Imports	1,954	2,222	3,209	3,162	3,977

Most imports come from South Africa. One-third of exports go to countries outside the South African Customs Union, the United Kingdom being the most important market.

MARKETING AND COOPERATIVE SOCIETIES

The Swaziland Milling Company imports, buys locally, and mills maize and maize products. Prices are controlled by the government.[19]

There were 3 cooperative societies in 1959: the Swaziland Tobacco Cooperative Company, which handles virtually the whole tobacco crop of the territory; the Swaziland Civil Servants Cooperative Society Ltd., and the Swaziland Citrus Cooperative Company Ltd.

LIVESTOCK [20]

1959 estimate

Cattle	503,915
Horses	2,333
Mules	594
Donkeys	16,741
Sheep and goats	215,557
Pigs	11,682
Poultry	282,977

Industry

MANUFACTURES

Processing firms include a creamery, two bone-meal factories, an oil-expressing plant, a timber factory, a pineapple-canning factory, a clothing factory, a tannery, two engineering concerns, and a ginnery. Tourist articles also are manufactured.

MINING

Swaziland has one of the largest asbestos mines in the world. Tin and barites are worked at present; and deposits of anthracite coal, high-grade calcite, and iron ore are known to exist. The Geological Survey Department is successfully prospecting for iron and coal.

POWER [21]

There are two hydroelectric stations: one on the Mbabane River—in 1959 the consumption was 1,118,800 kwh.; and one on the Usushwana River—consumption 860,500 kwh. in 1959.

Finance

CURRENCY

The same as the Union of South Africa—the rand: 2R equals 1£ sterling.

BANKING

The Standard Bank of South Africa and Barclay's Bank (D.C.O.) both have branches at Mbabane and Bremersdorp, and operate agencies elsewhere. There are post office savings banks throughout the territory.

BUDGET [22]

1961/62 estimate

Revenue	R. 3,335,256
Expenditure	R. 4,155,256

The main sources of ordinary revenue are income tax, customs and excise, native tax, base-metal royalty, and posts and telegraphs. Swaziland is treated as part of the Republic of South Africa for customs purposes and receives a fixed percentage of the total customs revenue collected by the Republic.

DEVELOPMENT PLAN [23]

United Kingdom Colonial development and welfare grants for the period 1955/60 equals £2,759,826. For the period 1948/59 loans totaled £1,708,656. Road development is the largest item of development expenditure.

LABOR [24]

The main occupations are agriculture, mining, building, trading, and employment in government services and on U.K. Colonial Development Corporation projects. About 15,000 persons are in wage-earning employment. In 1958, 7,600 Swazi were recruited for work in South Africa, and in March 1959 some 15,000 were employed in the territory, distributed as follows:

Havelock mine	1,627
Agricultural enterprises	9,281
Swaziland government	2,457

Although existing legislation covers settlements of disputes, registration of trade unions, workmen's compensation, etc., no trade unions have yet been formed in the territory.

SWAZILAND NOTES

1 Unless otherwise stated, all information obtained from Fact Sheets on the U.K. Dependencies, Reference Division, U.K. Colonial Office of Information, No. R, 4357, *Swaziland*, Oct. 1959.

2 Swaziland Government: *Swaziland Census 1956*, High Commission Printing and Publishing Co. (PTY) Ltd., p. 6, Table 1(a). A census was taken in 1959, but its results are not yet available.

3 R. Segal, *Political Africa*, Stevens & Sons Ltd., London, 1961, p. 480.

4 Swaziland Government: *Swaziland Census 1956, op. cit.*, p. 23, Table 5(c).

5 *Ibid.*

6 *Ibid.*, p. 6, Table 1(a).

7 *Ibid.*, pp. 45–47, Tables 2(a), (b), and (c).

8 *Ibid.*, p. 6, Table 1(a).

9 *Ibid.*, pp. 9–10, Tables 2(a), (b), and (c).

10 Swaziland Government: *Annual Report of Summary by the Director of Education, 1959*, Mbabane, Feb. 1960, pp. 1–4, and Tables IA, B, and

C, and VA, B, and C; Basutoland, Bechuanaland Protectorate, and Swaziland: *Report of an Economic Survey Mission*, H.M.S.O., London, 1960, p. 449.

11   Swaziland: *Annual Medical and Sanitary Report 1959*, p. 19.

12   *Ibid.*, pp. 5–13.

13   *Ibid.*, pp. 47–49, Appendices VI and VII.

14   U.K.: *Swaziland 1959*, London, H.M.S.O., 1960, pp. 91–92.

15   *Ibid.*, pp. 70–71.

16   U.N.: *Progress in Non-Self-Governing Territories Under the Charter*, Territorial Surveys, Vol. 5, New York, 1960, p. 117; U.K.: *Swaziland 1959*, *op. cit.*, p. 94.

17   U.K.: *Swaziland 1959*, *op. cit.*, p. 29.

18   *Ibid.*, pp. 29–30; and *Report of an Economic Survey Mission*, *op. cit.*, pp. 547 and 549.

19   U.K.: *Swaziland 1959*, *op. cit.*, pp. 41–42.

20   *Ibid.*, p. 43.

21   *Ibid.*, p. 88.

22   Swaziland: *Estimates of Revenue and Expenditure April 1961–March 1962*, p. 4.

23   *Report of an Economic Survey Mission*, *op. cit.*, pp. 544–45.

24   *Ibid.*, pp. 446–47; also U.K.: *Swaziland 1959*, *op. cit.*, pp. 16–17.

Tanganyika[1]

> **AREA:** 362,688 sq. m.
> (including some 20,000 sq. m.
> of inland water)
> **POPULATION:**[2] 9,238,600 (1960 estimate)
> Density:[3] 26 per sq. m.

GEOGRAPHY

Tanganyika has some 500 miles of coastline. Mount Kilimanjaro, with a permanent icecap, rises to 19,340 feet above sea level. The deep troughlike depression filled by Lake Tanganyika (the world's second deepest lake) lies 2,534 feet above sea level. Along the coast lies a plain 10 to 40 miles wide. Behind this the country rises to the great central plateau some 4,000 feet high. Along the eastern and western escarpment ridges, the plateau forms narrow belts of high country; in the east this is cut by the Great Ruaha River, and in the west by the Valley of the Malgarasi River. The main rivers are the Pangani or Ruvu, Wami, Rufiji, Great Ruaha, Matandu, Mbemkuru, Lukeledi, Ruvuma, and Mori. There are three climatic zones: (a) the coastal area and immediate hinterland where conditions are tropical, average temperature is 76 degrees F., and rainfall 40 inches; (b) the central plateau where humidity is low (rainfall is 20–40 inches annually), mean temperature high over 70 degrees F., and daily variations are great; and (c) semitemperate regions in the mountain areas where the climate is healthy and bracing, with cold nights.

HISTORICAL SKETCH

Localities such as Dar es Salaam and Tanga were probably inhabited in prehistoric times. Active colonization was begun by Arabs from Oman in the 8th century A.D. Persian remains and Chinese coins have also been found. Turks and Portuguese had transitory settlements in the 16th and 17th centuries. In 1884–1885 Tanganyika came under German influence when treaties were negotiated with the local chiefs and their land was declared German. Throughout the period 1889–1905, the Germans were faced with continual uprisings, which they finally managed to subdue. When World War I broke out, clashes between the British and German troops occurred and German forces were completely expelled in November 1917. Following the Versailles Peace Treaty, Germany renounced her rights over her overseas territories, and Tanganyika was placed under the Mandate system of the League of Nations, with Britain as the Mandatory Power. In 1946 the country was placed under United Nations Trusteeship. A Legislative Council had been established in 1926 which at first had no African representation, and in 1945 two Africans were nominated to it for the first time. In 1947 Tanganyika joined the East Africa High Commission and its Central Legislature, which had powers of control over certain strictly defined matters such as customs and tariffs and postal services. In 1958 Tanganyika held its first elections. It became independent on December 1, 1961 and was admitted to the United Nations on December 14, 1961.

GOVERNMENT

Present Status
Independent state.

Constitution [4]
Executive power is vested in a Cabinet consisting of the Prime Minister and 12 elected ministers. Legislative power is vested in the National Assembly of 81 members—71 elected, 2 European ex-officio, 8 nominated (4 Europeans, 2 Africans, 1 Arab, and 1 Goan). The 71 elected members are returned by 50 constituencies (50 represent open seats, 11 Asian, and 10 European reserved seats). All seats but one held by an Independent are held by TANU.

Franchise
Qualifications: 21 years of age; ability to read or write English or Swahili, or income of £75 per annum, or holder of a prescribed office.[5] Universal adult suffrage was introduced at the time of independence.

Local Government
Dar es Salaam has had a municipal council since 1949. In 1960 its 24 members were elected for the first time. There are 10 town coun-

cils, in several of which a proportion of the councilors are elected. An Ordinance of 1957 provided for the establishment of nonracial district and rural councils where the people want them. They are intended to replace existing local or native authorities. The setting up of district councils is now proceeding.

Political Parties [6]

Tanganyika African National Union (TANU), led by Julius Nyerere, Prime Minister.

African National Congress (ANC), led by Zubedi Mtemvu.

POPULATION BREAKDOWN

Main Cities

1957 census

Dar es Salaam (capital)	128,742
Tanga	38,053
Mwanza	19,877
Tabora	15,361
Morogoro	14,507
Moshi	13,726
Dodoma	13,445
Mtwara	10,459
Lindi	10,315
Iringa	9,587

Urban-rural Distribution [7]

	Percent
Total population	3
African population	2
European population	40
Indian/Pakistani	74
Other	38

Ethnic Distribution [8]

	1957 census	1960 estimate
Asian (including Goan)	76,536	87,300
European	20,598	22,300
Arab	19,100	25,400
Other	6,896	4,600
African	8,662,684	9,099,000

Tribal groups (1957)

Sukuma	1,093,767
Nyamwezi	363,258
Makonde	333,897
Haya	325,539
Chagga	318,167
Gogo	299,417
Ha	289,792
Hehe	251,875
120 other tribes	5,389,875

Religious Affiliation

Not available.

Languages

Masai, Sukumu, and other local vernacular languages are spoken, as well as Swahili (lingua franca); Hindu, Pakistani, Arabic. English is the official language.

Sex Distribution [9]

1957 census

	Male	Female
African	4,165,101 (48.1%)	4,497,583 (51.9%)
European	11,151 (54.1%)	9,447 (45.9%)
Asian	40,463 (52.9%)	36,073 (47.1%)
Arab	11,411 (59.7%)	7,659 (40.3%)
Other	3,686 (53.4%)	3,210 (46.6%)

Age Distribution [10]

1957 census

	Under 16	16+
African	3,840,248	4,822,436

	Under 15	15+
European	5,529	15,069
Asian	32,249	44,287
Arab	7,255	11,845
Other	3,040	3,856

SOCIAL DATA

TABLE I

Education [11]   1959

African	Primary schools	Enrollment	Teachers
739	Government and Native Authority		
1,871	Aided schools	375,008	6,604
71	Unaided schools		

	Middle schools		
138	Government and Native Authority		
212	Aided schools	38,413	1,910
9	Unaided schools		

	Secondary schools		
12	Government and Native Authority	4,132	247
16	Aided schools		
30	African teacher-training colleges	1,467	132
11	African technical and vocational schools	1,836	148
European: 44 schools		3,945	165
Indian/Pakistani, 152 schools		24,864	825
Other 12 schools		1,564	51

In 1959 there were about 260 students from Tanganyika studying in the United Kingdom. Proposals for the establishment of a University College are being considered.

In 1958, 24.1% of the African school-going population (5–14 years of age) was at school.

Expenditure 1959: £4,112,673 (1948—£373,047).

Health and Social Services

VITAL STATISTICS [12]

Per 1,000

	Crude birth rate	Crude death rate	Infant mortality rate
European	+24	5–6	24
Asian	33–38	8–11	90
Arab	42	—	—
African		Not available	

MAIN DISEASES [13]

Malaria, tuberculosis, venereal disease, yaws, sleeping sickness, small-pox, plague, and helminthic and intestinal diseases.

HEALTH SERVICES

TABLE II
1958

		Beds
57	Government hospitals	6,047
38	Mission hospitals	3,469
26	Industrial hospitals	874
20	Government dispensaries	395
84	Mission dispensaries	3,076
5	Government outpatient dispensaries	
643	Native authority outpatient dispensaries	
136	Mission outpatient dispensaries	
299	Industrial outpatient dispensaries	
120	Government maternity and child health centers	
183	Native authority maternity and child health centers	
204	Mission maternity and child health centers	
24	Leprosaria	

There were 460 registered medical practitioners in 1958.

SOCIAL WELFARE SERVICES [14]

In urban centers the policy of the Social Welfare Department is to establish revenue-earning community centers with adult education, social, cultural, and sports facilities. In rural areas emphasis is placed on community-development projects. Women's clubs are run throughout the country. There is a probation service in operation. In addition numerous social welfare services are undertaken by voluntary social welfare organizations.

ECONOMY

Tanganyika's economy is based mainly on the production and export of primary produce. Modern farming methods are being introduced.

Transport and Communications

WATERWAYS

Lake steamer services link Tanganyika with Kenya, Uganda, the Congo, Rwanda, Burundi, and Northern Rhodesia.

PORTS [15]

Dar es Salaam (3 deep-water berths, one of which was constructed for the Belgian Government); Mtwara (2 deep-water berths); Tanga (lighterage), and Lindi (lighterage). In 1959 the total tonnage handled was 1,051,696.

ROADS [16]

In 1959 the total mileage was 28,530, of which 3,588 were territorial main roads, 4,781 local main roads, 11,033 district roads, 8,500 village roads, 490 municipal and township roads, and 138 roads in other settlements. There were 22,883 public and private cars registered in the same year.

RAILROADS [17]

Route mileage at December 31, 1959, was 2,207. The longest line is that linking Dar es Salaam to Kigoma, 779 miles.

AIRWAYS [18]

The East African Airways Corporation, owned by the British East African Government, operates internal services connecting the main centers of Kenya, Uganda, Tanganyika, and Zanzibar, and services connecting Tanganyika with other parts of Africa, the United Kingdom, India, and Pakistan. There are 10 international and 45 other airports.

POSTS, TELECOMMUNICATIONS, AND BROADCASTING [19]

In 1959 there were 89 post offices and 86 postal agencies in the territory; 65 telephone exchanges and 7,659 subscribers, and 215 telegraph establishments. A statutory Tanganyika Broadcasting Corporation was established in 1956. Programs are broadcast in Swahili, English, Gujerati, and include programs for schools.

Resources and Trade

MAIN EXPORTS [20]

Sisal (two-fifths of the world's production, and 25% of the value of exports from 1954/58), coffee, cotton, diamonds, hides and skins, and gold.

MAIN IMPORTS

Machinery, vehicles, metal goods, textiles, petroleum, cement, and chemicals.

VALUE OF TRADE [21]

In £'000's

	1956	1957	1958	1959	1960
Exports	44,884	39,481	41,730	45,287	54,854
Reexports	1,423	1,614	2,098	1,931	1,747
Imports	33,885	39,275	33,568	34,456	29,523

Over 50% of Tanganyika's exports go to the sterling area, and specifically to the U.K.; half of the imports come from the U.K.

MARKETING AND COOPERATIVE SOCIETIES [22]

In addition to 8 main groups of primary marketing societies, Marketing Boards exist for cotton (territorial), coffee (Bukoba, Moshi, Rungwe), and tobacco (Nyamirembe).

In 1959 there were 617 cooperative societies with a membership of 324,904. Their services include bulk marketing facilities, bulk purchase of trade goods, distribution of consumer goods, seed and planting material, loans, crop finance, savings facilities, and education.

LIVESTOCK [23]

1959 census

Cattle	7,719,995
Sheep and goats	7,208,828
Pigs	14,680
Donkeys	130,645
Horses	204

Industry

MANUFACTURES

There were 4,327 registered factories in December 1958. The greatest number were tailoring and/or dressmaking establishments, followed by flour-milling, woodworking, sisal-processing, and motor-vehicle repairing establishments.

MINING

The main minerals at present being mined are diamonds, gold and silver, lead and copper, concentrates, mica, salt, tin, and building minerals. Other known mineral resources include coal, garnet, graphite, gypsum, iron, kaolin, lime, magnesite, meerschaum, niobium, and tungsten.

POWER

The total generating capacity of installations operating at the end of 1958 was 40,392 kw., of which about half was produced by water power.

Finance

CURRENCY

East African shilling: 20 EAsh equal 1£ sterling.

BANKING [24]

National Overseas and Grindlay's Bank, Standard Bank of South Africa, Barclay's Bank D.C.O., Nederlandsche Handel Mij, Bank of Baroda, Ottoman Bank, and Bank of India Ltd.

BUDGET [25]

1960/61 estimate in £'000's

Revenue	20,278
Expenditure	20,718

DEVELOPMENT PLAN [26]

Estimated total cost, £23,930,000

1960/63
Sources

U.K.D.&W.	4,500,000
Loans	11,500,000
Local resources	5,000,000

About £14 million has been allocated to communications and public works; £7 million to social services and urban housing; and the rest for agriculture, rural water supplies, bush clearing and resettlement, forestry, veterinary training, cooperative development, and research projects.

LABOR

A large proportion of the population is self-employed in agriculture. The number of paid Africans in the principal occupations in 1958, was:

Agriculture, forestry, and fishing	213,092
Public services	97,170
Manufacturing	13,701
Mining and quarrying	12,182
Construction	10,438
Commerce	11,800
Transport and communications	7,891
TOTAL	366,274

At the end of 1959 there were 35 registered trade unions with a total membership of about 47,000. These included 8 employers' trade unions, 2 European employees' trade unions, 6 Asian employees' trade unions, and 35 African trade unions. There were also 2 non-racial unions.[27]

Labor legislation covers such matters as terms and conditions of employment, conciliation and arbitration, employment contracts, hours of work, wage protection, medical inspection, compensation, employment of women and juveniles.[28]

TANGANYIKA NOTES

1 Unless otherwise stated, all information obtained from Fact Sheets on the U.K. Dependencies, Reference Division, U.K. Central Office of Information, No. R. 4363, *Tanganyika*, October 1959.

2 The East Africa Statistical Department: *Quarterly Economic and Statistical Bulletin*, No. 50, Dec. 1960, E. A. Printers (Boyds) Ltd., Nairobi, 1960, p. 3, Table A2.

3 International Bank for Reconstruction and Development: *The Economic Development of Tanganyika*, Johns Hopkins Press, Baltimore, 1961, p. 12.

4 Communication received from the British Embassy, Washington, D.C., July 1961; U.K.: Colonial Office. *The Colonial Territories 1960–1961*, H.M.S.O., Cmnd. 1407, London, January 1961, p. 14, para. 74.

5 Communication received from the British Embassy, *op. cit.*

6 R. Segal, *Political Africa*, Stevens & Sons Ltd., London, 1961, pp. 451–53.

7 U.K.: *Tanganyika, 1959, Part II*, H.M.S.O., London, COL. No. 346, 1960, p. 6; Tanganyika: *Report on the Census of the Non-European Population Taken on the Night of 20/21 February 1957*, Government Printer, Dar es Salaam, 1958, p. 7.

8 U.K.: *Tanganyika 1959, Part II, op. cit.*, pp. 8–9; *Quarterly Economic and Statistical Bulletin*, No. 50, Dec. 1960, *op. cit.*, p. 3, Table A2.

9 U.K.: *Tanganyika 1959, Part II, op. cit.*, pp. 8–9.

10 *Ibid.*

11 *Ibid.*, pp. 113–31; U.N. Commission for Africa, UNESCO: *Final Report of the Conference of African States on the Development of Education in Africa*, Addis Ababa, May 15–25, 1961, "Outline of a Plan for African Educational Development," p. 7, Table I, UNESCO/ED/181. "Outline of a Plan for African Educational Development," p. 7, Table I.

12 Tanganyika: *Report on the Census of the Non-European Population, op. cit.*, pp. 37–43.

13 U.K.: *Tanganyika 1959, Part I, op. cit.*, pp. 93–94.

14 *Ibid.*, pp. 87–88.

15 U.K.: *Tanganyika 1959, Part II, op. cit.*, p. 67.

16 *Ibid.*, p. 64.

17 *Ibid.*, p. 65.

18 *Ibid.*, p. 66.

19 *Ibid.*, p. 63.

20 Tanganyika: *Statistical Abstract 1959*, Government Printer, Dar es Salaam, 1959, p. 31.

21 U.K.: *Tanganyika 1959, Part II, op. cit.*, p. 43; Tanganyika: *Monthly Statistical Bulletin*, Vol. XI, No. 5, May 1961, Government Printer, p. 8, Table 13; Tanganyika: *Statistical Abstract 1959, op. cit.*, p. 30, Table E1.

22 U.K.: *The Colonial Office List 1961*, H.M.S.O., London, 1961, p. 168; U.K.: *Tanganyika 1959, Part II, op. cit.*, p. 62.

23 U.K.: *Tanganyika 1959, Part II, op. cit.*, p. 50.

24 S. H. Steinberg (Ed.), *The Statesman's Yearbook 1961*, Macmillan & Co., Ltd., London, 1961, p. 340.

25 Tanganyika: *Monthly Statistical Bulletin, op. cit.*, p. 10, Table 20.

26 U.K.: *The Colonial Territories 1960–1961, op. cit.*, p. 120.

27 U.K.: *Tanganyika 1959, Part I, op. cit.*, p. 85.

28 *Ibid.*, pp. 81–84.

The Republic of Togo

AREA: [1] *21,853 sq. m.*
POPULATION: [2] *1,094,000 (1957 estimate)*
Density: 74 per sq. m.

GEOGRAPHY [3]

Mountain ranges seldom rising above 3,500 feet cut across the country from Palime to Lama-Kara. To the north lies the valley of the Ote River. The Mono River running north to south is the only river of importance in the territory. There are two rainy seasons in the southern region, from May to June and in October. In the north the rainy season lasts from August to September. There is high humidity throughout the year. Average rainfall in the coastal region is 600–800 mm. and in the mountain region 1,500–1,700 mm.

HISTORICAL SKETCH [4]

Togoland was proclaimed a German Protectorate in 1884 and its boundaries were fixed by 1899. During World War I it was occupied by the French and British and divided into British (west) and French (east) spheres. In 1922 what is now Togo was placed by the League of Nations under French Mandate and in 1946 placed by the United Nations under French Trusteeship. French Togoland, in 1956, voted for autonomy within the French Union and the end of the Trusteeship system. On April 27, 1960, it gained its independence as the Republic of Togo and the Trusteeship was ended. It became a member of the United Nations on September 20, 1960. British Togoland joined with Ghana in 1957.

GOVERNMENT

Present Status

Independent republican state.

Constitution [5]

The country is governed by a Prime Minister, selected by and responsible to the unicameral legislature, and by the Chamber of Deputies, consisting of 46 members.

Franchise

Universal adult suffrage.

Local Government [6]

The country is divided into 17 districts, each headed by a "Chef de Circonscription" appointed by the Prime Minister.

Political Parties [7]

Comité de l'Unité Togolaise (C.U.T.), led by Sylvanus Olympio, President of the Republic.

Mouvement de la Jeunesse Togolaise (Juvento), led by Anani Santos.

Union Démocratique des Populations Togolaises (U.D.P.T.), led by Nicholas Grunitsky.

POPULATION BREAKDOWN

Main Cities [8]

1957 estimate

Lomé	38,100
Vegan	15,400
Tsévié	10,600
Anfouin	10,300
Bassari	9,800

Urban-rural Distribution [9]

About 7% of the population lived in towns of 10,000 or more inhabitants in 1957.

Ethnic Distribution [10]

1955 estimate

Non-African	1,277

1957 estimate

African	1,092,800

Of which the main tribal groups (to the nearest '000) are:

Cabrai	200,000
Ewe	195,000
Watchi	160,000
Moba	70,000
Cotocoli	60,000
Others (including such tribes as the Gurma, Mina, Lamba, Bassari, Tamberma, etc.)	615,000

Religious Affiliation [11]

Christians	19%
Muslims	5%
Animists	76%

Languages

Fon and Yoruba. French is the official language.

Sex Distribution [12]

1957 estimate

	Male	Female
African	554,400 (50.7%)	538,400 (49.3%)

1955 estimate

Non-African	758 (51.5%)	519 (48.5%)

Age Distribution [13]

1957 estimate

	Under 15	Adults	Aged
African	4,567,000	600,300	35,800

1955 estimate

	Under 20	20–59	60+
Non-African	309	962	6

SOCIAL DATA

Education [14]

As of January 1, 1958

TABLE I

	Enrollment	Public School Teachers
249 Public primary schools } 223 Private primary schools }	70,618	705
4 Public secondary schools } 5 Private secondary schools}	1,500	18
7 Public technical schools } 5 Private technical schools}	533	4

There were 288 students studying abroad.

In 1957, 44% of the children of school-going age were at school, of which 24.1% were girls. Educational expenditure amounted to 16.6% of the annual budget.

Health and Social Services

VITAL STATISTICS

Not available.

MAIN DISEASES [15]

Malaria, respiratory diseases, skin diseases, eye diseases, and tropical ulcers.

HEALTH SERVICES [16]

As of January 1, 1958

TABLE II

	Beds
1 Secondary hospital	455
11 Medical centers	1,046
109 Dispensaries	—
6 Private institutions	—

There were 41 medical practitioners, 1 per every 27,000 of the populations, and 14 beds per every 10,000 inhabitants.

SOCIAL WELFARE SERVICES [17]

Social assistance is given under family-allowance schemes and the provision of medical social services.

ECONOMY [18]

Togo's economy is essentially agricultural. Recently phosphate production for export has been undertaken.

Transport and Communications

WATERWAYS [19]

The Mono River is navigable by small vessels near its mouth.

PORTS [20]

Lomé is Togo's main port. It handled 106,700 tons of cargo in 1959.

ROADS [21]

At the beginning of 1958 Togo had 76 km. of bituminized roads, 1,100 km. of unbituminized roads, and 3,300 km. of trails.

RAILROADS [22]

There are 491 km. of railroad tracks in the country.

AIRWAYS [23]

The only airport is situated at Lomé.

POSTS, TELECOMMUNICATIONS, AND BROADCASTING [24]

At the beginning of 1958 there were 17 post offices and 14 postal agencies; 28 telegraph offices; 742 telephone subscribers, and 454 telephone branch lines. Radio Togo offers a 64-hour-per-week service.

Resources and Trade

MAIN EXPORTS [25]

Palm kernels and oil (representing 28.3% of the total value of exports for the years 1949–58), coffee, cocoa, copra, manioc, and cotton.

MAIN IMPORTS [26]

Consumer goods, capital goods, foodstuffs, energy, raw materials, and semifinished products.

VALUE OF TRADE [27]

In millions of C.F.A. francs

	1956	1957	1958	1959	1960
Exports	2,336	2,164	3,157	4,348	4,348
Imports	2,668	2,888	3,776	3,755	1,707

France is Togo's chief trading partner.

LIVESTOCK [28]

As of January 1, 1958

Cattle	128,000
Sheep and goats	649,000
Horses	640
Donkeys	3,720
Pigs	328,000

Industry

MANUFACTURES [29]

Industries are negligible apart from some cotton-ginning and kapok-processing, vegetable-oil extracting, and native handicrafts.

MINING [30]

Exploration of phosphate deposits was begun in 1956 and production started at the end of 1960.

POWER [31]

In 1959 the combined plants at Lomé and branches at Anecko generated 3,414,000 kwh., while 2,782,000 kwh. were consumed.

Finance

CURRENCY

One C.F.A. franc equals 2 old Metropolitan French francs.

BANKING [32]

La Banque d'Afrique Occidentale, La Banque Nationale pour le Commerce et l'Industrie, le Crédit Lyonnais.

BUDGET [33]

In millions of C.F.A. francs

1957

Revenue	1,448.0
Expenditure	1,807.2

DEVELOPMENT PLAN

See Appendix III.

LABOR

The employment of wage earners in 1957 was estimated to be distributed as follows: [34]

Public Sector

Civil service	2,040	
Non-Civil service	3,420	5,460

Private Sector

Agriculture, fishing, and forestry	470	
Mining and quarrying	260	
Industry	300	
Building and public works	620	
Commerce, banking, and professions	1,410	
Transport and storage	1,780	
Domestic service	1,650	6,490
TOTAL		11,950

In 1957 there were 2 employers' unions with 35 members and 14 employees' unions with some 7,200 members. In 1958 the Family Equalization Allowance scheme had 700 employers contributing, with 3,269 workers benefiting.[35]

Preindependence labor legislation covered such matters as minimum wages, trade unions, disputes, etc. Postindependence information is not available.

THE REPUBLIC OF TOGO NOTES

1   *The Journal of Negro Education*, Vol. XXX, No. 3, Howard University Press, p. 282.

2   *Ibid.*

3   République du Togo: Service de la Statistique Générale du Togo, *Inventaire Economique du Togo 1958*, Lomé. Pages are not numbered. Also Ministère de la France d'Outre-Mer, Ministère de l'Education Nationale, *Cameroun et Togo sous Tutelle Française*, Imprimerie Oberthier, Rennes, n.d., p. 56.

4   *Columbia Lippincott Gazetteer of the World*, Columbia University Press, New York, 1952, p. 1923; also S. H. Steinberg (Ed.), *The Statesman's Yearbook 1961*, London, 1961, Macmillan & Co., Ltd., pp. 1436–37.

5   U.S. Department of State: *Togo*: The Newly Independent Nations' series, Department of State publications 7135, African Series 10, April 1961, Bureau of Public Affairs, Washington, D.C.

6   *Ibid.*

7   R. Segal, *Political Africa*, Stevens & Sons, Ltd., London, 1961, pp. 456–58.

8   Service des Statistiques d'Outre-Mer, *Outre-Mer 1958*, Paul Dupont, Paris, Nov. 1959, p. 815, Table 3.

9   Figures computed from *Ibid.*, p. 813, Tables 1, 3, and 4.

10 *Ibid.*, pp. 814–15, Tables 1 and 4; *Inventaire Economique du Togo 1958*, *op. cit.*, Chapter 1.

11 *Outre-Mer 1958*, *op. cit.*, p. 140, Table 1.

12 *Ibid.*, pp. 814–15, Tables 1 and 4.

13 *Ibid.*

14 *Ibid.*, pp. 816–17, Tables 7 and 8.

15 *Inventaire Economique du Togo 1958*, *op. cit.*, Chapter I.

16 *Outre-Mer 1958*, *op. cit.*, p. 816, Table 5.

17 *Rapport Annuel du Gouvernement Français a l'Assemblée Générale des Nations Unies par l'Administration du Togo Placé sous la Tutelle de la France, Année 1957*: Imprimerie Chaix, St. Ouen, 1959, p. 168.

18 International Labor Office, *African Labor Survey*, Geneva, 1958, p. 22.

19 *Columbia Lippincott Gazetteer of the World*, *op. cit.*, p. 1230.

20 *Inventaire Economique du Togo 1958*, *op. cit.*, Chapter IV.

21 *Outre-Mer 1958*, *op. cit.*, p. 817, Table 9.

22 *Ibid.*, p. 818, Table 11.

23 *Ibid.*, p. 818, Table 13.

24 *Ibid.*, p. 818, Table 15.

25 *Inventaire Economique du Togo 1958*, *op. cit.*, Chapter IV.

26 *Outre-Mer 1958, op. cit.,* p. 839, Table 18.

27 *Inventaire Economique du Togo 1958, op. cit.,* Chapter IV; France: Service des Statistiques, *Bulletin de Conjectures d'Outre-Mer,* Paris, No. 21, August 1960, p. 22; and France: Service des Statistiques, *Résumé des Statistiques d'Outre-Mer, Bulletin Accéleré,* Paris, No. 7, April 1958, and No. 29, May 1961, p. 3.

28 *Outre-Mer 1958, op. cit.,* p. 819, Table 17.

29 *Columbia Lippincott Gazetteer of the World, op. cit.,* p. 1923.

30 *Inventaire Economique du Togo 1958, op. cit.,* Chapter II.

31 *Ibid.,* Chapter III.

32 *Rapport Annuel . . . Année 1957, op. cit.,* p. 85.

33 *Ibid.,* p. 78.

34 *Outre-Mer 1958, op. cit.,* p. 209, Table 3.

35 *Ibid.,* p. 207, Table 1, and p. 217, Table 15.

Tunisia

AREA:[1] *48,195 sq. m.*
POPULATION:[2] *3,965,000 (1960 estimate)*
Density: 82 per sq. m.

GEOGRAPHY [3]

Tunisia is a country of plains, seldom rising above 700 feet for half the entire area. The highest point is the Djebel Chambi of 1,544 meters. Apart from the northern coastal region, the geography is steppe-like, with the semiarid influence of the Sahara prevailing to the east and south of Dorsale. The comparatively higher region of the northeast enjoys the heaviest rainfall, averaging 1,575 mm. per annum, while the southeastern region has a rainfall of below 100 mm. per annum.

HISTORICAL SKETCH [4]

Carthage, founded in the 7th century B.C., became the capital of a powerful maritime republic which was finally destroyed by the Romans after a struggle which ended in the 6th century A.D. After a Vandal interlude it became part of the Byzantine Empire. The Arab invasions over this part of Africa during the 7th, 8th, and 9th centuries saw the spread of Islam, and the diminishing influence of Christianity. The Hilalian invasion at the end of the 10th century brought about the complete Islamization of the country. Until the 12th century Tunisia had been intermittently part of a larger complex. At this time, the country declared its independence from the Almohad Caliph and founded the Hafsid Dynasty. From the 16th century to 1883 it was nominally part of the Turkish Empire, but usually enjoyed autonomy. French influence started in 1869, when an international commission was appointed to control the financial situation of the country. In 1883 the Convention of Marsa resulted in France's taking over the entire administration of the

411

area, under protectorate status. Tunisia remained a French protectorate until its independence on March 20, 1956. A year later it became a Republic, and in November 1959 held its first general election. Tunisia was admitted to the United Nations on November 12, 1956.

GOVERNMENT[5]

Present Status

Independent republican state.

Constitution

Executive power is vested in the popularly elected President. He choses members of government, makes civil and military appointments, ratifies all legislation, is commander-in-chief of the armed forces, and makes orders in council, assisted by a Permanent Commission elected by the National Assembly, which must be placed before the Assembly for ratification. Legislative power is vested in the National Assembly of 90 deputies, elected at the same time as the President for a period of five years. Laws may be initiated by both the President and the Assembly, with those of the latter taking precedence.

Franchise

Universal adult suffrage.

Local Government

The constitution provides for the setting up of municipal and regional councils to deal with matters of local or regional interest.

Political Parties [6]

The Neo Destour, led by Habib Bourguiba, President of the Republic.
The Communist Party.

POPULATION BREAKDOWN

Main Cities [7]
1960 estimate

Tunis (capital)	680,000

1956 census

Sfax	65,635
Sousse	48,172
Bizerte	46,681

Urban-rural Distribution [8]
More than one-third of the total population lives in cities.

Ethnic Distribution [9]
1960 estimate

Tunisian	3,734,000
Muslim foreigners	102,000
Other foreigners	129,000

Religious Affiliation [10]
Islam is the state religion. There are some 160,000 Roman Catholics under the Archbishop of Carthage; and the Greek, French Protestant, and English churches are also represented.

Languages
Arabic is the official language; French is also spoken.

Age Distribution [11]
1960 estimate

Under 15	15–64	65+
40%	50%	10%

Sex Distribution [12]
Statistics are not available, but it is estimated that there are 1,000 more men than women.

SOCIAL DATA

Education [13]

TABLE I
1959/60

		Enrollment	Teachers
993	Elementary schools	320,362	6,155
165	Middle-level classes	4,928	
12	Secondary schools	11,803	
51	Vocational schools	6,303	
33	Modern Zeitonian colleges	1,031	
179	Traditional Zeitonian colleges	5,629	Not available
6	Teacher-training colleges	1,940	
4	Technical institutions	3,738	
6	Institutions of higher learning	2,333	

The University of Tunisia is to integrate all the six institutions of higher learning into one.

In 1954, 7% of the Tunisians and 20.7% of the foreigners of school-going age were at school.

About 20% of the budget is earmarked for education.

Health and Social Services

VITAL STATISTICS [14]

Per 1,000

Birth rate	Death rate	Rate of population growth
478	107	2%

MAIN DISEASES [15]

Tuberculosis, trachoma, and ringworm.

HEALTH SERVICES [16]

As of Sept. 1960

TABLE II

	Beds
64 Hospitals	10,539
347 Rural dispensaries	
54 City dispensaries	
4 Mobile dispensaries	
76 Mother and infant protection centers	
17 Special anti-ringworm centers	
14 Health education centers	

There are 2.25 beds per 1,000 of the population.

SOCIAL WELFARE SERVICES [17]

Welfare services are centered primarily around the provision of security to workers. In addition the state has made itself responsible for the physically and mentally handicapped, the aged, and the blind. For the last-named, a number of vocational centers have been established. Each region has a social solidarity center coordinating the activities of private associations.

ECONOMY [18]

Tunisia is essentially an agricultural country. In 1952, 70% of its active population was engaged in agricultural activities. Mining and processing industries are well developed and are being expanded.

Transport and Communications

WATERWAYS [19]

The Medjenda River provides the chief route of access (road and railroad) to Tunis from the west.

PORTS [20]

Tunisia has 4 major ports: Tunis–La Goulette, with a harbor able to handle 3 million tons of cargo annually; Bizerte, which is of military importance; Sousse; and Sfax. A fifth, La Skirra, is in the process of construction. In addition there are 22 minor port facilities along the coast.

ROADS [21]

Tunisia has a total of 15,000 km. of roads.

RAILROADS [22]

Tunisia has a total of 1,243 miles of railroads. Two companies control the network: The Gfasa Railroad Co. (to revert to state control in 1966), which operates the line from Sfax to Gfasa in the south; and the state-controlled system, administered by the Tunisia Railroad Co., which links all the principal ports and cities of the country.

AIRWAYS [23]

There are two main airports—at Tunis and Sfax. At the airport of Tunis–El Aouin, a 3,330-yard runway is under construction to accommodate jetliners. Tunisia has started its own airline, Tunis-Air. There are additional airports at Gabes and Dherba and new airfields are being built at Monastir and Tozeur.

POSTS, TELECOMMUNICATIONS, AND BROADCASTING [24]

There were 267 post offices in 1956. In 1957 there were 33,710 telephones. The Postal, Telegraph, and Telephone Administration controls all services.

The Tunisia Radio and TV network is located in Tunis. Programs in Arabic and French are provided.

Resources and Trade

MAIN EXPORTS [25]

Wines (14.4% of the total value of exports in 1960), phosphates, olive oil, wheat, iron, superphosphates, and mineral products.

MAIN IMPORTS [26]

Textiles, motor vehicles and tractors, iron, lead and steel, petroleum products, and foodstuffs.

VALUE OF TRADE [27]

In dinars '000's

	1956	1957	1958	1959	1960
Exports	32,292.7	54,187.1	64,405.3	59,584.9	50,266.6
Imports	67,999.7	63,351.7	64,885.7	64,202.5	80,091.7

France is Tunisia's principal trading partner. In 1960 it imported 60% of Tunisia's total exports and supplied 71.5% of its imports.

LIVESTOCK [28]

1959 estimate

Cattle	600,000
Sheep and goats	5,076,000
Horses, mules and asses	334,000
Camels	217,000
Pigs	15,000

Industry

MANUFACTURES [29]

Fertilizers are Tunisia's chief manufactured products. In addition the country has various food-processing industries, among them cereal, olive oil, fish, fruit and vegetable canning, sugar, and live-stock products undertakings. Building materials such as cement, lime, plaster, bricks, and tiles are also produced locally.

MINING [30]

Tunisia is the world's fourth largest producer of phosphates, mined at Metaoui, Redeyet, Moulares, Djebel, Medilla, Kalaat Djeida, and Ain Karma. In addition it mines an average of 1 million tons of iron annually and also mines lead and zinc.

POWER [31]

There are electric generating plants at La Goulette, Nebeu, Fernana, and El Arouissa. These supply the country's present demand. In 1958 total consumption in northeast Tunisia alone was 245 million kw.

Petroleum prospecting and drilling date back to the thirties, but it is as yet not a major source of energy.

Finance

CURRENCY [32]

One Dinar equals 11.75 old Metropolitan French francs.

BANKING [33]

Central Bank of Tunisia (issuing bank) and some 31 others, includ-ing the Banque de Tunisie, Banque Nationale Africole, Banque Franco-Tunisienne, British Bank of the Middle East, Arab Bank, and Crédit Lyonnais.

BUDGET [34]

In dinars '000's

1959/60

Revenue	48,600
Expenditure	48,600

The main sources of revenue are import duties.

DEVELOPMENT PLAN [35]

A 30-year plan was formulated in 1956, the total cost of which was estimated at 600,000 million francs. Projects under consideration include an esparto grass pulp plant, a sugar refinery, and a castor bean plantation.

LABOR

The following was the distribution of the active population according to the census of 1956: [36]

Agriculture	872,000	67%
Industry and commerce	92,000	7%
Professions and management	10,000	1%
Civil service	61,000	5%
Laborers	228,000	17%
Domestic service	25,000	2%
Others	9,000	1%
TOTAL	1,297,000	100%

In December 1957 Tunisia had some 226,000 trade-union members, 225,000 of whom were affiliated with the International Confederation of T.U. and 1,000 affiliated with the International Federation of Christian Trade Unions. Locally the majority are combined into the General Union of Tunisian Workers (U.G.T.C.).

Regional labor inspectorates have been set up to deal with problems of labor, conciliation, etc. A Labor Code dealing with agricultural workers in particular was passed in 1956. Legislation covers such matters as conciliation, trade unions, accidents, and compensation.[37]

TUNISIA NOTES

1 L. D. Stamp, *Africa: a study in Tropical Development*, John Wiley & Sons, Inc., New York, 1959, p. 531.

2 *L'Economie de la Tunisie en Chiffres*, Année 1960, Secrétariat d'Etat au Plan et aux Finances, Tunis, p. 1.

3 Secretariat of State for Information of the Tunisian Government, *Tunisia*, 1957, p. 110; also *Tunisie Nouvelle: Problèmes et Perspectives*, Imprimerie Sefan, Tunis, 1957, pp. 7–16.

4 A *Few Dates in the History of Tunisia*, included in a folder of Fact Sheets issued by the Embassy of Tunisia, Washington, D.C., 1961.

5 Secrétariat d'Etat à l'Information, *Constitution of the Tunisian Republic*, n.d.

6 R. Segal, *Political Africa*, Stevens & Sons Ltd., London, 1961, pp. 459–61.

7 S. H. Steinberg (Ed.), *The Statesman's Yearbook 1961*, Macmillan & Co., Ltd., London, 1961, p. 1439.

8 *Tunisian Republic*, Fact Sheet issued by the Embassy of Tunisia, Washington, D.C., 1961. Pages not numbered.

9 *L'Economie de la Tunisie en Chiffres, op. cit.*, p. 1.

10 S. H. Steinberg (Ed.), *op. cit.*, p. 1439.

11 *L'Economie de la Tunisie en Chiffres, op. cit.*, p. 1.

12 Communication received from the Tunisian Embassy, Washington, D.C., 1961.

13 République Tunisienne, Service des Statistisques: *Bulletin Mensuel de Statistiques*, Nouvelle Série, Jan. 1960, No. 62, pp. 1–5; Secretariat of State for Information of the Tunisian Government: *Tunisia Works*, Sept. 1960, pp. 190–91; S. H. Steinberg (Ed)., *The Statesman's Yearbook 1959*, Macmillan & Co., Ltd., London, 1959, p. 1424; République Tunisienne; *Tunisie 1958*, La Documentation Tunisienne, August 1958, p. 46.

14 *Tunisian Republic*, Fact Sheet, *op. cit.*

15 Secretariat of State for Information of the Tunisian Government, *Tunisia Works, op. cit.*, p. 39.

16 *Ibid.*, pp. 39, 41.

17 *Ibid.*, pp. 44–47.

18 *Ibid.*, p. 79.

19 *Columbia Lippincott Gazetteer of the World*, Columbia University Press, New York, 1952, p. 1172.

20 *Tunisia Works, op. cit.*, p. 140.

21 *Ibid.*, pp. 136–37; *Tunisian Republic*, Fact Sheet, *op. cit.*

22   *Tunisia Works, op. cit.,* p. 134.

23   *Ibid.,* pp. 142–43.

24   *Ibid.,* pp. 143–44; S. H. Steinberg (Ed.), *op. cit.,* p. 1441.

25   *L'Economie de la Tunisie en Chiffres, op. cit.,* p. 12.

26   *Ibid.,* p. 13.

27   *Ibid.,* pp. 10–11; République Tunisienne: *Bulletin Comparatif Trimestrel du Mouvement Commercial de la Tunisie pendant les années 1957 et 1956,* p. 4; *1959 et 1958,* p. 4; and *1960 et 1959,* p. 4.

28   *Tunisian Republic,* Fact Sheet, *op. cit.*

29   *Ibid., Tunisia Works, op. cit.,* pp. 120–27.

30   *Tunisia Works, op. cit.,* pp. 120–23.

31   *Ibid.,* pp. 162, 164.

32   S. H. Steinberg (Ed.), *op. cit.,* p. 1441.

33   *Tunisia Works, op. cit.,* p. 170.

34   *L'Economie de la Tunisie en Chiffres, op. cit.,* p. 8.

35   *Oxford Regional Economic Atlas,* "The Middle East and North Africa," prepared by the Economic Intelligence Unit Limited and the Cartographic Department of the Clarendon Press, O.U.P., London, 1960, p. 110.

36   *L'Economie de la Tunisie en Chiffres, op. cit.,* p. 1.

37   *Tunisia Works, op. cit.,* pp. 44–46; Africa: United States Department of Labor, Office of International Labor Affairs, *Directory of Labor Organizations, Africa,* February 1958, p. x, Table 1.

Uganda [1]

AREA: 93,981 sq. m.
(includes 13,689 sq. m. of water)
POPULATION: [2] 6,536,616 (1959 census)
Density: 84 per sq. m.

GEOGRAPHY

Uganda lies astride the equator in the heart of East Africa. Nearly half of the world's second largest lake, Lake Victoria, is in Uganda, and the White Nile has its source there. Other large lakes are Lake George, Lake Edward in the southwest, Lake Albert, and Lake Kyoga. On the western frontier lies the 60-mile-long Ruwenzori Range, and on the eastern frontier Mount Elgon. Forests cover 6,266 square miles, of which 3,344 square miles are savanna woodlands. The climate is equable with temperatures in most parts ranging from 60 to 80 degrees F. the year round. Rainfall averages 50 inches a year.

HISTORICAL SKETCH

The first European contact with this area was made in 1862 when the explorers Speke and Grant reached the capital of the Bugunda Kingdom. After the failure of the Imperial East Africa Company to administer the territory, finding the cost of occupation too high, the British Government assumed the company's obligations in 1893. A year later the territory was formally given protectorate status. In 1896 this status was extended to cover the whole country, the term Uganda being thereafter applied to the entire territory. Mwanga's kingdom, the present Buganda, became formally known by that name in 1908. In 1900 an agreement was concluded between the United Kingdom and the Kabaka (King), chiefs, and people of Buganda, laying down principles governing the administration by the Crown. In 1953, following disagreement between the protectorate government and the Kabaka, the British Government exiled the

Kabaka. In 1955 a new Buganda agreement was signed, redefining the status of Buganda as a province of the protectorate and making the Kabaka a constitutional ruler. A ministerial system was introduced in the same year for the whole of Uganda. In 1958 the first direct elections were held in a limited number of constituencies. Uganda is to attain independence in 1962.

GOVERNMENT

Present Status
British protectorate.

Constitution
The country is governed by a Governor assisted by a Council of Ministers and a partially elected Legislative Council. The Council of Ministers consists of the Governor, 3 ex-officio Ministers, and 10 unofficial Ministers. The Legislative Council consists of 82 elected members, 9 members elected by the whole council, and 3 ex-officio members. The government has a right to nominate additional members.

Franchise
Qualitative franchise.

Local Government [3]
Buganda: The Kabaka, a constitutional monarch, acts on the advice of the Katikiro (Prime Minister) and the other Ministers of the Government. Subject to the Governor's consent, the Kabaka and the Lukiko (Parliament) have power to make laws binding on all natives of Buganda.

Other provinces: In three districts which have native rulers, a system similar to that in Buganda prevails. Elsewhere district councils, consisting of chiefs, elected members (forming the majority in all cases), and nominated persons of standing are now the most important organs of local government.

Political Parties [4]
Democratic Party, led by Benedicto Kiwanuka.
Uganda People's Congress (UPC), led by A. M. Obote.
Uganda National Congress (UNC), led by Joseph William Kiwanuka.

Union National Party (UNP), led by Abu Mayanja and Apollo
   Kironde.
Progressive Party (PP), led by E. K. K. Mulira.
Bataka Party.

POPULATION BREAKDOWN

Main Cities [5]
   1959 census

Mbale	13,569
Kampala	46,735
Jinja	29,741

Urban-rural Distribution [6]

According to the 1959 census, urbanization figures for the various
communities were as follows: African 2.3%, European 63%, Indian
75.1%, Pakistani 66.1%, Goan 81.8%, and other non-African 60.9%.

Ethnic Distribution [7]

   1959 census

Asian (including Goan)	71,933
European	10,866
Other non-African	4,259
African	6,449,558

Divided into the following tribal groups:

	Percent
Baganda	16.2
Banyankola	8.1
Itese	8.1
Bagoga	7.8
Bakiga	7.1
Banyaruanda	5.9
Lungo	5.6
Bagisu	5.1
Acholi	4.4
Lugbara	3.7
Batero	3.2
Banyere	2.9
Rundi	2.2
Karamosong	2.0
Others	17.7

Religious Affiliation
Mainly Christian and pagan.

Languages
Luganda, Lwo, Ateso, Runyoro, and Runyonkole. English is the official language.

Sex Distribution [8]
1959 census

	Male	Female
African	3,236,902 (50.1%)	3,212,656 (49.9%)
Asian (including Goan)	38,238 (53.1%)	33,695 (46.9%)
European	5,702 (52.4%)	5,164 (47.6%)
Other non-African	2,388 (56.5%)	1,871 (43.5%)

Age Distribution [9]
1959 census

	Under 5	5–14	15–29	30–44	45+
African *	1,119,000	1,551,000	1,667,000	1,228,000	885,000
Asian	12,002	21,439	18,582	11,988	7,922
European	1,489	1,313	1,832	4,196	2,036
Other non-African	933	1,167	1,153	655	351

* To the nearest thousand.

SOCIAL DATA

Education [10]

TABLE I

1959

African

	Enrollment	Teachers
5,495 Primary schools	484,183	16,576
263 Junior secondary schools	25,450	922
20 Senior secondary schools	3,412	208
35 Teacher-training colleges	3,671	284
12 Junior secondary technical schools	756	180
83 Rural trade schools, homecraft centers, and farm schools	2,763	267

TABLE I—Continued

	Enrollment	Teachers
Asian		
115 Primary schools	16,312	625
27 Junior secondary schools	3,149	105
7 Senior secondary schools	2,143	152
1 Teacher-training college	95	9
European		
12 Primary schools	1,204	59

In 1959, 60% of African children between the ages of 6–11 were at school.

Educational expenditure (Africans only) £316,355 in 1959; (£76,000 in 1935).

Health and Social Services

MAIN DISEASES

Malaria, respiratory infections, diseases of the digestive system, trachoma, tropical ulcers, venereal disease, tuberculosis, leprosy, and trypanosomiasis.

VITAL STATISTICS [11]

Per 1,000

1958

	Crude birth rate	Crude death rate	Infant mortality rate
European	27	2	—
Indian and Goan	49	4	14
Arab	53	2	—
Other	91	15	—
1959			
African	42	20	—

HEALTH SERVICES [12]

TABLE II

1958

	Beds
26 Government hospitals	3,519
24 Mission hospitals	1,708
161 Government dispensaries	—
43 Mission dispensaries	—

In December 1958 there were 371 registered doctors in the protectorate.

SOCIAL WELFARE SERVICES [13]

Welfare work in the rural areas falls under the control of the Community Development Division of the Ministry of Social Development, which organizes rural centers for the training of leaders, community development projects, adult education and literacy work, and women's clubs. The Family and Child Care Service is the responsibility of the Ministry of Social Development: probation officers, remand homes, and case work are all part of this program.

ECONOMY

Uganda is primarily an agricultural country of peasant farmers whose main cash crops are coffee and cotton. More coffee is produced than in any other Commonwealth country and more cotton than in any other United Kingdom dependency.

Transport and Communications

WATERWAYS

Steamer service on Lake Victoria operated by East African Railways and Harbors Administration connects Uganda with Kenya, Tanganyika, and the Congo.

PORTS

Entebbe, Jinja, Bukakata, Port Bell, and Mjanji on Lake Victoria.

ROADS [14]

The Public Works Department maintains 2,989 miles of main roads, and the provincial and local authorities 8,300 miles of roads of variable standard. By 1960 there were 606 miles of bituminized roads.

RAILROADS

The railways form part of the system administered by the East African Railways and Harbors Administration. There are one main line of 1,081 miles from Kasese to Mombasa and two branch lines from Tororo to Soroti, 100 miles; and Mbulamuti to Namasagali, 19 miles.

AIRWAYS

There is an international airport at Entebbe and 10 additional secondary airfields.

POSTS, TELECOMMUNICATIONS, AND BROADCASTING [15]
There were 154 post offices in 1960. Uganda has a well-developed internal and foreign telegraph service, as well as telephone system. In 1960 there were 14,079 private and public telephones in the country. In 1954 the Uganda Broadcasting Service, operated by the Information Department, commenced regular transmission and daily news broadcasts in English and four local languages.

Resources and Trade

MAIN EXPORTS [16]

Coffee (representing about 44% of the annual value of exports from 1955 to 1959), cotton, copper, animal feed, tea, oilseeds, nuts, and kernels.

MAIN IMPORTS

Machinery, vehicles, cotton piece goods and other textiles, base metal manufactures, rubber tires and tubes, fuels and lubricants.

VALUE OF TRADE [17]

In £'000's

	1955	1956	1957	1958	1959
Domestic exports and reexports	42,305	41,508	46,832	46,389	43,228
Net imports	33,975	28,106	28,869	27,002	25,534

The United Kingdom is Uganda's chief trade partner, followed by South Africa and India.

MARKETING AND COOPERATIVE SOCIETIES [18]

The Lint Marketing Board controls the purchase and sale of lint cotton. The Coffee Marketing Board handles the produce of the African coffee crop and its sale.

Estate coffee factories, owned and operated on a cooperative basis by associations of African owners, are being developed. The products are marketed through commercial channels.

In 1960 there were 1,640 registered cooperative societies with a membership of 210,000. The vast majority of them are concerned with the marketing and processing of cotton and coffee. Most of these are affiliated with cooperative unions which operate cotton ginneries and coffee factories. In addition some societies deal with peanuts, tobacco, milk, cattle, and fish.

1960 estimate

Cattle	3,590,000
Goats and sheep	3,725,000

Industry

MANUFACTURES

Processing industries include the production of cement, bricks and tiles, soaps, and textiles. In addition there are engineering, printing, and sawmill firms. In 1957 there were 1,176 registered factories in the protectorate.

MINING

The Kilembe Mine in western Uganda came into production in 1956 and in 1957 produced 11,930 long tons of copper.[20] Deposits of pyrochlore, magnetite, and apatite, near Tororo, are now being explored. Small deposits of gold, tin, tungsten, and bismuth are mined for export.

POWER [21]

The Owens Falls Dam at Jinja on the Nile, opened in 1954 and had a capacity of 120,000 kw. by the end of 1959. It will eventually produce 150,000 kw. A new generating set is being installed at Kigati, which will have a capacity of 460 kw.

Finance

CURRENCY

British East African shilling, divided in 100 cents. 20 EAsh equal £1 sterling.

BANKING [22]

The National Bank of India Ltd. (9 branches), the Standard Bank of South Africa (7 branches), Barclay's Bank D.C.O. (19 branches), Bank of India, Bank of Baroda, and Netherlands Trading Society.

BUDGET [23]

In £'000's

	1960
Revenue	19,496
Expenditure	21,311

DEVELOPMENT PLAN [24]

1960/63

Total estimated cost, £16,929,000

Sources	£ millions
Capital development fund	3.9
C. W. & D. grants	3.0
Vehicle advances fund	0.4
Local borrowing	3.5
Capital budget revenue	0.3

Allocations: Economic services (including roads, technical services and education) £7.0 million; social services £4.8 million; urban development £1.6 million; law and order £1.0 million; administration £0.6 million.

LABOR

Most of the population is engaged in agriculture and cattle raising. In 1959 the distribution of the African wage earners was as follows: [25]

Agriculture	46,055
Government	14,665
African local government	38,328
Cotton ginning	3,950
Coffee curing	1,774
Forestry and fishing	3,582
Transport and communication	9,677
Wholesale and retail trade	8,554
Manufactures	24,311
Mining and quarrying	5,136
Building and construction	31,778
Education and medical services	21,560
Other services	14,890
TOTAL	224,260

Domestic service and peasant agriculture are not covered in this census, and it is estimated that if included they would bring the total up to some 298,000.

By the end of 1959 there were 22 registered trade unions with an estimated total membership of over 10,000; 16 of these unions were members of the Uganda Trade Union Congress. Joint staff councils or work councils had been introduced in 109 establishments, covering some 99,000 employees.[26]

Labor legislation covers such matters as minimum wages, hours of work, safety, health and welfare in mines and factories, workmen's compensation, conditions of employment of women and young persons, apprenticeship, and trade-testing.[27]

UGANDA NOTES

1   Unless otherwise stated, all information obtained from Fact Sheets on the U.K. Dependencies, Reference Division, U.K. Central Office of Information, No. R. 4205, *Uganda*, May 1959.

2   U.K.: *Uganda 1960*, H.M.S.O., London, 1961, p. 17.

3   Communication received from the British Embassy, Washington, D.C., July 1961.

4   R. Segal, *Political Africa*, Stevens & Sons Lt., London, 1961, pp. 462–64; Communication received from the British Embassy, *op. cit.*

5   U.K.: *Uganda 1960*, *op. cit.*, p. 18.

6   The East Africa Statistical Department, *Quarterly Economic and Statistical Bulletin, No. 50, Dec. 1960*, E. A. Printers (Boyds) Ltd., Nairobi, 1960, p. ix, Table 6.

7   *Ibid.*, p. v, Table 1; Uganda Protectorate: *Statistical Abstract 1960*, Government Printer, Entebbe, p. ii, Table 7.

8   *Quarterly Economic and Statistical Bulletin, op. cit.*, p. ix, Table 7.

9   *Ibid.*

10   Uganda Protectorate: *Annual Report of the Education Department 1959*, published by Command of His Excellency the Governor, p. 2; pp. 14–18, Table I; pp. 19–25, Table II; pp. 31–32, Table V.

11   Uganda: *Annual Report of the Medical Department, Vol. 1*, Government Printer, Entebbe, 1959, p. 7. U.K.: *Uganda 1960, op. cit.*, p. 19.

12   Uganda: *Annual Report of the Medical Department, op. cit.*, p. 34.

13   U.K.: *Uganda 1960, op. cit.*, pp. 87–89.

14   *Ibid.*, p. 106.

15   *Ibid.*, pp. 110–11, 115–16.

16   Uganda Protectorate: *Statistical Abstract 1960, op. cit.*, p. 21.

17   *Ibid.*, p. 20, Table UD 2.

18   U.K.: *Uganda 1959*, H.M.S.O., London, 1960, pp. 46–48; U.K.: *Uganda 1960, op. cit.*, p. 46.

19   U.K.: *Uganda 1960, op. cit.*, p. 59.

20   U.K.: *Uganda 1959, op. cit.*, p. 71.

21   *Ibid.*, p. 109; U.K.: *Uganda 1960, op. cit.*, p. 102.

22 S. H. Steinberg (Ed.), *The Statesman's Yearbook 1961*, London, 1961, Macmillan & Co., Ltd., p. 344.

23 U.K.: Colonial Office, *The Colonial Territories 1960–1961*, p. 121, Appendix II.

24 U.K.: *The Colonial Office List 1961*, H.M.S.O., London, 1961, p. 174.

25 *Ibid.*, p. 175.

26 U.K.: *Uganda 1959, op. cit.*, p. 22.

27 *Ibid.*, pp. 19–24.

The Republic
of the Upper Volta

AREA: *105,900 sq. m.*

POPULATION:[2] *3,543,000 (1958 estimate)*

Density: ±30 per sq. m.

GEOGRAPHY

Upper Volta lies in the heart of West Africa, 500 miles from the Gulf of Guinea and 1,000 miles from Dakar. The country is a wedge-shaped plateau, varying in altitude from 650 to 1,000 feet. The main rivers are the Leraba; Comoe; Black, White, and Red Volta; and the Oti. None is navigable. The climate is markedly seasonal—cool and dry in the winter from November to March, hot and dry from March to May, and hot and wet the remainder of the year. Rainfall decreases steadily inland, from about 40 inches in the south to less than 10 inches in the extreme north and northeast, where a hot wind from the desert adds to the aridity of the region.

HISTORICAL SKETCH

In the 11th century the empire- building Mossi extended their control to the Upper Volta in the form of feudal empires and kingdoms. By the time the French arrived at the end of the 19th century, the Mossi states were on the brink of dissolution. First, a protectorate was established in 1896 over the Empire of Ouagadougou; then, in 1919, the provinces were united into a territory designated as the Upper Volta and made part of French West Africa. After 1956 the political development of the country was rapid. The Loi Cadre of 1956 gave the Upper Volta universal adult suffrage; in May 1957 it had its first Cabinet of Ministers and on August 5, 1960, it became independent. On September 20, 1960, it was admitted to the United Nations. It is a member of the Conseil de l'Entente.

432

GOVERNMENT

Present Status
Independent republican state.

Constitution
The Upper Volta has a unicameral, parliamentary form of government with the Legislative Assembly as the principal instrument of power. The executive power is exercised by the President of the Council nominated by the Legislative Assembly. He has power to designate and dismiss ministers, to initiate and execute laws, appoint public officials, dispose of the armed forces, and negotiate agreements with foreign powers; but he is responsible at all times to the Legislative Assembly. An amendment to the constitution is under consideration which would make the Upper Volta a presidential system of government. The Legislative Assembly is composed of 75 deputies elected for 5 years.

Franchise
Universal adult suffrage.

Local Government
The country is divided into 37 districts (cercles) which in turn are subdivided, and these territorial units are headed by officials of the general and local administration.

Political Party [3]
L'Union Démocratique Voltaique (UDV), local branch of the RDA, led by Maurice Yameogo, President of the Council.

POPULATION BREAKDOWN

Main Cities [4]

1958	
Ouagadougou (capital)	31,705
Bobo-Dioulasso	41,717
Ouahigouya	8,686
Koudougou	8,784
Yako	6,011

Urban-rural Distribution [5]

About 2% of the total popuation lives in towns of more than 10,000 inhabitants.

Ethnic Distribution [6]

1958 estimate

Non-African	3,543
African	3,468,800

The main tribal groups are

	Million
Mossi	1.7
Bobo	.3
Gurunshi	.2
Lobi	.1
Mande	.23
Fulani	.2

Religious Affiliation [7]

Christians	4.5%
Muslims	19.0%
Animists	76.0%

Languages

Mole is the main African vernacular language spoken. French is the official language.

Sex Distribution [8]

	Male	*Female*
African	1,758,200 (50.6%)	1,710,600 (49.4%)
Non-African	2,108 (59.4%)	1,435 (41.6%)

Age Distribution

Not available.

SOCIAL DATA

Education [9]

As of January 1, 1958

TABLE I

	Enrollment	Public School Teachers
168 Private elementary schools 99 Public elementary schools	38,143	553
5 Public secondary schools 6 Private secondary schools	1,554	15
1 Public technical school 2 Private technical schools	199	6
3 Teachers' colleges 1 Catholic teachers' college for girls	500 } 1959 82	

In 1957, 7.8% of children of school-going age were at school, of which 28.2% were girls. Education expenses represented 16.4% of the local annual budget.

In 1959 fifty scholarships were awarded to persons for studies abroad. In 1958 a total of 106 students were furthering their studies outside the country.

Health and Social Services

VITAL STATISTICS

Not available.

MAIN DISEASES

Smallpox, yellow fever, and malaria.

HEALTH SERVICES [10]

As of January 1, 1958

TABLE II

	Beds
2 Hospitals	670
22 Medical centers	635
16 Maternity and specialized services (maternity beds)	145
90 Dispensaries	74
21 Private institutions	46

In 1958 there were 45 medical practitioners, 1 to every 77,000 of the population, and 4 beds to every 10,000 of the population.

SOCIAL WELFARE SERVICES

To meet the problems which the growth of industry, the development of urban centers, and the pressure of change toward modern ways of life bring with them, a social welfare program is carried on through five centers at Ouagadougou; at the principal one, social workers receive training. There are also three centers at Bobo-Dioulasso and a home for children at Orodara.

ECONOMY

More than 90% of the population is involved in agricultural activities. Farmers are hampered by unproductive soil, erosion, primitive methods of agriculture, lack of water, and are dependent on a few subsistence crops for their livelihood.

Transport and Communications

WATERWAYS

No navigable rivers.

PORTS

None.

ROADS

10,000 miles of roads; 1,300 miles are well-paved highways and 5,000 miles are dirt roads.

RAILROADS

225 miles of track link the Upper Volta with the Ivory Coast from Ouagadougou.

AIRWAYS

International airports at Ouagadougou and Bobo-Dioulasso connect the Upper Volta with Paris, Marseilles, Dakar, and Abidjan. About 25 secondary airfields serve local needs.

POSTS, TELECOMMUNICATIONS, AND BROADCASTING [11]

At the beginning of 1957 there were 21 post offices and 16 postal agencies in the country; 28 telegraph offices and 24 telephone bureaus.

A new 25-kw transmitter was recently installed, with a relaying transmitter at Bobo-Dioulasso.

Resources and Trade

MAIN EXPORTS [12]

Livestock on the hoof (representing about 30% of the total value of exports for 1959), fish, shelled peanuts, almonds, kapok, shells, hides, and ginned cotton.

MAIN IMPORTS

Vegetables, fruits, sugar, cotton and other fabrics, manufactured goods.

VALUE OF TRADE [13]

In millions of C.F.A. francs

	1956	1957	1958	1959	1960
Exports	1,067	897	1,131	1,121	1,064
Imports	1,563	1,612	1,800	2,071	2,027

Most of Upper Volta's trade is carried on within the franc zone. In 1958, three-fourths of Upper Volta's imports came from the franc zone and the rest from the sterling area.

LIVESTOCK

Cattle	1,500,000
Sheep and goats	2,500,000
Horses and donkeys	280,000
Pigs	31,000

Industry

MANUFACTURES

Fat- and oil-processing, rice-polishing, cotton-ginning, and the production of sisal twine. Most secondary industries are situated in and around Bobo-Dioulasso.

MINING

Gold fields extend from some 60 miles around Poura and the deposits vary in thickness from 5 to 10 feet. A pilot plant for the processing of auriferous quartz began operation in November 1957. Large manganese deposits discovered at Kiere are estimated at 700,000 tons, with a metal content of 35%. Bauxite deposits are found in the Kaya region and in the Bobo-Dioulasso region; and copper is known to exist at Goundoudy.

POWER

Electricity is supplied to Ouagadougou and Bobo-Dioulasso by 4 generators: one of 55 kw., one of 504 kw., and two of 273 kw. each.

Finance

CURRENCY

C.F.A. franc. 1 C.F.A. franc equals 2 old Metropolitan French francs.

BANKING [14]

Banque de l'Afrique Occidentale, Banque Commerciale Africaine, Banque Nationale pour le Commerce et l'Industrie, Société Générale, Crédit Lyonnais, and Banque Belge d'Afrique.

BUDGET [15]

In millions of C.F.A. francs

	1958
Revenue	4,081
Expenditure	4,081

DEVELOPMENT PLAN

See Appendix III.

LABOR

The Upper Volta is one of the major centers of labor migration in Africa. Much of this migration goes to the Ivory Coast and Ghana, where employment is found on coffee and cocoa plantations. In 1956 a Labor Office was set up to control labor movement and distribution, etc. It is managed by a council consisting of representatives of the administration, employers and workers under the authority of the Ministry of Labor, with headquarters at Bobo-Dioulasso and a branch at Ouagadougou.

The employment of the wage-earning population in 1957 was estimated to be as follows: [16]

Public Sector

Civil service	2,650	
Non-Civil service	9,050	11,700

Private Sector

Agriculture, fishing, and forestry	1,130	
Mining and quarrying	320	
Industry	1,570	
Building and public works	5,210	
Commerce, banking, and professions	2,240	
Transport and storage	690	
Domestic service	1,790	12,850
TOTAL		24,550

In 1953 there were 1,800 trade-union members; 1,500 belong to independent unions and 300 to unions affiliated with the Confédération de Travailleurs Chrétiens.[17]

In 1956 a fund was set up at Bobo-Dioulasso to deal with workmen's compensation and family allowances, the prevention of occupational diseases, accidents at work, and the implementation of welfare programs for workers' families.

Labor legislation covers such matters as hours of work, trade unions, compensation, wages, among other things.[18]

THE REPUBLIC OF THE UPPER VOLTA NOTES

1 Unless otherwise stated, all information obtained from Ambassade de France, Service de Presse et d'Information, *The Republic of Upper Volta*, New York, Oct. 1960.

2 Service des Statistique d'Outre-Mer, *Outre-Mer 1958*, Paul Dupont, Paris, Nov. 1959, p. 740, Table 1.

3 R. Segal, *Political Africa*, Stevens & Sons Ltd., London, 1961, pp. 471–72.

4 *Outre-Mer 1958, op. cit.*, p. 740, Table 2.

5 *Ibid.*, p. 740, Tables 1 and 2.

6 *Ibid.*, p. 740, Table 1.

7 *Ibid.*, p. 140, Table 1.

8 *Ibid.*, p. 740, Table 1.

9 *Ibid.*, p. 741, Tables 5 and 6.

10 *Ibid.*, p. 740, Table 3.

11 *Ibid.*, p. 742, Table 10. Also *Marchés Tropicaux et Méditerranéans*, 17ᵉ année, No. 798, February 25, 1961, Paris, p. 483.

12 *Africa Trade and Development*, Jan. 1961, Vol. 3, No. 1, London, p. 17.

13   S. H. Steinberg (Ed.), *Statesman's Yearbook 1959*, Macmillan & Co., Ltd., London, 1959, p. 1008; also France: Service des Statistiques, *Bulletin de Conjecture d'Outre-Mer*, Paris, No. 21, Aug. 1960, p. 25; also France: Service des Statistiques, *Résumé des Statistiques d'Outre-Mer Bulletin Accélére*, Paris, Nos. 8, May 1959, and 28, April 1961, p. 3.

14   S. H. Steinberg (Ed.), *op. cit.*, pp. 1018–19.

15   *Ibid.*, p. 1014.

16   *Outre-Mer 1958, op. cit.*, p. 209, Table 3.

17   International Labor Office, *African Labor Survey*, Geneva, 1958, p. 236, Table XII.

18   *Ibid.*, p. 654.

Zanzibar[1]

AREA: *consists of 3 islands*
Zanzibar: 640 sq. m.
Pemba: 280 sq. m.
Latham: 920 x 280 ft.
POPULATION: *299,111 (1958 census)*
Density: ±32 per sq. m.

GEOGRAPHY

The protectorate consists of the islands of Zanzibar and Pemba, the islets within their territorial waters, and the small uninhabited island of Latham. Zanzibar is the largest coralline island off the East African coast, and is separated from the mainland by a channel 22½ miles across its narrowest part. Both islands are low-lying, the highest point being only 390 feet above sea level. Temperatures vary between 76 and 86 degrees F. There is no real dry season, but the rainy seasons are well marked from March to May and November to December. Average annual rainfalls are 58 inches in Zanzibar and 73 inches in Pemba.

HISTORICAL SKETCH

The first recorded visit of an English ship to these parts was in 1591, when the Edward Bonaventure called there. During the 18th and 19th centuries Zanzibar came under the control of Arabs from Masqat in Oman. In 1747 Ahmed bin Said-el-Busaidi founded the Busaidi dynasty, which is still reigning in Zanzibar. By the mid-19th century Zanzibar had become, both politically and commercially, the principal town in East Africa. In 1861 it separated from Oman and in 1886 Britain, France, and Germany recognized the Sultanate of Zanzibar over the islands off the coast and a 10-mile-wide strip on the mainland. In 1888 part of this strip was leased to the British East African Association, whose administration eventually passed to the government of Kenya, which continues to pay an annuity of £10,000 to the Zanzibar government. Following the proclamation of the protectorate in 1890, a constitutional government was established with a British Representative as First Minister. In 1914 an advisory Protectorate Council was established and the post of British Resident created. In 1926 Executive and Legislative Councils were constituted to replace the Protectorate Council, and in 1956 a new constitution introduced a more democratic form of government.

GOVERNMENT

Present Status

British protectorate.

Constitution [2]

The present constitution provides for an Executive Council consisting of the British Resident as President, 3 ex-officio, and 5 unofficial members; and a Legislative Council of 23 elected, 3 ex-officio, and up to 5 appointed members.

Franchise [3]

Qualified male suffrage, 25 years and over, 12 months' residency, and ability to read English, Arabic, or Kiswahili; or 40 years and over and certain property qualifications; or ex-member of the Legislative Council; or ex-local government authority member; or holder of an approved civil or military decoration.

Local Government

There are 6 representative local councils which have the power to collect rates and to make bylaws. There has been a single Zanzibar Township Council since 1950, with 19 nominated members drawn from all racial groups. There is a plan to set up municipal councils with considerably increased powers and responsibilities.

Political Parties [4]

Zanzibar Nationalist Party (ZNP), led by Ali Muhsin—10 seats.
Zanzibar and Pemba People's Party (ZPPP)—3 seats which together with the ZNP have formed a coalition government.
Afro-Shirazi Party, led by Abeid Karume—10 seats.

POPULATION BREAKDOWN

Main Cities [5]
1958 census

Zanzibar (capital)	57,923
Chake	7,167
Wete	7,507
Mkoani	1,977

Urban-rural Distribution [6]
About 25% live in towns of 5,000 or more inhabitants.

Ethnic Distribution [7]
1958 census

Arab	15.7%
Asian	6.1%
European and other	1.7%
African	76.5%

The main tribal groupings are:

Wapemba	59,768
Watumbatu	46,131
Wahadimu	41,766
Wanyamwezi	8,253
Wazamaro	5,410

Religious Affiliations
The population is almost exclusively Muslim with some Christians, Hindus, and others.

Languages
Kiswahili, Arabic, Gujurati; English is the official language.

Sex Distribution [8]
1958 census

Male	Female
157,502 (59.4%)	141,609 (40.6%)

Age Distribution [9]
1958 census

Under 15	15–45	46+	Unknown
106,737	150,911	41,179	284

SOCIAL DATA

Education [10]

TABLE I
1959

		Enrollment	Teachers
50	Government primary schools	12,410	535
10	Aided primary schools	2,864	98
5	Unaided primary schools	258	15
3	Government secondary schools	598	44
1	Muslim Academy secondary school	104	6
2	Aided secondary schools	297	16
2	Unaided secondary schools	140	5
2	Government teacher-training colleges	142	32
3	Government technical and vocational schools	110	17
	MIOME technical and vocational schools	16	—
2	Unaided technical and vocational schools	98	2
684	Private Koran schools	±16,000	—
6	Nursery schools	624	—

In 1959, 29% of the children of school-going age were at school.
In 1958, 227 students were studying abroad.
Expenditure: £393,956 (1959), (£27,220–1953).

Health and Social Services

VITAL STATISTICS

Not available.

MAIN DISEASES

Malaria, infections of the respiratory and digestive systems, tropical ulcers, anemia, and yaws.

TABLE II
1958

		Beds
4	General hospitals	422
1	Mental hospital	185
1	Isolation hospital	30
1	Prison hospital	17
2	Leprosaria	200
3	Dispensaries	26
22	Rural treatment centers	
2	Maternity and child-welfare centers	

In 1958 there were 18 private practitioners in the protectorate; and 1 bed to every 850 inhabitants.

In addition the government ran school medical and dental services.

SOCIAL WELFARE SERVICES [12]

There is a Civic Center at Raha Leo with activities for adults and children. Provincial Administrations run welfare staff dealing mainly with case work among the poor. There are two voluntary organizations, one in Zanzibar and one in Pemba. A poorhouse with 160 beds is run by the Roman Catholic Church at Walezo. The Justice Department has a probation officer responsible for juvenile delinquents.

ECONOMY

The economy of Zanzibar is based on agricultural and marine products. By far the most important crop is cloves, with cotton second.

Transport and Communications

WATERWAYS

None.

PORTS

Zanzibar is the main port and from it there are regular services to all parts of the world.

ROADS

Zanzibar has 328 miles of roads, of which 276 miles are bituminized; Pemba has 277 miles of roads, of which 81 miles are bituminized.

RAILROADS

None.

AIRWAYS

There is one airport at Zanzibar and one at Chake Chake in Pemba. The East African Airways Corporation operates scheduled service to and from the protectorate.

POSTS, TELECOMMUNICATIONS, AND BROADCASTING [13]

There are 7 post offices in the protectorate and smaller offices in rural areas. A direct cable line links Zanzibar with the Seychelles, Durban, Dar es Salaam, and Mombasa; and telephone communications exist with London and up the East African coast. The telephone system is operated by the government, which has an automatic exchange in Zanzibar with a capacity for 800 subscribers, and a magneto system in Pemba. Voice of Zanzibar provides 4 hours per day of broadcasting service in Swahili.

Resources and Trade

MAIN EXPORTS [14]

Cloves, clove buds, and stem oil (representing 83% of the total export value in 1957); coconut oil, copra, oil cake, and fibers.

MAIN IMPORTS

Rice and grain, textiles, gasoline and petroleum, sugar, tobacco and cigarettes, flour, ghee, sesame, cattle.

VALUE OF TRADE [15]

In millions of U.S.$

	1952	1953	1954	1956	1957
Exports	12.0	22.1	16.6	16.3	16.4
Imports	14.0	16.4	15.1	17.0	18.1

While most of Zanzibar's imports come from the U.K. and other Commonwealth countries, the bulk of exports go to Indonesia and India.

MARKETING AND COOPERATIVE SOCIETIES

The Clove Growers' Association assists in stabilizing the price of cloves and distills and markets clove oil. It also assists in the marketing of tobacco, chilies, derris roots, and cacao. The Copra Board administers the proceeds of a tax on exported copra products for the benefit of the copra industry.

In 1957 there were 37 registered cooperative societies including 2 cooperative stores, 1 clove-marketing and 18 rural-credit societies, with a total membership of 1,187. Over 40 societies were in the process of formation in 1958.

LIVESTOCK

Approximately 24,000 cattle in Pemba and 8,000 in Zanzibar. Other livestock data are not available.

Industry

MANUFACTURES

Zanzibar processes clove and coconut oil, coconut fiber, and manufactures soap and coir.

MINING

There are no known mineral resources in Zanzibar, except for coral limestone which is burned for lime.

POWER

Electricity has been supplied by an independent Electricity Board since 1958. Output in Zanzibar Town was 3.8 million kw. in 1956. In Pemba electricity is being installed.

Finance

CURRENCY

East African shilling, divided in 100 cents. 20 EAsh equal £1 sterling.

BANKING

Two joint stock banks: The National and Grindlay's Bank Ltd., and the Standard Bank of South Africa Ltd. There is also one private Indian Banking firm of Messrs. Jetha Lila.

BUDGET
   1959 estimate in £'000's

Revenue	2,568
Expenditure	2,796

The chief sources of revenue are export duty on cloves and stems.

DEVELOPMENT PLAN
   Total cost £1,380,000

1955/59

Local resources	907,000
Colonial Development and Welfare Fund	473,000

LABOR

The majority of the rural population is engaged in agriculture. Fishing also occupies a large number, but they usually cultivate as well. In urban areas the principal occupations are in transport, building, port and dock labor, employment in sanitation and public works, domestic work, clerical work, and business.

At the end of 1957 there were 15 employees' trade unions with a total membership of 3,053 and one employers' union with a membership of 10.

Labor legislation covers such matters as the employment of women and children, minimum wages, conditions of work, workmen's compensation.

ZANZIBAR NOTES

1   Unless otherwise stated, all information obtained from: Fact Sheets on the U.K. Dependencies, Reference Division, U.K. Central Office of Information, R. 4128, *The Protectorate of Zanzibar*, March 1959.
2   Communication received from the British Embassy, Washington, D.C., July 1961.
3   *Ibid.*
4   R. Segal, *Political Africa*, Stevens & Sons Ltd., London, 1961, pp. 473–75; Communication received from British Embassy, *op. cit.*
5   Communication received from British Embassy, *op. cit.*
6   *Ibid.*

7   *Ibid.*

8   *Ibid.*

9   U.K.: *Zanzibar 1957 and 1958*, H.M.S.O., London, 1959, p. 29.

10 Zanzibar Protectorate: *Annual Report of the Department of Education 1959*, Government Printer, Zanzibar, 1960, p. 4; pp. 7–9, Tables I and II A; p. 14, Table V; U.K.: *Zanzibar 1957 and 1958, op. cit.*, p. 26.

11 U.K.: *Zanzibar 1957 and 1958, op. cit.*, pp. 30–32.

12 *Ibid.*, pp. 33–34.

13 *Ibid.*, pp. 46, 50, 52.

14 George H. T. Kimble, *Tropical Africa*, The Twentieth Century Fund, New York, 1960, Vol. I, p. 505.

15 *Ibid.*, pp. 498–501.

Appendix I

COLONIAL POLICIES IN AFRICA

APPENDIX I-A

BELGIAN COLONIAL POLICY IN AFRICA[1]

Belgium was the last of the metropolitan powers to enter the field of colonial rule in Africa. It assumed responsibility for the Belgian Congo following the ill-fated control of the area of Leopold II, and after World War I was given mandatory power over Ruanda-Urundi, part of the former German East African Colony.

Its policy in the Congo can best be described as one of cautious empiricism based primarily on the development of the country's economic potential. This emphasis resulted in the almost total neglect of political objectives per se. Much time and effort were spent evolving successful state-private enterprises to develop the mineral resources of the region and to improve the standard of living of the population. Legal authority was vested in the Belgian Government's local representatives, notably the King's representative in Leopoldville, and at no time did either white or African colonial subjects enjoy any political rights. *De facto* power in the Congo was in the hands of the Administration, the private companies, and the Roman Catholic Church, and remained so until 1959, because seldom did colonial questions arouse partisan political interests in Belgium. Until that time, also, a very clear social and legal distinction was maintained between the European residents and the African mass, except for a few African "immatriculés" who enjoyed legal equality with the Europeans but not necessarily social equality. No attempt was made to evolve local political institutions capable of assuming control in the future. The sudden handing over of power to the Africans in 1959 was due more to local and Belgian political exigencies than to any preconceived philosophy of colonial rule or plan for eventual independence.

---

[1] Lord Hailey: *An African Survey Revised 1956*, O.U.P., London, 1957, pp. 148, 217, 218; also T. Hodgkin: *Nationalism in Colonial Africa*, Frederick Muller Ltd., London, 1956, pp. 48–52.

In Ruanda-Urundi the policy was much the same as that followed in the Belgian Congo, except that it was conditioned, first, by its mandatory status and then by its status as a Trust Territory.

BRITISH COLONIAL POLICY IN AFRICA[2]

British policy in Africa reflects an acceptance of the notion of pluralism. It therefore differs widely from French policy, with its emphasis on assimilation and unity. British policy developed rather out of specific situations and as a means of resolving certain problems than from predetermined principles. It followed rather than preceded practice, and is often referred to as pragmatic and empirical. As a result, there is a lack of uniformity in the colonial institutions which Britain came to establish in its African territories, but two definite approaches may be discerned: one toward the black territories of West Africa and one toward the multiracial territories of East, Central, and South Africa.

The recognition of pluralism, coupled with a lack of desire for a logical unity of policy, made it possible to treat each colony as a separate, autonomous entity. Until World War II each colony managed its own budget according to local sources of revenue. Under the Colonial Development and Welfare Acts, Britain came to the financial assistance of her colonies, but development plans[3] were mapped territorially and not regionally. Similarly each colony had its own legislative and executive institutions, controlled by the metropole through its local representative, the governor or governor general, who exercised extensive powers and was able to exert considerable personal influence on the development of local policy. Finally, the notion of pluralism enabled Britain to evolve the loosely knit association of independent sovereign states, the Commonwealth, to which all newly independent African states belong.

In British West Africa, the achievement of self-government as a goal for Africans was accepted in the twenties. But the tempo at which this process took place varied according to the different stages of political evolution and local pressures in each territory. In this area of British influence, "self-government within the Commonwealth" involved a compara-

[2] Lord Hailey: *An African Survey Revised 1956*, O.U.P., London, 1957, pp. 146–47. Also, Thomas Hodgkin: *Nationalism in Colonial Africa*, Frederick Muller Ltd., London, 1956, pp. 40–45.
[3] See Appendix III-A.

tively easy sequence of steps. At the local level the system of "indirect rule" developed in its purest form. Starting in Northern Nigeria, during the rule of Sir Frederick Lugard, local indigenous political structures (Native Authorities) were used as pivotal institutions in the administrative machinery. These were adjusted to meet new requirements by changing their powers, functions, and membership until they became full-fledged local government units. At the central level, advisory legislative and executive councils were early established, at first under the direct control of the governor or governor general, who exercised full executive and legislative power. Over the years these councils were transformed into the democratic parliaments of independent states by altering their powers, functions, and membership. Today (end 1961), except for Gambia, the British Colonies in West Africa have all become independent sovereign states, freely associated "within the Commonwealth."

In British East and Central Africa, the process of achieving the goal of "self-government within the Commonwealth" has been much slower. The existence of "racial" communities has made the problem of the balance of political power extremely complex. The policy of paternalism, evident in early colonial practice in British West Africa, persisted much longer. The discharge of obligations by the Metropolitan power has been complicated by the lack of conception of common interests and loyalties and the unequal development of the various racial sections. "Self-government" does not necessarily mean self-government for all. In 1910, self-government for South Africa was given to the white minority. The extension of political rights in these areas could not be made in single and simple steps, but has involved a series of often complicated devices. The issue of the franchise has led to the formulation of such schemes as "parity voting" in Tanganyika, qualified as against universal adult suffrage in Kenya and the Federation of Rhodesia and Nyasaland, the creation of communal as against common voting rolls. Thus in this area of British influence the attempt to come to an equitable and just solution, i.e., one acceptable to all racial sections, has retarded the process of political evolution. Tanganyika is the only country in East and Central Africa to have achieved its independence.

APPENDIX I-C

FRENCH COLONIAL POLICY IN AFRICA[4]

Policy in French African territories was conditioned by a theoretical emphasis on cultural assimilation, a practical administrative acceptance of the need for working with traditional African institutions (instead of dissolving them, as the assimilationist theory would suggest), and a strong interpenetration of French Metropolitan and African party activity (except in Morocco, Tunisia, and the Trust Territories).

The theory of assimilation stems from France's egalitarian philosophy and its fundamental concept of the unity of the French Republic and dependencies. The theory provided a surface appearance of logical coherence, in patterns of colonial institutions lacking in British Africa. Assimilation and unity, in practice, were limited to the education of a small black African elite and its direct representation in Metropolitan parliamentary institutions, with the exercise of most legislative and executive control from Paris. Otherwise, in France's handling of the mass of its colonial subjects, there was more administrative decentralization and empiricism in French Africa than was usually recognized.[5] French colonialism in Africa, therefore, was not wholly antithetical to British colonialism, in spite of the theoretical differences between "direct" and "indirect" rule.

In French North Africa, there was also a theoretical commitment to assimilation, but there was a great contrast between administrative practices there and elsewhere in Africa. Algeria, with its large and heretofore politically dominant European minority, has been ruled as an integral part of France. Tunisia and Morocco, for various diplomatic and other political reasons, were never annexed to the French Republic, and their politicians never took part in the deliberations of the French National Assembly. The two countries remained as protectorates under the supervision of the French Foreign Office and received their independence from France in March of 1956.

The interpenetration of Metropolitan and black African politics since 1945 was a crucial factor in French African political development. It meant that the French National Assembly became the focus of African

[4] Lord Hailey: *An African Survey Revised 1956*, O.U.P., London, 1957, pp. 147, 206–16; also T. Hodgkin: *Nationalism in Colonial Africa*, Frederick Muller Ltd., London, 1956, pp. 33–38.
[5] *Vide* Delavignette, *Freedom and Authority in French West Africa*, O.U.P., London, 1950.

political activity, that individual Africans participated in the Assembly's deliberations, on its many committees, and as Government Ministers, and that the quarrels and affiliations of French politics were transferred to the African colonies. The major African political parties were affiliated with French parties.

The French Communist Party's encouragement of the *Rassemblement Démocratique Africain* (R.D.A.) gave that party its tone in its formative years. The tradition of interterritorial political organizations has continued to the present in such purely African parties as the *Parti de la Fédération Africaine* (P.F.A.), *the Parti du Regroupement Africain* (P.R.A.), and the R.D.A. (now purged of its Communist ties and considered in some territories the most conservative of the three), all of which had affiliates in a number of the Republics which were once territories of the French Union.

The Brazzaville Conference of January 1944 set a federalist tone for the French African territories, but the Constitution of the Fourth Republic which followed (December 1946) reemphasized assimilation via the means of the French Union. The territorial assemblies which were then established were much like the departmental *Conseils Généraux* in Metropolitan France. Economic development was considered a prime stimulant toward the creation of a viable union, and to achieve this end the *Fonds d'Investissement pour le Développement Economique et Social de la France d'Outre-Mer* (F.I.D.E.S.) were established. A series of assistance programs followed.[6]

Several reforms were offered after 1946, of which the Loi Cadre of 1956, providing for a greater degree of internal self-government, was the most important since it implied a departure from the assimilationist philosophy of the French Republic. The overthrow of the Fourth Republic in 1958 proved an opportunity for extensive constitutional change. A Referendum on the proposed Constitution of the Fifth Republic was presented in all French territories in September of that year. Three choices were open to all territories: status as a French Department, as an Overseas Territory (French Somaliland and the Comoro Islands accepted this), and status as a Member State of the Community (all other territories except Guinea accepted this). Guinea's rejection of these choices resulted in its attaining immediate independence. Acceptance of member-state status meant becoming an autonomous republic within the newly formed French Community, with issues of foreign policy, national defense, economic and financial policy, and higher education reserved to the Community as a whole. Since 1960, the Constitu-

[6] See Appendix III-B.

tion has been amended to allow for full independence *within* the Community on the British Commonwealth model.

All French-speaking African states, except the minor territories of French Somaliland and the Comoro Islands, are now independent. The former colonies of Senegal, Mauritania, the Malagasy Republic, Chad, the Central African Republic, Congo (Brazzaville), and Gabon are still in the Community. The former colonies of Guinea, Mali, Ivory Coast, Upper Volta, Dahomey, and Niger are not members nor are the former trust territories of Togo and Cameroon.

PORTUGUESE COLONIAL POLICY IN AFRICA[7]

Central to the policy of Portugal in her two main African colonies, Angola and Mozambique, is the emphasis placed on the unity and identity of Portugal and its dependencies. Since Portugal's political system is highly centralized and under the virtual dictatorial control of its Premier the principles of unity and identity are even more pronounced than in French Policy.

The principle of identity is illustrated in the Colonial Act of 1930, the Act of the Overseas Administrative Reform in 1933, and the declaration of the colonies as part of the territory of Portugal in 1935. The idea was carried further in 1951, when both colonies were made "overseas provinces" of Portugal. At that time all the inhabitants were given titular status of Portuguese citizens, entitling them to elect the President of the Republic and 3 Deputies to the National Assembly in Lisbon. But since citizenship depended upon high qualifications and the system of "indigenato" denied most Africans civil rights, very few became eligible.

Effective control rests with the Overseas Ministry in Lisbon, although the appointed Governors have extensive powers in administration and finance. The Legislative Councils of both colonies are important as safety valves for the sizable European population. The administrative structure is extensive and provides a ready means of overseeing and controlling the Africans, even at the small local level.

Following the revolt in Angola, beginning in 1961, the Portuguese Government promised sweeping reforms, subject to quelling the uprisings.[8] These include a granting of constitutional (legal) equality to all

[7] Lord Hailey: *An African Survey Revised 1956*, O.U.P., London, 1957, pp. 148, 228–33.

[8] *The New York Times*, July 27, 1961, p. 1; *Manchester Guardian*, August 29, 1961, p. 1.

Africans; eliminating the "indigenato" which placed the overwhelming majority of Africans under strict state paternalism; giving the franchise to those Africans able to qualify; opening public office and administrative posts to qualified Africans, and reorganizing the "Regedorias" (local administrative bodies) so as to allow for the election of administrators by the inhabitants according to the traditional manner. It is anticipated that implementing these reforms will take time, since so large a proportion of the population is illiterate and new rights are dependent upon educational qualifications.

Appendix II

REGIONAL GROUPINGS

BRITISH EAST AFRICA
(Tanganyika, Kenya, and Uganda)

Various proposals for the closer union of Uganda, Kenya, and Tanganyika, sometimes including the territories of Northern Rhodesia and Nyasaland, were made between World War I and World War II. But until World War II no formal structure was set up. The Governors of the three territories met for periodic conferences to discuss joint problems.

In 1948 the East Africa High Commission was created. It consisted of the Governors of Kenya, Tanganyika, and Uganda. At the same time the East African Legislative Assembly was set up with both nominated and elected representatives from each of the territories.

The High Commission services were divided into three groups falling under the Administrator, the Commissioner of Transport, and the Department of Meteorology. The control of these services by the High Commission involved no change in the constitution or administrative responsibilities of the governments of the three territories. They remained responsible for basic services such as administration, police, health and education, agriculture, animal husbandry, forestry, labor, housing, and public works.

The High Commission had power to legislate, with the advice and consent of the Legislative Assembly, on the following: appropriation for expenditure on services for which it was responsible; defense; income tax; interterritorial research; Lake Victoria Fisheries; Makerere College; meteorological services; benefits to its own employees; posts and telegraphs; telephones and radio communications; railways; harbor and inland water transport; statistics including census-taking; the Royal Technical College of East Africa; and merchant-shipping. In addition it established a number of research institutions, including a Literature Bureau, the Agricultural and Fisheries Research Council, the Veterinary Research Organization, the Council for Medical Research, Leprosy Research Center, Industrial Research Organization, Statistical Department, and Tourist Travel Association.[1]

In June, 1961, a conference of representatives of the three territories, the United Kingdom, and the High Commission met in London to discuss the future of the East African High Commission in the light of the forthcoming independence of Tanganyika (which was achieved in December 1961). It was agreed to set up the East African Common Services Authority to consist of the principal elected Minister responsible to the legislature of each of the three territories. The Authority is to be supported by 4 groups (responsible for communications, finance, commercial and industrial coordination, and social and research services), each consisting of one Minister from each of the three territories, known as the "Triumvirate."

There will also be a Central Legislative Assembly to consist of 12 Ministers (members of the four "Triumvirates"); nine members from each territory elected by the territorial legislatures; the Secretary General of the administration (the principal executive officer), and the Legal Secretary of the organization. The Assembly will have power to legislate on appropriation to finance itself and its services; civil aviation; customs and excise; income tax; interterritorial research; institutions of higher learning; meteorological services; pension schemes; posts and telegraphs, telephones and radio communications; loans; statistics; merchant shipping; legal proceedings by and against the organizations; allocations from the distributable pool; and the public service commission.[2]

APPENDIX II-B

THE UNION OF REPUBLICS OF CENTRAL AFRICA
[Central African Republic, Chad, Congo (Brazzaville)]

These three nations and Gabon comprise the former Afrique Equatoriale Française (A.E.F.) constituted in 1903 and governed on a federal basis by the French until 1958.

Under the Constitution of the Fourth French Republic of 1946, a Grand Council of the A.E.F. was formed, consisting of representatives from each of the territories, to handle matters of common interest. At

[1] U.K.: *The East Africa High Commission 1959*, H.M.S.O., London, pp. 1–2.
[2] U.K.: *The Future of the East Africa High Commission Services*, Colonial Office, *Cmnd. 1433*, H.M.S.O., London, 1961.

the territorial level each country was given an elected Representative Assembly, later transformed to a Territorial Assembly (1952), charged with managing territorial matters, in particular with voting on the local budget. In 1956 a measure of self-government was granted to the chief urban centers. The Loi Cadre of June 13, 1956, was a turning point in French policy regarding Overseas Territories. It established universal adult suffrage, eliminating the old system of electoral colleges, and instituted an African Government Council to exercise executive powers under the Head of the Territory, considerably broadening the powers of the Territorial Assembly.

The French Constitution of the Fifth Republic, established on October 4, 1958, created a new French Community under which colonial territories were given the right to self-determination for the first time. The four central African states decided by referendum to establish four autonomous republics within the Community.

Since 1958, these states have been preoccupied with the political problems of reconstructing an independent federation while retaining Community ties. Gabon, the most prosperous and least populous of the four, has refused consistently to participate in a political union. Nevertheless, in January 1959, it signed agreements with the other three states providing for a customs union, economic cooperation, and a joint administration of the common services that used to be administered by the federal government of A.E.F.

In May 1960, the Central African Republic (formerly Ubangi-Shari), the Republic of the Congo (formerly Middle-Congo), and the Republic of Chad constituted themselves into a confederation of independent states known as the "Union of Republics of Central Africa." The charter adopted by these three states, at the conference of Fort-Lamy of that year, was ratified subsequently by the Legislative Assembly of each country. The Union's jurisdiction covers foreign affairs, defense, the post office and telecommunications departments, the issuing of currency, and the coordination of economic matters.

APPENDIX II-C

THE CONSEIL DE L'ENTENTE
(Ivory Coast, Upper Volta, Niger, Dahomey)

Mr. Houphouet-Boigny, President of the Republic of the Ivory Coast, initiated the establishment, on May 29, 1959, of the Conseil de l'Entente which comprises the Republics of the Ivory Coast, the Upper Volta, the Niger, and Dahomey.

This Council meets twice annually and is presided over in turn by each of the Chiefs of State or Chiefs of Government of the four countries. The President serves one year and is assisted by an administrative secretariat. Mr. Houphouet-Boigny was the first President of the Entente in 1959, succeeded by Hamani Diori in 1960, President of the Council of Ministers of Niger.

The Conseil de l'Entente has already set up a Customs Union as well as a Solidarity Fund for financial assistance to each of the member states. It has also provided for the coordination of the development plans of the four states and of their policies in the fields of taxation, public administration, labor legislation, public works, transportation, and communications.

On June 11, 1959, the four member states of the Entente entered into a customs union agreement with the neighboring republics of Senegal, Mali, and Mauritania.

APPENDIX II-D

THE UNION OF AFRICAN STATES[3]
(Ghana-Guinea-Mali Union)

On November 23, 1958, the Ghana-Guinea Union was brought into being following Guinea's decision to remain outside the newly formed French Community of the Fifth Republic. In May 1959, a Joint Communiqué issued in Conakry laid down the practical basis for the achievement of such a Union and set out the basic principles for a wider African Community.

At the end of 1960 the Mali Republic, former French Sudan, became the third member of the Union. At the first meeting of the three Heads of State, held in Conakry on December 24, 1960, a Special Committee was set up to formulate concrete proposals for implementing such a Union.

On April 27, 28, and 29, 1961, the Heads of the three states held their

[3] Ghana: *Charter for the Union of African States and a Joint Communiqué issued later, after a Summit Conference between the leaders of the Union,* Ministry of Information, Government Printing Department, Accra, 1961. See also: *Ghana,* Ghana Information and Trade Center, New York, Press releases numbers 117, May 1, 1961, and 152, July 17, 1961; *West Africa,* Harrison & Sons Ltd., London, numbers 227, January 1, 1961; 2292, May 6, 1961; 2301, July 8, 1961, and 2321, November 25, 1961.

first quarterly meeting of the year at Accra and agreed on a Charter for the Union of African States to be submitted to their respective Parliaments for ratification. The draft Charter was published simultaneously in Accra, Bamako, and Conakry on July 1, 1961. The Charter provides for the defense of the territorial integrity of members, and for cooperation in diplomatic, economic, cultural, and research activities. It does not provide for common institutions, but conferences of the Heads of States are regarded as the Union's supreme executive body. It also provides for admitting new member states who accept the aims and objectives of the Charter.

Dr. Nkrumah, speaking at the state opening of the Ghana Parliament on July 4, 1961, said that the three states had agreed "to pool our resources in order to consolidate our independence and work jointly for the liquidation of colonialism and neocolonialism in Africa by harmonizing our domestic and foreign policies," and had "taken steps to install direct telecommunication links between our capitals in order to eliminate delays in our consultation." [4]

[4] Republic of Ghana: *State Opening of Parliament*, July 4, 1961.

Appendix III

METROPOLITAN AID TO AFRICA

APPENDIX III-A

UNITED KINGDOM AID TO AFRICA[1]

Traditionally, Britain's policy in the field of development has been one in which colonies are expected to finance the development of their infrastructures from their own local resources, Britain assisting from time to time with grants-in-aid while other economic activities are left to private enterprise. In 1929 the Colonial Development Act was passed to "promote commerce with, and industry in, the United Kingdom." A fund of £1 million per annum was set up for schemes of economic development. Schemes of welfare were not included at that time. By 1939 it had become clear that Britain would have to play a far greater role in creating the necessary social and economic conditions for eventual self-government. Thus in 1940 the Colonial Development and Welfare Act was passed, subsequently amended in 1946, 1950, 1951, 1955, and 1959. A C.D. & W. fund was set up to finance country-wide development plans, research and other centrally administered services and to build up a general reserve. The amount set aside under each successive act was increased, as was the sum ceiling for annual expenditure and under the 1959 act a scheme of Exchequer loans for newly independent states was introduced. In all, the sum of £315 million from United Kingdom taxation will have been made available to African territories by 1964, starting in 1946.

Until 1946 Colonial Governments were unable to plan far ahead owing to the fact that all unspent annual balances had to be returned. Under the 1946 Act this clause was repealed and funds were provided to cover the ten-year period 1946 to 1956. In 1955 the period was extended to March 1960 and the 1959 Act further extended the period to March 1964. This has meant that Colonial Governments have been able to form

---

[1] U.K.: *The United Kingdom Colonial Development and Welfare Acts*; British Information Services, Reference Division, I.D. 892 (revised), March 1960; Colonial Development Corporation: *Partners in Development*, The Fanfare Press Ltd., n.d.

a nucleus of development finance with a certain sense of security and to embark on long-term projects.

Until 1950 the various acts had provided that only dependencies could benefit under the scheme. In that year the clause making newly independent states ineligible was repealed, but in 1959 a proviso was introduced, viz., that funds could not be used for schemes for their sole benefit but would be made available for interterritorial schemes provided the country was able to contribute its fair share. In that same year the Exchequer loan schemes for independent states was also introduced, available to March 1964.

The contribution of C.D. & W. funds vary from country to country depending upon local conditions, needs, and wealth and do not represent the sole nor the greater source of finance for development. While the bulk of C.D. & W. funds are used for countries' development plans; e.g., £100.5 million of the £140.5 million available for the years 1959/1964—the balance goes into research and centrally administered services and a general reserve. Other sources of development finance representing a greater proportion of the total are obtained from loans raised on the London Market; loans from the International Bank of Reconstruction and Development guaranteed by the United Kingdom Government; capital from the Colonial Development Corporation established in 1948 and more recently, Exchequer loans.

The Colonial Development Corporation whose functions were consolidated in the Overseas Resources Development Act of 1959, operates as a commercial organization. It invests funds in development projects that will help increase the wealth of territories and also yield a reasonable return on the money invested. It has borrowing powers up to £150 million on long term and £10 million on short term. It obtains most of its capital from the United Kingdom Government—£130 million—and the rest from nongovernment sources.

Development Plans

At first most plans were drawn up on a ten-year basis but this proved unrealistic and the C.D. & W. Act of 1955 introduced a shorter planning period, normally of five years. The responsibility for framing plans and deciding on priorities rests with the territories themselves. Projects financed in whole or part by C.D. & W. funds generally form part of larger programs, but individual schemes must be approved by the Secretary of State for Colonies. Their initiation and implementation is primarily a local responsibility.

The contributions made by the C.D. & W. funds do not operate on a fixed scale of assistance and represent a relatively small part of total development finance. Other sources used are loan funds and local resources. Since 1959 Exchequer loans are provided from the Consolidated Fund, repayable to the Exchequer, for a period not exceeding 30 years and at a rate of ¼% above the rate at which government provides loans for a number of public corporations. The only proviso concerning these loans is that local laws provide reasonable facilities for trade-union organizations and fair conditions of labor.

Examples of Finance of Development Plans in Operation in 1958 in some African Countries in £'000's:

| Country | Planning Period | Total | Sources of Finance | | |
			C.D. & W.	Loans	Local Resources
Federation of Nigeria	1955/62	120,723 *	4,103	29,300	68,441
Sierra Leone	1956/59	11,428	3,139	5,813	2,475
Kenya	1957/60	28,995	2,868	18,000	8,127 †
Tanganyika	1957/61	27,000	4,000	20,000	3,000
Northern Rhodesia	1957/61	35,478 *	525	18,538	14,415
Nyasaland	1957/61	12,569 *	1,386	7,420	2,566

* Includes anticipated expenditure, for which the source of finance is not yet known.

† Includes grants by U.S. International Cooperation Administration toward the Swynnerton Plan.

Examples of Colonial Development Corporation participation:

In East Africa it has 23 projects with a capital investment of £22,626,-000 covering mining, wattle, tea and cocoa estates, flour milling, soap and margarine, hotels, electricity supply, and housing. In Tanganyika on the Great Rusha River the CDC is associated with the International Finance Corporation interests in the Kilomboro Sugar Company, Ltd., for a project estimated to cost some £3 million to grow sugar cane and produce refined sugar.

In the Federation of Rhodesia and Nyasaland it has 10 projects with a capital investment of £22,857,000 covering production of tobacco, tung oil and cement, African housing schemes, an industrial promotion corporation and an airways corporation. In Nyasaland the Kasungu Tobacco Estates project in cooperation with the Nyasaland Government is developing a smallholder scheme thereby helping African farmers to produce and market flue-cured tobacco.

In West Africa it has 17 projects with a capital investment of £13,-952,000, covering rubber, cement, factory development, hotels, fabricated steel, housing and local development companies. In Sierra Leone together with the government it has opened a new modern hotel.

In the High Commission Territories it has 8 projects with a capital investment of £15,880,000 covering forestry, pulp production, irrigation for citrus and other crops, sugar, cattle ranching, and abattoir. The CDC is equal partner with Courtaulds Ltd., in the Usutu Pulp Co., Ltd., formed in 1959 to put to commercial use 95,000 acres of pine forest which the CDC has planted over eleven years. It planned to produce 100,000 tons per annum of kraft pulp in a pulp mill which started production toward the end of 1961. This should add some £3 million to Swasiland's annual exports.

It is estimated that of the United Kingdom's national income of $47 billion in 1956, $300 million (public and private) was invested in under-developed areas representing 0.6% of the national income.[2]

FRENCH AID TO AFRICA[3]

France's contribution to the development of its African colonies has been considerable but, as in the case of the United Kingdom, it became a prominent feature of its colonial policy only after World War II. Until then, of the total $6 billion spent on its territories, Africa had received $2.1 billion.

Previous to 1946, France's colonies had autonomous budgets and were able to float loans on the Metropolitan financial market. Development was financed by either reserve funds or loans or sometimes by both.

In 1946 Metropolitan France accepted the principle of economic aid and social development of its colonies at public expense. A Law of April 30, 1946, created the Fonds d'Investissement pour le Développement Economique et Social des Territoires d'Outre-Mer (F.I.D.E.S.), which was to carry out its tasks with the cooperation of the Caisse Centrale de la France d'Outre-Mer (C.C.F.O.M.). In 1959, F.I.D.E.S. was replaced by the Fund for Aid and Cooperation (F.A.C.), with reference to French Territories that had acquired independence, while F.I.D.E.S. continued

[2] A Decade of Progress: 1948–1958; Ambassade de France, Service de Presse et d'Information, New York, Nov. 1958, p. 3.

[3] Unless otherwise stated, information obtained from Service des Statistiques d'Outre-Mer, Outre-Mer 1958, Paul Dupont, Nov. 1959, Paris, pp. 578–580; René Servoise: "French Economic Aid to Africa," in International Development, Jan. 1961, Vol. 11, No. 1, International Development Society, Cambridge, Mass.

to function in relation to the remaining overseas territories. At the same time, C.C.F.O.M. was replaced by the Caisse Centrale de Coopération Economique.

Up to 90% of F.I.D.E.S. funds were provided by Metropolitan France, the rest being contributions by the territories themselves. A part of F.I.D.E.S. funds are supplied by C.C.F.O.M. in the form of loans repayable at low interest rates over 25 years. C.C.F.O.M., which may participate in development either by direct participation or through loans, utilizes advances obtained from the Treasury and the Metropolitan budget.

F.I.D.E.S. funds operate at two levels—the general, and the local or overseas sections. At the general level it finances, on a grant basis, undertakings benefiting all or more than one territory, such as scientific research, public development corporations, and major public works studies. At the local or territorial level, grants and loans finance basic local equipment expenditure such as roads, ports, airports, power, schools, hospitals, housing, and so on. In addition F.I.D.E.S. assists by making available loans to non-F.I.D.E.S.-financed development, to communes; to state and/or private enterprises; and capital for investment.

In all local, i.e., territorial development projects, territories are supposed to make a contribution. Initially Metropolitan France paid 55% of all expenditure; in 1954 it raised its contribution to 75% and in 1956 to 100% on production and social services, and 75% of expenditure on infrastructure.

For the period 1947 to 1958 public aid to Africa totaled $3.74 million, covering two plans. The first plan, 1947/1951, was designed to build up and modernize the existing infrastructure by applying 50% of the investment for this purpose. The second plan, 1952/1958, concentrated on production, 45% of the total credits going to this sector. Expenditure on social services such as public health, town planning, housing, etc., rose from 16% in the first plan to 20% in the second plan.

In addition, there has been a substantial flow of public investment funds from France to Africa for purposes which, technically speaking, fall outside the scope of the plans, as well as financial assistance for purposes other than investment. By and large, the magnitude of France's financial aid to African countries appears to be substantially greater than that of Britain's in the postwar period. These statements do not take into account the flow of private investment into French-speaking African countries. No precise figures are available for private investment, but, in general, it appears to have been quantitatively less important than public aid.

The system of financing and implementing territorial development plans in French Africa differs from the British system. Most, if not all, finance comes from F.I.D.E.S. Each territory has to submit annual requirements to F.I.D.E.S. in Paris, and allocations are subsequently made on a yearly basis. Projects undertaken, whether the building of a dam or road, have to be completed within a four-year period.

At the present moment most of the newly independent former French territories have not yet completed the preliminary studies necessary to establishing and framing a definitive development plan.[4]

Illustration of finance development in two former French African territories:

Upper Volta

For the year 1961

Contributions

Local Budget—total, 742 million C.F.A. francs

Allocations—Roads and bridges	350
Posts and telecommunications	100
Customs posts	60
Building	151

F.A.C. (formerly F.I.D.E.S.)—total 994.5 million C.F.A. francs

Allocations—Research and mining survey	23%
Production	51%
Infrastructure	18%
Social equipment	8%

In addition the Fonds Européen de Développement contributed about 5,533 million C.F.A. francs over the years 1958 to June 1, 1961, for projects, of which 45% was allocated to social equipment.[5]

Chad

Local resources are so modest that none can be used for finance development.

O.C.R.S. (Organisation Communes de Régions Sahariennes) authorizations for 1961/62, in million C.F.A. francs

Agriculture	131.3
Hydraulics	488
Public works	119
Telecommunications	18
Health and education	35

[4] Communication received from Ministère de la Coopération, Division de l'Information, Paris, Feb. 1962.

[5] Républiques de la Haute Volta: Ministère de la Coopération, *Economie et Plan de Développement,* Paris, Sept. 1961, pp. 25–26, 29, 31.

| Mineral research | 20 |
| Miscellaneous | 20 |

F.A.C. total for 1961—798.9 million C.F.A. francs

Allocations—General expenditure	16.4%
Radio	3.1%
Production	26.0%
Infrastructure	26.6%
Health and education	27.9%

Fonds Européens de Développement 1961—1.780 million C.F.A. francs for hydraulic development.

United Nations 1961/63—total, 105,000 million C.F.A. francs of which the most important allocations will go to:

Medical training	16.8
Economic, social development, and public administration	15
Telecommunications	11.6 [6]

It is estimated that of France's national income of $40 billion in 1956, $600 million (public and private) was invested in underdeveloped areas representing 1.5% of the national income.[7]

[6] République du Tchad: Ministère de la Coopération, *Economie et Plan de Développement*, Paris, Nov. 1961, pp. 14–16 and 18–19.

[7] *A Decade of Progress 1948–1958*, Ambassade de France, Service de Presse et d'Information, New York, Nov. 1958, p. 3.

Appendix IV

BRITISH AND FRENCH TRADE AND MARKETING SYSTEMS

The trade pattern and marketing systems which exist between the United Kingdom and Metropolitan France and their respective dependencies and former dependencies in Africa reflect once more a different approach to the "colonial relationship."

French African countries are treated as an integral part of the Franc Zone, with the exception of Guinea. On the import side, a system of tariff regulations restricts imports from dollar and sterling areas into the countries, protecting French exports to members of the Zone. On the export side, France protects most of the products of overseas members of the Zone through a regime which compels the metropolitan buyer to purchase them at full or above world market prices. Thus French African countries accord to France preference both in terms of their imports and exports, and all marketing is done through private enterprise.

In British countries the export trade is handled largely through statutory export monopolies known as marketing boards. These in turn often work closely with the well-developed cooperative movements in channeling the sale, purchase, and export of local products. The prices offered the producers are usually below those obtaining on the world market, but the system compensates by ensuring a steady and reliable market for local products. Britain discriminates on behalf of British African countries in terms of their exports, but they do not have to discriminate in favor of the Commonwealth for their imports.

The result of these two systems is twofold. In the first place, trade between Metropolitan France and African members of the Franc Zone is much more integrated than is the case between the United Kingdom and its dependencies and former dependencies. It is estimated that France buys 60% of its former overseas territories' exports, and they in turn obtain 70% of their imports from France.[1] For the years 1957–1959, trade figures between the United Kingdom and Ghana, Nigeria, and British East Africa (Uganda, Tanganyika, and Kenya) combined reveal that Britain bought some 41% of their exports while they in turn took only about 30% of their imports from Britain.[2] In the second place, the cost of living index is generally lower in British than in French Africa, since French countries sell and buy at high prices whereas British countries buy and sell at low prices.

[1] René Servoise: "French Economic Aid in Africa," in *International Developments,* Jan. 1961, Vol. 11, No. 1, International Development Society, Cambridge, Mass., pp. 19–20.

[2] U.N.: *Economic Bulletin for Africa,* June 1961, Vol. 1, No. 2, Addis Ababa, Percentages computed from figures Table 5A, pp. 8 and 10, and Table 5B, pp. 9 and 11. See also *U.N.: Economic Bulletin for Africa,* Vol. 1, No. 1, Part B, E/CN. 14/67, December 21, 1960—especially pp. 3–5 for French marketing arrangements; U.K.: *Cooperation in the U.K. Dependencies,* Reference Division, U.K. Central Office of Information, London, June 1961, R.F.P. 4498.

Appendix V

TABLES OF MEASURES AND CURRENCY

MEASURES

Centimeter	0.394 inch	1 foot	0.305 meter
Meter	1.094 yards	1 yard	0.914 meter
Kilometer	0.621 mile	1 mile	1.609 kilometer

CURRENCY *

Ethiopian dollar	41	U.S. cents
Ghana pound	2.81	U.S.$
Moroccan derham	19	U.S. cents
South African rand	1.41	U.S.$
Egyptian pound	2.88	U.S.$
U.K. pound	2.80	U.S.$
French new franc	0.2040	U.S. cents
Tunisian dinar	2.40	U.S.$

* As of January 31, 1962. Obtained from the First National Bank of Boston.